Archaeologies of the Hea

Kisha Supernant • Jane Eva Baxter
Natasha Lyons • Sonya Atalay

Editors

Archaeologies of the Heart

Springer

Editors
Kisha Supernant
Department of Anthropology
University of Alberta
Edmonton, AB, Canada

Natasha Lyons
Ursus Heritage Consulting Ltd
Coldstream, BC, Canada

Jane Eva Baxter
Department of Anthropology
DePaul University
Chicago, IL, USA

Sonya Atalay
Department of Anthropology
University of Massachusetts Amherst
Amherst, MA, USA

ISBN 978-3-030-36352-9   ISBN 978-3-030-36350-5   (eBook)
https://doi.org/10.1007/978-3-030-36350-5

This Springer imprint is published by the registered company Springer Nature Switzerland AG
The registered company address is: Gewerbestrasse 11, 6330 Cham, Switzerland

Preface

The volume you are about to experience was a labour of love. Emerging from a deep desire to change our disciplinary practices, both in how we engage with the archaeological record and in how we engage with one another, the chapters in this volume demonstrate the widespread and relevant nature of heart-centred archaeology. The seeds of the approach we define in this volume have long been germinating in both professional and personal contexts and were planted in several ways: through the interpersonal relationships between the editors and our colleagues and through our intellectual engagement with feminist and Indigenous archaeologies.

This volume originated from two different conference sessions: one at the World Archaeological Congress in Kyoto, Japan, in 2016, on the archaeology of emotion, and one at the Society for American Archaeology (SAA) Annual Meeting in Vancouver, British Columbia, in 2017, on heart-centred archaeology. We wish to thank everyone who participated in both sessions. We are grateful to Teresa Krauss at Springer for her enthusiastic support of this project from the beginning and to those who have attended our conference sessions. In the SAA session, Jami Macarty led a group of archaeologists in a heart-centred meditation, an event which was very powerful and memorable for all who attended. We thank Jami for her contribution to our session and her willingness to create a text that we could include in this volume to allow others to participate in her meditation. The SAA also hosted an online webinar on the topic, and we are grateful to the organization and the attendees for their engagement. Finally, we want to thank everyone who has taken the time to reach out in support and to reinforce the importance of changing our approaches to archaeological practice. The response to our conference session, our webinar, and a short piece published in the SAA Record has been beyond our expectations.

One of the greatest joys of working on this volume has been the relationships we have created with each other as editors, with our volume contributors, and with the reviewers. We are grateful for the careful and heart-centred ways our reviewers engaged with the materials and provided generous, thoughtful, and impactful feedback for us and for the contributing authors. All of the authors in the volume have shown great courage to share both their work and, in many cases, their hearts with us and with you, the readers. We appreciate how the authors embraced this project and put such care into their contributions. We are also grateful to the Killam Research Fund at the University of Alberta for providing financial support for the project.

The result of these heart-centred collaborations and relations is the volume you see before you. It explores the possibilities of an archaeology that originates from the heart by centring care, relationality, rigor, and emotion. The chapters range from deeply personal narratives about our relations with archaeology as a discipline and the living beings with whom we collaborate to rich engagements with the evocative power of the material past. Drawing on case studies from all around the globe, the chapters here ask us to feel as well as think, to imagine as well as to prove, and, fundamentally, to engage in good relations with each other, past and present. We invite you to enter this volume with an open heart and leave transformed.

Edmonton, AB, Canada   Kisha Supernant
Chicago, IL, USA   Jane Eva Baxter
Coldstream, BC, Canada   Natasha Lyons
Amherst, MA, USA   Sonya Atalay

Acknowledgements

Kisha: More than anything else, I am grateful for the strong bonds of love that have been forged with my coeditors through our co-creation of this volume. Our visits and heartfelt collaborations have been a touchstone for me, reinforcing my belief that we can change archaeological practice to celebrate that we are all whole people. The Heart-Centered and Emotional Archaeologies for Research and Teaching (HEART) collective represents, for me, a new way of doing archaeology, and I am excited to see where we will go next. All of my work would not be possible without the strong foundation of love and support provided by my husband, Casey, and my family. I am grateful to my wonderful mentors who have encouraged me to follow my heart throughout my career and to my relatives and ancestors of my homelands in and around Amiskwacîwâskahikan. Finally, this volume is an academic representation of the love, kindness, and empathy taught to me by my mother, Shanti, which I endeavour to pass on to my own heart, my daughter, Leia. May you always bring love and kindness to the world. Hiy hiy.

Jane: My heart is full of gratitude as we complete this volume project. I am most grateful to my coeditors who created a space for me to explore and expand my writing and thinking and who through our collaboration and friendship reinforced the importance of bringing one's whole self to an intellectual project while also maintaining a rich, full, and balanced life. The loving, supportive friendships we have forged in this process are lifelong and life-changing. Thanks also to my partner, Jim; my step-kids, Samantha and James; and my friends for making a balanced life one filled with love and happiness.

Natasha: It has been a truly amazing process to create this volume and the emerging body of work that surrounds it. My sincere thanks to each of our contributors as well as our reviewers, Alison Wylie, Eric Simons, and George Nicholas. I gratefully acknowledge, admire, and appreciate a number of friends in and out of the discipline for our conversations about life, love, and wellness: my coeditors, Kisha, Jane and Sonya, as well as Tanja Hoffmann, Melanie Piorecky, Grant Wardlow, Sandra Peacock, Kate Hennessy, Chelsey Armstrong, Lisa Hodgetts, Ian Cameron, and Bob Lyons, my Dad! As editors, we have been thrilled to engage with many of the heroes and heroines of our discipline through the process of making this book. I am grateful to my own mentors, Jane Kelley, Michael Blake, and John Welch, for their guidance and inspiration. And I thank my greatest teachers, my children, Hallie and Henry Cameron, for their love, light, and levity.

Sonya: Sincere Miigwech (thank you) to my coeditors and the contributors to this volume – our work together gave me space to imagine another world and to vision what is possible. To my mentors and teachers who help me learn and grow and to those who are there by my side when I stumble, especially Amy Lonetree, my boy bears (Ted, Niigani, Bonifacio, and Myles) and our fur babies, my supportive family, and our ancestors; to my mother for teaching me to live with an open heart, and to my mama, Syd, for showing me how to lead with an open heart; to Shannon for her words and reminders of ayangwamazin, be determined on your path and be a good ancestor every day; to Bawdwaywidun and the Three Fires Midewiwin Lodge for carrying and sharing teachings that bring us mide life and mino biimatiziiwin; to Dave Shananaquet for the powerful, gorgeous cover art; and to Nia:wen Owisokon Lahache for the permission to include her painting in my chapter and Lori Lambert for allowing the use of her heart web image. I acknowledge with deep gratitude and respect the land, water, and especially the strawberries of my homeland, ni kani gana – all my relations. This project led me to find joy in writing with hope for alternative futures founded in heart-centred practices.

Contents

About the Editors

Kisha Supernant, PhD is an Associate Professor in the Department of Anthropology at the University of Alberta and Director of the Institute of Prairie and Indigenous Archaeology. A Métis woman with ties to northern Alberta Cree and Métis communities, she works with Indigenous communities in Western Canada to explore how archaeologists and communities can build collaborative research relationships. An award-winning Teacher, Researcher, and Writer, her research interests include the relationship between cultural identities, landscapes, and the use of space, Métis archaeology, and heart-centred archaeological practice. She has published in local and international journals on GIS in archaeology, collaborative archaeological practice, Métis archaeology, and Indigenous archaeology in the post-TRC era.

Jane Eva Baxter, PhD is an Associate Professor in the Department of Anthropology at DePaul University in Chicago, IL. She is a Teaching Professor and a Researcher with long-standing research interests in the archaeology of childhood, gender, labour, and identity. She is the author of 3 books, editor/coeditor of 3 volumes, and author/coauthor of over 30 peer-reviewed book chapters and articles.

Natasha Lyons, PhD is a Founding Partner of Ursus Heritage Consulting and Adjunct Faculty in the Department of Archaeology at Simon Fraser University. She conducts collaborative, community-based research with First Nations throughout Western Canada and the Inuvialuit of the Canadian Western Arctic. She practices and publishes widely on critical community archaeology, ethical research practice, digital representation, and palaeoethnobotany. She sees an archaeology of heart, and heart-centred practice more generally, as an important way forward in research and contemporary life.

Sonya Atalay (Anishinaabe-Ojibwe) is an Associate Professor of Anthropology at the University of Massachusetts Amherst. She works in engaged anthropology, utilizing community-based participatory methods to conduct research in full partnership with Indigenous communities. Her scholarship crosses disciplinary boundaries, incorporating aspects of cultural anthropology, archaeology, critical heritage studies, and Native American and Indigenous Studies. She's coauthor of 'NAGPRA Comics', a series of research-based graphic narratives about repatriation. Centring Anishinaabe epistemologies and concepts of well-being, she is working on a series of land-based collaborative projects that involve intergenerational Indigenous knowledge production and knowledge mobilization practices.

Contributors

Callum Abbott, MA Department of Anthropology, University of Victoria, Victoria, BC, Canada

Hakai Institute, Heriot Bay, BC, Canada

Eugene N. Anderson, PhD Emeritus, University of California, Riverside, CA, USA

Chelsey Geralda Armstrong, PhD National Museum of Natural History, Smithsonian Institution, Washington, DC, USA

Sonya Atalay, PhD Department of Anthropology, University of Massachusetts Amherst, Amherst, MA, USA

Jane Eva Baxter, PhD Department of Anthropology, DePaul University, Chicago, IL, USA

Melanie L. Chang, PhD Portland State University, Portland, OR, USA

Margaret W. Conkey, PhD University of California, Berkeley, Berkeley, CA, USA

Anthony P. Graesch, PhD Department of Anthropology, Connecticut College, New London, CT, USA

Lisa Hodgetts, PhD Department of Anthropology, The University of Western Ontario, London, ON, Canada

Tanja Hoffmann, PhD, RPCA Postdoctoral Fellow, Indigenous Works and University of Saskatchewan, Saskatoon, SK, Canada

Laura Kelvin, PhD Department of Archaeology, Memorial University of Newfoundland, St. John's, NL, Canada

Torill Christine Lindstrøm Department of Psychosocial Science, Faculty of Psychology and SapienCE, Centre for Early Sapiens Behaviour, CoE Faculty of Humanities University of Bergen, Bergen, Norway

Natasha Lyons, PhD Ursus Heritage Consulting and Department of Archaeology, Simon Fraser University, Coldstream, BC, Canada

Jami Macarty, MFA Simon Fraser University (Creative Writing Program) & Integrative Restoration Institute, Burnaby, BC, Canada

Corbin Maynard Department of Anthropology, Connecticut College, New London, CT, USA

April Nowell, PhD University of Victoria, Victoria, BC, Canada

Uzma Z. Rizvi, PhD Department of Social Science and Cultural Studies, Pratt Institute, New York, NY, USA

Kisha Supernant, PhD Department of Anthropology, University of Alberta, Edmonton, AB, Canada

Sarah L. Surface-Evans, PhD Central Michigan University, Mount Pleasant, MI, USA

Avery Thomas Department of Anthropology, Connecticut College, New London, CT, USA

Ruth Tringham, PhD University of California, Berkeley, CA, USA

Leslie Van Gelder, PhD Senior Contributing Faculty, Walden University, Minneapolis, MN, USA

John R. Welch, PhD Simon Fraser University and Archaeology Southwest, Burnaby, BC, Canada

Chapter 1
Introduction to an Archaeology of the Heart

Natasha Lyons and Kisha Supernant

The Heart Berry

Our intention with this volume is to work toward an archaeology of the heart. This is an emergent practice, drawn from various strands of archaeology and other disciplines, which are unpacked below as we conceive and share our thoughts with you. These thoughts have been many years in the making. We aim to create an archaeology that speaks to the whole person—our intellectual, emotional, spiritual, and physical selves. We aim to put heart into our understandings of the past by reframing our analyses to consider the powerful roles of emotion, love, and connection, though not at the expense of rigor. We aim to center the heart in our modes of practice, through how we relate to one another as people, our students, other archaeologists, community members, and our diverse publics. We aim to take the best of what our whole selves offer and make an archaeology that makes us better people, better archaeologists, and a kinder and more inclusive community of practice (Fig. 1.1).

The image presented above and depicted on the cover of this volume is a heart berry, the name given to the wild strawberry (*Fragaria* spp.) by many cultures, from Indigenous nations to the ancient Romans, Greeks, and other Europeans, because of its shape and color, its literal power as a heart medicine, and its more figurative power as a source of healing (Atalay, Chap. 16, this volume; Surface-Evans, Chap 5, this volume). We chose this image, graciously produced by Anishnaabe artist David Shananaquet, as a metaphor for the work that we, as authors and editors, together with you, our readers, hope to do with this volume. Below, we present the seeds of our own heart-centered practice, telling the story of how the ideas explored

N. Lyons
Ursus Heritage Consulting and Department of Archaeology, Simon Fraser University, Coldstream, BC, Canada

K. Supernant (✉)
Department of Anthropology, University of Alberta, Edmonton, AB, Canada
e-mail: kisha.supernant@ualberta.ca

© Springer Nature Switzerland AG 2020
K. Supernant et al. (eds.), *Archaeologies of the Heart*,
https://doi.org/10.1007/978-3-030-36350-5_1

Fig. 1.1 Original artwork by Dave Shananaquet commissioned by editors

here germinated and grew through our scholarship, friendship, and archaeological experiences, both positive and negative. The midsection of our introduction forms the rhizomes, or runners, that comprise the different intertwined elements of an emergent heart-centered practice. The final section represents the berry itself, the fruits of our intellectual, emotional, spiritual, and physical labors of love as archaeologists, where we find themes that crosscut the expressions of heart-centered practice presented by our volume's contributors.

The Seeds of an Idea

Our personal experiences in the discipline of archaeology led us to envision, create, define, and begin to practice an archaeology of the heart. We recount here some of our formative experiences as a way to share the conditions, assumptions, and expectations we had of archaeology as we grew as scholars, in theoretical, emotional, and experiential terms (sensu Harding 1995). We suspect that many of the disciplinary influences we reference in keystone publications and movements are shared by archaeologists of our generation, particularly those trained in Western, English-speaking institutions.

As all young archaeologists, we both had vague ideas about what archaeology was when we started out. Kisha read about exploring "lost cities" and ancient places as a teenager and thought it would be an adventurous life, travelling the world, seeing places few people got to see. She decided then and there to be an archaeologist studying ancient civilizations, having no idea where it would take her, but determined to follow a path to the unknown. Natasha had read James Michener's *The

Source while hitchhiking across Central Australia and been struck by—what? The appeal of working outdoors, and perhaps, the apparently sexy atmosphere of working on a dig? Definitely, the unknown and spiritual element of seeing, feeling, and making meaning out of what was buried in the ground. At that time, she had little experience with but an outsized draw to the First Nations cultures she had connections to in her adolescence in the Pacific Northwest.

We came of intellectual age as undergraduates during the rise of the post-processual movement, as did our two co-editors and a good number of our volume contributors. For us, this was a time of great intellectual excitement as archaeologists who would become our heroes and heroines broke and entered the ecosystem of processualism (Brumfiel 1992); spoke for, about, and with women, two spirited peoples, and other genders (Gero and Conkey 1991; Walde and Willows 1991; Wylie 1992, 1997); began to question who has the right to speak for Indigenous and ethnocultural communities (Bond and Gilliam 1997; Deloria 1969, 1997; Mihesuah 1996; McGuire 1992; Trigger 1980; Trigger et al. 1984); and worked to construct critical and socially relevant archaeologies (Leone et al. 1987; Shanks and Tilley 1987).

Both of us did our undergraduate studies at the University of British Columbia in Vancouver, giving us many common experiences, though separated by about half a decade. Both of us also felt an acute draw to the calls of the post-processual movement. This clearly relates to that formative time in our intellectual and social development when we are very open, and certainly, what we read and discussed about democratizing, particularizing, and diversifying accounts and readings of the past had great appeal. Natasha knew from Dr. Kew's classes that anthropologists could care and that inequality and justice could be on the research table. She had very personal, very subjective feelings about what she read and heard and saw—books such as Brody's (1981) *Maps and Dreams* and Schmidt and Patterson's (1995) *Making Alternative Histories*—but it didn't occur to her that those feelings could motivate and organize both research and inquiry (later, Mark Leone's work would teach her that). Kisha encountered the nascent field of Indigenous Studies through work at the First Nations House of Learning and began to explore her own Indigenous heritage which had impacted her life in myriad ways. Reading Trigger's Alternative Archaeologies (Trigger 1984) was a major intellectual moment that called into question the very purpose of archaeology.

This theoretical knowledge was not put into action until our introduction to and fieldwork with an Indigenous community. Both of us did UBC field schools with the Sq'éwlets people of the Fraser Valley of British Columbia, an inaugural form of community practice motivated by Chief Clarence Pennier's invitation to assist the community to learn more about the ancestral history on contested pieces of land (Lyons et al. 2016). Here, as early 20-somethings, we both—at 5 years distance from each other—developed relationships and knowledges of lived experience (our own and community members', which were clearly very divergent). We were to see and feel structural violence, systemic injustice, and social marginalization in a very visceral and sometimes shocking way, although we didn't perhaps put these words to it. We also both experienced a great deal of love and acceptance and intense personal and intellectual learning through our relationships to Betty Charlie, Clifford Hall, Vi Pennier, and others. These community members generously shared their knowledge and experiences of being on ancient spiritual sites, as well as what happened when protocols were not followed, a teaching which followed us throughout our careers.

Natasha would go on to do a Master's degree at Qithyil, one of the Sq'éwlets community's most significant ancestral sites, a paleoethnobotanical analysis that while rigorous in design, attentive to the ethnobotanical literature, and conducted in a community-based field setting, still felt only partly engaged with community needs (though many friends at Sq'éwlets received the thesis warmly). Kisha failed to get into her first choice of Master's program (and the only one to which she had applied), still clinging to the idea of studying ancient civilizations of the Near East. This failure, while painful at the time, was one of the best things to ever happen to her, because it sets her on the path toward Indigenous archaeology. She instead went to the University of Toronto for a 1-year Master's program, where she wrote her Master's paper on warfare practice on the Northwest Coast. Only much later, and with some hindsight, maturity, and experience, were either of us able to develop our own programs of practice, and both determine and situate our own political, ethical, and social positionings.

Although our studies followed such a parallel track, we did not meet until the 2004 Society for American Archaeology meetings in Montreal, where we found ourselves in all of the same sessions. We like to say that we fell in love with one another at these meetings. We both consider the session held in honor of Bruce Trigger, in which the organizers asked contributors to revisit Trigger's keystone paper Alternative Archaeologies (1984), within the context of contemporary social heritage politics, to be among the most significant and influential conference sessions we have ever attended. During the session, we kept turning to each other in shared wonder and amazement at the vision of archaeology presented in the papers. The session was later published by Junko Habu and colleagues (Habu et al. 2008) as *Evaluating Multiple Narratives*.

The early 2000s were a period when community and Indigenous archaeologies were emerging as a major turning point in the discipline, motivated by such texts as Nicholas and Andrews (1997), Atalay (2006), Marshall (2002), Smith and Wobst (2005), and Watkins (2003, 2005). This movement flowed from earlier post-processual strands and was deeply reliant on the seminal texts of Indigenous scholars, beginning with Tuhiwai Smith's (1999) utterly transformative *Decolonizing Methodologies*, which has promulgated an immense amount of productive thinking and practice by Indigenous scholars and allies. Both of us initiated our PhD work hoping to do community-based archaeology and began to read Indigenous scholars and theory fervently, realizing that these expanding bodies of work, combined with participatory research and an ethics of care, were foundations for the way forward. Kisha would attempt, and fail at, community-based archaeology in what was at the time contested territory between the Yale and Shxw'owhamel First Nations in the Upper Fraser River Valley of British Columbia. She produced a more conventional thesis than she had envisioned that was not warmly received in all sectors and that led her to deep reflection on the discipline (Supernant and Warrick 2014). Natasha's PhD work would eventually lead, with seed funding from Nicholas's Intellectual Property in Cultural Heritage project, to the Inuvialuit Living History Project in the Canadian Western Arctic (Hennessy et al. 2013; Lyons 2013), which she currently directs with Lisa Hodgetts.

Natasha formed Ursus Heritage Consulting with Ian Cameron in 2008 and Kisha became faculty in the Department of Anthropology at University of Alberta in 2010. By this time, both of us had developed a deep sense of care and love that expanded beyond the archaeological record to those living community members with whom we worked, and we struggled finding places and ways to talk about this in our professional settings. Healing as a paradigm was then coming into the wider research vernacular due to the social moment created by the United Nations Declaration on the Rights of Indigenous Peoples (2008) and Canada's Truth and Reconciliation Commission on Residential Schools (Canada 2015; and see Supernant 2018b). Kisha's healing began personally through her work with her own ancestral places and materials.

This led her to her living family and put her in deep relations with both her corporeal and non-corporeal kin, and to her creation of the Exploring Métis Identity Through Archaeology (EMITA) project (Supernant 2018a). Natasha started to experiment with love as a prime mover in her interpretive work (Lyons et al. 2018) in an attempt to help shift the awkward circumventing of this very basic of human emotions—more likely to embarrass than to lead the charge; more likely to pin you as feminine and emotional—within social science research.

The ideas that led to this volume began with our wish to bring together these influences and approaches and to invite others to contribute their own visions of what an archaeology of heart could be. We have experienced an absolute outpouring of emotion, love, and rigorous intellectual output as a result of this invite that continues to grow and gather momentum (Lyons et al. 2019). Below, we describe a suite of elements, and their intellectual influences, that we see as together comprising the "rhizomes" of an emergent heart-centered practice.

The Intertwining Rhizomes of a Heart-Centered Practice

We envision a heart-centered practice to be drawn together from many different theoretical and methodological veins of archaeology and other disciplines, like the entwined runners shooting out from one strawberry plant to another, creating life and vitality and interconnection. We see an archaeology of the heart centered around care and emotion, rather than dispassion and rationality, and operating within a rigorous and relational framework. This framework provides a new ethical space (following Ermine 2007) for thinking through an integrated, responsible, and grounded archaeology, where we show care for the living and the dead. It animates what we do as archaeologists, uniting our intellectual, emotional, physical, and spiritual faculties and allowing us to bring our whole selves to practice (Conkey,

Chap. 17, this volume; Brownlee 2019). An archaeology of the heart, therefore, is not merely a theory or a methodology; it is a practice which expands to the entirety of the archaeological process, from excavation to lab work, from teaching students to sitting with Elders, from working with partners to publishing results. This position fundamentally changes how we consider other humans and non-humans in our practices, as well as how we interpret the past. In this section, we describe four primary elements of a heart-centered practice—rigor, care, relationality, and emotion—which crosscut many of the ideas developed by authors in ensuing chapters.

Rigor

We are acculturated as scholars and scientists to separate the intellectual mind from the physical body, a position which assumes there is an objective world to be studied and that humans must remove themselves from that world to find the truth. Most of the chapters in this volume, and in fact most post-processual archaeologies, critique the Western scientific value of neutrality as false and invalid. Such claims to objectivity and representative authority have both been sharply discredited by feminist philosophers of science, critical theorists, and Indigenous and postmodern scholars, due to the disregard of this position for the subjective role of lived experience, its abjuration of systemic and structural violence to marginalized peoples, and its denial of the more contingent and performative aspects of scientific practice (Bhattacharya 2008; Christians 2000; Habermas 1971; Harding 1986, 1995; Kelley and Hanen 1988; Tuhiwai Smith 2013; Wylie 2000). Sandra Harding (1995, p. 334) observes that "[t]he demand for objectivity, the separation of observation and reporting from the researchers' wishes, which is so essential for the development of science, becomes the demand for separation of thinking from feeling. This promotes moral detachment in scientists which, reinforced by specialization and bureaucratization, allows them to work on all sorts of dangerous and harmful projects with indifference to the human consequences."

We see a heart-centered archaeology following the "strong objectivity" endorsed by Sandra Harding (1995), which rejects both relativism and neutrality and instead begins with the assumption that social inequality exists, in the sciences as elsewhere. This position, which derives from a form of standpoint theory, recognizes that all science is practiced within a system of interests and values (Hanen and Kelley 1989; and see Wylie 2002, 2013). The (social) scientist's job is to position her work consciously and to practice a rigorous self-reflexivity in its conduct. It requires us to emphasize rigor in our research processes, in knowledge generation, and in relations with communities of practice, such as archaeologists, cultural resource managers, students, and various public audiences (c.f. Gero 2015). An archaeology of the heart will acknowledge different knowledge systems, recognize their constraints, and emphasize the role of vetting from multiple perspectives (Atalay 2012; Colwell-Chanthaphonh and Ferguson 2008b; Echo-Hawk and Zimmerman 2006; Habermas 1996; Habu et al. 2008; Lyons et al. 2010; Trigger

2006). All of the following chapters exercise a reflexive approach, to larger and smaller degrees, as contributors consider the challenges, successes, and failures of their research programs, as well as speak to the distinctive demands and rewards associated with heart-centered practice in the respective political, social, institutional, and emotional contexts in which they practice.

Harding's (1995, pp. 347–348) strong objectivity relies on generating multiple perspectives on truth; it is the combination of multiple claims and responding critiques that help unveil different values, stakes, and interests. This competition for truth, is, essentially, the science(s) at work. And in our present academic milieu, it is absolutely essential, because systemic and structural barriers entrenched between most scientific disciplines create silos that prevent the cross-fertilization of people and ideas. A pluralistic approach is what allows such cross-fertilization to operate. In seeking to formulate an archaeology of the heart, we pull a great deal of inspiration from the interplay between science and public policy modalities used by ecologists, biologists, and resource managers to great effect in theorizing and addressing large-scale social and environmental issues (Dietz et al. 2003; Lertzman 2009). A smaller coterie of these practitioners is bringing their hearts explicitly into these equations as part of the suite of theoretical and methodological tools that are intrinsic to collective problem-solving (Bekoff 2002; Kimmerer 2011, 2013; Turner 2008, 2020).

The present work is particularly indebted to Eugene Anderson's (1996) *Ecologies of the Heart*. Anderson employs both a reflexive scientific analysis of the ecological aspects of climate change and a plea to society and its institutions to look critically at how contemporary belief systems exacerbate the various dimensions of the problem by valuing short- over long-term thinking. We are fortunate to have a chapter by Chelsey Armstrong and Eugene Anderson in this volume that looks at similar issues in an archaeological context. Anderson draws on Gregory Bateson's (1972) earlier *Steps to an Ecology of Mind*, which examines how the social and emotional components of human thought often supersede the more conscious and rational ones in public debate and policy-making affecting aspects of our social and environmental worlds (Anderson 1996, p. vii). All of these practitioners encourage us to scrutinize our assumptions and beliefs about emotion-laden issues, be they public or private ones, to speak to each other more freely and arrive at plausible and rational courses of action. They also invoke love as a prime mover of human interest and action and incite us to larger roles in the public discourse (Welch, Chap. 2, this volume).

Care

We suggest that when we bring all of our selves to our practice(s), the interpretations we make about the past come from a place of profound strength rather than weakness. This idea draws on a long and robust lineage of feminist thought beginning with Hilary Rose's (1983) call to integrate the hand, head, and heart into the practice of the natural sciences (Hodgetts and Kelvin, Chap. 7, this volume). Rose saw that reproduction, and the caring labor required (conventionally of women) in raising children, should be the model for the production of a materialist science that combines our physical labor, our respective intelligences, and our love and care. Fully cognizant that science is produced by people who have thoughts, feelings, and their own unique perspectives (read: bias) on the world, she (1983, p. 83) stated: "the production of people is thus different from the production of things. It requires caring labor—the labor of love." Bringing our hearts into this labor helps create "an emancipatory science rather than an exterminatory science" (1983, p. 75), meaning that we will be discerning about the projects we select and how our results are deployed in the world.

We endorse an ethic of care in our approach to research, developed and applied first in social psychology in the 1980s (Gilligan 1982; Tronto 1993) to "emphasize the importance of context, interdependence, relationships, and responsibilities to concrete others" (Koggel and Orme 2010, p. 109). This body of literature critiques a foundational assumption of psychology that the autonomous self, or individual agent, is the primary unit of healthy social relationships. Unpacking this logic, feminist scholars showed that this idealization is not only untenable but that it deforms the theories based on it (no matter whose gender is considered). Gilligan (1995, p. 120) and others theorize "connection as primary and fundamental in human life," a position that hears the relational and interdependent voice between people and its socially embedded character. As a body of theory, feminist ethics of care have expanded broadly into the social sciences and humanities (e.g., Larrabee 2016; Christians 2005; Oleson 2005), informing policy and practice in contexts that focus on health and well-being, as well as contributing to the foundations of care-based science (Watson 2009).

In the field of nursing, Watson (2009, p. 466) has followed practitioners "seeking more authentic practices, giving meaning and purpose to their professional lives and work," as well as working toward more conscious patient care. In this latter regard, Watson (Watson 2009, pp. 467–468) states: "Nurses and practitioners who are literate with caring relationships are capable of having loving, caring, kind, and sensitively meaningful, personal connections with an increasingly enlightened public: a public seeking wholeness and spiritual connections for their wellbeing, not just sterile, depersonalized, medical technological interventions, void of human-to-human caring relationships." These are formative points for advocates of the integrative and narrative medicine movements (Charon 2001a, b, 2008; Rakel 2012). They apply equally to myriad disciplines and professions beyond the caring ones, such as the social and life sciences and arts and humanities: these issues are profound contemporary ones that affect us all.

Care encompasses responsibility for the health and well-being of self and others, as well as attentiveness and consideration so as not to cause harm through action. These values are not inherent to the social and disciplinary structures in which we are immersed; rather, competition for resources (e.g., grading student papers, competing for grant dollars, bidding for contracts) is a near-constant driving force, as is the "wild west" culture of archaeological practice (Hays-Gilpin 2000). Field schools and field contexts are a particularly critical arena where many students or junior archaeologists experience harassment, discrimination, and assault (Clancy et al. 2014; Green et al. 1993; Hodgetts et al. 2020; Nelson et al. 2017). Often considered a rite of passage for archaeologists, field settings present unique challenges that are not found in typical classroom settings, and prospective archaeologists are evaluated on how well they can cope under these often deeply hierarchical conditions. Creating safe spaces for students to learn and engage in archaeological fieldwork requires an ethic of care approach, where we are cognizant that blurring of boundaries can happen in field projects and therefore have clear policies and agreements in place that define and, when necessary, enforce those boundaries. One way to accomplish this is to set out principles of community from the beginning of the field work process and have participants agree to those principles. Making explicit the ways in which we treat ourselves, each other, and the archaeological record creates caring and conscious teaching and learning environments that put the well-being of all involved at the core of the work (Abbott, Chap. 11, this volume; Surface-Evans, Chap. 5, this volume).

Care ethics have not conventionally extended to university-level pedagogy and training, nor collegial relationships, nor certainly to field contexts. We envision an archaeology where care is not a liability but a strength, where careful listening is deeply valued (Kehoe and Schmidt 2017; Schmidt and Kehoe 2019; Hodgetts and Kelvin, Chap. 7, this volume), where good sense and structure create an environment where students know what is expected from their part of the learning relationship (Baxter 2009), where practitioners model care for self and others in the demanding contexts of archaeology, and where "culturally safe" practices that respect the concerns and perspectives of individuals and communities are fully integrated into research relationships (Rigney 2003; Tuhiwai Smith 2013).

Relationality

Relationships are central to human cultures, and our lives are utterly contingent upon how we conceive and conduct them. Indigenous scholars and thinkers have long emphasized the importance of relationality among humans, between humans and other-than-human beings, and between non-humans, including material objects and landscapes (Archibald 2008; Atalay 2012; Todd 2016). The social sciences are currently undergoing an "ontological" turn (Graeber 2015; De Castro 2015; Holbraad et al. 2014), where Indigenous and other scholars of color undermined by the hegemony of the "whitestream" academic establishment are voicing their thoughts and intervening through other ways of being and relating (e.g., Grande 2003; Simpson 2014; Tuck and Yang 2012; Rizvi 2008; Todd 2016; Watts 2013). Feminist scholars see the relational voice—the ability to be and speak for yourself at the same time as nurturing relationships to and cooperation with those around you—as central to a healthy sense of self, community, and ultimately, survival as a species (Gilligan 2014).

Archaeologists build relationships through practice, whether it be with colleagues, students, community members, clients, or with the cultural materials we excavate, handle, and curate. Without the relationships we build, archaeology would not be possible, yet we do not always appreciate the impacts those relations have on the ways knowledge gets generated in our field and the ways we interpret the past (e.g., Holtorf 2010, 2013). These relational elements should be considered part of the messier whole of what we do rather than be conveniently tidied and/or denied (Gero 2015; Piccini and Schaepe 2014). We also need to acknowledge the relationships other people or communities might have with each other and with the archaeological record. For many Indigenous scholars, research is considered ceremony and must be viewed and conducted as such, with an emphasis on relationship-building (Wilson 2008). Many Indigenous communities have a sacred relationship with the places and objects of their ancestors, and when these relations are disrupted, the health and well-being of the community itself can be impacted, as is often the case with ancestral remains. In this context, Atalay (2019, p. 81) stresses the "importance of connecting intellectual work with spiritual and emotional aspects of reclaiming, and with embodied practices, such as physical engagement with cultural items—walking the land, recording or mapping sacred places, or hearing and telling stories about repatriation and reclaiming."

Archaeologists do not have to share such beliefs to recognize the sacred relations held between communities and their cultural materials and relations, and they can make space for those practices without feeling that their own set of disciplinary practices are being threatened. Rather, we need to bring to light the complexities of the space between different ways of knowing and relating to the past and find ethical spaces for engagement (Ermine 2007). For "what remains hidden and enfolded are the deeper level thoughts, interests and assumptions that will inevitably influence and animate the kind of relationship the two can have. It is this deeper level force, the underflow-become-influential, the enfolded dimension that needs to be acknowledged and brought to bear in the complex situation produced by confronting knowledge…systems" (Ermine 2007, p. 195).

We see heart-centered archaeologists working in a deliberate fashion to understand the complex webs of relations in which we are embedded. Relationships can be challenging, difficult, and fall apart due to our emotions, perceptions, and actions, however well intentioned; as practitioners, we need to understand the state of both our hearts and minds as we think and act (Rizvi, Chap. 6). To this end, a heart-centered archaeology may draw on concepts and practices from leadership, community-building, therapy, and contemplative pedagogy (Palmer 2009; Palmer et al. 2010; Palmer 2017; Barbezat and Bush 2013; Petrucka et al. 2016) in order to construct practices that emphasize the roles of openness, accountability, and responsibility across all forms of relationships (and see Colwell-Chanthaphonh and Ferguson 2008a; Zimmerman 2005). Many of our contributors, including Tanja Hoffmann, Uzma Rizvi, Leslie van Gelder, Melanie Chang, and April Nowell, explore the expectations and perceptions they hold of their relationships to communities with whom they practice, or between communities that existed in the past, in the chapters that follow.

Emotion

Emotions are part of the human experience and, in contemporary Western culture, are closely tied to how we conceptualize the heart (although this is not necessarily true across time and space). Emotions play a role in how we make decisions, both in our personal and our professional lives (Barbezat and Bush 2013; Biagetti and Lugli 2016; Fleisher and Norman 2015; Harris and Sørensen 2010; Murphy 2011; Tubb 2006). We recognize that while there are gendered and cultural differences in how emotions are expressed, acted upon, and controlled, emotions nevertheless played just as significant a role in the past as in the present.

Drawing on emotion research in other disciplines, Sarah Tarlow (2000) proposed in her seminal paper "Emotion in Archaeology" that exploring emotion was both necessary and possible in archaeology. Since that time, emotion research has rapidly expanded in our discipline to speak to a variety of human states, such as sorrow, anxiety, happiness, and empathy, as well as to probe more deeply into a variety of topics, like gender, identity, and childhood (Baxter 2005, 2008, 2013; Baxter, Chap. 9, this volume; Fleisher and Norman Fleisher and Norman 2015; Tarlow 2012; Tarlow et al. 2000). Many papers in this volume venture into that taboo arena of love, including reclaiming the feeling of doing the work we do as a true labor of love (Tringham, Chap. 15, this volume; Welch, Chap. 2, this volume; and Atalay, Chap. 16, this volume; Naumann 2017). Cultural heritage projects of various kinds are looking to bring emotion into our representations and portrayals of heritage sites, objects, people, and processes (Graesch et al., Chap. 10, this volume; Lindstrøm, Chap. 12, this volume; Brownlee 2019; Perry 2018). And perhaps most importantly, exploring our own emotions as practitioners helps us identify the emotional nature of disciplinary debates, for instance, about scientific vs. humanistic approaches to archaeology or the moral and legal status of ancestors such as the Ancient One, also known as Kennewick Man (Rasmussen et al. 2015; Watkins 2004), as well as the personal ones happening in our own institutional, field, and research contexts.

We are confident that an archaeology of the heart can create spaces for the emotions of practitioners, stakeholders, and peoples of the past. It can, for instance, create space for understanding the role of how intergenerational trauma impacts Indigenous communities and influences their ability to engage with archaeologists, as well as recognizing the possibilities for a responsible archaeology that can aid the healing process from historical trauma (Atalay, Chap. 16, this volume; Supernant 2018b). To this end, David Schaepe and colleagues (2017) have developed a framework for "Archaeology as Therapy." This working group of Coast Salish community members of the Pacific Northwest, clinicians, and archaeologists is currently translating this framework into a program for practice that engages youth with their cultural landscapes and belongings as a way to build confidence, identity, and well-being (Chatterjee and Noble 2016; Schaepe et al. in press).

The Fruits of Our Heart-Centered Labors

Archaeologists, as we have noted, often take on projects that we consider labors of love. However, we tend to talk about this emotional labor in interpersonal terms rather than in formal contexts, such as presentations and publications. Why is that? In this section, we discuss themes that arise in this volume as the fruits of our heart-centered labors of love. We are speaking of fruits as the outcomes of our intellectual, social, emotional, and spiritual work in archaeology, in the form of relationships, processes, projects, and products that we value and take pride in.

Below we discuss different and often crosscutting expressions of heart-centered practice that emerge in the following chapters, which are then taken up again by Sonya Atalay in our closing chapter and interpreted under different lights. Overall, the volume is divided into two substantive parts composed of six papers each— "Heart-Centred Guidance for Practice and Engagement" followed by "Heart-Centred in Encounters with the Archaeological Record"—whose content generally represent a movement from more internal and personal types of narratives, analyses, and reflections to more external and material-based ones. Our volume is bookended with a commentary section that includes three papers, one of which you must also seek online [link]. One prominent theme of this work is healing and transformation. Healing, as the process of making or becoming sound or healthy again, relates to myriad contexts, from the individual to the collective, from the very personal to the institutional. Becoming whole again usually implies change and transformation. In Western society, we are becoming more attuned and open to diverse healing practices than we have been for many centuries; in other cultures, there exist long-standing healing traditions that have long kept their members in tune and balance (with each other, with nature). Western-trained archaeologists have often confronted profound difference working with Indigenous and ethnocultural communities that causes them to transform their priorities and paradigms, but this can certainly happen in other contexts and situations as well. Several contributors use rigorous self-reflective analyses to speak to critical events that have caused transformations and/or greater awareness in their practices: Uzma Rizvi contemplates the harm we may cause in the betrayal of research relationships; Tanja Hoffmann, as well as Lisa Hodgetts and Laura Kelvin, considers major lessons learned from their relationships with Indigenous communities; and, Sarah Surface-Evans documents the steps she has taken to defend and articulate her research and pedagogical practices.

A second theme of this volume relates to motivations for practice. From a critical archaeology perspective, Mark Leone (2010, pp. 8–9; Wilson 2008, p. 8) asks us to name our circumstances and motivations at the outset of research. The motivations for archaeological work vary widely, of course, from the commercial to the ego-driven to the (sometimes seemingly) altruistic to the purely curious to the pursuit of knowledge unknown. None of these is inherently wrong, but recognizing our emotions and intentions around these motivations is certainly a critical starting place—a standpoint—for pursuing robust research and research relationships. Several authors in this volume explore their research motivations in different ways and employ tactics that span a scale of action from intense reflexivity to overt and more covert forms of activism (cf. Atalay et al. 2014; Hogg et al. 2017). Chelsey Armstrong and Eugene Anderson are motivated by the damage caused by extractive industries to advocate an archaeological practice tied to environmental ethics. John Welch is motivated by "what-if" scenarios to put appreciative inquiry to work exploring pathways toward structural change and desired futures. Meg Conkey examines her twin fears and hopes for the future of our discipline (and culture) and dares to root for a time when the heart takes over.

A third theme of this volume is the relationships that archaeologists create between people of the present (themselves and others) and those of the past. These chapters attend most closely to recognizing and expressing love, care, and other emotional states conveyed through the material record of those left behind. Contributors imagine, suggest, depict, and specify how these relationships are conceived and operationalized through different forms of inquiry. Leslie van Gelder articulates the relationship between Paleolithic communities and the cave walls that formed their homes. Jane Baxter claims an emotional space for interpreting the archaeology of childhood, Anthony Graesch and colleagues use emotional resonance to develop an archaeology focused on contemporary illegal discard, and Torill Christine Lindstrøm tests a facial coding system in the analysis of the emotions represented by faces on Roman frescos. Callum Abbott envisions a communities-of-practice approach to lithic analysis. And Ruth Tringham—whose multimedia contribution can be viewed online—investigates what has set her heart beating fast as she excavated closely observed layers through many years of archaeological practice.

The fourth and final theme of this volume relates to the production process itself. For the past 3 years, Natasha and Kisha have met routinely with co-editors Jane and Sonya, and in this time, life has happened to all of us. We've become close friends, and we've developed a way of working that fills our hearts as well as our minds and bodies and spirits, in the process forming the Heart-Centered and Emotional Archaeology in Research and Teaching (HEART) collective. This work has been a labor of love. We've had similarly positive, constructive, and engaging interactions with our contributors, and we thank them profusely for thinking through the tenets of an archaeology of the heart with us and for being so brave, open, creative, rigorous, and heartfelt in their writing and practices. We owe a great deal of appreciation to some of the discipline's mentors and leaders—Meg Conkey, Ruth Tringham, Alison Wylie, George Nicholas, John Welch, and Susan Kus—many of them our own heroes and heroines, who took a chance on this work as contributors and reviewers. We have experienced a remarkable intergenerational dialogue with them through the writing, editing, and review processes characterized by all the elements of a heart-centered practice asserted in this chapter. The production of this volume brings to mind the story of the gift of heart berries shared by Sonya Atalay in the closing chapter of this volume, which tells us why each part of the strawberry plant is important, beautiful, and necessary. You'll find it well worth the read, as are all the chapters in between.

References

Anderson, E. N. (1996). *Ecologies of the heart: emotion, belief, and the environment.* Oxford: Oxford University Press.

Archibald, J.-A. (2008). *Indigenous storywork: Educating the heart, mind, body, and spirit.* Vancouver: University of British Columbia Press.

Atalay, S. (2006). Indigenous archaeology as decolonizing practice. *American Indian Quarterly, 30*(3/4), 280–310.

Atalay, S. (2012). *Community-based archaeology: Research with, by, and for indigenous and local communities.* Berkeley: University of California Press.

Atalay, S. (2019). Braiding strands of wellness: How repatriation contributes to healing through embodied practice and storywork. *The Public Historian, 41*(1), 78–89.

Atalay, S., Clauss, L. R., McGuire, R. H., & Welch, J. R. (2014). *Transforming archaeology: Activist practices and prospects.* Walnut Creek: Left Coast Press.

Barbezat, D. P., & Bush, M. (2013). *Contemplative practices in higher education: Powerful methods to transform teaching and learning.* New York: Wiley.

Bateson, G. (1972). *Steps to an ecology of mind: Collected essays in anthropology, psychiatry, evolution, and epistemology.* Chicago: University of Chicago Press.

Baxter, J. E. (2005). Introduction: the archaeology of childhood in context. *Archeological Papers of the American Anthropological Association, 15*(1), 1–9.

Baxter, J. E. (2008). The archaeology of childhood. *Annual Review of Anthropology, 37,* 159–175.

Baxter, J. E. (2009). *Archaeological field schools: A guide for teaching in the field.* New York: Routledge.

Baxter, J. E. (2013). Status, sentimentality and structuration: An examination of 'intellectual spaces' for children in the study of America's Historic Cemeteries. *Childhood in the Past, 6*(2), 106–122.

Bekoff, M. (2002). The importance of ethics in conservation biology: Let's be ethicists not ostriches. *Endangered Species Update, 19*(2), 23–26.

Bhattacharya, H. (2008). New critical collaborative ethnography. In S. N. Hesse-Biber & P. Leavy (Eds.), *Handbook of emergent methods* (pp. 303–322). New York: Guildford Press.

Biagetti, S., & Lugli, F. (2016). *The intangible elements of culture in ethnoarchaeological research.* New York: Springer.

Bond, G. C., & Gilliam, A. (Eds.). (1997). *Social construction of the past: Representation as power.* London: Psychology Press.

Brody, H. (1981). *Maps and dreams: Indians and the British Columbia frontier.* Vancouver: Douglas & McIntyre.

Brownlee, K. (2019). *Dibaajimindww Geteyaag: Ogiiyose, Noojigiigoo'iwe gaye Dibinawaag Nibiing Onji – Stories of the old ones: Hunter and fisher from sheltered water.* Winnipeg: Manitoba Museum.

Brumfiel, E. M. (1992). Distinguished lecture in archeology: breaking and entering the ecosystem—gender, class, and faction steal the show. *American Anthropologist, 94*(3), 551–567.

Canada, T. a. R. C. o. (2015). *Honouring the truth, reconciling for the future: Summary of the final report of the Truth and Reconciliation Commission of Canada.* Winnipeg: Truth and Reconciliation Commission of Canada.

Charon, R. (2001a). Narrative medicine: A model for empathy, reflection, profession, and trust. *JAMA, 286*(15), 1897–1902.

Charon, R. (2001b). Narrative medicine: Form, function, and ethics. *Annals of Internal Medicine, 134*(1), 83–87.

Charon, R. (2008). *Narrative medicine: Honoring the stories of illness.* Oxford: Oxford University Press.

Chatterjee, H., & Noble, G. (2016). *Museums, health and well-being.* London: Routledge.

Christians, C. G. (2000). Ethics and politics in qualitative research. In N. K. Denzin & Y. S. Lincoln (Eds.), *Handbook of qualitative research* (pp. 133–155). Thousand Oaks: Sage.

Christians, C. G. (2005). Ethics and politics in qualitative research. In N. K. Denzin & Y. S. Lincoln (Eds.), *Handbook of qualitative research* (pp. 139–164). Thousand Oaks: Sage Publications.

Clancy, K. B., Nelson, R. G., Rutherford, J. N., & Hinde, K. (2014). Survey of academic field experiences (SAFE): Trainees report harassment and assault. *PLoS One, 9*(7), 1–9.

Colwell-Chanthaphonh, C., & Ferguson, T. J. (Eds.). (2008a). *Collaboration in archaeological practice: Engaging descendant communities.* Plymouth: AltaMira Press.

Colwell-Chanthaphonh, C., & Ferguson, T. J. (2008b). *Collaboration in archaeological practice: The collaborative continuum* (pp. 1–34). Lanham: AltaMira Press.

De Castro, E. V. (2015). Who is afraid of the ontological wolf? Some comments on an ongoing anthropological debate. *Cambridge Anthropology, 33*(1), 2.

Deloria, V. (1969). *Custer died for your sins: An Indian manifesto.* Norman: University of Oklahoma Press.

Deloria, V. (1997). *Red earth, white lies: Native Americans and the myth of scientific fact.* Golden: Fulcrum Publishing.

Dietz, T., Ostrom, E., & Stern, P. C. (2003). The struggle to govern the commons. *Science, 302*(5652), 1907–1912.

Echo-Hawk, R., & Zimmerman, L. J. (2006). Beyond racism: Some opinions about racialism and American Archaeology. *American Indian Quarterly, 30,* 461–485.

Ermine, W. (2007). The ethical space of engagement (article). *Indigenous Law Journal, 6*(1), 193–203. http://login.ezproxy.library.ualberta.ca/login?url=https://search.ebscohost.com/login.aspx?direct=true&db=edshol&AN=edshol.hein.journals.ilj6.12&site=eds-live&scope=site.

Fleisher, J., & Norman, N. (2015). *The archaeology of anxiety: The materiality of anxiousness, worry, and fear.* New York: Springer.

Gero, J. M. (2015). *Yutopian: Archaeology, ambiguity, and the production of knowledge in Northwest Argentina.* Austin: University of Texas Press.

Gero, J. M., & Conkey, M. W. (Eds.). (1991). *Engendering archaeology: Women and prehistory.* New York: Wiley-Blackwell.

Gilligan, C. (1982). New maps of development: New visions of maturity. *American Journal of Orthopsychiatry, 52*(2), 199.

Gilligan, C. (1995). Hearing the difference: Theorizing connection. *Hypatia, 10*(2), 120–127. https://doi.org/10.1111/j.1527-2001.1995.tb01373.x.

Gilligan, C. (2014). Moral injury and the ethic of care: Reframing the conversation about differences. *Journal of Social Philosophy, 45*(1), 89–106. https://doi.org/10.1111/josp.12050.

Graeber, D. (2015). Radical alterity is just another way of saying "reality" a reply to Eduardo Viveiros de Castro. *HAU: Journal of Ethnographic Theory, 5*(2), 1–41.

Grande, S. (2003). Whitestream feminism and the colonialist project: A review of contemporary feminist pedagogy and praxis. *Educational Theory, 53*(3), 329–346.

Green, G., Barbour, R. S., Barnard, M., & Kitzinger, J. (1993). "Who wears the trousers?": Sexual harassment in research settings. *Women's Studies International Forum. Elsevier, 16*(6), 627–637.

Habermas, J. (1971). *Knowledge and human interests* (trans: J. Shapiro). London: Heinemann.

Habermas, J. (1996). *Between facts and norms: Contributions to a discourse theory of law and democracy* (trans: W. Rehg). Cambridge: Polity Press.

Habu, J., Fawcett, C., & Matsunaga, J. M. (2008). *Evaluating multiple narratives: Beyond nationalist, colonialist, imperialist archaeologies.* New York: Springer.

Hanen, M., & Kelley, J. (1989). Inference to the best explanation in archaeology. In V. Pinsky & A. Wylie (Eds.), *Critical traditions in contemporary archaeology* (pp. 14–17). Cambridge: Cambridge University Press.

Harding, S. (1986). *The science question in feminism.* Ithaca: Cornell University Press.

Harding, S. (1995). "Strong objectivity": A response to the new objectivity question. *Synthese, 104*(3), 331–349.

Harris, O. J., & Sørensen, T. F. (2010). Rethinking emotion and material culture. *Archaeological Dialogues, 17*(2), 145–163.

Hays-Gilpin, K. (2000). Feminist scholarship in archaeology. *The Annals of the American Academy of Political and Social Science, 571*(1), 89–106.

Hennessy, K., Lyons, N., Loring, S., Arnold, C., Joe, M., Elias, A., et al. (2013). The inuvialuit living history project: Digital return as the forging of relationships between institutions, people, and data. *Museum Anthropology Review, 7*(1–2), 44–73.

Hodgetts, L., Supernant, K., Lyons, N., & Welch, J. R. (2020). #MeToo and more: Preliminary results of the equity and diversity in Canadian Archaeology Survey. *Canadian Journal of Archaeology.*

Hogg, E. A., Welch, J. R., & Ferris, N. (2017). Full spectrum archaeology. *Archaeologies, 13*(1), 175–200.

Holbraad, M., Pedersen, M. A., & de Castro, E. V. (2014). The Politics of Ontology: Anthropological Positions. Theorizing the Contemporary, *Fieldsights*, January 13. https://culanth.org/fieldsights/the-politics-of-ontology-anthropological-positions.

Holtorf, C. (2010, August). Meta-stories of archaeology. *World Archaeology, 42*, 381–393.

Holtorf, C. (2013). On pastness: a reconsideration of materiality in archaeological object authenticity. *Anthropological Quarterly*, 427–443.

Kehoe, A. B., & Schmidt, P. R. (2017). Introduction: Expanding our knowledge by listening. *The SAA Archaeological Record, 17*(4), 15–19.

Kelley, J., & Hanen, M. (1988). *Archaeology and the methodology of science*. Albequerque: University of New Mexico Press.

Kimmerer, R. W. (2011). Restoration and reciprocity: The contributions of traditional ecological knowledge. In *Human dimensions of ecological restoration* (pp. 257–276). New York: Springer.

Kimmerer, R. W. (2013). *Braiding sweetgrass: Indigenous wisdom, scientific knowledge and the teachings of plants*. Minneapolis: Milkweed Editions.

Koggel, C., & Orme, J. (2010). *Care ethics: New theories and applications*. New York: Taylor & Francis.

Larrabee, M. J. (2016). *An ethic of care: Feminist and interdisciplinary perspectives*. Routledge.

Leone, M. P. (2010). *Critical historical archaeology*. London: Routledge.

Leone, M. P., Potter, P. B., Jr., Shackel, P. A., Blakey, M. L., Bradley, R., Durrans, B., et al. (1987). Toward a critical archaeology. *Current Anthropology, 28*(3), 283–302.

Lertzman, K. (2009). The paradigm of management, management systems, and resource stewardship. *Journal of Ethnobiology, 29*(2), 339–358.

Lyons, N. (2013). *Where the wind blows us: Practicing critical community archaeology in the Canadian North*. Tuscon: University of Arizona Press.

Lyons, N., Dawson, P., Walls, M., Uluadluak, D., Angalik, L., Kalluak, M., et al. (2010). Person, place, memory, thing: How Inuit Elders are informing archaeological practice in the Canadian North. *Canadian Journal of Archaeology, 34*(1), 1–31.

Lyons, N., Hoffmann, T., Miller, D., Huddlestan, S., Leon, R., & Squires, K. (2018). Katzie & the Wapato: An archaeological love story. *Archaeologies, 14*, 7–29.

Lyons, N., Schaepe, D. M., Hennessy, K., Blake, M., Pennier, C., Welch, J. R., et al. (2016). Sharing deep history as digital knowledge: An ontology of the Sq'ewlets website project. *Journal of Social Archaeology, 16*(3), 359–384.

Lyons, N., Supernant, K., & Welch, J. R. (2019). What are the prospects for an archaeology of the heart? *SAA Archaeological Record, 19*(2), 6–9.

Marshall, Y. (2002). What is community archaeology? *World Archaeology, 34*(2), 211–219.

McGuire, R. H. (1992). Archeology and the First Americans. *American Anthropologist, 94*(4), 816–836.

Mihesuah, D. A. (1996). American Indians, anthropologists, pothunters, and repatriation: Ethical, religious, and political differences. *American Indian Quarterly, 20*(2), 229–237.

Murphy, E. M. (2011). Children's burial grounds in Ireland (Cillini) and parental emotions toward infant death. *International Journal of Historical Archaeology, 15*(3), 409–428.

Naumann, A. (2017). Doing your heart's work. *SAA Archaeological Record, 17*(3), 26–28.

Nelson, R. G., Rutherford, J. N., Hinde, K., & Clancy, K. B. (2017). Signaling safety: Characterizing fieldwork experiences and their implications for career trajectories. *American Anthropologist, 119*(4), 710–722.

Nicholas, G. P., & Andrews, T. D. (1997). *At a Crossroads: Archaeology and First Peoples in Canada*. Vancouver: Simon Fraser University.

Oleson, V. (2005). Early millennial feminist qualitative research: Challenges and contours. In N. K. Denzin & Y. S. Lincoln (Eds.), *The Sage Handbook of Qualitative Research* (pp. 235–278). Thousand Oaks: Sage Publications.

Palmer, P. J. (2009). *A hidden wholeness: The journey toward an undivided life*. New York: Wiley.

Palmer, P. J. (2017). *The courage to teach: Exploring the inner landscape of a teacher's life*. New York: Wiley.

Palmer, P. J., Zajonc, A., & Scribner, M. (2010). *The heart of higher education: A call to renewal*. New York: Wiley.

Perry, S. (2018). *EMOTIVE: Storytelling for cultural heritage*. http://emotiveproject.eu/. Accessed 6 Apr 2018.

Petrucka, P. M., Bickford, D., Bassendowski, S., Goodwill, W., Wajunta, C., Yuzicappi, B., et al. (2016). Positive leadership, legacy, lifestyles, attitudes, and activities for Aboriginal youth: A wise practices approach for positive Aboriginal youth futures. *International Journal of Indigenous Health, 11*(1), 177–197.

Piccini, A., & Schaepe, D. M. (2014). The messy business of archaeology as participatory local knowledge: A conversation between the Stó:lō Nation and Knowle West. *Canadian Journal of Archaeology, 38*(2), 466–495. http://www.jstor.org/stable/43487310.

Rakel, D. (2012). *Integrative medicine e-book: Expert consult* (Premium edn.) Amsterdam: Elsevier Health Sciences.

Rasmussen, M., Sikora, M., Albrechtsen, A., Korneliussen, T. S., Moreno-Mayar, J. V., Poznik, G. D., et al. (2015). The ancestry and affiliations of Kennewick Man. *Nature, 523*(7561), 455.

Rigney, L. I. (2003). The First Perspective: Culturally safe research practices on or with Indigenous Peoples. In T. Peck, E. Siegfried, & G. Oetelaar (Eds.), *Indigenous People and archaeology: Honouring the past, discussing the present, building the future* (pp. 226–244). Calgary: University of Calgary Archaeological Association.

Rizvi, U. Z. (2008). Conclusion: Archaeological futures and the postcolonial critique. In M. Liebmann & U. Z. Rizvi (Eds.), *Archaeology and the postcolonial critique* (pp. 197–203). New York: Altamira.

Rose, H. (1983). Hand, brain, and heart: A feminist epistemology for the natural sciences. *Signs: Journal of Women in Culture and Society, 9*(1), 73–90.

Schaepe, D. M., Angelbeck, B., Snook, D., & Welch, J. R. (2017). Archaeology as therapy: Connecting belongings, knowledge, time, place, and well-being. *Current Anthropology, 58*(4), 502–533. https://doi.org/10.1086/692985.

Schaepe, D. M., Lyons, N., Chan, A. S., Phillips, A., & Hennessy, K. (in press). The Sq'éwlets Youth Origins Experience: Providing Tangible and Intangible Experiences of Ancestral Places and Belongings in Supporting Wellness among Indigenous Youth and Community. In *Material Connections: Exploring the role of objects in learning and wellbeing*, edited by T. Kador and H. Chatterjee. London: Routledge.

Schmidt, P. R., & Patterson, T. C. (1995). *Making alternative histories: the practice of archaeology and history in non-Western settings*. Santa Fe, NM: School of American Research Press.

Schmidt, P. R., & Kehoe, A. B. (2019). Archaeologies of Listening. Gainsville, FL: University Press of Florida.

Shanks, M., & Tilley, C. Y. (1987). *Social theory and archaeology*. Cambridge: Polity Press.

Simpson, A. (2014). *Mohawk interruptus: Political life across the borders of settler states*. Durham: Duke University Press.

Smith, & Wobst. (2005). *Indigenous archaeologies: Decolonizing theory and practice*. London: Taylor & Francis.

Supernant, K. (2018a). 'Archaeology of the Métis' S. Silliman historical archaeology Oxford Handbook online. Oxford: Oxford University Press.

Supernant, K. (2018b). Reconciling the past for the future: The next 50 years of Canadian archaeology in the post-TRC era. *Canadian Journal of Archaeology, 42*(1), 144–153.

Supernant, K., & Warrick, G. (2014). Challenges to critical community-based archaeological practice in Canada. *Canadian Journal of Archaeology, 38*(2), 563–591.

Tarlow, S. (2012). The archaeology of emotion and affect. *Annual Review of Anthropology, 41*, 169–185.

Tarlow, S., Averill, J. R., Campbell, F., Hansson, J., Cowgill, G. L., Harré, R., et al. (2000). Emotion in archaeology. *Current Anthropology, 41*(5), 713–746.

Todd, Z. (2016). An Indigenous feminist's take on the ontological turn: 'Ontology' is just another word for colonialism. *Journal of Historical Sociology, 29*(1), 4–22.

Trigger, B. G. (1980). Archaeology and the image of the American Indian. *American Antiquity, 45*, 662–676.

Trigger, B. G. (1984). Alternative archaeologies: Nationalist, colonialist, imperialist. *Man, 19*(3), 355–370. http://www.jstor.org/action/showPublication?journalCode=man.

Trigger, B. G. (2006). *A history of archaeological thought*. Cambridge: Cambridge University Press.

Trigger, B. G., Series, N., & Sep, N. (1984). Alternative archaeologies: Nationalist, colonialist, imperialist. *Man, 19*(3), 355–370. http://www.jstor.org/action/showPublication?journalCode=man.

Tronto, J. C. (1993). *Moral boundaries: A political argument for an ethic of care*. London: Psychology Press.

Tubb, K. W. (2006). Artifacts and emotion. In N. Brodie, M. M. Kersel, C. Luke, & K. W. Tubb (Eds.), *Archaeology, cultural heritage, and the antiquities trade* (pp. 284–302). Gainsville: University of Florida Press.

Tuck, E., & Yang, K. W. (2012). Decolonization is not a metaphor. *Decolonization: Indigeneity, Education & Society, 1*(1).

Tuhiwai Smith, L. (1999). *Decolonizing methodologies: Research and Indigenous Peoples*. London: Zed Books Limited.

Tuhiwai Smith, L. (2013). *Decolonizing methodologies: Research and Indigenous Peoples*. London: Zed Books Ltd.

Turner, N. J. (2008). *The Earth's Blanket: Traditional teachings for sustainable living*. Seattle: University of Washington Press.

Turner, N. J. (2020) *Plants, People, and Places: The Roles of Ethnobotany and Ethnoecology in Indigenous Peoples' Land Rights in Canada and Beyond*. Montreal: McGill-Queen's University Press.

United Nations Declaration on the Rights of Indigenous Peoples. (2008). United Nations: New York.

Walde, D., & Willows, N. D. (1991). *1989 'The Archaeology of Gender: Proceedings of the twenty-second annual conference of the Chacmool Archaeological Association of the University of Calgary' D. Walde, & N. D. Willows Chacmool*. Calgary: University of Calgary Archaeological Association.

Watkins, J. (2003). Beyond the margin: American Indians, First Nations, and Archaeology in North America. *American Antiquity, 68*(2), 273–285. https://doi.org/10.2307/3557080.

Watkins, J. (2004). Becoming American or becoming Indian? NAGPRA, Kennewick and cultural affiliation. *Journal of Social Archaeology, 4*(1), 60–80.

Watkins, J. (2005). Through wary eyes: Indigenous perspectives on archaeology. *Annual Review of Anthropology, 34*, 429–449.

Watson, J. (2009). Caring science and human caring theory: Transforming personal and professional practices of nursing and health care. *Journal of Health and Human Services Administration, 31*, 466–482.

Watts, V. (2013). Indigenous place-thought and agency amongst humans and non humans (First Woman and Sky Woman go on a European world tour!). *Decolonization: Indigeneity, Education & Society, 2*(1), 20–34.

Wilson, S. (2008). *Research is ceremony: Indigenous research methods*. Black Point: Fernwood Publishing.

Wylie, A. (1992). Rethinking the quincentennial: consequences for past and present. *American Antiquity*, 591–594.

Wylie, A. (1997). The engendering of archaeology: Refiguring feminist science studies. *Osiris, 12*, 80–99.

Wylie, A. (2000). Questions of evidence, legitimacy, and the (dis)unity of science. *American Antiquity, 65*(2), 227–237. https://doi.org/10.2307/2694057.

Wylie, A. (2002). Archaeological cables and tacking: Beyond objectivism and relativism. In A. Wylie (Ed.), *Thinking from things: Essays in the philosophy of archaeology* (pp. 161–167). Berkeley: University of California Press.

Wylie, A. (2013). Why Standpoint Matters. In S. Harding & R. Figueroa (Eds.), *Science and other cultures: Issues in philosophies of science and technology* (pp. 34–56). London: Routledge.

Zimmerman, L. J. (2005). First, be humble: Working with Indigenous Peoples and other descendant communities. In C. Smith & H. M. Wobst (Eds.), *Indigenous archaeologies: Decolonizing theory and practice* (pp. 301–314). London: Routledge.

Part I
Heart-Centered Guidance for Practice and Engagement

How do we follow a heart-centered approach to engage with the discipline of archaeology, with each other as colleagues and community partners, and with the diverse people impacted by our work? The chapters in this section focus on personal stories and experiences to illustrate the unique ways that the authors incorporate heart-centered practices into their research, mentoring, or teaching. For some, we are allowed a glimpse into the intimate and moving ways that archaeology has captured their heart. For others, we see the care and humility of practice that are central for deep roots of relationality to settle and grow.

John Welch proclaims his love for archaeology, taking an appreciative inquiry approach to imagine all archaeology could become, if we focus on heart and love. Emphasizing archaeology focused on care, for each other, for the past, and for the environment, Welch brings all the potential of archaeology to the fore, outlining six areas where a heart-centered practice could move archaeology into a new relevance for the future.

Chelsey Armstrong and Eugene Anderson address the discipline of archaeology, calling for a broader environmental ethic to infuse cultural resource management practices, especially in North America. Drawing on their deep and long-standing work with First Nations communities, they emphasize how their research experiences center the interconnectedness of land, water, plants, animals, and the archaeological record. They note how the structure of most CRM does not provide time or resources to develop heart-centered practice but use a case study with the Gitxsan and Wet'suwet'en First Nations of British Columbia to illustrate the possibilities when efforts are made to engage an environmental ethic grounded in community knowledge.

Tanja Hoffmann also places relationships with Indigenous communities as central to developing an archaeology of the heart. She shares lessons in humility and persistence in doing community archaeology. Vulnerability, teachability, honoring in/dependence, and holding your place are core practices that have allowed her to develop and maintain strong relationships with her Katzie partners.

Participating in archaeological field work often leads us to develop strong connections, both between members of the field team and with project partners. Sarah

Surface-Evans considers heart connections in community-based practice. Surface-Evans tells a story about how the discipline of archaeology made it hard for her to truly be herself in her practice—a women who wears her heart on her sleeve—because heart and emotion were both feminized and devalued in her training. When she had the chance to teach and develop a collaborative research program, she focused on developing an epistemology of the heart that would create different pedagogical spaces and more authentic relationships with her peers and students. Surface-Evans uses the example of a research project on the Mount Pleasant Indian Industrial Boarding School to show how a heart-centered approach allowed her to create the necessary relationships to carry out research that was deeply emotional.

Uzma Rizvi looks at our capacities for disruption and betrayal. Rizvi's experiences of relationship-building and archaeology focus on the ways in which the structure of the discipline disrupts relationships by its very methodological processes. She uses the story of her PhD research to illustrate how limited time and resources led to a betrayal of the connections and friendships she was building with her collaborators in India. Even though her focus and commitment were on a decolonized archaeology, the realities of trying to build a career in archaeology meant she could not maintain the relationships and intimacies she had created. The privileged position of the academic archaeology can often hold promise for our collaborators, but what happens when we cannot follow through? The emotional impacts of this failure can be profoundly felt both by the archaeologist and the community members with whom we work.

Field work can be transformative both personally and professionally for archaeologists, and Lisa Hodgetts and Laura Kelvin share stories that allow us to see this in action. In working with the Inuvialuit community in Sachs Harbour in the Canadian Western Arctic, their chapter illustrates how these experiences caused them to shift their thinking about how archaeology should be practiced. The relationships they built with community partners began to strongly impact the types of archaeological research they were doing, moving toward work that was emotionally and spiritually meaningful for community members. Breaking down boundaries between the intellectual pursuit of archaeology and the heart work of connecting with other people, past and present, became essential for them to continue fieldwork. They provide specific examples of how this shift has changed the focus of their archaeology to a more holistic and activist practice.

Chapter 2
I ♥ Archaeology

An Experiment in Appreciative Inquiry

John R. Welch

> The most valuable possession you can own is an open heart. The most powerful weapon you can be is an instrument of peace. –Carlos Santana

This is not a mystery story, so I'll cut to the chase: I ♥ (love) archaeology. What began as a juvenile infatuation has deepened into a long-term committed relationship, adult in its complexities and contingencies. There are many reasons why the relationship has "worked" for almost a half-century (golden anniversary in 2022!). One of these is the simple truth that archaeology has done a great deal for me. Archaeology has enabled and enriched my wanderlust, kept the refrigerator mostly full, and rescued me from a career in retail management at a Brooklyn department store (my only job prospect coming out of college). Less materialistically, archaeology has illuminated pathways for my emphatically kinesthetic predispositions in thinking, imagining, and creating—hyperactive routes to contribution less open in more sedentary and purely cerebral fields. Archaeology has introduced me to innumerable terrific colleagues and afforded me career-defining opportunities to serve people possessing extraordinary grace and integrity and to preserve places endowed with inspiring significance and recurring promise. Archaeology has encouraged me to follow lofty stars while employing me gainfully as a CRM shovel bum and project director, US government agency staffer, White Mountain Apache Tribe historic preservation officer, social entrepreneur, professor, advocate, and expert witness.

Neither is this (really) a love story. I certainly profess love for archaeology, but I write not to make sure archaeology knows how I feel or loves me back (notions even sillier than my chapter title). Instead, because I'm a forward-thinking, mission-oriented sort of archaeologist (a preservation crusader above all else), the offered love seeks to highlight what I see as the best of archaeology's many extraordinary and broadly beneficial attributes. I especially want to highlight archaeology's capacities, increasingly recognized, to teach and guide humans about how to take care of the world and of one another. I hope my candidly personal professions of love may

J. R. Welch (✉)
Simon Fraser University and Archaeology Southwest, Burnaby, BC, Canada
e-mail: welch@sfu.ca

© Springer Nature Switzerland AG 2020
K. Supernant et al. (eds.), *Archaeologies of the Heart*,
https://doi.org/10.1007/978-3-030-36350-5_2

spark further discourse relating to the best and most meaningful reasons for doing archaeology and to the best practices and methods for realizing individual and collective potentials to create and mobilize knowledge about past and present human relationships with our material worlds.

In this sense the chapter is an excursion (for me) and invitation (to you) into appreciative inquiry (the other AI!), a mode of deliberation that encourages purposeful identification of the best the world has to offer (Bushe 2012). Appreciative inquiry is a logical extension of positive psychology—i.e., the nurturing of mental health and vitality through clear focus on pleasant and constructive internal emotions—to the external domains of social groups and institutions. The essential principle underlying AI's theory of group and organizational wellness and change is that identifying and amplifying desirable and beneficial qualities and attributes in any endeavor will naturally accentuate and accelerate those "goods." Persons with no interest in how their thoughts and emotions affect their worlds, or no interest in social change, or no interest in archaeology's roles and possibilities to effect positive social change need read no further. For those who see themselves, archaeology, or both as actual or potential agents of change—especially peace, justice, environmental-historical awareness, sustainability, and intercultural reconciliation—please read on.

Questions, Disclaimers, and Enjoinders

This is not a science fiction essay (I hope!), but some "what if…?" inquiry seems apt. What if love can enhance archaeology and help archaeology to make the world better? What if love and appreciation are keys to enabling and expanding archaeology's contributions to protecting and carrying forward the places, belongings, and ways of thinking and doing that most people want to pass on to their successors? What if love and appreciation can build connections and reveal continuities and interests shared among diverse archaeologists and archaeologies? What if, in other words, love and appreciation provide blueprints and foundations for collaborative constructions of mutualistic understandings, relationships, and desired futures? How will we know unless we try? How might we go about trying?

With these initial questions in mind, I join the other contributors to this volume in advancing propositions to bring heart and devotion closer to the surface in archaeological method, theory, and practice. How can love operate in archaeology? The suggestion here and across other chapters is that positive emotional engagement with and through archaeology promises to carry benefits on levels ranging from quotidian individual behavior (loving acts) and collaborations (loving relationships) to disciplinary refinement (loving practices) and public policy (collective cherishing of heritage of all varieties at all governance scales). The words and concepts I deploy pay tribute to archaeologies I love and invite readers to participate in an experiment to cultivate and share their loves with and about their archaeologies. My goal, following Johnson (2014) and each and all of the authors whose work appears in this book, is to spark further discourse about love and appreciation in and of archaeology. Indeed, I seek to inveigle all archaeologists to broaden, deepen, and mobilize their special loves with their particular archaeologies in their distinctive ways. My ultimate purpose is to plant kernels of confidence, even conviction, in the power of heart-centered practice and the potency of disciplinary love and appreciation— seeds I hope will grow, perchance to flower, fruit, proliferate, sustain, and empower…

Before hitting the reset button for the Summer of Love or declaring victory over disaffection and anomie, however, three paired disclaimer-exhortations seem in order. I recognize, first, that other disciplinary practitioners—from astronomers to zoologists—love their lives and works. On behalf of archaeology, I hereby challenge one and all to friendly interdisciplinary rivalry to demonstrate love's powers to enhance practitioner satisfaction, mobilize intra-disciplinary cooperation, accelerate extra-disciplinary engagement, multiply disciplinary service to society, and so forth. To planetary scientists, ornithologists, and professional practitioners everywhere, I say, "Let the games of disciplinary love begin!" May that discipline win that is doing the greatest good for the mental, emotional, and physical well-being of practitioners, stakeholders, and humanity!

Second, I recognize that some people and groups do not share appreciation for archaeology or fascination with the past. Some see archaeology as a cog in the wheel of industrial land alteration and natural resource consumption (Ferris and Welch 2014; Welch and Ferris 2014). Some see archaeology as a leech on the vital arteries of enterprise and economic growth. Some cultural traditions, including Apache contexts where I have worked for several decades, discourage interests directed toward those who have passed away (Welch 2000). Many Apaches have good reasons to be concerned about archaeology in general and the research-driven excavation of burials in particular (Welch 2015). My approach to detractors is to welcome general distain for archaeology as an opportunity to show a particular good that archaeology and its practitioners can do. My specific position regarding cultural concerns with archaeology, one honed through discussions with Apache colleagues and revealed in various ways throughout this chapter and my career, is that the preservation-oriented values and preferences of those who own a given archaeological record or who are descended from that record's creators take precedence over demands for destructive treatment of that record on the part of either scientists or land alteration proponents. My experience is that there are many ways of doing archaeology that embrace proscriptions to avoid all intrusive and disrespectful treatments of the dead and their belongings. Preservation archaeology, for example, routinely optimizes respect for both pasts and futures through applications of minimally invasive methods for site detection, assessment, and conservation (Doelle 2012; Welch 2000; Welch et al. 2009). Preservation archaeology accommodates local preferences through common-sense, well-mannered, good-neighbor approaches to owners and descendants concerned with appropriate treatment of places, objects, and ancestors.

My third and final disclaimer-exhortation is the recognition that some will judge the convictions offered here as out of bounds in scientific discourse. In response, I respectfully challenge my objectivist-empiricist colleagues to consider and assess their devotion to science as a valid form of love and to measure, quantify, and otherwise assess the effects of love and appreciation on whatever disciplinary dimension seems apt—method, theory, practice, societal impact, job satisfaction, sustainability, etc. Let these be the initial criteria applied by the judges of the disciplinary love rivalries invoked above. I am a romantically inclined optimist, obviously, but even the cynical realist that is my feisty flipside cannot find much downside in experimenting with declarations and promulgations of disciplinary devotions. Upsides might ultimately include paradigmatic shifts in contemplating, doing, and mobilizing research, perhaps culminating in variously upscaled organizational cultures (i.e., from work groups, small CRM companies, and academic departments to regional, national, and international associations and subdisciplines) structured by and for loving and appreciating the best that archaeology, or whatever other field, has to offer.

My hope is that this windy preamble has cleared mists to reveal the question at the core of this appreciative inquiry: how do I love thee, archaeology? Well, let me count the ways. Six. I find in my heart-mind six things I most love and appreciate about archaeology: archaeology is unique, social, youthful, relevant, widely admired, and generally humble. These six attributes provide a basis for structuring each of the following declarations of my love. The discussions also suggest, I think, ways and means for expanding, refining, and mobilizing these attributes to make it possible, and even plausible, for archaeology to be loved and appreciated by more people, for more good reasons, and to more good ends. While I have no illusions that all people can or should come to love archaeology, I see no reason why its proponents and practitioners should reserve, discount, or downplay any love or appreciation in our individual and collective hearts. What have we to lose in celebrating and building upon the best and most meaningful aspects of our individual and collective archaeologies? If you do not like my list of six, please make one of your own.

Archaeology Is Unique

I love archaeology because it is at once utterly distinctive and wildly diverse. Early archaeology developed through fruitful associations with geology, paleontology, and anthropology and then proceeded to define and reinforce critical analytic separations from these sister disciplines. On the basis of fundamental shared interests and overlaps with earth and social sciences, archaeologists have gone on to carve out, defend, occupy, and enliven a distinctive and effectively global domain of study and practice that seeks to understand the quintessentially human dedication to making and using things and places. Archaeology's devotion to the relationship between humans and our material worlds has produced awesome arrays of methods, theories, tools, practices, practitioners, partnerships, projects, and programs dedicated to investigating, reporting upon, and assisting in the stewardship of this endlessly fascinating relationship. Only archaeology exists to grasp the metes and meanings of how humans shape material worlds and are then shaped by them, to track that variation in materiality across the vastness of time, and to assist communities and societies in making good decisions about how and how much to conserve of the aesthetic, cultural, economic, educational, and scientific values embedded in material legacies. Archaeology has itself emerged as an important contributor to place-making at innumerable scales, and archaeologists make ourselves at home virtually everywhere, from urban metropoles to the central Gobi (McAtackney and Ryzewski 2017; Wang and Zhao 2013). Done well, archaeology is chameleon-like and service-oriented, effortlessly assimilating and adding value and dimension to local ways of thinking, doing, learning about the past, and making plans for the future (see Lyons 2013).

Archaeology Is Super Social

I love archaeology because it has matured to become extroverted, inclusive, and increasingly proactive. Archaeology did not define and differentiate itself in isolation. Instead, individuation has come through iterative engagements with its sister disciplines and through both entrepreneurial quests and collaborative ventures to build audiences and clienteles. As David Schaepe (2007) astutely quipped, "archaeology is a social science—we do it in groups." Archaeology takes a village, sometimes literally. If ever there was a quaint academic stereotype that has outlived its utility and validity, it's that of the "lonesome cowboy archaeologist" on a heroic odyssey in search of lost civilizations. Although inspirationally grounded in Western mythology and nominally useful as a spark for heroism, it ignores the realities of collective heritage ownership and the truths that few if any civilizations have ever been truly lost, much less found by archaeologists. Popularized notions of solo practitioners discount the importance of traditional knowledge and other local contributions to archaeology and otherwise deny the collaborative realities of most archaeological practice. Today and forevermore, archaeology is and must be a social enterprise, both in doing the work and in making the resultant knowledge relevant and beneficial. Like all social enterprises, archaeology requires context-specific social licenses to operate. Most archaeology is and should be practiced under prevailing national and local mandates to demonstrate legitimacy and produce results having societal (i.e., extra-academic) benefits, including befits over and above making way for the next subdivision, power-line, highway, mine, etc. This requirement to transcend the proximal purpose of a given project is or should be a siren song that plays to archaeologists' heartstrings. Invitations and demands to create local and spinoff benefits from research- and compliance-driven projects are sparking archaeologists' creative and collaborative pursuit of practices and programs that bring real advantages to our clients and hosts and especially to descendant and steward communities (Atalay 2012; Canuto and Yaeger 2000; Greer et al. 2002). Shifts in archaeological field schools, from socially and intellectual insulated, sink-or-swim student proving grounds to contexts for broad engagements with local needs for technical assistance, youth training, and information needed for community and economic development, signal many of these changes (Baxter 2009;

Mills et al. 2008; Silliman 2008). Whenever it is done with open minds and open hearts, archaeology can be a big group hug, an ideal context for diverse, mutually satisfying, and endlessly proliferating social, intellectual, and practical transactions (Lyons et al. 2016; see also chapters in this volume by Hodgetts and Kelvin, Rizvi, Surface-Evans, and others).

Long histories of formal and informal relationships within and beyond academic circles have produced archaeologies that are convivial as well as polyamorous. Even as archaeology continues to cultivate its long-term, committed relationships—i.e., with anthropologists, classicists, geologists, and historians—it inveterately seduces biologists, chemists, engineers, materials scientists, sociologists, statisticians, and others into pursuits of mysteries entombed in societal and behavioral offal. Collaborations with social, biophysical, and applied sciences have enabled archaeologists' shameless use of everything from social theory and backhoes to DNA, GIS, XRF, and AI (at least two types now!). If the smile frequencies, decibel levels, or per capita beer consumption at archaeological conferences are valid proxies for assessing sociability, then it seems clear that archaeologists enjoy one another's company and relish opportunities to deepen relationships, expand networks, mobilize social capital, and solicit new research partners and audiences.

Archaeology Is Still Young, Adaptable, and both Easily Inspired and Inspirational

Archaeology can maintain and diversify all these relationships and experiment with growing arrays of newfangled conceptual and technical playthings because it remains young. I love archaeology because it is still becoming and reinventing itself, developing in dynamic and constructive response to stimuli from within and well beyond disciplinary boundaries. I am not a philosopher or historian of science, but only geography comes to mind as a discipline inherently endowed with the awesome advantages of liberal access to and effectively global use of ideas, methods, and technologies from the arts, humanities, social sciences, and biophysical sciences. Archaeology has sometimes been guilty of exercising this advantage either to show off or to hide in shadowy borderlands among these seldom-overlapping domains. More often than not, however, archaeology can be found busily retooling itself to integrate, expand, and enhance methods, clienteles, audiences, partners, and applications. Archaeology remains in a continuous and downright exciting process of transformation in response to advances in sister disciplines, to clever internal innovations, and to mounting societal demands for relevance, inclusivity, justice, knowledge, and meaningful connections with authentic places, histories, and cultural developments (Atalay et al. 2014). Archaeology, in other words, is exuberant, dynamic, apparently adaptable, and intrinsically hooked into authenticity—a scarce and wondrous attribute treasured at least as much by human spirits as it is by cash markets for genuine goods and experiences (Scannell and Gifford 2017).

Should proof or clarification of the desirability of agility be required, consider the substantial and still-unfolding transformation of archaeology since about 1990. In three short decades, archaeology has morphed from a quaint, mostly gentlemanly pastime and stodgy academic "den of antiquity" to a still-small but clearly potent source of evidence for righting past wrongs, advancing intercultural reconciliation, embracing diversity, and planning just and sustainable futures (Atalay et al. 2014; Little and Shackel 2007; Sabloff 2008). The rapidly expanding commitments to self-examination and institutionalized auto-correction, however incomplete and in-progress thanks to #MeToo and other social forces, are enabling new types and levels of collaborations, notably relationships freed from the debilitating tyrannies of age-, sex-, and race-isms. Altruistic engagements are proliferating with, among others, Indigenous peoples, local communities, collectors, advocates for limiting the effects of climate change, purveyors of heritage tourism, and social entrepreneurs of all stripes. Apparent secular trends in archaeology toward appreciation and advocacy for instrumental values linked to heritage (e.g., justice, reconciliation, therapy, resource management), and away from exclusive attention to intrinsic and narrowly scientific and commerce-related values, are demonstrating change and inspiring new archaeologies and archaeologists (Little 2002; Schaepe et al. 2017; Welch 2017).

Archaeology Is a "Player"

I love archaeology because it gets around as much politically as it does socially. The steadfast stewardship investments archaeologists have made on behalf of places and associated belongings, traditions, and communities have enabled us to negotiate modest shares of power with governments and industries. Perhaps the most central factor in these negotiations are the international, national, and regional rules that mandate archaeological efforts to identify, assess, protect, and present cultural heritage affected by proposed land alterations. These rules give archaeologists seats at tables with cultural, economic, artistic, and community movers and shakers. Few other disciplines benefit from governmental policies that provide structural guarantees of access to and participation in broadly consequential decision-making. Notwithstanding critiques of archaeology as a pawn in late modern statecraft (Hutchings and Dent 2017) and pleas for attention to sustainability principles in CRM (Ferris and Welch 2014; Welch and Ferris 2014), archaeologists regularly represent and advocate for cultural heritage in diverse planning contexts around the world (Welch and Lilley 2013).

Archaeology's privileged access to and use of information from the full span of human history and full range of human-environmental interactions attract welcome attention to archaeological processes and products. Archaeology routinely parlays inherent advantages of unique knowledge and perspective into diverse and mutually beneficial relations with lots of smart and savvy people. Archaeology's structural advantages endow archaeologists with opportunities to enlist and serve diverse allies, most especially those with interests in justice, intercultural reconciliation, and the mitigation of pernicious effects of late modernity and environmental change (see Hogg et al. 2017 and accompanying papers). Even as a perhaps unfortunate preponderance of archaeology is done simply to enable land alteration and commodity extraction, archaeologists are increasingly committed to ethical codes and performance standards that recognize cultural, economic, political, and educational as well as scientific and instrumental values embedded in ancient lands and landscapes (Chandler 2017). "Stewardship," which got a bad rap as a result of arrogance on the part of a small number of self-aggrandizing archaeologists, is gradually reclaiming its rightfully and inherently altruistic position as an essential ethical principle (Wylie 2005). There's room for improvement, still and always, but archaeology and its potent practitioners have made and are making positive differences in the world through political engagements in communal, institutional, administrative, and legal processes.

Everybody (Almost) Loves Archaeology

I love archaeology because, well, virtually everybody loves archaeology. Leaving aside the detractors and critics mentioned above, archaeology inspires and captivates the imaginations and individual dreams of billions of people. An extraordinary number of grade schoolers place archaeology at or near the top of their intended careers. Most adults who meet archaeologists profess some measure of fascination with archaeology or with the romantic ideals of earthbound time travel or with prospects for dis- and uncovering the lost and forsaken. Throughout the Americas and many other world regions, most people have spaces in their hearts and imaginations for the awesomeness of human diversity across time and for the effectiveness of Western and non-Western scientific methods in assigning names, dates, categories, and significances to fragmentary remains and erstwhile elusive pasts. Few will deny at least passing desires to pursue or perpetuate connections to ancestors' and forebears' lives, arts, homes, and legacies. Archaeology is a big and open access "tent" where few fear to enter, linger, and dream.

As if the mysterious allures of forgotten civilizations, buried treasures, and reconnecting with ancestors is not enough, Hollywood has pimped archaeology via various, predominantly favorable makeovers. Archaeologists are generally cast as clever and public-minded explorers, diggers, and curators of heritage. The widely distributed fascination with and respect for the potency of archaeology—however naïve and however distorted and commodified by the *Indiana Jones* franchise and *Treasure Quest: Snake Island*—endows practitioners with the enormous privilege of inspirational exchanges with individual and collective imaginations and of public confidence and resulting social licenses to operate. The net effect of archaeology's enduring popular appeal is public admiration and trust. Paleontologists have also earned this sort of confidence, but must concern themselves with millions of species and epochs. Archaeologists enjoy a comparative advantage in our focus on a single keystone species and its (our!) development over a few hundred thousand years. I'll put my money on the victory, however imaginary, of our best and most cooperative indigenous hunters against their cold-blooded roadrunner ancestors and other bizarre biota.

Archaeology Is Humble

Despite all of these extraordinary advantages, archaeology is (or is becoming more) humble, grounded in uncertainty, and cognizant of its own limitations without ceding its powers and capacities to discover, reveal, connect, safeguard, and inspire. Archaeology sustains long and fruitful intra-disciplinary traditions of open-mindedness and modesty in the face of unmistakably daunting uncertainties. At its best, archaeology mobilizes this humility through ever-more diverse, creative, satisfying, and broadly beneficial collaborations—interdisciplinary, intercultural, and international. These collaborations increasingly extend across boundaries that once rigidly separated many descendent and indigenous owners and stewards from their cultural heritage and from others who care about and for it. The line between indigenous and non-indigenous archaeologies, always blurry, continues to fade as most younger archaeologists now internalize inclusive professional ethics and routinely defer, as I do, to the wishes and preferences of owner and descendant communities.

To these six admirable and potent attributes of archaeology arising from our subject matter and from dynamics at the interface of scholarship, social critique, and governance, I would add the provocative truth of our personal touch. Most archaeologists embrace self-identification as students and curators of the past and of human-material relations. Most archaeologists spend time away from their offices and project areas visiting archaeological sites and museums. Most recognize that our short lifetimes and cognitive capacities are insufficient to achieve our broadest research goals. I see the intellectual and professional humility demonstrated by most archaeologists as one product of continuous engagement with the ambiguities inherent in most archaeological records. Here, too, younger practitioners seem especially prone to realism and its attendant humilities. Those who have come of age in the 1990s and later seem especially willing to espouse personal attitudes and make professional investments tightly linked to archaeology's ethical codes, imperfect and evolving as they are. Recognized rules for professional practice encourage respectful treatment of our subjects and of one another; they discourage selfish practices and imperious attempts to assert authority or limit competing uses and values of places and materials, including those claimed, linguistically, as "archaeological." Again at the risk of overoptimism or simplification, I think archaeologists are rapidly learning how to share our ever-more connected discipline and our distinctive skills and capacities for positive contributions in and to our increasingly crowded world. I love it and the endless promises it speaks for dissolving outmoded and often counterproductive binary distinctions between savage and civilized, past and present, nature and culture, human and nonhuman, etc.

So What?

I love archaeology, but I've previously refrained from saying those three magic words. So, why say them now? My answer stems from various sources: real personal gratitude, a vague sense that many others love archaeology at least as much as I do, and an admittedly half-baked notion that archaeology deserves recognition for all it has done for archaeologists and for all it has the potential to do in and for the world at large. The appreciative inquiry missionary in me is enticed and motivated by the hypothesis that fostering, collectivizing, and harnessing love and its emotional cousins will allow archaeology and archaeologists to achieve new levels and types of service and integrity on individual and collective levels. At the very least, professions of love for archaeology should prompt neurons to fire and pheromones to flow in new ways, hopefully at or near some cortical centers for pleasure, altruism, justice, and strategic and critical thinking.

What importance, if any, should be attached to archaeology's semi-unique, structurally enshrined privileges of access to and use of both the human past and the present human imagination? In a word, *duty*. Swirls of popular appeals, disciplinary developments, professional ethics, and personal commitments endow archaeology and archaeologists with unique rights. As with most other prerogatives, these rights are naturally accompanied by, and can only be sustained through, judicious and diligent attention to concomitant responsibilities. There can be no doubt that archaeology and archaeologists have, to date, been the principal beneficiaries of advocacy for heritage preservation and study. As recognized experts in the identification, assessment, and treatment of the material legacies of all previous human generations, archaeologists have accepted, at varied scales of consciousness and jurisdiction, the de facto rights and concomitant duties to serve collective interests in what we have claimed as "The Archaeological Record." Archaeologists are, surely if sometimes still too slowly, relinquishing prior claims to exclusive use and control of the past. Our personal inclinations, disciplinary training, public profile, and legal status afford us unique access to and responsibilities for the archaeological record. It is our job and our duty, more than it is for any other category of persons, to lead endless and often fruitless quests to identify and interpret the values of that record, to identify and assess the actual and potential threats to those values, and to create and advocate for appropriate treatments to avoid and reduce such threats. Archaeologists are ideally positioned to guide our diverse clientele—real and potential audiences of people who care about the past as prologue, as refuge, as inspiration, as data, as cautionary tale, or as some combination—into relationships with archaeological processes (fact creation), products (fact validation and other "testimony of the spade"), and dialogues (fact critique and significance assessment). The take-home lesson is that archaeology holds vast, extraordinary, and far-from-realized potentials to connect people to senses of places, belongings, and ways of being and doing across vast and otherwise seldom traversed dimensions of time, space, culture, and power (Agbe-Davies 2010; Sabloff 2008; Schaepe et al. 2017).

Why don't we do more of this? Why is so much of our work done only for other archaeologists and otherwise doomed to obscurity by self-limiting focus on intra-disciplinary communications? At least part of the answer to this complex question seems clear as my career as a professional archaeologist traverses its fourth decade: put simply, archaeology is hard. I think the intellectual and practical challenges of doing good archaeology are responsible in large part for archaeologists' collective hesitation to step confidently forward as public intellectuals. On the other hand, I think the same challenges foster and account for archaeologists' formidable qualities of mind and temperament: observational acuity, organizational skill, investigative rigor, and procedural perseverance. These attributes are necessary, of course, in the navigating of vast landscapes to find sites, in the sifting of deep sediments to find evidence, in the targeting of optimal methods to find those tools most suited to the demands of specific contexts, and in the foregrounding of crucial questions to find interpretive purchase. Such rigor-making attributes are embedded in and integral to standard archaeological training and practice. They are important tools for professional archaeologists, trainees, and others engaged in field- and laboratory-based pursuits of knowledge from or about the past. They are part of our collective persona and popular identity.

But do these attributes and tools serve archaeologists in all times and places? Is it possible that the industrious intensity that enables success in some archaeological research and practice settings thwarts it elsewhere? Is it time for critical reconsideration of when and how to exchange or soften our disciplinary commitments to rigor, precision, and perseverance, perhaps by placing greater focus on alternative ways of learning, finding, and relating? How can archaeology and archaeologists harness and deploy the full complement of our disciplinary attributes, personal interests and skills, and interpersonal potentialities to enhance and expand our effectiveness as researchers, community partners, teachers, colleagues, and citizens?

Answers to such sweeping questions may require nods to the truths that there are only personal, relational, and local answers. The challenge, of course, is to carry forward the best and most useful aspects of minds and temperaments in order to counter the intrinsic ambiguities in the archaeological record and without allowing these to impede collaborative and community processes. One good way forward, as discovered on countless projects by innumerable archaeologists, involves recognition and adoption, in whole or part, of the essential social and emotional dimensions of archaeology. The other chapters in this volume, along with the collective works of my fellow authors, provide clear and compelling indications that this is not just possible, but happening now, in real time (see also American Anthropological Association 2018). Like any decent social scientist greeted with evidence of an apparently incongruent social phenomenon, in this case the "power of love and appreciation in archaeology," or some such, questions arise as to the source and general applicability of the phenomena. This is a job for theory!

Love Theory

One way to sum up the central claim advanced in this essay is that much is to be gained, with little risk or sacrifice, by giving love and appreciation (even) more and better chances in and through archaeology. "My" theory, in other words, is that archaeology and archaeologists will be more effective on multiple fronts—e.g., public support, research productivity, and private satisfaction—to the extent that:

1. Archaeologists love and appreciate ourselves.
2. Archaeologists love and appreciate our colleagues and collaborators.
3. Archaeologists love and appreciate what we do and how we do it.
4. Archaeologists share our loves, celebrate our appreciations, and otherwise re-invest positive affect in our discipline, practice, students, collaborators, and clientele.

What is not being advanced here is any recipe or prescription for pursuing, enhancing, or expressing love or appreciation. Nor am I suggesting that love displace the observational, organizational, and investigative acumen that define archaeology and archaeologists. Making and sharing love is and must be as varied as the constitutive individuals and relational dynamics in which it unfolds. Archaeology love is no different, and no specific program is presented here for self-, other-, or work-love. The general program of giving kind and concerted attention to love- and heart-centric work in all its forms is presented here as a way to create and apply a branch of appreciative inquiry in and to archaeology. This theory of institutional change is not just emphatically personal, but is also essentially pragmatic, meaning it is explicitly intended to bring about good and practical benefits extending well beyond disciplinary boundaries. The theory is also effectively middle-range (sensu Merton 1968; c.f. Binford) and may be restated as the hypothesis, eminently testable, that archaeology done with and through love creates broader ranges of deeper values and benefits—cultural, educational, scientific, etc. These values, unlike love itself, are measurable, and it seems to me that many archaeologists, especially those of us engaged in supporting decision-making about what to conserve in the face of global change, are getting good at measuring them (Shaw 2016).

If for no other reasons than to illustrate and substantiate my love and to stimulate comparable affirmations or critiques on the subject, I have seen fit to reveal why and how I love and appreciate archaeology. That said, finding and "seeing" love in archaeology is seldom straightforward. The following example of an application of love theory is offered to show that love can and does find its way into even contentious archaeological discourse, contexts apparently bereft of positive affect. The example is from a project that emerged from consultations with Chairman Terry Rambler of the San Carlos Apache Tribe, in 2017. Chairman Rambler asked me to complete a review of cultural, historical, and archaeological evidence for the Apache occupation and use of a part of the central Arizona mountains targeted by the Rio Tinto subsidiary, Resolution Copper, for a massive new mine (Welch 2017). Apaches had expressed concerns about prospective damages to ancestral lands and mining proponents had responded to Apache claims about the importance of the project impact area with questions about the legitimacy of the Apache claims. Because the area had never been part of any reservation or otherwise officially recognized as aboriginal land, it seemed at least possible that the Apache concerns, which centered on a place known as Chí'chil Bildagoteel (Oak Flat), were being inflated by environmentalists or otherwise promoted simply to thwart the mining proposal. The problem was vexing and important enough to prompt my systematic examination of available cultural, historical, and archaeological evidence. Conclusions seemed elusive until I decided to tally up the casualties from the roughly 70 different episodes of violent conflict between Apaches and non-Apaches in the greater Oak Flat region. My eyes teared as I realized the truth of what a many Apache colleagues had attempted to explain to me through the years: the so-called Apache Wars were, at least in this region, nothing more or less than an instance of state-sponsored genocide against people who refused to yield their land to miners. Government troops and vigilantes killed more than 380 Apache women, children, and men between 1859 and 1874; during the same period, and over a much larger area, Apaches were responsible for the deaths of about 70 non-Apaches, all of them men. The unusual and poignant convergence of archaeological and historical data opened my mind, my eyes, and most especially my heart to a stark and horrific truth that has been reverberating through Apache stories, lives, communities, landscapes, and external relationships for at least five generations. It is now possible, even necessary, for me to expand the dispassionate analysis that allowed me to "discover" a genocide hidden in plain sight by seeking ways to link archaeological and historical data to familial recollections and oral traditions. Perhaps my change of heart will help the miners to change theirs, and to accept partial responsibility for the sins of their industrial forebears?

Onward!

The final thing that this chapter is not is a treatise on future archaeologies. That said, archaeologists are invited and encouraged to maintain and where appropriate expand archaeology's still-nascent and tenuous social and political currencies. I cannot see how or why this can or should be done without at least a touch of love. I do not think archaeology is in imminent peril, but nevertheless see merit in active appreciation, personal as well as collective, for the best and most promising of archaeology's attributes and applications. Peer review, government policy standards, and ethical codes provide important institutional foundations for guiding practices and practitioners, but each and all of these directional indicators and quality controls derive from and depend on personal integrity and dedication. It is for this reason that appreciative inquiry is recommended here as a means for recognizing and harnessing the powers of personal preferences in intellectual and practical pursuits. In the final analysis, love and true appreciation are inherently personal. Pathways forward in archaeology will be gentler and more readily and fearlessly travelled to the extent we can cultivate wholehearted emotional intentions and fuse these with incisive intellectual pursuits and impeccably ethical and altruistic practice. Commitments to open-eyed, open-minded, open-armed, and open-hearted archaeologies are sturdy and splendid foundations for maintaining and accelerating extra-disciplinary influence along with exceptional recent disciplinary growth, diversification, and inclusivity.

References

Agbe-Davies, A. S. (2010). An engaged archaeology for our mutual benefit: The case of New Philadelphia. *Historical Archaeology, 44*(1), 1–6.

American Anthropological Association. (2018). *Field school opportunities.* http://www.american-anthro.org/LearnAndTeach/ResourceDetail.aspx?ItemNumber=12949

Atalay, S. (2012). *Community-based archaeology: Research with, by, and for Indigenous and local communities.* Berkeley: University of California Press.

Atalay, S., Clauss, L. R., McGuire, R. H., & Welch, J. R. (Eds.). (2014). *Transforming archaeology: Activist practices and prospects.* Walnut Creek, CA: Left Coast Press.

Baxter, J. E. (2009). *Archaeological field schools: A guide for teaching in the field.* Walnut Creek, CA: Left Coast Press.

Bushe, G. R. (2012). Appreciative inquiry: Theory and critique. In D. Boje, B. Burnes, & J. Hassard (Eds.), *The Routledge companion to organizational change* (pp. 87–103). London: Routledge.

Canuto, M.-A., & Yaeger, J. (Eds.). (2000). *Archaeology of communities: A new world perspective.* London: Routledge.

Chandler, S. (2017). *Comments on environmental and social framework draft guidance notes for borrowers.* International Government Affairs Committee, Society for American Archaeology, 13 December 2017. http://www.saa.org/Portals/0/SAA/GovernmentAffairs/GUIDANCE_NOTES_COMMENTS_FINAL.pdf

Doelle, W. H. (2012). What is preservation archaeology? *Archaeology Southwest, 26*(1), 1–3.

Ferris, N., & Welch, J. R. (2014). Beyond archaeological agendas: In the Service of a Sustainable Archaeology. In S. Atalay, L. R. Clauss, R. H. McGuire, & J. R. Welch (Eds.), *Transforming archaeology: Activist practices and prospects* (pp. 215–237). Walnut Creek, CA: Left Coast Press.

Greer, S., Harrison, R., & McIntyre-Tamwoy, S. (2002). Community-based archaeology in Australia. *World Archaeology, 34*(2), 265–287.

Hogg, E. A., Welch, J. R., & Ferris, N. (2017). Full spectrum archaeology. *Archaeologies, 12*, 1–26.

Hutchings, R. M., & Dent, J. (2017). Archaeology and the late modern state: Introduction to the special issue. *Archaeologies, 13*(1), 1–25.

Johnson, M. (2014). *Lives in ruins: Archaeologists and the seductive lure of human rubble.* New York: Harper Perennial.

Little, B. J. (Ed.). (2002). *Public benefits of archaeology.* Gainesville, FL: University Press of Florida.

Little, B. J., & Shackel, P. (Eds.). (2007). *Archaeology as a tool of civic engagement.* Lanham, MD: Alta Mira Press.

Lyons, N. (2013). *Where the wind blows us: Practicing critical community archaeology in the Canadian North.* Tucson: University of Arizona Press.

Lyons, N., Schaepe, D. M., Hennessy, K., Blake, M., Pennier, C., McIntosh, K., Phillips, A., Welch, J. R., Charlie, B., Hall, C., Hall, L., Point, A., Pennier, V., Phillips, R., Williams, J., Jr.,

Williams, J., Sr., Chapman, J., & Pennier, C. (2016). Sharing deep history as digital knowledge: An ontology of the Sq'éwlets website project. *Journal of Social Archaeology, 16*(3), 359–384.

McAtackney, L., & Ryzewski, K. (Eds.). (2017). *Contemporary archaeology and the city: Creativity, ruination, and political action*. Oxford: Oxford University Press.

Merton, R. K. (1968). *Social theory and social structure*. New York: Free Press.

Mills, B. J., Altaha, M., Welch, J. R., & Ferguson, T. J. (2008). Field schools without trowels: Teaching archaeological ethics and heritage preservation in a collaborative context. In S. W. Silliman (Ed.), *Collaborating at the Trowel's edge: Teaching and learning in indigenous archaeology* (pp. 25–49). Tucson: University of Arizona Press.

Sabloff, J. (2008). *Archaeology matters: Action archaeology in the modern world*. Walnut Creek, CA: Left Coast Press.

Scannell, L., & Gifford, R. (2017). The experienced psychological benefits of place attachment. *Journal of Environmental Psychology, 51*, 256–269.

Schaepe, D. (2007). *Personal communication to Welch*. Vancouver.

Schaepe, D., Angelbeck, B., Snook, D., & Welch, J. R. (2017). Archaeology as therapy: Connecting belongings, knowledge, time, place, and well-being. *Current Anthropology, 58*(4), 502–533.

Shaw, J. (2016). Archaeology, climate change and environmental ethics: Diachronic perspectives on human: Non-human : Environment worldviews, activism and care. *World Archaeology, 48*, 449–465. https://doi.org/10.1080/00438243.2016.1326754.

Silliman, S. W. (Ed.). (2008). *Collaborating at the Trowel's edge: Teaching and learning in indigenous archaeology*. Tucson: University of Arizona Press.

Wang, S., & Zhao, X. (2013). Re-evaluating the silk Road's Qinghai route using dendrochronology. *Dendrochronologia, 31*(1), 34–40.

Welch, J. R. (2000). The White Mountain Apache Tribe heritage program: Origins, operations, and challenges. In K. E. Dongoske, M. Aldenderfer, & K. Doehner (Eds.), *Working together: Native Americans and archaeologists* (pp. 67–83). Washington, D.C.: Society for American Archaeology.

Welch, J. R. (2015). The last archaeologist to (almost) Abandon Grasshopper. *Arizona Anthropologist* (Centennial Edition), 107–119. https://webcache.googleusercontent.com/search?q=cache:XkNrK4Tk2I0J:https://journals.uair.arizona.edu/index.php/arizanthro/article/download/18856/18499+&cd=1&hl=en&ct=clnk&gl=ca

Welch, J. R. (2017, October–December). Earth, wind, and fire: Pinal Apaches, miners, and genocide in Central Arizona, 1859–1874. *Sage Open*, 1–19. http://journals.sagepub.com/doi/full/10.1177/2158244017747016

Welch, J. R., & Ferris, N. (2014). 'We have met the enemy and it is us': Improving archaeology through application of sustainable design principles. In S. Atalay, L. R. Clauss, R. H. McGuire, & J. R. Welch (Eds.), *Transforming archaeology: Activist practices and prospects* (pp. 91–113). Walnut Creek, CA: Left Coast Press.

Welch, J. R., & Lilley, I. (2013). Beyond the equator (principles): Community benefit sharing in relation to major land alteration projects and associated intellectual property issues in cultural heritage. Report on a forum at the annual meeting of the Society for American Archaeology, 5 April 2013, Honolulu, Hawai'i. *International Journal of Cultural Property, 20*(4), 467–493.

Welch, J. R., Altaha, M. K., Hoerig, K. A., & Riley, R. (2009). Best Cultural Heritage Stewardship Practices by and for the White Mountain Apache Tribe. *Conservation and Management of Archaeological Sites, 11*(2), 148–160.

Wylie, A. (2005). The promise and perils of an ethic of stewardship. In L. Meskell & P. Pells (Eds.), *Beyond ethics: Anthropological moralities on the boundaries of the public and the professional* (pp. 47–68). London: Berg Press.

Chapter 3
Ecologies of the Heart

People, Land, and Heritage Management in the Pacific Northwest

Chelsey Geralda Armstrong and Eugene N. Anderson

Background

The concept and practice of resource management are often conceived of as a physical science dominated by bureaucrats and scientists and focused on controlling a specific object or space. In 1996, I (Anderson) published a contribution in the fields of ethnobiology and ecological anthropology, entitled, *Ecologies of the Heart: Emotion, Belief, and the Environment*. Here, I argued that resource management is not about managing or controlling resources: it is about managing people. For millennia, humans have been carving out a niche in almost every bioregion in the world (Balée 2013; Rick et al. 2013; Tømmervik et al. 2010). Our ability to adapt to diverse environments, to one another, and to live relatively cohesively required some form of resource management that was typically codified into spirituality, religion, and other belief systems. Those societies that have been more or less successful in managing resources and maintaining a livelihood in the same place for hundreds or even thousands of years necessarily developed sophisticated resource management practices to sustain or even increase the biodiversity and functions in the ecosystems they inhabited (Anderson 2005; Balée 2013; Armstrong 2017). This does not mean people did not make mistakes—rather, some mistakes were learned from, altered, and delineated into stories and practices to improve management strategies. Broadly, this is reflected in some Indigenous communities where the concept of "taking only what you need" has been so deeply engrained it is almost too taboo to write. Coincidentally even the term "taboo," Polynesian in origin, refers to overfished reefs, orchards of unripe fruit, or overharvested plant and animal species

C. G. Armstrong (✉)
National Museum of Natural History, Smithsonian Institution, Washington, DC, USA

E. N. Anderson
Emeritus, University of California, Riverside, CA, USA
e-mail: eugene.anderson@ucr.edu

© Springer Nature Switzerland AG 2020
K. Supernant et al. (eds.), *Archaeologies of the Heart*,
https://doi.org/10.1007/978-3-030-36350-5_3

that are declared *tapu* or *kapu* and off limits until they can recover or be harvested from again (Anderson 1996). It is perhaps unsurprising that some of the most eco-logically intact landscapes remaining on Earth are owned and managed by Indigenous peoples (Garnett et al. 2018). Everyone must practice management. Even the most dispersed hunter-gatherer groups had to deal with overharvesting, overhunting, and competition for resources. The communities that succeeded in maintaining moderately high human populations, and over a long period of time, can be considered relatively successful managers (Anderson 1996, 2016).

The Northwest Coast of North America is one of the most consistently occupied places in the world (e.g., Cannon 2003; McLaren et al. 2015). Complex and dynamic systems of resource management have been necessarily codified into oral stories and histories, legal codes, and kinship systems characterized by judicious land own-ership and tenure systems (Trosper 2002; Turner 2014). Much archaeology in the region is tied to and informed by extensive ethnographic and ethnohistoric records, yet rarely do archaeologists consider how the archaeological record, and heritage valuation, may be tied to social and environmental ethics in resource management (but see Gauvreau et al. 2017; Lepofsky and Armstrong 2018). For example, when archaeologists manage heritage resources, they are also, consciously or not, making decisions about the fate of the entire landscape, including water systems, biota, geologic features, and the *people* that encompass a so-called archaeological site. This chapter, by an ecological anthropologist (Anderson) and an archaeologist (Armstrong), considers lessons from *Ecologies of the Heart* and ponders how a heart-centered approach to managing heritage resources is not merely about the resources, but about the land and people too. Although archaeologists can be emo-tionally tied to the material remains from a site (Abbott, this volume), we argue that an emotional archaeological practice in settler nations like Canada should consider the human and nonhuman entities tied to the archaeological "stuff" being surveyed, studied, or managed.

Most archaeology conducted in North America falls under the purview of cul-tural resource management/archaeological resource management (CRM or consult-ing archaeology)—a top-down, government-mandated practice driven by researchers and managers but with obligations, first and foremost, to industry and commercial development (Atalay et al. 2014; Little and Shackel 2007). It was a cliché even a decade ago to point out that the rise and dominance of commercial and consulting archaeology changed the face and fabric of the practice (Ferris 2003, 2007). Many archaeological consultants have taken strides to have more material collaborations with, and opened decision-making powers to, Indigenous communities (e.g., Lynott and Wylie 1995; Shackel and Chambers 2004; Martindale and Lyons 2014). However, in some contexts (e.g., oil and gas development) where a good business climate means culling environmental and heritage regulations (Van Hinte et al. 2007), archaeologists may not have room or resources to develop an emotional practice tied to people or to the landscape.

Heritage valuation often focuses on rarity, fragility, and esthetic, instead of char-acteristics like culturally attributed meaning and value and environmental or land-scape setting (see Darvill 2005). The definition of archaeological heritage is contentious, and its valuation for government protection is complicated by both overt and nuanced power relations and the political and economic contexts within which researchers and consultants work (Nicholas and Hollowell 2016; McGuire 2008; Meskell and Preucel 2008). Indeed, even the concept of heritage has changed drastically in conjunction with globalization (Appadurai 2001). Consider archaeological artifacts and sites as part of the "flow" of objects, places, ideologies, and technologies in a globalized world. The heritage valuation of a site or object in an "uncontested" landscape is more likely to produce collaborative partnerships between researcher and descendant community (e.g., Lepofsky and Lertzman 2019). Alternatively, in contested spaces, for example, where Indigenous communities are actively defending their land (e.g., through direct or legal actions) from oil and gas development, archaeological heritage may be seen as bureaucratic red tape or extractive and destructive and can further disenfranchise people from their lands and cultural inheritance (Angelbeck and Jones 2018; Armstrong and Brown 2019).

This contribution considers social and environmental ethical codes and management protocols on the Northwestern Coast rich and critical resources for archaeologists yet generally underutilized and absent from the toolkits archaeologists use to survey, document, and evaluate archaeological heritage. Without these tools, we argue, archaeologists are missing key elements of the landscapes they intend to evaluate or manage and mitigate. Consequently, some archaeologists end up neglecting or missing important places and sites for descendent communities, and at worst, contribute to the erasure of Indigenous communities from their homelands. We first review the resource management practices and protocols among Indigenous communities throughout the northwest of North America and then showcase how, in two contexts, a resource use and management practices and protocols flowed from a heart-centered approach. This approach leads to a more productive archaeological practice; we located more sites and undercut several of the colonial and sometimes violent practices associated with heritage management in contested places.

Resource Management in the Pacific Northwest

Indigenous peoples throughout the Americas developed institutions for managing and conserving animal and plant resources. These included, most obviously, agriculture and domestication, which, by definition, involve conserving and reproducing stock for future multiplication. There was a range in most of the hemisphere from purely agricultural crops that required extensive care (maize was the foremost) to less demanding crops and then to managed wild plants and ultimately unmanaged wild resources (Minnis and Elisens 2001). The Northwest Coast of North America presents special challenges for management. It appears a land of abundance when one considers the huge runs of fish and the fertile root prairies, but these are separated by miles of evergreen forest with extremely low value as a source for human food. Also, fish runs and other massive resource concentrations are prone to fluctuate, sometimes quite dramatically because of migratory habits that lead to bottlenecks and constrain movement (Suttles 1968). This creates problems for human management.

In the Pacific Northwest, the only carefully managed and carefully protected domesticated crop was tobacco (*Nicotiana attenuata*), grown very locally and sporadically (Turner 1995; Tushingham et al. 2013). However, many wild crops were so intensively managed that they probably changed genetically in a "domesticated" direction (Anderson 2017). Camas (*Camassia quamash*), for instance, flourishes so well in garden environments—especially compared to other wild Northwest Coast plants—that it appears to have been semidomesticated (see also Lyons and Ritchie 2017). Bitterroot (*Lewisia rediviva*), glacier lily (*Erythronium grandiflorum*), springbeauty (*Claytonia lanceolata*), spiny wood fern (*Dryopteris expansa*), springbank clover (*Trifolium wormskioldii*), and Pacific silverweed (*Potentilla anserina* ssp. *Pacifica*) all have underground storage organs (corms, roots, bulbs) managed and harvested for their rich complex and simple carbohydrates (Turner and Kuhnlein 1982; Norton et al. 1984; Deur 2002; Turner et al. 2013).

Northwest Coast management practices are reflected in codified social and environmental ethics based on mutual aid relationships of profound communal respect for nonhuman kin. For example, when nonhumans are eaten, they empower humans; there are rites, songs, and ceremonies that are generations old witnessing these relationships (Drucker 1955; Book Builders of 'Ksan 1980; Anderson 1996; Turner 2005). Protocol is deeply embedded in practices like fishing, hunting, and harvesting roots and berries (Deur and Turner 2005; M.K. Anderson 2005; Turner 2014). As early as 1826, William Brown observed that a hunter "is particularly careful neither killing too many himself nor allowing any to do so" (William Brown, quoted Fiske and Patrick 2000:128). He is speaking of Babine First Nations, among whom clans maintained fishing weirs and owned very specific fishing stations within carefully delineated territories. By introducing individual nets, Canadian settlers undermined this arrangement. Enforcing conservation was easy with clan-owned weirs but difficult when individually owned nets were involved. Salmon populations spiked after the Pleistocene and survived in large numbers for millennia in British Columbia and were considered "superabundant" at the time of colonial contact, only to have their numbers dwindle by the twentieth century with overharvesting practices of colonial settlers (Campbell and Butler 2010).

The ethnographic record shows good management: fish populations were sustained, trees were kept healthy, berries and root crops flourished and were managed for multiplication, and game was not overhunted (Anderson 2005; Turner 2005). Conservation was based on the simple principle of "leave some for others." The Nuu-chah-nulth phrase was *uh̲-mowa-shitl*, "keep some and not take all" (George 2003:74). There are enough exceptions, credible stories of resource waste and depletion (Krech 1999), to show that this was not a matter of idyllic children of nature playing an Edenic vision but the decisions of individuals who knew perfectly well what the options were and made informed choices (Anderson 2016). Communities had to self-govern restraint. This degree of self-control is hard to square with the modern Euro-American idea that people act in their material self-interest, let alone with the more cynical ideas of Thomas Hobbes that life for "savages" was a "warre of each against all" (Hobbes 1950 [1651]) or John Locke's milder but still overblown idea that Indigenous peoples could not have managed anything because they did not have private property (Locke 1924 [1690]). Of course, they did (and do) have private property (e.g., Glavin 2000), but what is more interesting is the extent of moral management of common-pool property like bow trees, salmon, and cedars. To some extent these could be privatized—groves and fishing stations were owned—but even then the ownership was usually collective.

Elinor Ostrom (1990, 2005, 2009) showed that collective management of common-pool resources is not only possible, but is common; however, it requires several conditions to function. One of these conditions is motivation. People must be invested enough in the project to self-regulate. There must also be some recourse—some guardian group or set of rules. Transaction costs for managing collective resources can become severe. The worldview of Indigenous peoples in Northwestern North America is one in which plants and animals are owed respect as fellow persons and relations. The Nlaka'pamux metaphor that the Earth's wealth is linked to flowers, grass, and human action recognizes that living things ought to be used, but only with careful and thoughtful attention (Turner 2005). For example, the leaves of non-fruiting cattail (*Typha latifolia*) and basket sedge (*Carex obnupta*) were harvested and fruiting portions left to seed and propagate. Throughout the northwest, cultural prohibitions ensure plants are only harvested at specific reproductive stages (Turner and Peacock 2005).

Another problem recognized by Ostrom is knowing when a resource is being depleted (Ostrom et al. 1999). A strong ethic of taking no more than necessary, backed up by moral sanctions, partially dispenses with this problem: people do not push the resource base. If they did, they quickly observed it, in the times when they depended on immediate resources for survival. One must only look to the Haida who had the population numbers and technology to destroy the salmon fishery— Haida Gwaii had small streams and few salmon—and yet did not (Anderson 2016). As Walter Wright, a Tsm'syen chief and community leader, accounted in of the Wars of Medeek, people are continuously penalized (and often brutally killed) when they mistreat salmon, goat, and other important food resources (Robinson and Wright 1962).

Social and environmental ethic was directed toward respect and care via stories, songs, dances, ceremonies, and religious activity. Emile Durkheim (1995 [1912]) showed long ago that religion—whatever else it may be—is universally directed toward getting people emotionally involved in their societies, so that they will not only internalize ethical codes but will be emotionally and personally attached to and involved with those codes. Northwest Coast ceremonies serve very well indeed to accomplish this end. They are highly emotional. They often involve masked dances by individuals portraying the animal powers and mythical beings. They often teach conservation messages or dramatize moral tales about the dangers of resource misuse (Robinson and Wright 1962).

Notably important were stories of famine following overhunting or overfishing. Apparently, every community had such tales. The Tahltan knew of a hunter who was turned to stone with his dog for hunting too many mountain goats (Teit 1919:241–242). One widespread story concerns Tsm'syen people who showed disrespect for animals by taking too many and treating them poorly. The animals, often taking human form, destroy the community except for one or two children who refused to follow the people in disrespectful behavior. These children go on to find a new community and teach their descendants not to repeat the errors of the past (Robinson and Wright 1962).

James Teit noted among Tahltan people:

> The Meat-Mother watches her children, the game, and also the people. When people do not follow the taboos, and do not treat animals rightly, the latter tell their mother; and she punishes the people by taking the game away for a while, or by making it wild, and then the people starve…the Moose children are the most apt to tell their mother of any disrespect shown them: therefore people have to be very careful [as] to how they treat moose. (Teit 1919:231–232, as cited in McIlwraith 2012:68–69)

Thomas Thornton's Tlingit friend Herman Kitka noted that when a weir blocks the river totally, the salmon leave because they are "insulted," not because they are physically stopped: "Those little sockeye get offended if you don't leave them a hole in your [fish] weir; they won't come back…" (Thornton and Sealaska Heritage Institute 2008:173–174). Tlingit often tell guests, in formal contexts, *Tleil dagák' ahwateeni yík*, "Don't leave insulted like those little sockeyes" (Thornton and Sealaska Heritage Institute 2008:173).

On the Northwest Coast, conservation depended on developing a social and emotional relationship with the world. Plants, animals, and sometimes mountains and rivers were persons—"other-than-human persons"—but owed respect and good treatment like other persons. Animals hunted and taken were often thanked for giving themselves to the hunter. Myths and stories routinely portrayed a time when animals (and often plants and mountains) were human or humanoid. This reinforced the idea of personhood. A boy's first kill, a girl's first harvest of berries, and the first fish of the season were usually shared by everyone in the community, to teach not only the virtues of sharing but also respect for the items themselves (Anderson 2016). The rich knowledge of the land was critically important to maintaining the local economy (Thornton 2012; Anderson 2016). Native American biologist Raymond Pierotti has written: "A common general philosophy and concept of community appears to be shared by all of the Indigenous peoples of North America, which includes: 1) respect for nonhuman entities as individuals, 2) the existence of bonds between humans and nonhumans, including incorporation of nonhumans into ethical codes of behavior, and 3) the recognition of humans as part of the ecological system" (Pierotti 2011:198–199).

Manuel Andrade, collecting Quileute language texts in 1928, recorded a "speech…spontaneously offered" by Jack Ward,

> when he found out that the texts which he was dictating would be published." Ward, speaking elegant Quileute, called on the Whites "to observe conservancy of the products of the land…you should take good care of the trees…. Let no one…destroy too much trout, stealhead [sic], salmon, and all other kinds of fish. Proud and happy I am knowing that my people, the Indians, are moderate in the use of nature's supplies, never killing wantonly the fish in the waters…. But you, White people, are wasteful. You are not mindful of what you

do in your camps, and consequently, many trees are often destroyed by fires. It is heart-breaking to us Indians to see how the country around us has changed...all the animals in the land are beginning to disappear. Much of the fish in the...waters is [sic] disappearing. Many of the good trees are disappearing.... (Andrade 1969 [1931]:12)

This wide concept of respect—*iisʔak̓* in Nuu-chah-nulth, and the word covers far more than English "respect"—is found throughout the northwest and, indeed, much more widely. A touching example of respect is the custom of leaving something for the rodents when raiding their caches. People often find and steal the caches of seeds, nuts, and roots that rodents make, but they are expected to leave enough to keep the animals alive (Armstrong et al. 2018). Ross (2011:249) reports that cattail leaves were left for squirrels for nesting material.

Stories on the Northwest Coast ranged from myths and legends to actual happenings. Here is a rather grim story of a real person who violated the rules. The story was told (in English) by Lawrence Aripa, a Coeur d'Alene tribal member from Northern Idaho (quoted in Frey 1995:177–179). The ellipses represent pauses in the story, not material left out; italics represent spoken emphasis.

"A person named Cosechin
    was just *cruel*...to animals.
  He would knock down trees
    and not use them.
  He would grab leaves from the trees in the springtime
    and scatter them to try to kill the trees.
  And you know it's the custom of the Indian that when they're going to use
  something from a tree
    or...even fish or hunt,
    they...ask permission first...
    'Mr. Tree may I use some part of you
    or I need it...for warmth for my children,'"
And so on. Cosechin treated humans just as badly, but notice the animals and plants come first.
  Cosechin was told to reform, and threatened. He shaped up for a while, but
    "he went back to his old ways like.
  And then...all of a sudden...he disappeared...."

The implication is that someone did away with him. Such enforcement of basic principles was sometimes necessary.

Emotional engagement with local landscapes was deep and intense (see Johnson and Hunn 2010), as these spiritual teachings show. Myths, spiritual power quests, and religious teachings, as well as personal stories, informed everyday experience with (nonhuman) people, trails, places, and spaces.

Archaeology and Environmental Management

Globally, the transformation of natural environments into cultural landscapes has resulted in a composite range of heritage that is at the nexus of culture and nature (Swetnam et al. 1999; Erickson 2010; Fairclough 2018). Regardless of the term used to describe such heritage—ecocultural heritage, landscape heritage, and dynamic heritage—there is an increasing recognition of the complex interplay between cultural resource and natural resource management and the governance systems and colonial structures that define such heritage (Kearsley and Middleton 2006). For example, some natural resources are threatened when people are removed or prevented from managing them (A. Ross 2011), climate change and environmental management strongly impact heritage resources (Howard et al. 2016), and archaeological sites are critical to understanding modern ecosystem services and functions and preparing for future resource variability (Rick et al. 2018). In a globally crowd-sourced project that asked historical ecologists the 50 most important research questions for future research in their field, the top ranked was "How can we better integrate heritage management laws and policy with those of natural resource management and conservation?" (Armstrong et al. 2017). In natural resource extraction and development contexts (oil and gas, mining, etc.), the concept of ecocultural heritage fundamentally contradicts with the ambition and scope of most extraction projects. Unlike stone tools, materials that can be removed from their landscape and analyzed later, a forest garden, trapline, or berry patch, cannot be. The long-standing emphasis on material culture has skewed our understanding of heritage and how it ought to be valued and preserved, and this is especially true in the context of Indigenous cultural and hereditary property (Nicholas and Hollowell 2016).

The *remnants* of managed ecosystems are now recognized throughout the Pacific Northwest and include both obvious and subtle changes to the landscape such as clam gardens (Toniello et al. 2019), intertidal marsh gardens (Deur 2002), wapato gardens (Hoffmann et al. 2016), and forest gardens (Armstrong 2017). Intensively managed berry patches, trail networks, and sites of isolation such as those used in puberty rights were in some cases used for centuries and continue to be used (Mack and McClure 2002; Johnson 2010). The landscape was cultivated to varying degrees (Anderson 2005; Deur and Turner 2005; Turner 2005). Today there are community and lineage-specific management practices that continue to adapt and flourish (Arias-Bustamante 2013). While traditional management practices might seem challenging to document archaeologically (Lepofsky and Lertzman 2008), such challenges are overcome by consulting ethnographic and ethnohistoric records (Lepofsky and Armstrong 2018), utilizing any number of impressive developments in bioinformatics and innovative technologies and collaborating with ecologists (e.g., Fisher et al. 2019). Perhaps more importantly, the heritage legacies of management practices are easy to identify and protect if archaeologists actually listen and talk to the people whose land they are working on (Deur et al. 2015; Lepofsky et al. In press).

In British Columbia, culturally modified trees (CMTs) are the most recorded site type and the most dominant feature on the archaeological landscape. Documenting and recording living and natural heritage are therefore not inconceivable, burdensome, or unrealistic. Other sites like forest gardens, burned berry patches, and intertidal marsh gardens are likely ignored because (1) such sites are not always visible to an untrained archaeologist, (2) such sites have not yet been considered under legal frameworks for protection (government guidelines, policies, agreements, and bulletins, as written by mostly non-Indigenous people), and (3) dating human modifications to landscapes and biota (for the ever controversial protection time stamp of 1846) requires a complex suite of historical-ecological methods (Lepofsky and Armstrong 2018). While there are exceptions, where archaeologists have gone to great lengths to protect heritage that is environmentally ensconced or "environmental" in nature, generally such managed sites are not regarded. We are at a crossroads in British Columbia where there has been a massive expansion in liquefied natural gas (LNG) exploration and export and a simultaneous expansion and recognition of the rich archaeological heritage that is utterly entangled and conveyed in natural environments. Ignoring Indigenous peoples' forms of ecocultural heritage, denying them direct and meaningful engagement with ecological management decisions, or separating communities from such heritage not only results in considerable economic and cultural harms but is a form of colonial violence (Nicholas 2017).

According to legal requirements, archaeological and environmental assessments are conducted in advance of any proposed infrastructure development such as pipelines, pumping stations, work camps, and export terminals in order to evaluate potential adverse effects. Communities must be consulted in accordance with policy and legislation. From 2011 to 2019, archaeological assessments in Wet'suwet'en and Gitxsan communities in Northwestern British Columbia concluded that the archaeological heritage of some territories was largely insignificant, of no teaching or heritage value (as specified in the BC Heritage Conservation Act), and, therefore, not worth protecting. In both cases, none of the chiefs or house representatives were consulted or even aware of the archaeology occurring on their territories. In response to potential pipeline development, two communities—Madii Lii (House[1] Luutkudziiwus, Gitxsan) and Unist'oten (Dark House, Wet'suwet'en)—set up checkpoints or cultural immersion camps (culture camps) to prevent LNG projects from proceeding on their unceded[2] territories. These checkpoints include self-contained cabins, smokehouses, gardens, traplines, fish stations, and healing centers built directly on the paths of pipelines. Chief and house/lineage members, allies, and spokespeople permanently live at the camps. They routinely hold feasts, organize youth leadership activities, and provide cultural training for community members to fish, hunt, and harvest plant foods and medicines on their territories.[3] In both cases I (Armstrong) was asked to "assess the assessments" conducted by consulting archaeologists. According to the house representatives, it was impossible that their land "had no heritage worth protecting." It was clear that the heritage valuation of both territories was done poorly or not at all. Perhaps unsurprisingly, "when archaeology is done only for the advancement of an industry, and obligatory compliance with regulations, we waste time, resources, and public trust. This becomes more harmful than beneficial" (Atalay et al. 2014:111). Below we review the harm

---

[1] House groups are the foremost unit of Gitxsan and Wet'suwet'en socioeconomic organization

[2] Unlike the "number treaties" signed elsewhere in Canada, in British Columbia First Nations have never extinguished any rights to their territories (with some exceptions).

[3] In both cases, no treaty has ever been signed, and therefore rights to territories were never extinguished by house/clan chiefs.

archaeologists had (and are still inflicting) on communities and the heart-centered management approach that emerged in response to it.

Madii Lii

Madii Lii is the traditional territory of House Luutkudziiwus (and recognized as such in the Supreme Court of Canada), a House group (Wilp) in Gitxsan territory in Northwestern British Columbia. Consulting archaeologists were flown in to survey a fraction of the 354 km^2 of Madii Lii territory in advance of a proposed LNG pipeline and, according to the community, purportedly missed archaeological heritage and sites worth protecting. I (Armstrong) was asked to review the reports that consulting archaeologists submitted. My review (conducted with fisheries biologist, Ken Rabnett) contained faulty predictive models (e.g., using Interior Plateau models for a transitional coastal people) to calculate archaeological potential in the territory and inconsistent methods for locating sites (test pitting on bedrock). Following up with the community's complaints, I (Armstrong) went out on the land with a community member, and we located three discrete archaeological sites where the report said there were none (this community member and his family have lived and trapped in the area for centuries). These sites were located by talking with Elders, identifying aggregations of ethnobotanically important plants, and targeting ecologically significant areas like river canyon pools (the best honey holes for fishing). We (Armstrong and the house representatives) wrote our own archaeological assessment and submitted it to the legal team involved in a judicial review for House Luutkudziiwus' right to be consulted on any development in their territories.

Our heart-centered archaeology began by working backward. Backcasting is a planning method derived from ecology and was used to design an innovative archaeological program that was community-based and community-oriented (e.g., Martindale and Lyons 2014). Backcasting begins by identifying what an ideal future looks like and then works backward to define the actions and resources needed to get there (Robinson 1990; Atalay this volume). This is a particularly useful method since the current trends and practices of archaeology in contested landscapes are a systemic problem (see Holmberg and Robert 2000) rather than a specific or isolated factor. In other words, rather than have an archaeologist (Armstrong) redesign a new scheme for recording archaeological sites—a scheme that would appease consultants, band councils, lawyers, or the Provincial Archaeology Branch overseeing the management of heritage resources—we co-created and implemented a heart-centered archaeology built around the community's desired futures, their environmental resource ethic and management practices, and Gitxsan-specific protocol.

We began by asking Elders, "What does an ideal Gitxsan future look like?" In every instance the same three themes emerged: language, land, and youth. Specifically, there was a desire to empower youth and for them to engage with language and land. By focusing on these themes, we involved youth in assessing the

Fig. 3.1 "Field cards" were placed around the territory for a pace and compass exercise that was conducted in Gitxsan language. Forest gardens (ancient managed groves of native perennials e.g., Armstrong 2017) were discovered by youth who used the cards to identify plants. (Photo: C.G. Armstrong)

cultural and ecological significance of the Madii Lii landscape and infused it with Gitxsan language at every opportunity (Fig. 3.1).

In collaboration with *Tam Giist*, a "back to the land" cultural camp at nearby Gitsegukla Lake, we integrated archaeology into the numerous cultural programs (medicine walks, hunting and fishing trips, etc.) offered to Gitxsan community members that participated in themed weeks (women's week, men's week, youth week, and family week). Together, we sought out grease trails (the sometimes obvious and sometimes ephemeral ancient highway networks that connected many communities in the northwest, [Johnson 2010]), forest gardens, berry burning patches, medicine patches, bear wallows, historic traplines, mountain goat nests, and natural boundary markers between house-owned territories. These exercises taught everyone (including the archaeologists) how connected archaeological sites were to place (not space) and to the entire Gitxsan landscape.

In one instance, we accessed a remote huckleberry patch on a forest service road that was directly on the path of the proposed pipeline (Fig. 3.2). One of the cultural facilitators, Wally Morgan (Gitxsan), noted, "this place was recently burned, that's why the berries are so juicy and the size of marbles" (referring to cultural burning, see Trusler and Johnson 2008 for this site specifically). Roughly 200 meters from the epic berry patch, we located the Babine grease trail—a massive trail network with fire-cracked rock that connects the Skeena and Babine watersheds—and two

Fig. 3.2 Tam giist cultural immersion camp participants picking black huckleberries (gadimis/ simmaa'y; *Vaccinium membranaceum*) and identifying archaeological and cultural sites on House Luutkudziiwus territory, zoned for the Prince Rupert Gas Transmission Pipeline. (Photo C.G. Armstrong)

archaeological sites that were missed, or simply not recorded by the proponent-paid archaeological consultants. The living legacy of the berry patch was intimately tied to the archaeological heritage. Many were grateful to their ancestors for "building the path" to the berries in the past and maintaining the berries for the youth to harvest in the present.

The archaeology only came after a desired future was designed and after we were immersed in the landscape, and as Ruby Morgan pointed out, "only after we were able to connect with youth and matriarchs and support them in a strong, fun, practical, and healing experience." The land was primary—constructing a pipeline in a land that was populated with food, family, powerful beings, water, and remnants from the ancestors did not compute with camp participants. A heart-centered archaeology in Madii Lii meant connecting to Gitxsan values and protocols of harvesting, which in turn were part of the archaeological and cultural landscape that has been Luutkudiiwus' home for millennia. Managing heritage resources was not about the resources—it was about land, youth, and language. Tapping into an ecology of the heart, the environmental ethic in Gitxsan cultural discourse, was not only a satisfying and transformative exercise; it was also good practice—we recorded more archaeological sites (as defined by the BC Heritage Conservation Act) that the archaeological consultants missed.

Unist'ot'en

Roughly 125 km southwest from Madii Lii is Unist'ot'en or Dark House territory. In order to halt the construction of multiple pipelines,[4] since 2009 community members have permanently established a culture camp in the territory. In 2019, militarized police forcibly removed and arrested community members so that contractors for a recently proposed pipeline (Coastal Gaslink, LNG Canada) could enter and conduct permitting assessments for their project.[5] No assessments were conducted. Contractors began bulldozing the site immediately and within 2 weeks destroyed multiple archaeological sites and traplines. Unist'ot'en people routinely contacted the BC government and oil and gas regulators about the potential for archaeological sites in the area and the lack of assessments but work only stopped after a site was destroyed in 2019. Stone tool artifacts (~3500–2400 BP) were recovered from the destroyed site, the government designated the construction area as a "legacy site," and construction promptly continued (Sutherland-Wilson et al. 2019).

Consulting archaeologists originally designated the Unist'ot'en construction area as having "high" archaeological potential. Citing access difficulties (they could not get into the territory to assess the archaeological potential), archaeologists changed the designation potential from high to "low" (Sutherland-Wilson et al. 2019). When the stone tools were recovered, the oil and gas regulators in charge of permitting for the project released a bulletin insinuating (but not claiming) that the artifacts were planted and inauthentic. When construction began, the Office of the Wet'suwet'en (the governing body in Wet'suwet'en territory) published multiple cease and desist orders citing the high archaeological potential of the area. However, when the BC provincial government and oil and gas regulators examined the destroyed sites, they removed all the artifacts before the site could be properly inspected. A woefully inadequate mitigation plan was enacted, and within weeks, construction continued (Sutherland-Wilson et al. 2019). This was *not* a heart-centered approach to archaeology.

In response to the destroyed sites and ongoing construction at Unist'ot'en, a process of "frontline archaeology" ensued (Angelbeck and Jones 2018; Armstrong and Brown 2019). I (Armstrong) was tasked with reviewing the permit applications and reports, and the extensive cultural heritage files stored with the Office of the Wet'suwet'en. These files included archaeological sites, place names, and ethnobiologically significant sites recorded and inventoried, first for the Delgamuukw Supreme Court case proceedings (1980s–1990s [Delgamuukw v. the Queen]) and then by the Office of the Wet'suwet'en Lands and Resources department (2000–to present). None of this data was available to the consulting archaeologists, largely

---

[4] The ill-fated Northern Gateway pipeline was first proposed in the early 2000s but was halted in 2016. Currently, the Coastal Gaslink pipeline for LNG Canada (following a similar route as Northern Gateway) has been tentatively approved, but no Wet'suwet'en Hereditary Chiefs have consented to its construction.

[5] All charges were dropped for the 14 community members that were arrested.

because those archaeologists never consulted with the community, and as such, missed archaeological sites which were then destroyed. Reports, affidavits, and endless exhibitions were written for court proceedings citing the failure of archaeologists to comply with the Heritage Act—in some cases, doing poor archaeological assessments or doing none at all.

Unist'ot'en spokespeople and camp defenders were trained to identify culturally modified trees (CMTs), cultural depressions, trails, and modified forest gardens (Fig. 3.3). In many cases, most people already knew what to look for—active traplines are along trails that are thought to be hundreds of years old. They were given GPSs and mapped out sites while they were checking their traplines, fishing, hiking trails, or harvesting other plant foods. In doing so, an Unist'ot'en cultural heritage inventory filled the otherwise empty maps on the government's archaeological database. For example, in one report, consulting archaeologists noted,

> The investigative area has minimal potential for CMTs due **to the absence of mature cedar and hemlock trees**. (emphasis added, 2013-0033-1023, Appendix DD)

This could be a sound observation in some areas on the Coast, but Wet'suwet'en peoples' homelands are in transitional coastal and interior zones, and CMT species in this specific bioregion are from lodgepole pine (*Pinus contorta*), whitebark pine

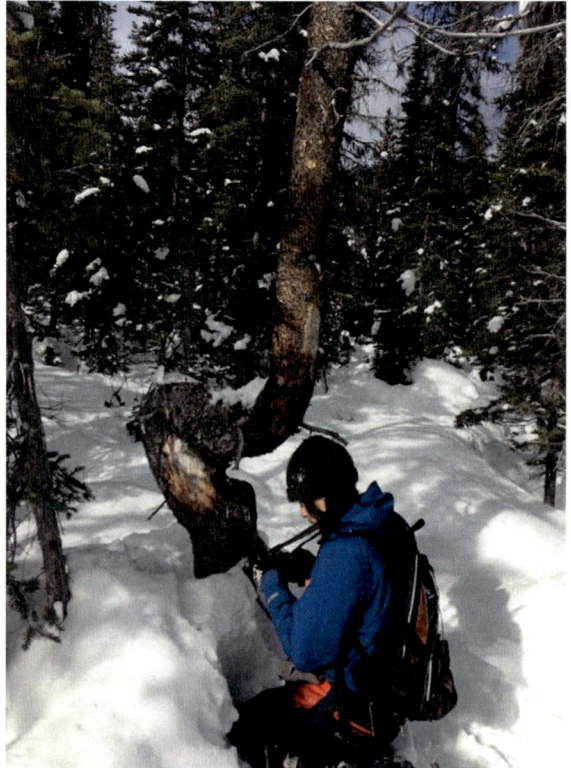

Fig. 3.3 Unist'ot'en supporter Denzel Sutherland-Wilson (Gitxsan) locates multiple CMTs along a precontact trail

(*Pinus albicaulis*), firs (*Abies* spp.), and spruces (*Picea* spp.). Wet'suwe'ten peoples marked their trails on trees in many different ways according to very specific family traditions and practices (Morin 2011). Sure enough, every CMT that Unist'ot'en people recorded on the frontline of their territories were on spruce, balsam, and pine and consisted of unique bending, snapping, and splitting markers (Fig. 3.3). One does not expect every archaeologist to be an expert in all regions of the British Columbia—but surely we can expect them to *consult with the experts*. That is at the core of a heart-centered approach. Not mere consultation or notification with communities—but an active engagement with the people and land that archaeological resources come from (Zimmerman and Branam 2014). Once again, this was not only more collaborative and just archaeology; it was better practice—we identified over 40 sites consulting archaeologists missed. Managing archaeological heritage is not about managing resources, it is about engaging and managing people.

A Heart-Centered Future

In the Pacific Northwest, the pragmatic "leave some for others" approach not only makes sense but also is necessary for survival. In the absence of formal state-level government, individual conscience was the only mechanism that could guarantee forbearance and restraint, but this codified ethic entirely removed (and at odds with) large-scale oil and gas development assessments (e.g., Belanger and Lackenbauer 2014). Northwestern BC has been home to countless postwar development schemes that have gone "bust" (asbestos mines, hydroelectric projects, abandoned railways, see Peyton 2017). In its current iteration, aggressive resource extraction and LNG development will be no different. Such resource developments in contested territories do not "leave some for others" but destroys and compromises the land for future generations, and archaeologists are complicit in this if they are removed entirely from heart-centered approaches. We cannot determine whether or not consulting archaeologists would still have missed sites in Madii Lii or circumvented the Heritage Act in Unist'ot'en if they were practicing a heart-centered approach. However, modern resource management—by that we mean the management of any landscape—requires at least some form of emotion or ideology.

Biotic management today is largely the responsibility of consultants, engineers, bureaucrats, and others who often share the narrowest of rational views. This point has been amply discussed by "sensitive" conservation biologists such as David Ehrenfeld and David Orr, who note that most field biologists love their subjects, and study them because they love them, yet seem afraid to admit this in public or to talk of emotions in their writings. As we consider what a heart-centered archaeological practice looks like, particularly in the Pacific Northwest, we must first confer with the heart-centered ecologies and environmental protocol and ethic of the people whose ancestors we study and seek to understand.

We argue that understanding peoples' land-based ethos and ecologically managed landscapes is a heart-centered approach to archaeology that ultimately leads to a better practice. This practice requires archaeologists to (1) think of the cultural, religious/spiritual, legal, and traditional constituents of all living entities in peoples' territories, (2) consider such constituents as integral to archaeological landscapes, and (3) go beyond rote and compliance practice of archaeology and ask, "archaeology for whom?" (Panameno and Nalda 1978). Heritage is complex and culturally variable, but the heritage of peoples who have been colonized, disenfranchised, and disempowered is uniquely a question of human rights (Hillerdal et al. 2017). The BC Heritage Act is imperfect at best, and so archaeologists are tasked with challenging the practices that *continue* to colonize, disenfranchise, and disempower.

Taken together, we consider how *Ecologies of the Heart* informs and inspires *Archaeologies of the Heart* both methodologically, through heart-centered approaches, and theoretically by understanding the deeply intertwined valuations of Indigenous heritage as land based—both in the past and in the present (Lepofsky et al. In press). We must consider the hearts of those who entrust us to good with the heritage left by their ancestors—this trust is indeed a heart-centered relationship onto its own.

References

Anderson, E. N. (1996). *Ecologies of the heart: Emotion, belief, and the environment.* New York: Oxford University Press.

Anderson, M. K. (2005). *Tending the wild: Native American knowledge and the management of California's natural resources.* Berkeley: University of California Press.

Anderson, E. N. (2016). *Caring for place: Ecology, ideology, and emotion in traditional landscape management.* Walnut Creek: Left Coast Press.

Anderson, M. K. (2017). Geophytes and human evolution. *Fremontia, 44*(3), 39–41.

Andrade, M. (1969). *Quileute texts.* Orig. 1931, Columbia University Press. New York: AMS Press.

Angelbeck, B., & Jones, J. (2018). Direct actions and archaeology: The Lil'wat peoples movement to protect archaeological sites. *Journal of Contemporary Archaeology, 5*(2), 117–206.

Appadurai, A. (2001). The globalization of archaeology and heritage: A discussion with Arjun Appadurai. *Journal of Social Archaeology, 1*(1), 35–49.

Arias-Bustamante, J. (2013). *Indigenous knowledge, climate change and forest management: The Nisga'a nation approach.* Doctoral dissertation, Faculty of Forestry University of British Columbia, Vancouver, BC.

Armstrong, C. G., & Brown, C. (2019). Frontiers are frontlines: An ethnobiology against ongoing colonialism. *Journal of Ethnobiology, 39*(1), 14–31.

Armstrong, C. G., Shoemaker, A. C., McKechnie, I., Ekblom, A., Szabó, P., Lane, P. J., et al. (2017). Anthropological contributions to historical ecology: 50 questions, infinite prospects. *PLoS One, 12*(2), e0171883. https://doi.org/10.1371/journal.pone.0171883.

Armstrong, C. G., Dixon, M., & Turner, N. J. (2018). Management and traditional production of beaked hazelnut (k'áp'xw-az', Corylus cornuta; Betulaceae) in British Columbia. *Journal of Human Ecology, 46*(4), 547–559.

Armstrong, C. (2017). Historical ecology of cultural landscapes in the Pacific Northwest. Doctoral Dissertation, Department of Archaeology, Simon Fraser University, Burnaby, BC.

Atalay, S., Clauss, L. R., McGuire, R. H., & Welch, J. R. (2014). *Transforming archaeology: Activist practices and prospects.* London: Routledge.

Balée, W. (2013). *Cultural forests of the amazon: A historical ecology of people and their landscapes*. Tuscaloosa: University of Alabama Press.

Belanger, Y. D., & Lackenbauer, P. W. (2014). *Blockades or breakthroughs? Aboriginal peoples confront the Canadian state*. Montreal: McGill-Queen's University Press.

Book Builders of 'Ksan. (1980). *Gathering what the great nature provided: Food traditions of the Gitksan*. Medeira Park, BC: Douglas & McIntyre.

Campbell, S., & Butler, V. (2010). Archaeological evidence for resilience of Pacific Northwest salmon populations and the socioecological system over the last~ 7,500 years. *Ecology and Society, 15*(1), 1–20.

Cannon, A. (2003). Long-term continuity in Central Northwest Coast settlement patterns. In R. L. Carlson (Ed.), *Archaeology of Coastal British Columbia* (pp. 1–12). Burnaby: Archaeology Press, Simon Fraser University.

Darvill, T. (2005). Value systems in archaeology. In J. Carman, M. Cooper, A. Firth, & D. Wheatley (Eds.), *Managing archaeology* (pp. 59–69). London: Routledge.

Deur, D. (2002). Rethinking precolonial plant cultivation on the northwest coast of North America. *The Professional Geographer, 54*(2), 140–157.

Deur, D., Dick, A., Recalma-Clutesi, K., & Turner, N. J. (2015). Kwakwaka'wakw "Clam Gardens". *Human Ecology, 43*(2), 201–212.

Drucker, P. (1955). *Indians of the Northwest Coast (No. 970.1 D8)*. American Museum Science Books.

Durkheim, E. (1995) [1912]. *The elementary forms of religious life*. Translated by Karen E. Fields. New York: Free Press.

Erickson, C. L. (2010). The transformation of environment in to landscape: The historical ecology of monumental earthwork construction in the Bolivian Amazon. *Diversity, 2*, 618–552.

Fairclough, G. (2018). Landscape and heritage: Ideas from Europe for culturally based solutions in rural environments. *Journal of Environmental Planning and Management, 62*, 1149. https://doi.org/10.1080/09640568.2018.1476026.

Ferris, N. (2003). Between colonial and Indigenous archaeologies: Legal and extra-legal ownership of the archaeological past in North America. *Canadian Journal of Archaeology/Journal Canadien d'Archéologie, 190*, 154–190.

Ferris, N. (2007). Always fluid: Government policy making and standards of practice in Ontario archaeological resource management. In W. J. H. Willems & M. van den Dries (Eds.), *Quality management in archaeology* (pp. 78–99). Oxford: Oxbow Books.

Fisher, J. A., Shackelford, N., Hocking, M. D., Trant, A. J., & Starzomski, B. M. (2019). Indigenous peoples' habitation history drives present-day forest biodiversity in British Columbia's coastal temperate rainforest. *People and Nature, 1*, 103–114.

Fiske, J.-A., & Patrick, B. (2000). *Cis Dideen Kat (when the plumes rise): The way of the Lake Babine Nation*. Vancouver: University of British Columbia Press.

Frey, R. (1995). *Stories that make the world: Oral literature of the Indian peoples of the Inland Northwest*. Norman, OK: University of Oklahoma Press.

Garnett, S. T., Burgess, N. D., Fa, J. E., Fernández-Llamazares, Á., Molnár, Z., & Robinson, C. J. (2018). A spatial overview of the global importance of Indigenous lands for conservation. *Nature Sustainability, 1*, 369–374.

Gauvreau, A., Lepofsky, D., Rutherford, M., & Reid, M. (2017). Everything revolves around the herring: The Heiltsuk-herring relationship through time. *Ecology and Society, 22*(2), 10. https://doi.org/10.5751/ES-09201-220210.

George, E. M. (2003). *Living on the edge: Nuu-Chah-Nulth history from an Ahousaht Chief's perspective*. Winlaw, BC: Sono Nis Press.

Glavin, T. (2000). *A death feast in Dimlahamid*. Vancouver, BC: New Star Books.

Hillerdal, C., Karlström, A., & Ojala, C.-G. (2017). *Archaeologies of 'us' and 'them' — Debating the ethics and politics and indigeneity in archaeological and heritage discourse*. New York: Routledge.

Hobbes, T. (1950) [1651]. *Leviathan*. New York, NY: Dutton.

Hoffmann, T., Lyons, N., Miller, D., Diaz, A., Homan, A., Huddlestan, S., & Leon, R. (2016). Engineered feature used to enhance gardening at a 3800-year-old site on the Pacific Northwest Coast. *Science Advances, 2*(12), e1601282.

Holmberg, J., & Robèrt, K. H. (2000). Backcasting—A framework for strategic planning. *International Journal of Sustainable Development & World Ecology, 7*(4), 291–308.

Howard, A. J., Knight, D., Coulthard, T., Hudson-Edwards, K., Kossoff, D., Malone, S., & A. (2016). Assessing riverine threats to heritage assets posed by future climate change through a geomorphological approach and predictive modelling in the Derwent Valley Mills WHS, UK. *Journal of Cultural Heritage, 19*, 387–394.

Johnson, L. M. (2010). *Trail of story, traveller's path: Reflections on ethnoecology and landscape.* Edmonton: Athabasca University Press.

Johnson, L. M., & Hunn, E. S. (2010). *Landscape ethnoecology: concepts of biotic and physical space.* New York, NY: Berghahn Books.

Kearsley, G., & Middleton, M. (2006). Conflicted heritage: Values, visions and practices in the management and preservation of cultural and environmental heritage. *Public History Review, 13*, 23–34.

Krech, S. (1999). *The ecological Indian: Myth and reality.* New York, NY: W. W. Norton.

Lepofsky, D., & Armstrong, C. G. (2018). Foraging new ground: Documenting ancient resource and environmental management in Canadian archaeology. *Canadian Journal of Archaeology, 42*(1), 57–73.

Lepofsky, D., & Lertzman, K. (2008). Documenting ancient plant management in the northwest of North America. *Botany, 86*(2), 129–145.

Lepofsky, D., & Lertzman, K. (2019). Through the lens of the land: Reflections from archaeology, ethnoecology, and environmental science on collaboration with first nations, 1970s to the present. *BC Studies, 200*, 141–160.

Lepofsky, D., Armstrong, C. G., Mathews, D., & Greening, S. (In press). Understanding the past for the future: Archaeology, plants, and first nations' land use and rights. In N. J. Turner (Ed.), *Indigenous peoples' land rights and the roles of ethnoecology and ethnobotany: Strategies for Canada's future.* Montreal: McGill-Queen's University Press.

Little, B. J., & Shackel, P. A. (Eds.). (2007). *Archaeology as a tool of civic engagement.* Lanham, MD: Rowman Altamira.

Locke, J. (1924) [1690]. *Two treatises on government.* New York, NY: Everyman.

Lynott, M. J., & Wylie, A. (1995). *Ethics in American archaeology: Challenges for the 1990s.* Washington, D.C.: Society for American Archaeology Monograph. ISBN 0932839126.

Lyons, N., & Ritchie, M. (2017). The archaeology of camas production and exchange on the Northwest Coast: With evidence from a Sts'ailes (Chehalis) village on the Harrison River, British Columbia. *Journal of Ethnobiology, 37*(2), 346–368.

Mack, C. A., & McClure, R. H. (2002). *Vaccinium* processing in the Washington Cascades. *Journal of Ethnobiology, 22*(1), 35–60.

Martindale, A., & Lyons, N. (2014). Community-oriented archaeology. *Canadian Journal of Archaeology, 38*(2), 425–433.

McGuire, R. H. (2008). *Archaeology as political action* (Vol. 17). Berkley: University of California Press.

McIlwraith, T. F. (2012). *"We are still Didene:" Stories of hunting and history from Northern British Columbia.* Toronto, ON: University of Toronto Press.

McLaren, D., Rahemtulla, F., Gitla, E. W., & Fedje, D. (2015). Prerogatives, sea level, and the strength of persistant places: Archaeological evidence for long-term occupation of the Central Coast of British Columbia. *BC Studies, 187*, 155–191.

Meskell, L., & Preucel, R. W. (2008). *Companion to social archaeology.* Hoboken: Wiley.

Minnis, P. E., & Elisens, W. J. (Eds.). (2001). *Biodiversity and Native America.* Norman, OK: University of Oklahoma Press.

Morin, M. (2011). *Niwhts'ide'nïhibi'it'ën, the ways of our ancestors: Witsuwit'en history and culture throughout the millennia.* School District No. 54, Bulkley Valley, BC.

Nicholas, G.P. (2017). *Activism, education, and the protection of Indigenous heritage.* Shephard Krech III Lecture, Haffenreffer Museum of Anthropology, Brown University. Available online: https://www.academia.edu/34624002/_Activism_Education_and_the_Protection_of_Indigenous_Heritage_2017_

Nicholas, G., & Hollowell, J. (2016). Ethical challenges to a postcolonial archaeology: The legacy of scientific colonialism. In Hamilakis, Y. & Duke, P. (Eds.) *Archaeology and Capitalism* (pp. 59–82). New York, NY: Routledge.

Norton, H. H., Hunn, E. S., Martinsen, C. S., & Keely, P. B. (1984). Vegetable food products of the foraging economies of the Pacific Northwest. *Ecology of Food and Nutrition, 14*(3), 219–228.

Ostrom, E. (1990). *Governing the commons: The evolution of institutions for collective action.* New York, NY: Cambridge University Press.

Ostrom, E. (2005). *Understanding institutional diversity.* Princeton, NJ: Princeton University Press.

Ostrom, E. (2009). A general framework for analyzing sustainability of social-ecological systems. *Science, 5939*(325), 419–422.

Ostrom, E., Burger, J., Field, C. B., Norgaard, R. B., & Policansky, D. (1999). Revisiting the commons: Local lessons, global challenges. *Science, 284*(5412), 278–282.

Panameno, R., & Nalda, E. (1978). Arqueologia, Para Quien? *Nueva Antropologia, 12*, 111–124.

Peyton, J. (2017). *Unbuilt environments: Tracing postwar development in Northwest British Columbia.* Vancouver, BC: University of British Columbia Press.

Pierotti, R. (2011). *Indigenous knowledge, ecology, and evolutionary biology.* New York: Routledge.

Rick, T. C., Kirch, P. V., Erlandson, J. M., & Fitzpatrick, S. M. (2013). Archaeology, deep history, and the human transformation of island ecosystems. *Anthropocene, 4*, 33–45.

Rick, T. C., Braje, T. J., Erlandson, J. M., Gill, K. M., Kirn, L., & McLaren-Dewey, L. (2018). Horizon scanning: Survey and research priorities for cultural, historical, and paleobiological resources of Santa Cruz Island, California. *Western North American Naturalist, 78*(4), 1–12.

Robinson, J. B. (1990). Futures under glass: A recipe for people who hate to predict. *Futures, 22*(8), 820–842.

Robinson, W., & Wright, W. (1962). *Men of Medeek.* Kitimat, BC: Northern Sentinel Press.

Ross, J. A. (2011). *The Spokane Indians.* Spokane: Library of Congress Online Catalogue (980 875).

Shackel, P. A., & Chambers, E. (2004). *Places in mind: Public archaeology as applied anthropology.* New York: Routledge.

Sutherland-Wilson, D., Spice, A., & Armstrong, C. G. (2019). Compliance archaeology fails Indigenous peoples in British Columbia: An example from Unist'ot'en territory. *The Midden, 49*(1), 26–29.

Suttles, W. (1968). Coping with abundance: Subsistence on the Northwest Coast. (tDAR id: 134177).

Swetnam, T. W., Allen, C. D., & Betancourt, J. L. (1999). Applied historical ecology: Using the past to manage for the future. *Ecological Applications, 9*(4), 1189–1206.

Teit, J. (1919). Tahltan Tales. *Journal of American Folk-Lore, 32*, 198–250.

Thornton, T. F. (2012). *Haa Léelk'w Hás Aaní Saax'ú: Our grandparents' names on the land.* Juneau/Seattle: Sealaska/University of Washington Press.

Thornton, T. F., & Sealaska Heritage Institute (2008). Being and place among the Tlingit (Culture, Place, and Nature). Seattle, WA: University of Washington Press.

Tømmervik, H., Dunfjeld, S., Olsson, G. A., & Nilsen, M. Ø. (2010). Detection of ancient reindeer pens, cultural remains and anthropogenic influenced vegetation in Byrkije (Børgefjell) mountains, Fennoscandia. *Landscape and Urban Planning, 98*(1), 56–71.

Toniello, G., Lepofsky, D., Lertzman-Lepofsky, G., Salomon, A. K., & Rowell, K. (2019). 11,500 y of human-clam relationships provide long-term context for intertidal management in the Salish Sea, British Columbia. *PNAS 116*(4), 22106–22114.

Trosper, R. L. (2002). Northwest coast indigenous institutions that supported resilience and sustainability. *Ecological Economics, 41*(2), 329–344.

Trusler, S., & Johnson, L. M. (2008). "Berry patch" as a kind of place—The ethnoecology of black huckleberry in northwestern Canada. *Human Ecology, 36*(4), 553–568.

Turner, N. J. (1995). *Food plants of coastal First Peoples*. Vancouver, BC: University of British Columbia Press.

Turner, N. J. (2005). *The earth's blanket*. Vancouver, BC/Seattle: Douglas and McIntyre/University of Washington Press.

Turner, N. J. (2014). *Ancient pathways, ancestral knowledge: Ethnobotany and ecological wisdom of Indigenous peoples of Northwestern North America*. Montreal and Kingston: McGill-Queen's University Press.

Turner, N. J., & Kuhnlein, H. V. (1982). Two important "root" foods of the Northwest Coast Indians: Springbank clover (*Trifolium wormskioldii*) and Pacific silverweed (*Potentilla anserina* ssp. *pacifica*). *Economic Botany, 36*(4), 411–432.

Turner, N. J., & Peacock, S. (2005). Solving the perennial paradox: Ethnobotanical evidence for plant resource management on the Northwest Coast. In D. Deur & N. J. Turner (Eds.), *Keeping it living: Traditions of plant use and cultivation on the Northwest Coast of North America* (pp. 101–150). Seattle/Vancouver: University of Washington Press/University of British Columbia Press.

Turner, N. J., Deur, D., & Lepofsky, D. (2013). Plant management systems of British Columbia's First Peoples. *BC Studies, 179*, 107–133.

Tushingham, S., Ardura, D., Eerkens, J. W., Palazoglu, M., Shahbaz, S., & Fiehn, O. (2013). Hunter-gatherer tobacco smoking: Earliest evidence from the Pacific Northwest Coast of North America. *Journal of Archaeological Science, 40*(2), 1397–1407.

Van Hinte, T., Gunton, T. I., & Day, J. C. (2007). Evaluation of the assessment process for major projects: A case study of oil and gas pipelines in Canada. *Impact Assessment and Project Appraisal, 25*(2), 123–137.

Zimmerman, L. J., & Branam, K. M. (2014). Collaborating with stakeholders. In Balme, J. & Paterson, A. (Eds.), *Archaeology in Practice: A Student Guide to Archaeological Analyses* (pp. 1–25). Hoboken, NJ: Wiley-Blackwell.

Chapter 4
"We Ask Only That You Come to Us with an Open Heart and an Open Mind"

The Transformative Power of a Humble Archaeology of the Heart

Tanja Hoffmann

I was 25 years old. It was my second year as a graduate student, and I had been hired by the Saik'uz First Nation of North-Central British Columbia to conduct some interviews with community Elders about local archaeology. I was thrilled. Here was my chance to put all my hard-earned knowledge and skills into practice. So I packed my carefully crafted non-leading questions, my informed consent forms and my tape recorder into my big bag of good intentions, threw the whole lot into my Ford Pinto and drove out to the Reserve. At the Band Office, I met my first interviewee, Mrs. Sophie Thomas, an Elder, traditional plant expert and healer with far more experience in anthropology and with archaeologists than I will ever have. I began.

I did it all right. Forms were signed, and appropriate buttons on the tape recorder were pressed. I had my questions in front of me, and boy, they were good ones! Mrs. Thomas patiently answered the first few, and I, buoyed on the wave of this early success, asked more. With each pause I interjected with another of my cleverly crafted questions, anxious to fit them all in before the interview time was up. Then it happened. Suddenly Mrs. Thomas sat up taller in her chair, leaded forward and, her voice ringing out, frustrated she said, "you know girlie, if you shut up and stop asking so many questions, you might actually learn something!"

I remember little else of that particular interview except the cool wash of shame that rushed over my body. Yet, despite this early gaff, the Saik'uz Nation continued to employ me for the duration of my graduate studies. Months later I asked Mrs. Thomas why, despite her admonishment in that first interview, she and the community had decided to keep me around. "Well", she replied slyly, "you keep coming back to learn some more".

T. Hoffmann (✉)
Postdoctoral Fellow, Indigenous Works and University of Saskatchewan,
Saskatoon, SK, Canada

© Springer Nature Switzerland AG 2020
K. Supernant et al. (eds.), *Archaeologies of the Heart*,
https://doi.org/10.1007/978-3-030-36350-5_4

As difficult as that first interview with Mrs. Thomas was, I realize now how fortunate I was to have had such a transformative experience so early in my career. In reflecting on what I learned from this and the other experiences I have had in the intervening 20 years, I have come to realize that an "archaeology of heart" is grounded in, and practiced through, humility.

Indigenous and non-Indigenous scholars list humility as essential to successful and sustained partnerships with Indigenous communities. Colwell-Chanthaphonh and Ferguson (2004:21) suggest that the virtues of tolerance, humility and reasonableness should motivate the archaeologist. This is particularly so in situations where naming, classifying and transmitting the meaning of sites come into conflict. These virtues can be used to guide equitable consideration of competing or conflicting meaning, as opposed to seeking ways to synthesize or impose one meaning over another. Martindale and Lyons (2014:431) suggest that community-oriented archaeology requires practitioners to exercise honesty, reflexivity, integrity and humility so as to make way for true partnerships capable of fostering new interpretations of the past. Humility is listed as a prerequisite, requiring vulnerability and creation of unsettling process, for community-oriented work (Martindale and Lyons 2014; Nicholas 2012). Zimmerman (2005:295) equates a humble practice as one that rejects absolutist approaches for those that help us understand descendant communities and the pasts they create.

Though frequently listed as a fundamental to community-based practice, there is less attention given to an explicit definition of humility. In Western secular terms, humility is defined variously as "a state", "a quality" or "condition". The Cambridge English Dictionary (2008) defines humility as "the quality of not being proud because you are aware of your bad qualities". Similarly, the Oxford English Dictionary notes humility is "the quality of having a modest or low view of one's importance". Etymology suggests humility references the Latin *humilis* meaning "lowly, humble and literally on the ground" or *humus* meaning "earth".

Western definitions of humility are largely grounded in Judeo-Christian reflections on the relationship of the human to the divine. In Christian thinking, humility is the virtue through which one recognizes the "wretchedness of the human condition" in juxtaposition to the perfection of God (Weinstein 2015). Self-abasement serves to place humans in appropriate relationship to God and godliness, such that humans might recognize that all good comes from God (Weinstein 2015). Thomas Aquinas, thirteenth-century Catholic priest and scriptural theologian, asserts that humility is part of the spiritual foundation, making humans open to the influx of divine grace (Overmyer 2015:655). In a Jewish worldview, humility is the practice of getting past the self or ego, to reveal inherent godliness. Judaism views human beings as intermediaries between God and creation – superior to animals and the physical world but lower than God. Humility, rather than demanding destructive self-abnegation, is a superior moral virtue requiring one to transfer emphasis away from the self to nurture a giving nature that is incompatible with self-love (Berenbaum and Skolnik 2007). Thus "Humility is not an isolated trait, but rather a life-style, which encompasses and structures every aspect of human thought and behaviour" (AICE 2019).

An indigenous definition of humility engages a broader context, one that acknowledges the essential interrelatedness of self to whole and whole to self. Referencing her connection to the Seven Grandfather Teachings, Anishinaabe legal scholar Lindsay Borrows (2016:152) defines humility as "a state of being that can open hearts and minds to see a situation in different ways". Defined in this way, humility requires engagement of all aspects of the self. Here an open heart and mind are the internal prerequisites for a broadening of external perspective. To this end, Borrows (2016) suggests an Indigenous definition of humility encompasses four principles: vulnerability, teachability, critical self-reflection and the ability to "hold ones place". Each of these principles guides action and facilitates learning. In the following sections, I explore how these and other principles of humility have guided my own "archaeology of heart".

First, Be Vulnerable

Atalay (2012) suggests humility is about more than pursuing a humble practice. It is also about presenting *yourself* to the community. It is about imparting your research aspirations in a manner that is transparent and authentic. Here humility requires that what you *do* reflects who you *are*. This type of personal disclosure necessitates vulnerability and vulnerability's constant companion, discomfort. There is an old adage that goes: "there is no growing in a comfort zone, and no comfort in a growing zone" (Borrows 2016:149). Authentic engagement with a community means we open our core selves to "sticky" questions, the ones that make us "squirm" (Martindale and Lyons 2014; Nicholas 2012).

As an archaeologist working in cultural resource management, I am frequently required to assess the "significance" of an archaeological site. My disciplinary culture ranks large, intact and old (the older the better) sites as highly significant and ephemeral, disturbed or recent sites of less significance. In practical terms, "significant" sites are "managed" according to more rigorous sampling regimes than sites of low or moderate significance. In essence, significance evaluation facilitates the erasure of the "humble site" from the physical and interpretive landscape (Harrison 2006:94). For many Indigenous peoples, the significance assessment process is highly objectionable (Ferris 2003). It establishes hierarchy where none should exist via the application of Western scientific measures of importance (Beaudoin 2016; Gnecco and Langebaek 2013). Personal challenges from Indigenous leaders, Elders and spiritual advisors have forced me to accept the uncomfortable truth that my acquiescence to the potential assessment process has had a permanent impact on ancestral cultural landscapes.

Indigenous perspectives challenge the foundations, motivations and the "social distance" norms of mainstream social science (Coburn et al. 2013). Hamilakis (2016) suggests a re-conceptualization of archaeology as "archaeological ethnography". With critical reflexivity and community partnership as its theoretical and practical anchors, archaeological ethnography "forces us to 'excavate' our own collective subjectivity and disciplinary culture; like all true encounters, it is a mutually transformative process". This transformation might encourage the "epistemic humility" that Hamilakis (2016:679) argues still eludes the majority of archaeological enterprise.

The "sticky" problems, uncomfortable questions and lively debates concerning the role of cultural resource management (CRM) in heritage preservation and destruction (e.g. Martindale and Lyons 2014; La Salle and Hutchings 2016) or the value of Indigenous archaeology itself (e.g. McGhee 2008; Silliman 2010) provide ongoing sources of discourse vital to the future of archaeology (Ireland and Schofield 2015). While scholarly debate is important, so too are those personal experiences that "open the core" to expose the authentic self that shapes our actions. In working through the challenges and the uncomfortable situations, we come to expose existing orthodoxy and reveal new, creative understandings about the past, about each other and about ourselves (Gosden 2012; Lyons 2013; Martindale and Lyons 2014). As Brené Brown (2012:211) aptly notes, "Vulnerability is not winning or losing; it's having the courage to show up and be seen when we have no control over the outcome".

Second, Be Teachable

Second, humility is the condition of being teachable. While fostering vulnerability one remains open to new ideas, experiences and understanding. An Indigenous definition of humility requires that this state of openness must be maintained in both heart and mind, for an open heart is a potent antidote to an egotistical mind.

At a recent conference I attended, a paper was delivered by a South African anthropologist. She described in eloquent, narrative terms how a particular group of rock art panels might help us understand the spiritual coalescence that occurs between hunter and prey at the moment of an animal's death. Midway through her presentation, another anthropologist entered and unapologetically made his way to a seat at the rear of the room. Upon completion of her presentation, this same anthropologist, leaning back in his chair, congratulated her on her well-written romantic story then stated "in my considerable experience hunting with these people, they experience about as much emotion when killing these animals as they do when slicing a loaf of bread". While not for me to challenge the validity of their competing interpretations, his statement served as a reminder that vulnerability goes both ways. People are unlikely to present alternate perspectives when they sense a closed mind, and a closed mind is unlikely to invite them. Engagement in the "teachable moment" requires a willingness to surrender intellectual certainty, social distance and entrenched belief. Iwama (2009:7) aptly notes "As we learn together, the journey offers the sacred gift of humility".

Third, Recognize and Honour In/Dependence

Third, humility is "a state of positioning oneself in a way that does not favour one's own importance over another's" (Borrows 2016:153). An Indigenous colleague of mine is fond of reminding those that work with her (including me) of two things, (1) no one is indispensable, and (2) if it is starting to feel like yours, it is time to let it go. Over time I have come to understand that these statements reference her commitment to a long-term goal greater than the individuals who work towards it. It is her way of reminding us that our role as individuals is in service of something much bigger than ourselves.

Humility exercised in the context of partnerships with Indigenous communities encourages archaeologists to take inventory of the relative importance of their disciplinary contributions to community-driven research questions or political initiatives (Martindale and Lyons 2014). As Pyburn (2009:161) suggests "archaeologists need to be able to see themselves as one group of stakeholders with a right to advocate their position, but no right to ultimate control of the resources that they use to create an archaeological record". This type of intellectual humility must also extend to the interpretation of the material record, whereas Hogg et al. (2017:175) argue, archaeologists must exercise "humility borne of a high tolerance for the ambiguities inherent in the archaeological record and of the methodological rigour and diversity required to address these ambiguities".

Returning one day to the field laboratory established to process and curate a large collection of recently excavated 4000-year-old wood artefacts, I encountered a distraught archaeologist. She proceeded to tell me that the Elders had requested to visit the lab and to hold the artefacts. Not understanding her source of distress, I pressed for further details. "I only told the Elders that they needed to wear gloves to protect the artifacts" she said, then added, "and now the Elders are really upset with me". The archaeologist had been trained to prioritize the physical condition of the objects by limiting human contact. In contrast, the Elders viewed contact as an essential aspect of managing the disruption caused by the removal of the artefacts from their physical and spiritual context. Ensuing discussions quickly moved from the conflict over how the artefacts should be handled (since gloveless handling posed no real risk to the artefacts) but instead focused on the Elders' discomfort with the archaeologist's *belief in her authority* to dictate how the artefacts must be treated. For the Elders, this conflict raised powerful spectres of marginalization, disenfranchisement and loss. For the archaeologists, the conflict reminds us that we are never far from the legacies of colonialism. Though uncomfortable, the encounter over the artefact handling facilitated an important conversation about authority, reciprocity and respect. In this case, humility served of the broad arc of critical discourse about the past, the impact of that discourse on the present and the ways in which collaboration can affect the future (Colwell-Chanthaphonh et al. 2010; McNiven 2016).

Fourth, Hold Your Place

As Borrows (2016:164) states humility is "not about making yourself too small or too big. It is about taking up the right amount of space". In this context the definition of humility differs from the Christian concepts thereof. Here humility is not the constant pursuit of self-deprecation. It is about finding and holding one's place.

As archaeologists we are armed with a suite of general research skills that can be called into action as community objectives dictate. However, as part of holding one's place, archaeologist must be cognisant of, and vocal about, the constraints of our discipline (Nicholas 2005; Atalay 2008, 2012). This is particularly true in areas where Western legal frameworks place undue emphasis on archaeological interpretation to influence arguments about Aboriginal rights and title (Supernant and Warrick 2014; Thom 2009). Supernant and Warrick (2014) warn that archaeology can be detrimental to descendant communities when archaeological interpretation is used to privilege one Indigenous community's interpretation of the past over that of another or to silence dissenting voices within a community.

Critical here is the distinction between self-actualization and archaeological practice. Indigenous communities that engage, or engage with, archaeologists benefit from the maintenance of good scholarship. Moreover, they demand it (Atalay 2012; Atalay et al. 2016). A professional archaeologist armed with the tools of scientific method and academic voice has a role to play in community-centred work (e.g. Schaepe et al. 2017). A humble practice does not require archaeologists to lay down the tools of scientific rigour, but rather that we are humble enough to pick them up in order to build something that reflects a different design, vision or purpose (Colwell-Chanthaphonh et al. 2010; Bruchac et al. 2016).

In the spring of 2007, the Katzie First Nation faced an agonizing decision. Road construction would destroy an ancestral village site, and the community could excavate it themselves or watch as someone else did. Finally, after failed attempts to negotiate rerouting of the road to avoid the site, Katzie leadership decided that the spiritual, emotional and physical costs of disturbing the ancestors should be borne by those best equipped to manage the consequences—the Katzie people. For the next 2 years, a crew of more than 70 community members, with assistance from a team of archaeologists, embarked on the archaeological excavation and analysis of the site. Excavations revealed a remarkable history of 2500 years of occupation, including the first direct evidence of wild plant food production on the Northwest Coast in the form of the intact remnants of a 3800-year-old wetland garden (Hoffmann et al. 2016; Lyons et al. 2018). Publication of the garden find generated international press interest. In a conscious decision to foreground Katzie perspectives, press calls were deliberately channelled to Katzie representatives. The ensuing press coverage provided opportunity for the Katzie to communicate, in their own voices, the significance of the finding and their responses to the archaeological experience. Referencing the cultural significance of community involvement in the archaeological excavation, one community member reflected, "Culturally we talked about what it meant to be in the earth with our ancestors and touching their lives.

We've just walked into the house of the ancestors. It was for many, many of our people an absolute connection to their history, something that they couldn't have gained in any other way… We brought our ancestors home in our hearts and in our minds and in our conversations with our people" (D. Miller in Omand 2016). Despite the gifts it provided all involved, the experience was, and remains, bittersweet. For many Katzie people, the destruction of the site, however, sensitively managed, remains a painful reminder of persistent asymmetries in decision-making power between First Nations and government. As for the archaeologists, we learned that by doing the best archaeology we knew how, we held our place, and in doing so, we made a lasting contribution to the past, present and future of Katzie.

Finally, Soften Your Gaze

An essential element of the postcolonial agenda is the foregrounding of community-driven or at the very least, community-derived research programmes (Atalay 2012; Kovach 2015). The process of identifying and bounding community-based research priorities can be obvious and straightforward, but in many instances, it is emergent and complex. Furthermore, research agendas of community origin often morph mid-programme, necessitating flexibility of method and openness regarding outcome. For researchers trained in Western research methods, this process can be confusing and often frustrating. However, surrendering the requirement to set the agenda and control the process can take the outside researcher on unanticipated journeys that foster remarkable outcomes.

Several years ago I was asked by the St'at'imc Chief's Council to accompany a group of Elders into the mountainous regions of their territory in Interior British Columbia. I was tasked with recording the cadence of movement and conversation and to map some of the lifetime of hunting knowledge held by two of the nation's most knowledgeable Elders. In preparation for off-roading into high alpine hunting grounds, we had camped out for the night. The next morning, as I bumped along in the back seat of the crew cab with maps and tape recorder at the ready, I was hypnotized into a semi-conscious state, owing largely to the sleepless night on the cold tent floor but also to the fact that the Elders appeared to be saying a lot to one another without uttering a single word. Close friends and hunting companions all their lives, the Elders shared a unique language comprised of low murmurs, knowing looks and vague "over there" gestures as hypnotizing as they were indecipherable. Finally, we stopped, and I sleepily emerged from the back seat. I rolled out my maps on the hood of the truck, set up the tape recorder and looked up. Both Elders were gone—having seemingly vanished into the bush. I panicked. Calling names, I stayed close to the vehicle and tried desperately to see the flash of a jacket through the trees or to hear a noise that would signal their general location.

Ten minutes later both Elders re-emerged from the bush chuckling, slightly annoyed at my deer-repelling noisemaking.

"Where'd you go?" I asked.

"What do you mean? We went there", one of the Elders responded, pointing toward the trees by the side of the road.

"I looked for you and I couldn't see you!" I replied, still slightly panicked.

"Well, you were looking so hard for me, you missed the trail I left for you!" he said.

Exasperated, I blurted, "What trail?"

He sighed, grasped my shoulders and faced me towards the bunch of trees he'd disappeared into.

"Stop looking so hard" he said. "Soften your gaze. Don't look for just one thing, but rather, try and see everything at once. If you do that, you'll see the trail".

So I did just that, I softened my gaze. I allowed my eyes to relax and my focus to soften, then there it was, a broken branch just at eye level, then another behind it and yet another behind that. The trail. It was obvious…now.

Like the trail the Elders left for me, emergent research agendas are trails laid down by the community, towards a direction they wish to travel in pursuit of their own interests. This definition and underlying concepts are familiar to many who work in and with Indigenous communities, but the skill to see emergent community agendas requires the less familiar, possibly uncomfortable, yet eminently humble act of surrender. Softening your gaze requires you to release what you think you are trying to find and allow what needs to be known to reveal itself. Once you acquire the skill to see in this way, the trails come fast and furious, and the research avenues they lead you along are as fascinating as they are rewarding.

Conclusion: The Humble Archaeologist

Maori scholar Linda Tuhiwai Smith (2013:5) notes "If I have one consistent message for the students I teach and the researchers I train it is that Indigenous research is a humble and humbling activity". Undoubtedly many contributors to this volume, many of whom have been shaped by working with, for and amongst Indigenous communities, would agree with Smith. Vulnerability, "teachability", self-awareness and critical reflection are amongst those elements essential to a humble practice. The demands of humility are transformative; they are also uncomfortable, often profound and recurrent. Indeed, "Understanding and living the full meaning of humility is the work of a lifetime" (Borrows 2016:153).

A practice grounded in an Indigenous definition of humility demands we engage our whole selves, mind and heart. Embracing humility means advancing the conversation beyond what humility does for archaeology, to one that includes what humility does for archaeologists. A humble archaeologist honours the communities we work with and for by engaging in dialogues that challenge our personal and disciplinary boundaries (Kovach 2015; McNiven 2016). In opening our hearts through a humble practice, we subject ourselves and our scholarly endeavours to risk, to conflict but, ultimately, to growth. As Larry Zimmerman (2005) advises, "first be humble. Everything else follows more easily".

References

American-Israeli Cooperative Enterprise (AICE). (2019). Virtues in Judaism: Humility. Jewish Virtual Library. Online https://www.jewishvirtuallibrary.org/humility-jewish-virtual-library

Atalay, S. (2008). Multivocality and Indigenous archaeologies. In *Evaluating Multiple Narratives* (pp. 29–44). Springer, New York, NY.

Atalay, S. (2012). *Community-based archeology: Research with Indigenous and local communities*. Berkeley: University of California Press.

Atalay, S., Clauss, L. R., McGuire, R. H., & Welch, J. R. (Eds.). (2016). *Transforming archaeology: Activist practices and prospects*. London/New York: Routledge.

Beaudoin, M. A. (2016). Archaeologists colonizing Canada: The effects of unquestioned categories. *Archaeologies, 12*(1), 7–37.

Berenbaum, M., & Skolnik, F. (Eds.). (2007). *Encylopaedia Judaica* (2nd ed.). Detroit: Macmillan Reference, USA. 22 vols. (18,015 pp.).

Borrows, L. (2016). DABAADENDIZIWIN: Practices of humility in a multi-juridical legal landscape. *Special Issue: Indigenous Law, Lands and Literature*. Windsor Yearbook of Access to Justice, *33*(1), 149–165. http://ojs.uwindsor.ca/ojs/leddy/index.php/WYAJ/issue/view/464

Brown, B. (2012). *Daring greatly: How the courage to be vulnerable transforms the way we live, love, parent, and lead*. New York: Gotham.

Bruchac, M., Hart, S., & Wobst, H. M. (Eds.). (2016). *Indigenous archaeologies: A reader on decolonization*. Abingdon: Routledge.

Cambridge University Press. (2008). *Cambridge online dictionary*, Cambridge Dictionary online. Retrieved at April 23, 2008, from the website temoa: Open Educational Resources (OER) Portal at http://www.temoa.info/node/324

Coburn, E., Moreton-Robinson, A., Sefa Dei, G., & Stewart-Harawira, M. (2013). Unspeakable things: Indigenous research and social science. Socio. La nouvelle revue des sciences sociales, (2), 331–348.

Colwell-Chanthaphonh, C., & Ferguson, T. J. (2004). Virtue ethics and the practice of history: Native Americans and archaeologists along the San Pedro Valley of Arizona. *Journal of Social Archaeology, 4*(1), 5–27.

Colwell-Chanthaphonh, C., Ferguson, T. J., Lippert, D., McGuire, R. H., Nicholas, G. P., Watkins, J. E., & Zimmerman, L. J. (2010). The premise and promise of Indigenous archaeology. *American Antiquity, 75*(2), 228–238.

Ferris, N. (2003). Between colonial and Indigenous archaeologies: Legal and extra-legal ownership of the archaeological past in North America. *Canadian Journal of Archaeology / Journal Canadien d'Archéologie, 27*(2), 154–190. JSTOR, JSTOR, http://www.jstor.org/stable/41103447.

Gnecco, C., & Langebaek, C. (Eds.). (2013). *Against typological tyranny in archaeology: A South American perspective*. Springer Science & Business Media, New York.

Gosden, C. (2012). Postcolonial archaeology. In I. Hodder (Ed.) *Archaeological theory today* (2nd ed.) (pp. 251–266). Polity Press, Cambridge UK.

Hamilakis, Y. (2016). Decolonial archaeologies: From ethnoarchaeology to archaeological ethnography. *World Archaeology, 48*(5), 678–682.

Harrison, R. (2006). "It will always be set in your heart": Archaeology and community values at the former Dennawan reserve, Northwestern New South Wales, Australia. Proceedings of the Conservation theme at the 5th World Archaeological Congress, Washington, DC. 22–26 June 2003. In N. Agnew & Janet Bridgland (Eds.) *Of the Past, for the Future: Integrating Archaeology and Conservation*, Getty Conservation Institute, Getty Publications, pp. 94–101.

Hoffmann, T., Lyons, N., Miller, D., Diaz, A., Homan, A., Huddlestan, S., & Leon, R. (2016). Engineered feature used to enhance gardening at a 3800-year-old site on the Pacific Northwest Coast. *Science advances, 2*(12), e1601282.

Hogg, E. A., Welch, J. R., & Ferris, N. A. (2017). Full spectrum archaeology. *Archaeologies, 13*, 175. https://doi.org/10.1007/s11759-017-9315-9.

Ireland, T., & Schofield, J. (2015). The ethics of cultural heritage. In T. Ireland & J. Schofield (Eds.), *The ethics of cultural heritage. Ethical archaeologies: The politics of social justice* (Vol. 4). New York: Springer.

Iwama, M., Marshall, M., Marshall, A., & Bartlett, C. (2009). Two-eyed seeing and the language of healing in community-based research. *Canadian Journal of Native Education, 32*(2), 3–23.

Kovach, M. (2015). *Emerging from the margins: Indigenous methodologies*. Research as resistance: revisiting critical, indigenous, and anti-oppressive approaches, 43.

La Salle, M., & Hutchings, R. (2016). What makes us squirm-A critical assessment of community-oriented archaeology. *Canadian Journal of Archaeology, 40*(1), 164–180.

Lyons, N. (2013). *Where the wind blows us: Practicing critical community archaeology in the Canadian North*. Tucson: University of Arizona Press.

Lyons, N., Hoffmann, T., Miller, D., Huddlestan, S., Leon, R., & Squires, K. (2018). Katzie & the Wapato: An archaeological love story. *Archaeologies, 14*(1), 7–29.

Martindale, A., & Lyons, N. (2014). Community-oriented archaeology. *Canadian Journal of Archaeology, 38*, 425–433.

McGhee, R. (2008). Aboriginalism and the problems of Indigenous archaeology. *American Antiquity, 73*(4), 579–597.

McNiven, I. J. (2016). Theoretical challenges of Indigenous archaeology: Setting an agenda. *American Antiquity, 81*(1), 27–41.

Nicholas, G. (2005). The persistence of memory; the politics of desire: archaeological impacts on Aboriginal peoples and their response. In C. Smith & H. M. Wobst (Eds.), *Indigenous archaeologies: Decolonizing theory and practice One World Archaeology Series* (p. 75). New York: Routledge.

Nicholas, G. P. (2012). "Making us uneasy": Clarke, Wobst, and their critique of archaeology put into practice. *Archaeologies, 8*(3), 209–224.

Omand, G. (2016, December 21). Road project reveals millennia-old wetland-gardening site. *MacLeans Magazine*. Available online: https://www.mcleans.ca/news/canada/road-project-reveals-millennia-oldwetland-gardening-site/. Accessed 2 May 2019.

Overmyer, S. (2015). Exalting the Meek Virtue of Humility in Aquinas. *The Heythrop Journal, 56*(4), 650–662.

Pyburn, K. A. (2009). Practising archaeology — As if it really matters. *Public Archaeology, 8*(2–3), 161–175.

Schaepe, D. M., Angelbeck, B., Snook, D., & Welch, J. R. (2017). Archaeology as therapy: Connecting belongings, knowledge, time, place, and well-being. *Current Anthropology, 58*(4), 502–533.

Silliman, S. W. (2010). The value and diversity of Indigenous archaeology: A response to McGhee. *American Antiquity, 75*(2), 217–220.

Smith, L. T. (2013). *Decolonizing methodologies: Research and Indigenous Peoples*. London: Zed Books Ltd.

Supernant, K., & Warrick, G. (2014). Challenges to critical community-based archaeological practice in Canada. *Canadian Journal of Archaeology/ Journal Canadien d'Archéologie, 38*, 563–591.

Thom, B. (2009). The paradox of boundaries in Coast Salish territories. *Cultural geographies, 16*(2), 179–205.

Weinstein, J. A. (2015). Humility, from the Ground Up: A Radical Approach to Literature and Ecology. *Interdisciplinary Studies in Literature and Environment, 22*(4), 759–777.

Zimmerman, L. J. (2005). First, be humble: Working with Indigenous Peoples and other descendant communities. In C. Smith & H. M. Wobst (Eds.), *Indigenous Archaeologies: Decolonizing Theory and Practice* (pp. 301–314). New York: Routledge.

Chapter 5
"I Could Feel Your Heart"

The Transformative and Collaborative Power of Heartfelt Thinking in Archaeology

Sarah L. Surface-Evans

Introduction

As anthropologists we know that the heart is considered a source of strength in many cultures. Stories of the heart often derive strength from their power to teach and transform knowledge (Bruchac 1996). One such teaching is told by the Anishinabe of the Great Lakes region concerning the *odemin*, strawberry, or heart berry. The *odemin*, as a metaphor for the heart, is a symbol of life, healing, and forgiveness (see Atalay, Chap. 16, this volume, for the full telling). Yet in Western society and the culture of science, matters of the heart are generally feminized and as a consequence, devalued (hooks 2000). As critiques of science have pointed out, the philosophical privileging of reason and disconnect between the heart and mind often produces science without compassion (Kourany 2013). In this chapter, I advocate for reconnecting the heart and mind within the practice of archaeology.

My perspective is deeply influenced by "all about love," by bell hooks, in which she demonstrates the violence that an ethic of patriarchy and domination perpetuates in our society (2000). Her views about living by a love ethic, which includes "showing care, respect, knowledge, integrity, and the will to cooperate," is a useful way for considering the importance of the heart in archaeological practice (2000:101). Living by a love ethic is essential to transform the way we do science into a community-grounded and culturally aware practice. Guided by Feminist and Indigenous archaeological theory (Atalay 2010, 2012; Colwell-Chanthaphonh et al. 2010; Conkey 2010, 2007; Fawcett et al. 2008; Harris 2010; Hart 2012; Lyons 2013; Spencer-Wood 2001; Supernant and Warrick 2014), I seek to practice an archaeology that foregrounds heartfelt thinking as part of community-based heritage work. The practice and institutions of science perpetuate prevailing epistemologies of hierarchy, domination, and violence when they fail to acknowledge that we are both

S. L. Surface-Evans (✉)
Central Michigan University, Mount Pleasant, MI, USA
e-mail: surfa1sl@cmich.edu

© Springer Nature Switzerland AG 2020
K. Supernant et al. (eds.), *Archaeologies of the Heart*,
https://doi.org/10.1007/978-3-030-36350-5_5

rational and emotional beings (hooks 2000). An epistemology of the heart seeks to dismantle hierarchy and power structures that perpetuate violence through critical awareness and active community-based practice. Archaeologists, in particular, have an ethical imperative to recognize the consequences of their representations of the past on descendant communities and the colonial roots of our discipline (Conkey and Spector 1984; Little 2009; Trigger 2008). As the discipline of archaeology becomes increasingly multivocal and recognizes the richness of such an approach, an epistemology of the heart is essential to responsible practice in the discipline. Only by embracing the heart can we restore balance between the heart and mind, the rational and romantic within the discipline (see Supernant and Lyons, Chap. 1, this volume; Hodder 2008; Trigger 2008).

Archaeology is a practice that can bring powerful emotions to the surface, whether we wish to acknowledge these emotions or not. As anthropologists, we know that humans have emotional connections to the past and its physical remnants. The past is part of our individual and social identities (Sabloff 2008). The past is personed, filled with the ghosts of ancestors and the spirits of those who have come before us. The past is emplaced in the landscape; stories of the past are layered in a literal and figurative sense in the land we inhabit. As a professional archaeologist, I have seen the power of archaeology to open wounds of the past and/or heal them. Given this influence, archaeologists have the responsibility to acknowledge and be mindful of the wider impacts of our research.

The following essay is a personal reflection on how I came to a practice of *heart-felt thinking*. I will attempt to define what I mean by this term and discuss the benefits and challenges I have experienced in operationalizing such an approach. I hope to demonstrate the essential need for an epistemology of the heart for our discipline. To avoid the usual pitfalls of academic writing, in which the researcher and research are obscured (see Conkey, Chap. 17, this volume), I will share my journey as a series of personal stories.

Origin Story

Everyone has an origin story, and I'd like to share how I came to practice heartfelt archaeology. As a child, I was prone to wearing my heart on my sleeve and was quick to cry when emotions ran high. But I learned, often through the unkind reactions of adults, that my emotion and compassion made others uncomfortable. I learned that the heart was not valued. As a consequence, I tried not to allow my feelings get the best of me or allow my empathy to overwhelm me. Ultimately, however, what brought me into the discipline of archaeology was an emotional connection and love for the past (see Welch, Chap. 2, this volume).

I was fortunate enough to be able to go to college to study archaeology, despite financial challenges. My early experiences in archaeology were all in male-dominated spaces and worldviews, where once again I was taught that my emotions had no place, especially in science. My undergraduate training and field school were exclusively taught by male faculty who were self-identified processualists. I gained much technical skill from these mentors, but little in the way of theoretical grounding that was of interest to me. Between undergrad and grad school, I worked in cultural resource management in the Midwest, again mostly with men. In these contexts, I was indoctrinated into the competitive, masculinized perspective of "cowboy" archaeology, where expert knowledge was dispensed by the principal investigator of the project (Hays-Gilpin 2000). Here there was little room for different perspectives or interpretations, no consultation with the communities in which we worked, no acknowledgment of our feelings as researchers, and no exceptions to the hypothetico-deductive approach.

My graduate education exposed me, finally, to feminist theory and introduced me to Indigenous archaeology. My mentors and teachers were increasingly diverse, although not necessarily engaging in feminist or Indigenous practice. Public outreach was increasingly stressed and integrated into the research of my mentors, giving me an appreciation of the importance of interacting with the communities in which we work. My dissertation research ended up being far more grounded in processual theory than I had originally planned, but the important thing was that the degree opened doors to other opportunities.

At the end of grad school and the first few years as a newly minted PhD, I worked for state government and taught as a part-time adjunct at several 2- and 4-year schools. These experiences gave me additional insights into the various ways the teaching and practice of archaeology affect the public and communities. Eventually, an opportunity presented itself as a postdoc at a medium-sized state school. This is where I consciously took steps to take a different approach and move toward the mindful practice that is an archaeology of the heart.

New Beginning

In 2011 I was hired at Central Michigan University (CMU) first as a postdoc and later in a tenure track position. CMU wanted someone who had experience both in and outside the academy to establish what they were envisioning as an applied archaeology program. The North American archaeology program had been on hiatus at CMU for nearly 30 years, and they wanted to develop a new interdisciplinary master's program in heritage management with a Great Lakes focus. I was fortunate enough to be one of the principal faculty members tasked with developing this interdisciplinary program and the only Great Lakes archaeologist involved. I also had the opportunity to expand our undergraduate specialization in archaeology within the anthropology program by developing new curriculum and reinvigorating the field and lab experiences for undergraduate students. At the threshold of this new beginning, I had the privileged opportunity to create something innovative and purposefully sought to create something unlike what I had previously experienced during my education. I created an approach that in hindsight I would call an *epistemology of the heart*.

This work was not undertaken alone or in a vacuum. In part, it was guided by my previous experience working in CRM, which taught me that preservation is a matter of social justice. In particular, I embraced the perspective that *archaeologists must take an activist stance* – that we have an ethical imperative to be civilly engaged (Fawcett et al. 2008; Little and Schakel 2007; Sabloff 2008; Stottman 2010; Trigger 2008). As hooks states, "love is an action" (2000:165). Archaeologists should use their long-term perspectives on human social systems to inform policy (Sabloff 2008). Archaeologists have unique skill sets with which to recover "lost" components of history and, in doing so, to empower communities (Brighton 2011). Americanist archaeologists, in particular, have a responsibility to decolonize the discipline and narratives of the past by sharing the stories of those that colonialism tried to erase (Atalay 2010; Hart 2012; Little 2009; Lyons 2013; Oland et al. 2012; Silliman 2012).

A related component to an epistemology of the heart is a *public and community-based methodology to research*. Again, hooks reminds us that the path to living by a love ethic requires community and the skills of respect, care, and forgiveness that one develops in a loving community (hooks 2000:138). While conducting research at heritage sites in the Great Lakes region, I have sought to make meaningful community-based collaborations the foundation for these projects (cf. Surface-Evans 2013, 2015, 2016, 2017). Community archaeology places emphasis on creating partnerships to protect, investigate, and educate the public about cultural heritage. This approach reflects the core archaeological ethics of stewardship, accountability, and outreach (Lyons 2013). Community-based research reinforces the value of a heartfelt approach because it requires the decentering of the researcher as "expert" and foregrounds community needs, interests, and voices (Atalay 2012; Colwell-Chanthaphonh et al. 2010; Lyons 2013).

Several theoretical perspectives also form the basis of a heartfelt approach because of how these frameworks problematize patriarchal and heteronormative assumptions of the past (Conkey and Spector 1984). This is an essential step in a heartfelt approach because, as hooks reveals, these Western modes of thought and action perpetuate a culture of death and violence, rather than one of love (2000:193). Feminist, Indigenous, and queer theory (Aimers and Rutecki 2016; Atalay 2012; Blackmore et al. 2016; Bruchac et al. 2010; Conkey and Spector 1984; Conkey and Gero 1997; Conkey 2007; hooks 1994, 2000; Lyons 2013; McDavid 2010; Oland et al. 2012; Rutecki and Blackmore 2016; Spencer-Wood 2001) allow us to decolonize and question dominant narratives. These theoretical lenses achieve this by widening perspectives and interpretations and encouraging multivocality (Lyons 2013). A *multivocal approach to the interpretation of the past* is essential in order to draw out the voices and experiences of marginalized or underrepresented communities (Fawcett et al. 2008). At the center of this perspective is a reframing of research from individual to collective and a critical approach toward the creation of scientific knowledge. In other words, acknowledging the political nature of science and being explicit with one's personal biases.

While contextualizing one's research by being upfront with life experiences and identity is commonplace in cultural anthropology, this has yet to become a normalized practice in archaeology. On the whole, archaeology still privileges an etic perspective that claims moral authority from a supposedly objective and disengaged practice. Yet, a disengaged practice that does not acknowledge the fact that archaeology is still overwhelmingly male, white, and heterosexual perpetuates the colonialism of the discipline. Ignoring the voices and needs of diverse descendant communities cannot repair the damage caused by Western, colonial modes of thought. This is why a reflexive and heartfelt approach is integral to the future of archaeology. Nothing is lost in the intellectual rigor of archaeological research by bringing more voices to the table (see Supernant and Lyons, Chap. 1, this volume; Trigger 2008; Wylie 2007, 2008).

None of what I propose here is new in itself, but few university programs have operationalized a heart-centered practice. In my unique situation of being tasked with rebuilding the CMU archaeology program, I had the opportunity to create one based on a "love ethic." The essential components of a heartfelt approach that I sought to develop include:

1. Engaging in archaeological activism to affect local and regional policy to protect threatened cultural heritage and empower communities.
2. Foregrounding respectful, equitable, and compassionate dialog between collaborators, students, and community partners to prevent the privileging certain voices, including my own.
3. A critical and reflexive perspective of gender, sexuality, and identity.
4. Openly communicating personal experiences and biases so as to critically evaluate how they impact research.

Operationalizing an Epistemology of the Heart

How did I operationalize an epistemology of the heart in the archaeology program at CMU? There are three areas in which I focused my approach: (1) through research by organizing all projects to be community-based, public, and collaborative, (2) through curriculum and classroom pedagogy, and (3) by being a role model for respectful dialogue with my students, advisees, colleagues, and community. Each of these applications is, of course, a work in progress. There are many challenges to such an approach, not least of which is the perception that inclusive and reflexive practice is a sign of weakness to some. Another difficulty I have experienced is the effects of emotional burnout. I share the following stories of my personal successes, failures, and frustrations, in the hope that this will help us all work toward more heartfelt strategies in the future.

Listening and learning: Operationalizing in the Field

This story begins with a meeting. It was the July before my official position started with CMU and the dean of my college invited me to attend a meeting at the Ziibiwing Center of Anishinabe Culture and Lifeways, operated by the Saginaw Chippewa Tribe of Michigan. Other than the dean, I knew no one at this meeting, and she was running late. I entered the room and sat down. I was excited but nervous (my graduate institution did not exactly have a reputation for working well with Michigan tribes). I was immediately asked about my academic lineage, knowing that this might automatically damage my relationship with some in the room. I answered honestly and also explained that Pamela Gates, my dean, had invited me to the meeting. After a smudging ceremony, a prayer, and brief introductions, I spent the rest of the meeting listening and taking notes. To my surprise, by the end of the meeting, elders were sharing stories with me, and I was invited to participate in a road trip to the Lac du Flambeau Boarding School in Wisconsin, thus began my long-term collaboration with the Saginaw Chippewa Tribe for the Mount Pleasant Indian Industrial Boarding School project.

The meeting was the initial formation of the Mount Pleasant Indian Industrial Boarding School Committee. Only months earlier, the Saginaw Chippewa Tribe of Michigan acquired a portion of the former school and was beginning to organize and gather data about what to do next. At that meeting I became a consulting member of the boarding school committee established by tribal council. I participated in action planning, along with over a hundred tribal community members, to define the direction and goals of the project. The mission statement for the committee is "to transform, preserve, and finance the development of the Mount Pleasant Indian Industrial Boarding School to become a place for healing, education, wellness, and empowerment." Archaeological and archival research was viewed as an important component of this mission.

The committee and community helped define the areas of interest for archaeological research. A primary question was the location of unmarked student graves within the 320 acre school grounds. This work was extremely emotional for many community members because almost every family has a personal connection to the death of a child at the school. It was also complicated by the fact that most of the likely locations of the cemetery were owned by the City of Mount Pleasant. Multiple years of noninvasive investigations were carefully planned by the committee and negotiated with the city. Ultimately, by being sensitive to community concerns, an approach was developed to help answer the question of undocumented deaths and location of unmarked graves. Without a heart-centered approach, it would have been difficult to release control of the archaeological research plan and grasp the communities' concerns and needs. An epistemology of the heart shifts my role from that of expert authority to one of facilitator and co-collaborator, which helps to prevent the privileging of my voice in the research process.

For example, during ongoing consultation and collaboration for the Mount Pleasant Indian Industrial Boarding School project, a community member told me that she "could feel my heart" when I spoke. Later, she gifted me with a beautiful beadwork medallion of *odemin* or heart berry (Fig. 5.1). The *odemin* was an apt image given its meaning in Anishinabe culture because it illustrated the power of heartfelt work to bring about healing. The experience of working on this project has been powerful and transformative not only for the community that I am working with but also for me as an archaeologist. This gift reminded me of the importance of speaking from the heart and listening from the heart, for effective community-based engagement. It also taught me that we as researchers should not be afraid of or hide our emotion – that our hearts can in fact make us better researchers and conduct more sensitive archaeology.

While opening my heart has been a strength in the community-based work with the Saginaw Chippewa Tribe and other tribes affected by the Mount Pleasant Indian Industrial Boarding School, it has had a different impact on my relationship with the City of Mount Pleasant. The vulnerability of wearing my heart on my sleeve (Fig. 5.2, another gift, sewn by a department colleague) has led some with the city to question my motives and perhaps more damagingly, question my scientific integrity. City officials have repeatedly ignored my recommendations and have even sought outside review of the conclusions of the project research. While I welcome independent review of research, I am troubled by the fact that researchers hired by the city have made no attempt to collaborate with the Saginaw Chippewa Tribe or other tribes. As a consequence, they lack the contextual depth to understand the larger project and its ongoing impact on the community. Situations like this, where my credibility is questioned, could cause me to doubt the efficacy of my heartfelt

Fig. 5.1 Beaded medallion of odemin

Fig. 5.2 Hand sewn heart
to wear on my sleeve

approach. But this experience has shown me, more than anything, the potential damage of a disengaged, supposedly more rigorously scientific practice. Without understanding the deeper context and history of the boarding school site, these detached researchers propose strategies for investigation that trigger historical trauma in the Saginaw Chippewa community. Here we can see the emotional nature of archaeological inquiry – we are not simply reconstructing a disconnected and dispassionate past. Rather, the past and present are entangled in complex and emotional ways that archaeologists must acknowledge if we are to become more ethical researchers (see also Armstrong and Anderson, Chap. 3, this volume).

Mentoring the Next Generation: Operationalizing in the Classroom

This leads me to the topic of pedagogy and training students in a heart-centered approach. The only way to create change in the discipline is by training students to appreciate an epistemology of the heart. I view teaching as part of a larger practice of civic engagement. I encourage the cultivation of a love ethic by involving my undergraduate and graduate students in all aspects of my community-based research projects (Surface-Evans 2013, 2015). I strive to train the next generation of archaeology professionals to recognize the role of the heart in promoting an effective multivocal, critical, and civically engaged research perspective.

In the classroom, I promote respectful dialogue and seek to democratize the practice of learning. I focus on helping students understand the links between theory and practice. A fundamental question I pose to my students is whether or not accepting multiple interpretations of the past is somehow antiscientific? This question often leads to nuanced conversations, including what to do about "fringe" theories and white supremacists and how to evaluate or weigh different perspectives and the need for public engagement and education about heritage preservation. Ultimately, however, students unanimously recognize what many in our profession remain unwilling to that (1) science is always political (to pretend otherwise is unethical) and (2) interpretations of the past are not diminished by multivocal perspectives but are enriched by them.

Another way that I convey these lessons is through preparations for fieldwork. Prior to going to the field, all of my students participate in a daylong cultural sensitivity and privilege awareness training that was developed by my colleague Colleen Green, a Saginaw Chippewa Tribe member and director of the CMU Native American Program in the Office of Inclusion and Diversity. This training has several purposes. First, it introduces students to the concepts of privilege and intersectionality. Second, it sets the expectation that I value their experiences and voices and want them to feel that they can communicate with me openly. I make it clear from day one of field school that students' have a responsibility to share with me, each other, and our community partners what we are finding and how we are thinking about it. Third, it helps equip students with greater understanding (and hopefully more compassion) for those who are different. This last aspect is especially important because of the community and public presence at my research sites. I assign students rotations as public relations coordinators, where they are responsible for learning about the details of the project and overseeing the communication of appropriate aspects of it to the public. Oftentimes this includes working with community participants, volunteers, or visitors at the site. This task helps students develop communication skills, as well as shape their perspective to an engaged and activist stance.

Of course, not every student responds well to my heartfelt approach of teaching and mentoring. I have particularly struggled with mentoring graduate students. Part of the problem is that graduate students in our interdisciplinary program come already indoctrinated into patriarchal perspectives of domination typical of academic institutions. Academic institutions are often complicit with perpetuating patriarchy, elitism, and competition, because these are imbedded in academic culture (Hays-Gilpin 2000; Kourany 2013). As predominantly white, male, and heterosexual institutions, a culture of microaggressions on the basis of gender, race, class, ability, age, and sexual orientation is common because of implicit biases. While social scientists should be more aware of these biases, not all undergraduate programs prepare students with appropriate ethical and theoretical backgrounds to recognize their own worldviews. Additionally, because our graduate program accepts students from a variety of disciplines, those outside of anthropology are even less equipped to accept an epistemology of the heart. Sometimes it is difficult for these students (and other professionals) to see that there is value in taking a different approach to how we study, reconstruct, and talk about the past. As the demographic profile of archaeology becomes increasingly diverse, some of these problems will subside.

Implicit in the rejection of a heart ethic is the view that a heartfelt epistemology is a sign of weakness. Feminist theory teaches us that patriarchal modes of thought perpetuate the notion that respectful relationships between mentor and student are based on domination and hierarchy. I have had some students respond with anger and confess that they do not "respect" me because I do not "command" it. Having students reject my approach can feel like a personal attack, but I have to remind myself that change can be frightening for those who have not experienced another way of thinking and being. Even with these occasional setbacks, I continue to treat my students as colleagues, demonstrating that respectful relationships can be built on mutual trust and collaboration, rather than violence and domination. Overall, the majority of students are receptive to a heartfelt approach.

A parallel issue to the negative reaction from students is the long-term emotional toll that a heartfelt approach can have on us as researchers. When we intentionally make ourselves vulnerable, it can leave us open for injury and trauma which can come in many forms. For example, working in isolation, coping with a lack of institutional support, collaborating with communities who have dealt with centuries of systematic oppression, and working in a society where political trends are counter to an epistemology of the heart can all contribute to emotional burnout. Laura van Dernoot Lipsky's work *Trauma Stewardship* is an excellent resource for preventing emotional fatigue that is inevitable from a heartfelt approach (2009). She provides numerous tools for self-care for those who are regularly exposed to "secondary trauma," which is the response to repeated trauma exposure. I argue that the inherent activism of an archaeology of the heart will lead to trauma exposure. Consequently, it is essential for researchers using this perspective to be aware of the significant need for support and self-care (see also Welch, Chap. 2, this volume). My self-care routine includes seeking balance between professional obligations and personal life. For example, I have set boundaries with colleagues and students by not responding to emails after hours or on weekends. Creating these boundaries allows me to recharge and be fully present with my family. In my personal time, I also engage in hobbies that give me fulfillment, such as running and painting. Seeking counseling is also important self-care strategy for dealing with the long-term burnout and trauma of living by a love ethic.

A Disciplinary Imperative?

In the last 8 years, I have had the privileged opportunity to create an archaeology program that was centered around an epistemology of the heart. I have intentionally sought a different approach based on living by a "love ethic" (hooks 2000). I see the important theoretical components of a love ethic in archaeology as (1) acknowledging researcher biases, (2) seeking an activist stance by engaging in the community, and (3) practicing empathy, respect, and compassion for my students, colleagues, and research partners. While I had the opportunity to build a new program at CMU, it is possible to operationalize heartfelt practice within existing archaeology programs at other universities; however, doing so it takes conscious and careful action. The stories I shared illustrate what is successful about an epistemology of the heart and also how things can go wrong. Thankfully, I have the support of my institution and colleagues, at least up to a point; I am still held to the same professional and academic standards – which is a discussion for another time – for institutional evaluation and promotion.

Since 2011, I have conducted numerous community-based projects and have trained several cohorts of undergraduate and graduate students. My students are now entering graduate programs and the workplace, and many continue to carry the lessons they learned with them into these new contexts. For example, one of my recent master's program graduates contacted me to tell me that he was forming his own CRM firm named "Heart Song Archaeology." I am hopeful that archaeology can shift to embrace an epistemology of the heart as more students become practicing professionals.

While change is never immediate, I can see that my work is beginning to have a positive impact on the communities in which we are working. Although some local governments have been slow to open their hearts with us (such as the City of Mount Pleasant, discussed above), others have been much more accepting and participatory. In 2016, our community-based work at the Mount Pleasant Indian Industrial Boarding School was recognized for a state-wide preservation award in Michigan, primarily because of the heart-centered approach of this project.

The stories I shared show us that working from an epistemology of the heart may lead to moments in which we doubt ourselves or feel the full impact of allowing ourselves to be vulnerable. However, my experiences also show us that the future of our discipline depends on our ability to reach others and help them feel the presence of the past in meaningful, healing ways. I firmly believe that an epistemology of the heart is the most ethical way we can hope to impact policy, help communities, and preserve places that matter. The discipline of archaeology will only be made stronger if we are willing to acknowledge our biases, maintain a critical perspective, and engage in respectful and collaborative research to empower communities. We have to embrace the teachings of the *odemin* to recognize that the heart is the path to life, healing, and forgiveness (see Atalay, Chap. 16, this volume).

Acknowledgments I would like to express profound gratitude to the Saginaw Chippewa Tribe of Michigan for entrusting me to be a partner in the study and preservation of the Mount Pleasant Indian Industrial Boarding School, *Miigwetch*. Thank you to the members of the boarding school committee, staff of the Ziibiwing Center of Anishinabe Culture and Lifeways, Tribal Council, and the many elders and community members who have shared their knowledge with me. I also gratefully acknowledge all of the teachers who have influenced my life path. I appreciate the editors of this volume for asking me to be a part of this important work and for the anonymous reviewers for their insightful feedback.

References

Aimers, J., & Rutecki, D. M. (2016). Brave New World: Interpreting sex, gender, and sexuality in the past. *SAA Archaeological Record, 16*(1), 12–17.

Atalay, S. (2010). Indigenous archaeology as decolonizing practice. In M. M. Bruchac, S. M. Hart, & H. M. Wobst (Eds.), *Indigenous archaeology: A reader on decolonization* (pp. 79–86). Walnut Creek: Left Coast Press.

Atalay, S. (2012). *Community-based archaeology: Research with, by, and for indigenous and local communities.* Berkeley: University of California Press.

Blackmore, C., Drane, L., Baldwin, R., & Ellis, D. (2016). Queering fieldwork: Different and identity in archaeological practice. *SAA Archaeological Record, 16*(1), 18–23.

Brighton, S. A. (2011). Applied archaeology and community collaboration: Uncovering the past and empowering the present. *Human Organization, 70*(4), 344–354.

Bruchac, J. (1996). Strong stories. *AGNI, 44*, 167–169.

Bruchac, M. M., Hart, S. M., & Wobst, H. M. (2010). *Indigenous archaeology: A reader on decolonization.* Walnut Creek: Left Coast Press.

Colwell-Chanthaphonh, C., Ferguson, T. J., Lippert, D., McGuire, R. H., Nicholas, G. P., Watkins, J. E., & Zimmerman, L. J. (2010). The premise and promise of indigenous archaeology. *American Antiquity, 75*(2), 228–238.

Conkey, M. W. (2007). Questioning theory: Is there a gender of theory in archaeology? *Journal of Archaeological Method and Theory, 14*, 285–310.

Conkey, M. W. (2010). Dwelling at the margins, action at the intersection? Feminist and indigenous archaeologies, 2005. In M. M. Bruchac, S. M. Hart, & H. M. Wobst (Eds.), *Indigenous archaeology: A reader on decolonization* (pp. 91–98). Walnut Creek: Left Coast Press.

Conkey, M., & Gero, J. M. (1997). Programme to practice: Gender and feminism in archaeology. *Annual Review of Anthropology, 26*, 411–437.

Conkey, M., & Spector, J. (1984). Archaeology and the study of gender. *Advances in Archaeological Method and Theory, 7*, 1–38.

Fawcett, C., Habu, J., & Matsunaga, J. M. (2008). Introduction: Evaluating multiple narratives: Beyond nationalists, colonialist, imperialist archaeologies. In J. Habu, C. Fawcett, & J. M. Matsunaga (Eds.), *Evaluating multiple narratives: Beyond nationalist, colonialist, and imperialist archaeologies* (pp. 1–13). New York: Springer.

Harris, H. (2010). Indigenous worldviews and ways of knowing as theoretical and methodological foundations behind archaeological theory and method. In M. M. Bruchac, M. H. Siobhan, & H. M. Wobst (Eds.), *Indigenous archaeologies: A reader on decolonization* (pp. 63–68). Walnut Creek: Left Coast Press.

Hart, S. M. (2012). Decolonizing through heritage work in the pocumtuck homeland of northeastern North America. In M. Oland, S. M. Hart, & L. Frink (Eds.), *Decolonizing indigenous histories: Exploring prehistoric/colonial transitions in archaeology* (pp. 86–109). Tucson: The University of Arizona Press.

Hays-Gilpin, K. (2000). Feminist scholarship in archaeology. *Annals of the American Academy of Political and Social Science, 571*, 89–106.

Hodder, I. (2008). Multivocality and social archaeology. In J. Habu, C. Fawcett, & J. M. Matsunaga (Eds.), *Evaluating multiple narratives: Beyond nationalist, colonialist, and imperialist archaeologies* (pp. 196–200). New York: Springer.

hooks, b. (2000). *All about love.* New York: Harper Perennial.

Kourany, J. A. (2013). Meeting the challenges to socially responsible science: Reply to Brown, Lacey, and Potter. *Philosophical Studies: An International Journal for Philosophy in the Analytic Tradition, 163*(1), 93–10.

Little, B. J. (2009). What can archaeology do for justice, peace, community, and the earth — Response to comments. *Historical Archaeology, 43*(4), 128–129.

Little, B. J., & Schakel, P. A. (2007). *Archaeology as a tool of civic engagement.* Plymouth: Alta Mira Press.

Lyons, N. (2013). *Where the wind blows us: Practicing critical community archaeology in the Canadian north.* Tucson: The University of Arizona Press.

McDavid, C. (2010). Public archaeology, activism, and racism: Rethinking the heritage "Prodct". In M. Jay Stottman (Ed.), *Archaeologists as activists: Can archaeologists change the world?* (pp. 36–46). Tuscaloosa: University of Alabama Press.

Oland, M., Hart, S. M., & Frink, L. (2012). *Decolonizing indigenous histories: Exploring prehistoric/colonial transitions in archaeology.* Tucson: The University of Arizona Press.

Rutecki, D. M., & Blackmore, C. (2016). Towards an inclusive queer archaeology: An overview and introduction. *SAA Archaeological Record, 16*(1), 9–11.

Sabloff, J. A. (2008). *Archaeology matters: Action archaeology in the modern world.* Walnut Creek: Left Coast Press.

Silliman, S. W. (2012). Between the longue Duree and the short puree: Postcolonial archaeologies of indigenous history in colonial North America. In M. Oland, S. M. Hart, & L. Frink (Eds.), *Decolonizing indigenous histories: Exploring prehistoric/colonial transitions in archaeology* (pp. 113–131). Tucson: The University of Arizona Press.

Spencer-Wood, S. M. (2001). Views and commentaries: What difference does feminist theory make? *International Journal of Historical Archaeology, 5*(1), 97–114.

Stottman, M. J. (2010). *Archaeologists as activists: Can archaeologists change the world?* Tuscaloosa: University of Alabama Press.

Supernant, K., & Warrick, G. (2014). Challenges to critical community-based archaeological practice in Canada. *Canadian Journal of Archaeology, 38*(2), 563–591.

Surface-Evans, S. L. (2013). *Confronting the Legacy of the Mt. Pleasant Indian Industrial Boarding School: A Community-Driven Movement for Healing, Truth-Telling & Decolonization.* Invited panelist for the Historical Society of Michigan Annual Meeting, March 22, 2013, Livonia.

Surface-Evans, S. L. (2015). *Creating public partnerships: The benefits of community involvement in archaeology.* Poster presentation for the 2015 Annual Midwest Archaeological Conference, November 7–9, 2015, Millwaukee.

Surface-Evans, S. L. (2016). *Discourses of the haunted: Community-based archaeology at the Mount Pleasant Indian Industrial Boarding School.* Paper presentation for the Annual Meeting of the Society for American Archaeology, April 2016, Orlando.

Surface-Evans, S. L. (2017). *Archaeology lighting the way to responsible heritage tourism: Partnerships with three Michigan lighthouses.* Paper presentation, Michigan Historic Preservation Network's 37th Annual Conference, May 2017, Emmet County.

Trigger, B. (2008). "Alternative archaeologies" in historical perspective. In J. Habu, C. Fawcett, & J. M. Matsunaga (Eds.), *Evaluating multiple narratives: Beyond nationalist, colonialist, and imperialist archaeologies* (pp. 187–195). New York: Springer.

Van Dernoot Lipsky, L. (2009). Trauma stewardship: An everyday guide to caring for self while caring for others. In *Oakland.* Berrett-Koehler Publishers, Inc.

Wylie, A. (2007). Doing archaeology as a feminist: Introduction. *Journal of Archaeological Research Method and Theory, 14*(3), 209–216.

Wylie, A. (2008). Integrity of narratives: Deliberate practice, pluralism, and multivocality. In J. Habu, C. Fawcett, & J. M. Matsunaga (Eds.), *Evaluating multiple narratives: Beyond nationalist, colonialist, and imperialist archaeologies* (pp. 201–212). New York: Springer.

Chapter 6
Community-Based and Participatory Praxis as Decolonizing Archaeological Methods and the Betrayal of New Research

Uzma Z. Rizvi

Next time, bring your parents so we can meet them. – Shanta Bai, District Sikar, Rajasthan.[1]

I have worked, lived, and dreamed about Rajasthan for over two decades. During that time, I have met; mapped; laughed; surveyed; cried; categorized; ate; looked through archives; drank early morning chaach (yogurt drink); argued about postcolonialism, feminism, and Marxism; and had countless cups of chai with many women, men, children, queer people, families, communities, and schools, in the cities, towns, villages, and highways between Jaipur and Delhi, India. In a country that I never called my own, the people I was entangled with made me feel like I belonged in its cities, and its countryside, even as others within that same space made a point of making me feel unwelcome and unsafe on account of religious difference.

This chapter is about those encounters, those moments of feeling like I belonged, like I had a stake, and how that might change through time. It is about intimacy, it is about friendships, and it is about betrayal. Ultimately, it is also about how we do archaeology. When Shanta Bai (cited above) asks me to bring my parents when I next visit her village, as we bag and tag pottery, it is because in me she sees my family; through and with them, she places me into a social and cultural framework that is intimately part of her own sociality. In 2003, when I had first started living in the town of Neem Ka Thana to work on my PhD research, she, as an elder in that context, had spent many afternoons sitting, talking, and walking with me. She asked me who I was, gave me advice, and was generally around, particularly as our project team ebbed and flowed with participation. She kept an eye on us as if we were in her care and, in retrospect, collegially ensured that we were being careful in her space (see Lyons and Supernant, this volume). There was an everydayness to our interactions with her, and that quotidian interaction became an integral part of the project.

---

[1] Personal Communication, 2003. Please note: names have been changed in this text.

U. Z. Rizvi (✉)
Department of Social Science and Cultural Studies, Pratt Institute, New York, NY, USA
e-mail: urizvi@pratt.edu

© Springer Nature Switzerland AG 2020
K. Supernant et al. (eds.), *Archaeologies of the Heart*,
https://doi.org/10.1007/978-3-030-36350-5_6

It was also that everyday intimacy that allowed for a certain trust to develop that was not one hinged on labor but on living together. In her question of when my parents might visit was also embedded a chide – one that acknowledges that I had met and spoken to all of her ways of being and living, as represented by her family, and she has had to take me for my word, without the usual frameworks of knowing and social engagement. In this sense, she put more trust in me and our relationship than I had to – and as such, she was aware of the power differential in our relationship. Within her social world, however, taking care of a young woman who is in her social space, one who is without family there, has a different valence: one in which she is the one who is explicitly caring and vouching for me, in spite of other power relations I may read into this relationship (Rizvi 2006).

When Shanta Bai told me to bring my parents in my next visit (as cited above), I smiled at her and nodded. And I felt the pit of my stomach drop because I suspected I was never going to be able to bring my parents to her. Just that morning I received an email from my advisor saying it was time to "pack up and start writing." I knew that once I went back to Philadelphia and started writing my dissertation, I would have very little control on when I would be able to come back at all. Everything suddenly seemed so contingent upon finishing a dissertation, finding more funding, writing up a new project, getting another permit, and finding a job or a postdoc. All of this anxiety around my future fell into place and leaned on my desire to come back to see the people who supported, nurtured, and helped me along my way; to come back to see people who had made me and themselves intimate aspects of this project in their neighborhood and larger area.

In some sense, our social and emotional relationships were constitutive of the community-based and participatory archaeological practice we were engaged within: we were the project and the project was us (Nagar 2014).[2] Thus, once the project ended, so did our made pathways of relational intimacy. The traces of the project, however, were heavy and long-standing, emerging and revealing feelings of betrayal that now, with over two decades of experiencing such work, I can see as the emotional labor of archaeology.

Community-Based and Participatory Work in India: Decolonization, Care, and the Illusion of Choice

In an interview with T.J. Ferguson, Leigh J. Kuwanwisiwma speaks of collaborative research as work that bridges time (2008: 156). Community-based and participatory practices make archaeological work contemporary and thus entangled with and within social and political worlds of all those who engage with and through it and

---

[2] I have turned to Richa Nagar's work, *Muddying the Waters* (2014), many times to understand the impact of such intimate work with communities, in particular as my previous experiences in India bleed into my more contemporary research work with creative communities in the United Arab Emirates.

its effects (see also Surface-Evans, this volume). There is a different sense of community-based work when one belongs to the community in question (see Atalay 2012). Archaeologists like Tiatoshi Jamir, whose practice and research is embedded within his own Naga community at the site of Chungliyimti, exemplify such participatory ethics. Much of the impetus to do such work emerges from decolonial efforts that stem from past colonial experiences at indigenous Naga ancestral sites. Belonging to a community, however, does not take away from the need to do much of the emotional trust work that participatory ethics requires, made explicit in his recent writing on decolonizing archaeology in Northeastern India:

> With the aim of incorporating a more community-inclusive research and ascertain the level of mutual trust, several meetings were called with members of the village council to discuss ideas of the research program. With previous years of the site excavation, the community by now had removed all doubts that we were simply antique collectors, a remnant of the colonial past known in the region. Transparency of process increased the levels of trust among us, as did a collective social memory we shared with this ancestral site. (Jamir 2016)

Decolonization is an approach within archaeology that recognizes the relationship of colonialism to the development of a practice as a discipline and, as a method, proceeds to intentionally dismantle and reframe colonial forms of knowing. Unless we choose to decolonize archaeology, the systems by which we are taught research continue to reinstate older, oppressive, racist, chauvinist, and patriarchal models of being that gets coded into all of us and we continue to replicate it (Rizvi 2015). This is no easy task and requires an enormous amount of self-reflection at every step – it is asking more from us as practitioners than post-practice self-reflexivity. Moreover, it is complicated to decolonize archaeology because of the deep and intimate relationships colonial states have to their archaeological sites and collections as monuments to nation-building and authorized heritage (Gullapalli 2008; Chadha 2010). As such, our training to respect nations and their laws comes into direct conflict at times and must be carefully negotiated so that the communities we are working with and we, ourselves, are safe (Lorenzon and Zermani 2016). These relationships maintained by state vis-à-vis populations are locally specific; however, what unites the various geographies is the history of colonization and the continued violence on *othered* bodies in those locales (Sundberg 2014). *Othered* bodies are often marked by race and ethnic distinctions – and it is that "colonial difference" that Walter Mignolo argues is required for colonial power to be fully realized, and for what modernity was to base its existence upon (2002).

Holding true to these efforts, however, I was unable to foresee the future, nor was a mature enough scholar to understand what might happen if I was unable to return. The inability to return and the emotional labor related to new research feels like betrayal once it becomes clear that social relations may not be able to be maintained through time. In spite of the processes and methods of decolonizing archaeology, the ways in which my research and life ways have unfolded no longer include many of the collaborators with whom I first started and developed many archaeological theories alongside.

During and between 2000 and 2003, I intentionally engaged in a series of collaborative, participatory, and cooperative archaeological surveys with villages in

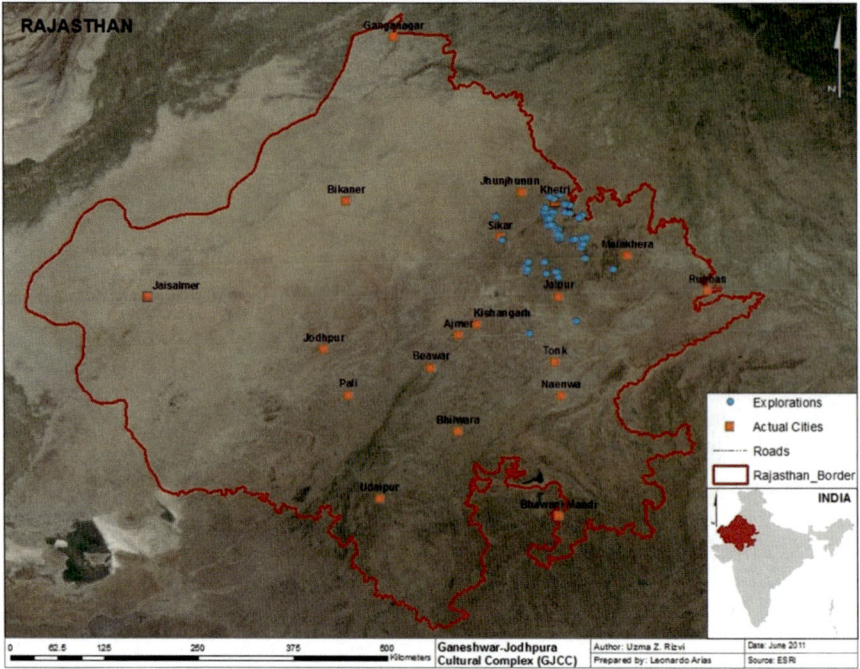

Fig. 6.1 Map illustrating sites explored during Ganeshwar Jodhpura Cultural Complex (GJCC) Survey 2003

Rajasthan that roughly fall between the cities of Jaipur and Delhi (Rizvi 2006, 2008; Fig. 6.1). At the time, I found that working on archaeological projects with communities could be an effective dismantling of research-based power structures; indeed today, there are many successful community-based, participatory projects around the world (Atalay 2012; Jamir and Vasa 2008; Mehari and Ryano 2016; Ross et al. 2013). It is important to keep in mind that such a methodology necessitates the active engagement with community concerns; in other words, when doing work with people, there are intimate and emotional concerns that emerge when speaking to people about *how* they belong: if they feel they do belong or are allowed to feel like their belonging has meaning. It is also just as important to keep in mind that often these conversations may also trigger traumatic memories (such as partition memories in the case of India/Pakistan). Thus, doing community-based participatory work and decolonizing archaeology and heritage projects means one has to learn how to manage affect and emotion.

Simultaneous to the archaeological project is a development of heritage, identity, and, in most cases, cultural resources management that leads to tourism opportunities. The management and public presentation of archaeological and other heritage resources created a situation in which heritage tourism might have been able to put money into the pockets of local communities rather than multinational corporations and develop local heritage resources in ways that are sensitive to the needs, interests, and abilities of the communities in question (Ibrahim, in review).[3]

A key component to the methodology employed during the survey in Rajasthan was realized through community participation and collaboration, which I have consequently considered to be alternating between community-based archaeology and public archaeology linked through a participatory ethic. A collaborative, community-based model worked very well in the village to village survey. Preliminary survey work took place in the summer of 2000, and in 2003 the full survey project commenced with (in total) 10 team members, which included doctoral students from the University of Rajasthan, Jaipur, and the New School University, New York. In addition to these team members, smaller collaborative projects were formed with participating villages and communities in order to conduct the archaeological survey (Fig. 6.2). These collaborative spaces were often realized through practices that documented the presence/absence of ancient artifacts on the surface during survey but also included 8 after-school programs, 64 *panchayat*[4] meetings, and countless

Fig. 6.2 Neem Ka Thana and Ladala Ki Dhani families after workshops and discussion, Spring 2003

---

[3] See also Anne Pyburn and Caroline Beebe's project on "Grassroots Resource Preservation and Management in Kyrgyzstan" http://www.sfu.ca/ipinch/project-components/community-based-initiatives/grassroots-resource-preservation-and-management-kyrgy/, Accessed 5 May 2019.

[4] *Panchayat* can be translated to the village council or council of five villages, and *sarpanch* is the head or chair of the *panchayat* in India. These are political positions and recognized by all levels of government. A *tehsildar* is the tax/revenue officer, often linked to the District Magistrates office,

discussions with individuals of all ages who would join us on our surveys, communities who chose to engage in discussions about copper mining, and publics that formed around the discourse of tourism, heritage management, and the use of archaeology in the contemporary world.

Each new survey began with a visit to the village *sarpanch* to discuss the overall project. This would often result in a discussion with other *panchayat* (village council) members and interested community leaders, including, and perhaps especially, farmers. Such discussions made each of these individuals stakeholders in the overall project, each with a particular point of view and specific interests in collaboration with the survey project (Fig. 6.3). In most cases, local history teachers would also join in the efforts and discussion, and their classes would join our surveys. In some instances, these students would actually become part of after-school programs in which the survey team would teach the students survey techniques and lessons in the general archaeology of South Asia. Our work involved interacting with a range of persons including officers of the Archaeological Survey of India (ASI), the State Government of Rajasthan, Secretary of Tourism, Art and Culture, the Directorate of Archaeology and Museums, the District Magistrate, the Assistant District Magistrate, *tehsildars*, *patwaris*, police officers at the stations where artifacts were stored after a chance find, the *panchayat*, individual *sarpanch*, school teachers (particularly his-

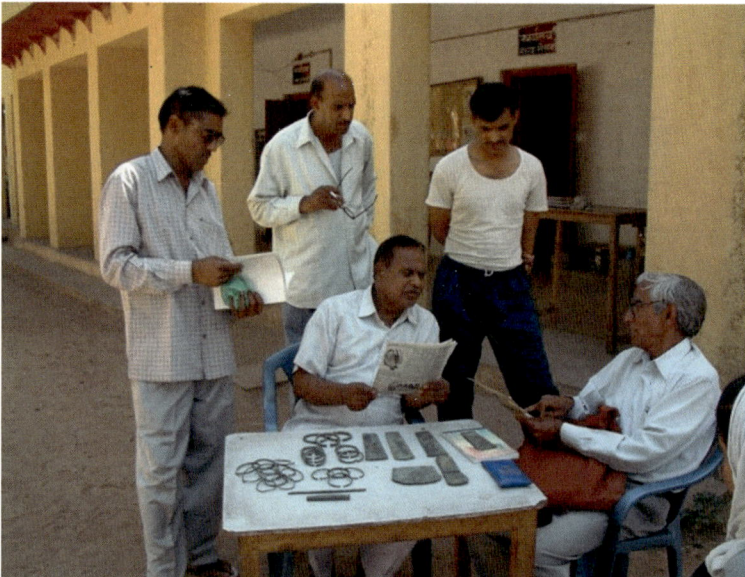

Fig. 6.3 Police Station with officers in conversation with Mr. Harphool Singh looking over copper material brought to them as chance find by a farmer, Spring 2003

and the *patwari* works close with them as a local authority who maintains the ownership records of a specific area, also to collect land taxes.

tory teachers), community leaders, elders, head of households and farmsteads, interested individuals passing by, and, most of all, children. These methods were developed through our interactions with these individuals and groups as an active mode of decolonization by incorporating community-based archaeology, public archaeology, and a change in the education and training of archaeologists (Marshall 2002; Atalay 2006).[5]

Sociality and Its Stakes

Archaeological graduate training has traditionally involved a form of stranger fetish that accompanies the idea of going to "the field." In *Strange Encounters: Embodied Others in Post-Coloniality* (2000), Sara Ahmed forces us to contend with the ways by which we have been taught to construct our own identities through difference and the forms it takes. Within an archaeological context, whether we become "foreigners" or "archaeologists," Ahmed's framework allows us to deconstruct the fetishization of difference or strangeness or, as she says, "strangers," with whom the encounter and the narration and articulation of that moment construct our identity as informed by that at the expense of such individuals/strangers. These positions of strangeness then are rendered static and lacking in agency and become tropes for pre-existing objects of knowledge (rather than allowing for subjective positionality). Ahmed proposes that "we can only avoid stranger fetishism . . . by examining the social relationships that are concealed by this very fetishism . . . [W]e need to consider how the stranger is an effect of processes of inclusion and exclusion" (2000: 6). Within community-based participatory work, that sociality, those stakes, or that life together has the potential to be opened up and considered in a way to undo (as a decolonial gesture) the static nature of these articulated relationships.

Living and working alongside the many stakeholders, we develop social relationships which have to be maintained within the framework of social relations within that specific context. There was a "daily intimacy" to our practice and relations that I consider integral to the archaeological research method (Dave 2012:24). Our work and new sociality had to address the impact of previous work done in the region, whether that be of the colonial time period, an antiquities dealer, or the MA or PhD candidate who came through the village just prior to our visit (Kersel and Chesson 2013; Rizvi 2006). These relationships and their legacy persist and often outlive us and our bodies as memories of interactions on an intimate landscape.

---

[5] I have long argued a distinction between community-based practice and public practice (see Rizvi 2006). For me, this distinction is important as "public" for me is a political/civil society term that is contingent upon citizenship. For many communities and populations who may be documented in different ways, I believe community praxis holds a different form of belonging through sociality in a different way than belonging to and with the state. More recently, I engaged in a conversation around the differences with Carol McDavid and Laurajane Smith, which may help elucidate the many ways of engaging with public and community (see McDavid et al. 2016).

Local populations that live within the area of the archaeological site are only ever referred to as significant if there are issues of "encroachment" or discussions of permits and boundaries. Often it is only in the context of community-based practices that people are considered to be relevant to the project. With a focus on such methods, however, what tends to get lost is that the people who live in these *other/othered* places still have lives that are not related to the project, that they exist even when archaeology does not code or consume them as a commodity fetish or instrumentalize them for the purposes of the project (Abu-Khawajah 2014). Prior to being coded as "community partners," our discipline *others* people, and populations that we work with and encounter on a daily basis are not treated or conceived of as existing except as an-*other:* a form of difference that is part of our (the archaeologists') experience. This approach impacts the ways in which relationships are formed, delineated, and consumed as commodity fetish of archaeological practice (hooks 1992).

Any attempt to move beyond this, from someone coming from a western practice, requires a particular care not to consume difference in a manner that approximates appropriation, while at the same time learning to respect and honor the cultural differences that make us unique. As Carol McDavid clearly states in a piece on archaeology, race and white privilege:

> ...those of us who work in this area of archaeology, have a responsibility, a mandate even, to do two things: to reflect upon how race and racism emerge in "everyday" public archaeology practice, and to find ways to discuss issues with our publics as we present our archaeological work. (2007:67)

Through such intentional critique, we are made aware then of our racial privilege that maps on to colonial traces of our practice on colonized landscapes. In this intentionality is the impetus not only of decolonization but also of care (Rizvi 2016). That care manifests itself within social relationships and engenders respect among all the people who encounter the project, including the archaeologist, herself. The interlinked space of care within a decolonial effort loosens the discipline, in some sense, undisciplining it (Haber 2012; Shepherd 2014). The impact of emotional labor that has a basis in ethical, anti-colonial, anti-racist praxis is one that creates a deeper recognition and sociality among the participants of any project. There is a different seeing of each other that simultaneously honors and respects them/us, their/our pasts, histories, and futures.

I want to contextualize the significance of this care in India – and in relation to this project. One of the lessons of care involves the generosity of time. In giving time, you honor people's time and their ways of being and understanding history and archaeology. Nothing exemplified this more than learning how to visit people and drink tea; this may seem counterintuitive if you operate in a capitalist, efficiency-driven mind-set, but, in fact, has proven to be one of the most efficient ways to work in most of the world. Drinking tea is both a metaphor and an action. It is about respecting the person sitting in front of you as a person first; it diffuses the instrumentalization of relationships that is so prevalent in a capitalist economy (I include contemporary knowledge production in this). It sets up reciprocity, social networks, and in some cases extended, fictive, academic/research kin.

Given these nuanced and deep relationships that informed our sociality, the stake that many of us had in the archaeological research actually had larger political ramifications (Lyons 2014). On numerous occasions, women of all ages (and some men) would come and tell me how much they wanted the project, the research, and for me to succeed because in me, they recognized the political stakes of such work. The work in this case then was not about pottery sorting or mapping; the work referred to here was the work of my body, the optic of my body, the performance of my body to do archaeology. And by entering into that visual field, we would then together inscribe new realities upon insistent traces of colonialism and patriarchy. In their support of me, they were vocal in saying that it was to provide a model for their girls to become directors of such projects. Through this practice, I became aware of the many different projects my dissertation work was engaged in – it was not just about doing archaeological research. The stakes of my body doing that research were being read as having a cultural and political impact.

Much of the research I write about is coproduced with communities of people in that it emerges from the many discussions and experiences we share; the engagement transforms all of us. In particular, I believe it was a significant transformative experience for me. For people who lived in those areas, there were already systems of power in play, alongside forms of dis/empowerment that were outside my academic world framing. Their engagement and willingness to work with me made me imagine my disciplinary practice in a completely different way. I saw the potential of a participatory model that went beyond archaeological knowledge production. It allowed me to imagine an archaeology that could have stakes beyond its own limits.

However, my experience also confirms that at each level of interaction, the coexistence of suspicion and curiosity is a traumatic remnant of a colonial past and a reiteration of an unequal present, in which information, power, and prestige have been continued to be stolen from the caretakers of the land (Nandy 2001). It was only at the highest levels of the Indian bureaucracy, and within the company of internationally recognized senior scholars, usually with some western training, that such a suspicion was not blatant and there was an expressed interest in my academic qualifications. At this privileged level, the individuals are recognized, legitimized, and authorized as some part of the elite on the national stage or international stage. In contrast, the vast majority of the middle-class Indian bureaucracy showed less interest in my academic prowess; rather, in order to gain access to locked cabinets, museum records, and information about previous excavations, I had to prove my trustworthiness by locating my spatial practice and performance within their social systems and cultural norms.

Through our training, archaeologists are transformed into vessels of power that signify promise, yet often we cannot live up to that potential. It is a performance of power that we reenact by occupying a specific space that is not local to us, which recalls in collective memory the colonial archaeologists and the power vested in their positions as embodiments of empire. I believe that a shift in methodology – one that accounts for privileged practice, the collective memory of the colonial archaeologist, and the context for any curiosity and suspicion – enables a dismantling of colonial structures upon which they stand. But this dismantling cannot happen alone. It, too, is a collaborative process, one that requires all parties and stakeholders to be able to transform that narrative into one that allows for a different sort of process to still have the same level of acceptance, authenticity, and experience in history making (Richardson and Almansa-Sánchez 2015).

These reflections beg the question of new research methods specifically around community-based practices, taking into account the amount of time, emotional investment, care, intimacy, and intentional strategies around participatory ethics. Although this chapter is not the place to propose such methods, I do think that in thinking through these issues, we will recognize that even within them, the ease with which one might slip into a neocolonial practice is clear. Community-based praxis is not about patronizing groups of people and claiming that your methods are the best way forward; it is very much about just the opposite – it is about having a methodology that forms and formulates around shared concerns, one that centers sociality and equity in a manner to inform process, and a discipline that recognizes that what is valued is not the end result (because really, research never ends), but that it is in the process that value is placed and understood as rigorous. And so what this really is about then is what we, as a discipline and community of peers, will review and code as valuable.

On the Betrayal of New Research

In 2013, a long-standing resident of the Emirates asked if I might shift my focus of research to the United Arab Emirates (UAE). I began to consider the impact of what leaving India might mean, and in order to contextualize this invitation and how it made me feel, I went back to Rajasthan to meet and talk to some of my collaborators about how this might roll out. I was no longer the graduate student they had first met in the late 1990s/early 2000s, and so our conversations had shifted as I was now a mature scholar with different expectations attached to my position as an Assistant Professor about to go up for tenure. It had been increasingly difficult to receive permits to work in India; state politics and communal focus made designing projects unsettling. Many of the issues around safety that had first been considered over a decade prior had, by then, become quite real and work within that context felt untenable. It was an emotional and traumatic issue which left many of my collaborators in awkward situations when trying to think through what it might mean to continue the relationships that had been forged a decade earlier. Many of the younger women I had worked with had grown, matured, and finished their PhDs. Throughout that decade, I had only been able to go back a handful of times, nothing like the consistent engagement that my graduate work had afforded me. There were many conversations with my collaborators about how little time we had been able to spend together since my early work, and even if I explained those through circumstance, the initial moment of my departure in 2003 kept resurfacing as the first break in an archaeological relationship. What was left unspoken but was very much felt was that they could not believe I actually left, even though I had consistently told them that I would. We had created new worlds of practice together, we had created new possibilities together, which hadn't been given enough time to form before I left (see Rizvi 2006 and 2018 for failed projects and how to value them). We all felt that loss acutely, and yet none of us had the capacity to articulate where those expectations came from because, intellectually, we all thought this was just about archaeology (Piccini and Schaepe 2014).

I now understand that it was not the archaeological project that was at the core of that loss – but it was the larger political project of what it meant for women of South Asian heritage to direct an archaeological project. In all my journal writing from that time, nowhere had I worked out what it meant for the feminist project to unwind. The inability to articulate a transnational feminist project led to many unclear stakes that blurred the lines of the decolonial method for archaeology. This was my own inability and lack of training and maturity in being able to articulate how transnational feminism and activism informed my archaeological practice (see Swarr and Nagar 2010). My leaving in 2003 could not have been seen as anything but betrayal by my many collaborators and friends because I had left and gone back to the privileged western world. And in turn, I felt betrayed by my own discipline for not having provided the structures for support or mentorship to help navigate such issues.[6]

Although my current work on decolonizing archaeology and heritage in the UAE seamlessly fits into the archaeological queries and critiques that have been at the core of my work for decades, the experience of my research does not. I learned a lot from carrying the feeling of betrayal and have allowed it to inform how I live, work, and collaborate with people in the UAE. I am aware and make others aware of the many projects that are embedded in any archaeological project that we may embark on. I am intentional about not talking as much about de-privileging the academic as it, in that statement, reinstates the hierarchy but rather investigate how we build solidarity and think about these questions together. And I am constantly aware that in our actions there are promises that are being made and enacted. I find myself constantly asking: What was promised to me and what did I promise?

Unresolved Resolutions

Whether or not I ever work in India again is not the point of this chapter. What is important to recognize is that the emotional labor that underpins anti-colonial, community-based, participatory work anywhere in the world leaves its mark and needs to be acknowledged and cared for in specific ways. As our discipline makes an effort to move toward a more inclusive, undisciplined, decolonized, and ethically just praxis, we must take into account the many systems and projects our own bodies are engaged in that have political ramification beyond archaeology. Those impli-

---

[6] This is why, in large part, I am choosing to write about this now – so that the next generation of scholars has access to the ways in which archaeological projects are simultaneously many other projects that need to be handled with the same rigor.

cations also have the power to transform our discipline and should be considered with just as much rigor as any other form of epistemic critique. Contending with embodied knowledge and privilege is emotional labor, which is a part of archaeological praxis for as long as your body is engaged in research. The recognition of such labor in praxis enhances the rigor of the project; it provides nuance to the multiple forms of diplomatic relationships we end up negotiating among stakeholders and, above all, provides some space for truth to the feeling that in new research is betrayal and loss of the previous form, which includes not only the topic but also all the other projects and people wrapped up into that experience, including a part of yourself.

Epilogue: A Short Note

Eventually, I did take my mother to meet Shanta Bai. It seemed uneventful and normalized ...and although not required, it felt important. They both enjoyed talking about me with a shared intimacy of knowing me, and when we were leaving, my mother thanked her "for taking care of me." That was probably better than any acknowledgment I could have given her in my written text.

Acknowledgments I want to thank the Heart Collective (Sonya Atalay, Jane Baxter, Natasha Lyons, and Kisha Supernant), for the invitation to be a part of this important conversation and turn toward a more emotionally intelligent archaeological praxis. I would also like to thank "Shanta Bai" for all the care and many hours of company, laughter, and cups of tea. Many thanks to the community-based programs and workshops in Neem ka Thana and Kot Putli, as well as the Panchayat in districts Alwar, Tonk, Sikar, and Jaipur. I would also like to acknowledge the collaborative efforts of my colleagues at the Rajasthan State Department of Archaeology and Museums and the Archaeological Survey of India offices (Jaipur and Delhi).

References

Abu-Khawajah, S. (2014). 'They are hiding it … Why do they hide it? From Whom, and for Whom?': Community heritage at work in the post-colonial context of Jordan. In S. Thomas & J. Lea (Eds.), *Public participation in archaeology* (pp. 149–160). Suffolk: Boydell and Brewer.
Ahmad, S. (2000). *Strange encounters: Embodied others in post-Coloniality*. London: Routledge.
Atalay, S. (2006). Decolonizing archaeology. *American Indian Quarterly, 30*(3 & 4), 269–279.
Atalay, S. (2012). *Community-based archaeology: Research with, by and for indigenous and local communities*. Berkeley: University of California Press.
Chadha, A. (2010). The Archaeological Survey of India and the Science of Postcolonial Archaeology. In J. Lydon & U. Z. Rizvi (Eds.),. Handbook of Postcolonial Archaeology *World Archaeological Congress Research Handbooks* (pp. 227–233). Walnut Creek: Left Coast Press.
Dave, N. (2012). *Queer Activism in India: A Story in the Anthropology of Ethics. Durham and.* London: Duke University Press.
Gullapalli, P. (2008). Heterogeneous encounters: Colonial histories and archaeological experiences. In M. Liebmann & U. Z. Rizvi (Eds.), *Archaeology and the postcolonial critique* (pp. 35–52). Lanham: Altamira Press.

Haber, A. (2012). Un-disciplining archaeology. *Archaeologies, 8*(1), 55–66.

hooks, b. (1992). *Black looks: Race and representation*. Boston: South End Press.

Ibrahim, A. (in review). The role of museums, design accessibility and community concerns: A case study of State Bank of Pakistan Museum and Art Gallery. Journal of Community Archaeology and Heritage.

Jamir, T. (2016). Decolonizing Archaeological Practice in Northeastern India: Towards a Community-Based Archaeology at Chungliyimti, Nagaland. Special series on Decolonizing Anthropology, Savage Minds. https://savageminds.org/2016/10/24/decolonizing-archaeological-practice-in-northeast-india-towards-a-community-based-archaeology-at-chungliyimti-nagaland/. Accessed 5 May 2019.

Jamir, T., & Vasa, D. (2008). Archaeology of local cultures: New findings and interpretations in Nagaland. In M. Oppitz, T. Kaiser, A. v. Stockhausen, & M. Wettstein (Eds.), *Naga identities: Changing local cultures in the northeast of India* (pp. 323–339). Snoeck Publishers: Gent.

Kersel, M., & Chesson, M. (2013). Tomato season in the Ghor es-Safi: A lesson in community archaeology. *Near Eastern Archaeology, 76*(3), 159–165.

Kuwanwisiwma, L. J. (2008). Collaboration means equality, respect, and reciprocity: A conversation about archaeology and the Hopi tribe. In C. Colwell-Chanthaphonh & T. J. Ferguson (Eds.), *Collaboration in archaeological practice: Engaging descendant communities* (pp. 151–169). Lanham: AltaMira Press.

Lorenzon, M., & Zermani, I. (2016). Common ground: Community archaeology in Egypt, interaction between population and cultural heritage. *Journal of Community Archaeology & Heritage, 3*(3), 183–199.

Lyons, N. (2014). Localized critical theory as an expression of community archaeology practice with an example from Inuvialuit Elders of the Canadian Western Arctic. *American Antiquity, 79*(2), 183–203.

Marshall, Y. (2002). What is community archaeology? *World Archaeology, 34*(2), 211–219.

McDavid, C. (2007). Beyond strategy and good intentions: Archaeology, race, and white privilege. In B. Little & P. Shackel (Eds.), *Archaeology as a tool of civic engagement* (pp. 67–88). Lanham, MD: Alta Mira Press.

McDavid, C., Rizvi, U. Z., & Smith, L. (2016). Community archaeology and heritage in Africa: Conversations inspired by a workshop. In P. Schmidt & I. Pikirayi (Eds.), *Community archaeology and heritage in Africa* (pp. 250–269). London: Routledge Press.

Mehari, A., & Ryano, K. P. (2016). Maasai people and Oldupai (Olduvai) gorge: Looking for sustainable people-centred approaches and practices. In P. Schmidt & I. Pikirayi (Eds.), *Community archaeology and heritage in Africa* (pp. 21–45). London: Routledge Press.

Mignolo, W. (2002). The geopolitics of knowledge and the colonial difference. *The South Atlantic Quarterly, 101*(1), 57–96.

Nagar, R. (2014). *Muddying the Waters: Coauthoring Feminisms Across Scholarship and Activism*. Urbana/Chicago/Springfield: University of Illinois Press.

Nandy, A. (2001). *Time warps: The insistent politics of silent and evasive pasts*. Delhi: Permanent Blacki.

Piccini, A., & Schaepe, D. M. (2014). The messy business of archaeology as participatory local knowledge: A conversation between the Stó:lō Nation and Knowle West. *Canadian Journal of Archaeology/Journal Canadien D'Archéologie, 38*(2), 466–495.

Richardson, L.-J., & Almansa-Sánchez, J. (2015). Do you even know what public archaeology is? Trends, theory, practice, ethics. *World Archaeology, 47*(2), 194–211.

Rizvi, U. Z. (2006). Accounting for multiple desires: Decolonizing methodologies, archaeology and the public interest. *India Review, 5*(3–4), 394–416.

Rizvi, U. Z. (2008). Decolonizing methodologies as strategies of practice: Operationalizing the postcolonial critique in the archaeology of Rajasthan. In M. Liebmann & U. Z. Rizvi (Eds.), *Archaeology and the postcolonial critique* (pp. 109–127). Lanham: Altamira Press.

Rizvi, U. Z. (2015). Decolonizing archaeology: On the global heritage of epistemic laziness. In O. Kholeif (Ed.), *Two days after forever: A reader on the choreography of time* (pp. 154–163). Berlin: Sternberg Press.

Rizvi, U. Z. (2016). Decolonization as care. In C. F. Strauss & A. P. Pais (Eds.), *Slow reader: A resource for design thinking and practice* (pp. 85–95). Amsterdam: Valiz Publishers.

Ross, A., Ulm, S., & Tobane, B. (2013). Gummingurru: A community archaeology knowledge journey. *Australian Archaeology, 76*, 62–68.

Shepherd, N. (2014). Undisciplining archaeological ethics. In A. Haber & N. Shepherd (Eds.), *After ethics: Ancestral voices and post-disciplinary worlds in archaeology* (pp. 11–26). New York: Springer.

Sundberg, J. (2014). Decolonizing Posthumanist geographies. *Cultural Geographies, 21*(1), 33–47.

Swarr, A. L., & Nagar, R. (Eds.). (2010). *Critical transnational feminist praxis*. Albany: SUNY Press.

Chapter 7
At the Heart of the Ikaahuk Archaeology Project

Lisa Hodgetts and Laura Kelvin

As part of the Western scientific tradition, the discipline of archaeology has always emphasized the intellectual aspects of our work as archaeologists. This volume provides a welcome opening for us to consider the emotional side of what we do. This chapter explores our personal trajectories towards a more heart-centred practice through our experiences as part of the Ikaahuk Archaeology Project – a community-focussed research project in the largely Inuvialuit[1] community of Sachs Harbour in Canada's Northwest Territories (Fig. 7.1). We document how we came to the project, what we have learned through it, and the implications for our future work and the discipline more broadly. We argue that a heart-centred approach to archaeology makes our research caring work – work done with and for others – and that its outcomes, while more personally rewarding for us as people, are not valued in the same way within academia as those of a mind-centred approach. A heart-centred archaeology therefore calls us to action to restructure not just our research lives but the institutional and legislative contexts within which many of us work.

Our reflections are inspired by the feminist call for knowledge production to be more of a work of the heart. Hilary Rose (1983) suggested that feminists should ground their epistemology in "hand, brain, and heart", by which she meant that it should not only be about the abstraction of thought (the brain) but also about activism (doing – the hand) and what she called "caring labour" (the heart). Caring labour is nurturing work, the intimate, emotionally demanding labour most often associated with raising children and with women. She argued that we need to break

---

[1] Inuvialuit are the Inuit of Canada's western Arctic.

L. Hodgetts (✉)
Department of Anthropology, The University of Western Ontario, London, ON, Canada
e-mail: Lisa.Hodgetts@uwo.ca

L. Kelvin
Department of Archaeology, Memorial University of Newfoundland, St. John's, NL, Canada

© Springer Nature Switzerland AG 2020
K. Supernant et al. (eds.), *Archaeologies of the Heart*,
https://doi.org/10.1007/978-3-030-36350-5_7

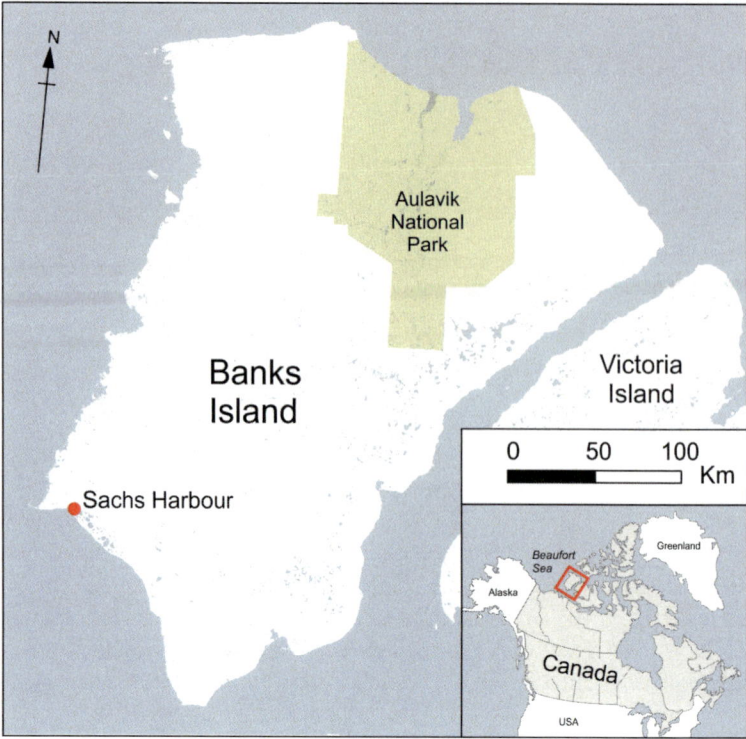

Fig. 7.1 Location of Sachs Harbour on Banks Island

down these divisions between labour of the mind, body, and heart to move towards a feminist epistemology of science. Within academia, teaching is often framed as caring labour, work done with and for others, but research rarely is. Park (1996: 47) argued that "a gendered division of labour exists within (as outside) the contemporary academy wherein research is implicitly deemed 'men's work' and is explicitly valued, whereas teaching . . . [is] characterized as 'women's work' and explicitly devalued". Over 20 years on, the gendered nature of that division may be less pronounced (though we note that 70% of Canada Research Chairs are held by men (Government of Canada 2017)), but our experience suggests that publication counts and traditional measures of research success still carry the greatest weight in decisions about research funding and tenure and promotion. We advocate for a more holistic and caring approach to archaeology by *all* archaeologists and ponder how to work for structural change within academia to support this more heart-centred practice.

In our Ikaahuk Archaeology Project research, we understand caring labour as putting our relationships with the Inuvialuit we work with at the centre of everything we do. These relationships require attention and nurturing, so we must tend them in the same way women tended the *qulliq*, the oil lamp that formed the symbolic heart of a traditional Inuvialuit dwelling and provided heat and light to all within. Our approach to caring relationships resonates with elements of Indigenous scholarship on education (e.g. Archibald 2008, Cajete 2000, 2015) and philosophical discourse on ethics of care (e.g. Held 2006). For us, caring involves acknowledging the context within which we work and the power dynamics that flow from it. We must be sensitive to the history of our discipline and of Inuvialuit within colonial Canada and our own privilege as White academics. It also means being attentive and responsive to the needs of Inuvialuit community members, which involves continuously reflecting on our practice, both individually and collectively. We strive to pay close attention to Inuvialuit understandings, values, and concerns and to understand things from their perspectives. We also strive to ensure that our work meets their needs as much as our own, continually adjusting our approach as our understanding of their needs deepens and as those needs change. Caring means always being open to new lessons and being willing to apply them. With care comes responsibility. We are continually reminded of the colonial institutions and processes that disadvantage the Inuvialuit we work with, as well as the rational, mind-centred foundations of the academy that create structural barriers to a holistic, heart-centred practice. We feel an obligation to do what we can to break down these barriers.

We agree with Rose (1983) that we should move beyond the mind/body division that underlies Western epistemology, grounding our knowledge in the hand, or perhaps more properly in the body, through doing and in the heart, through caring. This more holistic approach draws not just on the feminist critique of science (e.g. Haraway 1988; Harding 1986; Keller 1985; Longino 1990), which undermines traditional Western understandings of science as objective and rational, but also on Indigenous ways of knowing. While they vary from community to community, many Indigenous worldviews share a common understanding of knowledge as holistic, involving the heart, mind, body, and spirit (Archibald 2008; Cajete 2000). Moreover, many Indigenous philosophies emphasize that we create knowledge within the context of relationships and can therefore not separate it from those relationships. Caring, holistic approaches are defining characteristics of community-based archaeologies, a range of approaches that engage Indigenous and other local communities as research partners (cf. Atalay 2012, Nicholas and Andrews 1997). For us, a heart-centred practice means bringing this caring, holistic approach into all aspects of our work as academic archaeologists: research, teaching, and service (see also Lyons and Supernant, this volume). We believe that doing so will benefit archaeology, archaeologists, and the communities we work with, because it will guide us to support one another rather than serving only our own interests or competing with each other (see also Surface-Evans, this volume). The two of us have travelled different paths to these conclusions, though in recent years, our journeys have intertwined and informed each other. We begin by sharing how we both came to participate in the Ikaahuk Archaeology Project.

Lisa's Journey

I discovered archaeology as a first year undergraduate English major. I took one course in Classical archaeology that sold me on the discipline because it combined my interests in people, history, travel, and the outdoors. I had my first field experience in the traditional territories of the Heiltsuk and Nuxalk First Nations on the coast of British Columbia. It was my first direct exposure, as the great-great-granddaughter of British immigrants to Canada, to the rich culture and heritage of Canada's Indigenous peoples. As an undergraduate student on those projects, I had few opportunities to interact directly with First Nations community members, who for the most part did not join us in the field. I followed my interest in zooarchaeology to graduate studies in England, working on previously excavated 4000-year-old faunal collections from northern Norway. My graduate training was strongly in the processual tradition. The expertise I gained in identifying seal bones led me to a zooarchaeological postdoctoral project in Newfoundland, working on arctic-adapted groups who occupied Newfoundland during a period of cooler climate from roughly 2000 to 1000 years ago.

To this point, I had not had the opportunity to work closely with Indigenous descendant communities whose heritage I was studying. My younger self would have scoffed at the idea of an archaeology of the heart. The work I have done over the last 10 years with community members in Sachs Harbour has completely changed my perspective on what constitutes archaeology, my approach to research, and my place within the discipline.

In 2004, I got a tenure track job at the University of Western Ontario (Western) where several of my colleagues in the Anthropology department were engaged in community-based research. I could see the value in it and wanted to move my work in that direction but struggled because I had no pre-existing relationships with communities in the western Arctic where I hoped to work. I found myself in a bind. Community-based research works best when communities are involved in the research design from the beginning, but without a fully formed research proposal, how was I to get funding to travel north to build the relationships that would allow us to develop such a project? My compromise was to formulate a grant proposal that looked very broadly at changing interactions between people, animals, and the land on Banks Island over time. This approach built in enough flexibility to work with community members to focus the questions in ways that were meaningful to them. My application was successful, and I made my first trip to Sachs Harbour in 2008. It is a small, largely Inuvialuit community of roughly 100 people and is the only permanent settlement on Banks Island. Laura was an undergraduate student at Western at the time. I remember her as the quiet one in my Arctic archaeology class, who stood out for the quality of both her thinking and her writing in the final paper she wrote on community archaeology in the North. I did not know then that she would join me in Sachs Harbour in a few years.

I am so grateful that people in Sachs Harbour did not send me packing – I was painfully aware in the early years that I had imposed myself on them; they had not invited me in. It has taken a long time to build mutual understanding, trust, and friendship. More than a decade on, I still often feel like we are just getting started. I went in knowing that I had a lot to learn, though I did not appreciate how much. I still have a lot to learn. I am grateful for the kindness and generosity of so many people in the community who were willing to talk with me, feed me, and gently point out my misconceptions and set me straight. Throughout, I have tried to stay true to the caring values of attentiveness and responsiveness.

Over the course of the project, as I learned more about community members' values, beliefs and epistemologies, something Laura helped me to better understand, the research moved away from more traditional archaeological approaches to less traditional ones that are more community-driven. Our initial work involved survey, including geophysical survey in response to community members' wishes for less invasive methods, and some targeted excavation of a site threatened by erosion – which is accelerating in the region in response to climate change.

More recently, we focussed on increasing access to artefact collections from Banks Island housed in southern museums. We explored the potential of 3D modelling towards this end, utilizing low-cost, easy-to-use technologies in the hands of community members. Through listening and trying to respond to the needs of community members in Sachs Harbour, my research has become less about reconstructing past lives from material remains and more about working with community members to facilitate their access to their archaeological heritage and supporting them as they make meaning from those remains. It flows from my personal relationships with community members, which makes it a work of the heart, and it is about connecting them with things that have emotional and spiritual meaning and value for them – things of the heart. I have made new friends through this work, and because we are friends, I share in the joy that I see on their faces when they hold an artefact or they share a happy memory with me. I am emotionally invested in this work in a way I never was in any of the previous work I have done, which makes it more demanding at times, but also far more meaningful for me.

Laura's Journey

My parents always had a strong interest in archaeology, and they often brought my siblings and me to museums, which prompted my own interest in archaeology. What I hope to achieve with my work is strongly influenced by my grandmothers. My maternal grandmother was Hungarian and had a great love for her culture, and her heritage was a source of pride. She was always excited to share her heritage with me and taught me that heritage is an important part of self. She often stood in contrast to my paternal grandmother, who due to colonial processes was unable to learn much about her Indigenous heritage and family, and internalized racism often made her uncomfortable talking about it. In the long term, I hope to contribute to understandings of the past that better reflect the understandings and experiences of

Indigenous people as part of a greater effort to foster knowledge and appreciation of Indigenous heritage in North America.

I did my undergraduate degree at the University of Western Ontario in Anthropology and First Nations studies. In the beginning, I felt a disconnect between what was being taught in my classes and what I understood about contemporary Indigenous people. I became disillusioned with archaeology and thought it might not be for me. When I took Lisa's Arctic archaeology course in 2006, it was the first time I had an archaeology instructor explicitly discussing the colonial roots of archaeology and the continued impacts it has on Indigenous communities – issues that had deterred me from pursuing a career in archaeology. She also taught our class about ways that Indigenous communities and archaeologists (and Indigenous archaeologists!) are working together to build research projects that empower Indigenous communities and build holistic and inclusive understandings of the past. Her encouragement of my interest in these topics helped me find my voice and my place in archaeology.

I went on to do a Master's degree at Memorial University with Lisa Rankin. My MA project used oral history research and archaeological survey to examine the history of the Inuit-Metis in Sandwich Bay, Labrador (Kelvin 2011). It was part of the broader *Understanding the Past to Build the Future Community University Research Alliance Project* initiated by the Southern Inuit in Labrador (Kennedy 2014). Working on this large-scale collaborative project gave me a chance to see the ways archaeology can creatively benefit communities when it is guided by community aspirations and inspired me to continue my studies. After finishing my Masters, I came back to Western to do a PhD with Lisa, as part of the *Ikaahuk Archaeology Project*. My research explored how Sachs Harbour community members produce and maintain historical knowledge in order to determine how archaeological knowledge can best complement Inuvialuit understandings and ways of knowing the past (Kelvin 2016). I spent the summer of 2013, summer and fall of 2014, and spring of 2015 living in Sachs Harbour for my research, conducting interviews with community members focussing on archaeology, traditional knowledge, and Banks Island's past (Fig. 7.2). The relationships that I built and the teachings I received from Elders and community knowledge holders have shaped who I am as a researcher and a person.

Learning Through Doing: Together

Attentiveness to the needs of Sachs Harbour community members has taught us the importance of embodied action – doing – to their understanding of their history and identity as Inuvialuit. *Doing* has an important social element – it often happens with others and involves sharing stories and other knowledge. This is a common feature of many Indigenous knowledge systems, in which knowledge is understood as inseparable from the social relations within which it is created (Cajete 2015). Western academics study the past intellectually and know the past primarily in their

Fig. 7.2 Elder Lena Wolki, Laura Kelvin, and Elder Edith Haogak during a traditional knowledge interview at Haogak Lake, 2014

minds. Community members from Sachs Harbour tell us that they learn about the past through doing, the same way they traditionally learned about most things (Kelvin 2016). Learning the past through doing means engaging one's body and heart, as well as mind in the process. Betty Haogak told Laura that community members learn about the past "by living it", and Kevin Gully explained that learning through doing involves "going to the source of history". When they describe this concept of learning about the past through doing, community members are usually referring to "traditional" activities like sewing, hunting, trapping, and food preparation. By taking part in traditional activities, often on the land in places used by their ancestors, people experience and know the past in ways that cannot be learned through oral histories. Their present intersects with the past as they "do" as their ancestors did. One of the women who taught Laura to sew commented during a lesson that when she sews, she knows her past and is connected to her ancestors. Learning through doing also happens through "nontraditional" activities, for example, photography and participating in culturally themed Facebook groups (Fig. 7.3).

In all of these contexts, there is an important social element and stories play a key role. *Doing* on the land or in the home, whether it involves preparing a hide, hunting, or sharing a photograph, provides an opportunity to share stories and experiences that can inform and direct actions. This sharing, which traditionally happened face to face in real time, now also happens online through social media. Even when people engage in these activities alone, they remember learning these skills from family and friends, practising them at other times and places, and feeling connected

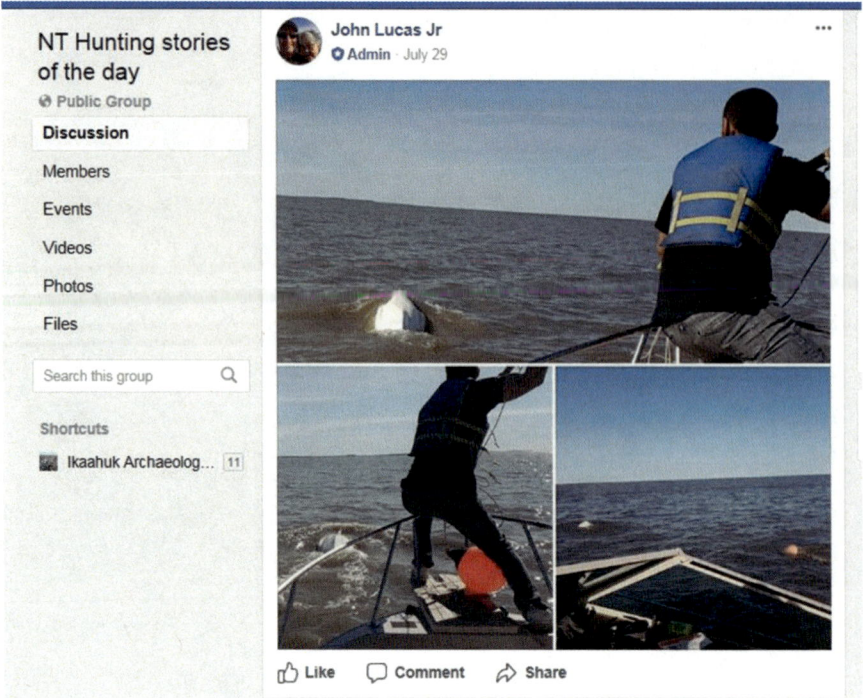

Fig. 7.3 Screenshot of NT Hunting Stories of the Day, a Facebook group with over 4000 members

to their community, their ancestors, and their heritage. This more holistic approach, incorporating the body, heart, and mind, is central to Inuvialuit ways of understanding, teaching, and learning about their past and to Inuvialuit identity.

To be responsive to Inuvialuit ways of knowing, we have attempted to incorporate learning through doing within the Ikaahuk Archaeology Project, embracing its holistic nature, and recognizing that Inuvialuit have a special relationship with their archaeological heritage because it is intimately tied to their individual and collective identities. We also frame the Ikaahuk Archaeology Project itself in these terms – we are learning how to do community-based archaeology with our Inuvialuit partners through doing it. This means that we all understand the project as a work in progress, and we reflect critically on our process throughout.

We have made several attempts to incorporate learning through doing in our research by involving Inuvialuit youth in the practice of archaeology. In 2009, we partnered with Parks Canada to host a youth camp in Aulavik National Park in the north of Banks Island. We brought youth to the park along with an Elder, Lena Wolki, who spent a lot of time in the area as a young girl. We visited several cultural sites, Lena shared stories about her childhood and her experiences on the land with her parents and sister, and the youth mapped archaeological features and recorded several previously unrecorded sites. During the 2013 survey field season and 2014 excavation field season, we hired Inuvialuit to join our field crew. These positions went primarily to local youth because community members told us youth needed summer work opportunities close to home.

We have had mixed success with this approach. Some students were very engaged, others less so. We recognize that these efforts simply involved Inuvialuit in Western archaeological ways of doing. Community members have suggested they would be more effective and meaningful if we could incorporate more traditional activities into this shared time on the land and find more ways to bring different generations together so they can share their knowledge. Both are elements that are featured in our current work.

We also incorporated this concept of learning through doing during a community visit to Prince of Wales Northern Heritage Centre (PWNHC) in 2015. In this instance, a stronger emphasis on storytelling led to greater youth engagement. The trip involved community members from multiple generations since people have told us it is important to focus not just on Elders and/or youth and have emphasized the importance of sharing knowledge across the generations. We held and examined artefacts from Banks Island. The Elders shared stories about their experiences with similar artefacts and about the past (Fig. 7.4). The youth used photogrammetry (a method of stitching together photographs taken from multiple angles) and 3D scanners to make 3D models of the artefacts, which we posted to the project Facebook page and shared on the project website. This approach allowed us to tap into the high levels of digital literacy and social media engagement among Inuvialuit youth.

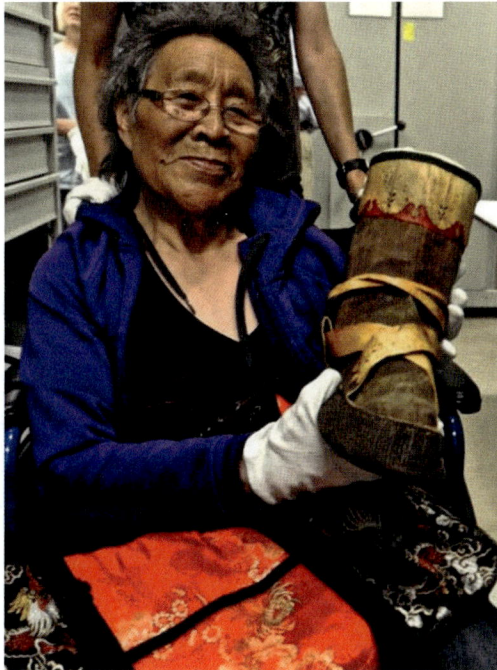

Fig. 7.4 Elder Lena Wolki holds up a kamik with waterproof soles during a community visit to Prince of Wales Northern Heritage Centre. It reminded her of learning to make similar ones from her mother. (Photo credit: Laura Kelvin)

The Inuvialuit adults on the trip felt that putting the digitization in the hands of youth was important in giving these young people a sense of ownership over their past and in empowering them to contribute to the documentation and interpretation of their cultural heritage. Beverly Amos, a linguist at the Inuvialuit Cultural Resource Centre who participated in the trip, said to Lisa: "They should be doing your jobs one day". We could not agree more.

While some of the students were very enthusiastic about creating the models, the process did not hold the attention of others as much as we thought it might. Drawing on the strong tradition of storytelling in Inuvialuit culture, we asked students to select an artefact and write and illustrate a story about it (Fig. 7.5). They had already heard the Elders' stories about many of these objects. Now they imagined for themselves how these artefacts featured in the lives of their ancestors. All of the students were highly invested in this activity, and their stories are featured on our project website (http://www.ikaahukarchaeologyproject.com/pwnhc.html).

Haudenosaunee scholar Patricia Monture (2009: 92-93) writes: "such-and-such content is not the essential ingredient of a good Aboriginal education . . . . Building confidence and teaching to empowerment are more important ideals because they are the tools that allow us to confront Whiteness, oppression, and colonialism". We aspire to achieve these ideals by putting our research tools in the hands of Inuvialuit youth and having them contribute directly to project outputs. If, in the process, we can help to support or spark their interest in their past and help them develop the skills to pursue those interests into a career, we will have succeeded beyond our wildest dreams. We were both excited to see that 2 years after our PWNHC trip, a Facebook post by one of the youth participants read: "Dream job: actress or archaeologist". It gave us hope that one day she or another student in the future might make our work their own and take it in new directions.

Fig. 7.5 Inuvialuit students create artefact stories at Prince of Wales Northern Heritage Centre while Lisa looks on. (Photo credit: Beth Compton)

Caring, Context, and Reflexivity

Building caring relationships with community members is a pillar of community-based approaches, and prioritizing our relationships with people in Sachs Harbour is at the core of our heart-centred practice. Building trusting relationships has been both a challenge and a pleasure, has taken (and continues to take) time, and means that we are emotionally invested in this work. These relationships have shaped the path of the Ikaahuk Archaeology Project and our future research.

As educated, White women from the south, our life experiences are substantially different from those of people in Sachs Harbour, who cope daily with transgenerational trauma, the effects of residential schools,[2] poverty, and a system that provides inadequate health care and housing. A heart-centred practice has meant confronting these experiences and our own privilege, rather than regarding them as outside the scope of a "mind-centred" archaeology. We recognize the structural racism Inuvialuit face in their daily lives and the negative impact it can have on their own perceptions of their culture and heritage. We have had to reflect on how archaeology and academia have played a role in this racism through the mining and removal of material culture, whitewashing of Inuit history, and academic gatekeeping and by contributing to popular misconceptions about the Inuit (Steckley 2009).

Community members have sometimes questioned our motives. Someone once suggested that we were reaching out to the community only to get an archaeology permit and ensure we could meet our goals as archaeologists. This was partly true, as community approval is required for research permits and licences in the Northwest Territories. However, the caring relations to which we aspire align our interests with those of our community partners: "those who conscientiously care for others are not seeking primarily to further their own interests, their interests are intertwined with the persons they care for. … They seek … to preserve or promote an actual human relation between themselves and particular others. Persons in caring relations are acting for self and other together" (Held 2006: 12). Obtaining research permits was never our sole purpose in attempting to build relationships with the community. As a research team, we genuinely wanted to develop projects with the community that would be of interest and use to them. However, given the history of archaeological and other research on Banks Island, largely framed in Western terms with traditional academic outcomes and limited meaningful engagement with the community, we understand why this approach was met with scepticism. We also recognize that our relationships with community members could very easily be one-sided. In many ways, we need them a lot more than they need us, not just for approval of our

---

[2] Canada's residential school system, which began in the 1880s and continued in some areas until 1996, was a government-sponsored religious education programme designed to assimilate Indigenous youth into Euro-Canadian society. Operated by the State and Christian Churches, it removed Indigenous children from their home communities, forbid them from speaking their own languages, and promoted conversion to Christianity.

research or logistical support but for guidance navigating an unfamiliar place and friendship and emotional support while we are far from home.

We worked past this initial scepticism by returning to the community and show-ing our commitment to attentiveness and responsiveness by continually asking for and applying community input, sharing our research results, building social rela-tionships through volunteering and participating at community events, and visiting with community members, often over tea. Nonetheless, there were still times when community members were critical of project efforts, suggesting we use our research funding to address more pressing community issues, such as improving housing. Sometimes those comments have been made in anger and have been hurtful to us as individuals in the moment. We remind ourselves that they reflect deeper frustrations with systemic injustices. Given the many challenges facing the community, we have often contemplated and sometimes questioned the value of our archaeological research on Banks Island.

Heart Work

We set out to build relationships through community-based research because we care that archaeology has been used as a tool for a colonial system in the past. Caring about something is not the same as caring labour. Our relationships with community members, the caring labour that we do together, means that we care about this colonial history in a deeper, more personal way than if we did not have these connections. As outsiders, we can never fully understand Inuvialuit experi-ences of colonialism or the full weight of its impact on their community, but what Inuvialuit have shared with us about their experiences, and the much more that goes unsaid, drives us to keep doing archaeology in a good way, as determined by Inuvialuit. We feel a responsibility, given our own privilege, to support Sachs Harbour community members in whatever small ways we can, in regaining some aspects of their history that have been lost through colonial processes and in their rights to self-determination with respect to their cultural heritage. We are very con-scious that they have their own ways of working towards these ends and that we must be cautious to avoid repeating the paternalistic approaches that characterize so many relationships between White outsiders and Indigenous communities in the past.

We are encouraged that community members tell us that the work we are doing together is important. While we recognize that archaeology can only ever be a small piece in a large puzzle when it comes to healing, many community members have shared with us the intellectual, spiritual, and emotional value that archaeological research has, or could have, for them. The care we bring to our work means that our interests are intertwined with theirs, so hearing them express these feelings brings us joy. The value that they see in the work we are doing together makes it very per-sonally rewarding for us.

Many community members see greater knowledge of the past as part of moving beyond the impacts of the residential school system, and archaeology as one way of enhancing that knowledge, and regaining some of what has been lost. Doreen Carpenter explained to Laura:

> Yeah, there is a big gap from residential school to now. . . .[T]here was a big gap in-between where our parents [were] never taught. So there is like a whole generation of kids that don't know how to teach them and having this [research] helps. Having all of this information and stuff helps us teach our kids, I think, better. Like how things used to be done long ago.

Some community members also feel that there is a disconnect between Inuvialuit youth and Elders, which they see as detrimental because Inuvialuit knowledge is passed down through the generations through storytelling and shared activities. Elder Roger Kuptana was disappointed in what he saw as a lack of interest among community members in their history: "Well, I think what it is… these people should show a little more interest in what their ancestors did". Several community members talked about the potential of archaeology to bring youth and Elders together to explore their history, something they saw as valuable.

Things of the Heart

Many people in Sachs Harbour have talked to us about the importance of artefacts as embodiments of the traditional knowledge and skills of their ancestors. They view them as touchstones that link the past with their own personal histories (see also Lyons (2013) for a rich discussion of these connections). These deep emotional connections make them things of the heart. In the following exchange during an interview with Laura about the value of archaeological research in their community, Lawrence Amos is initially unsure about its relevance for him, until his wife Beverly talks about the emotional connection it makes her feel to her ancestors:

> **Lawrence:** Yeah, I don't know how it is going to benefit me, like you know, how is it going to benefit our people? The work, sure I know it is interesting stuff.
> **Beverly**: It doesn't make you feel good inside? I'm not talking about other kind of benefits, but right here (points to heart).
> **Lawrence:** Yeah. That's, well that's the best part.
> **Beverly**: That's one of the only main parts, eh. Make you appreciate how, what they went through and how strong they are, so you would be more thankful.

Most community members feel that artefacts connect them to their ancestors or that the artefacts embody the spirits of their ancestors. Traditional Inuvialuit teachings therefore require that people avoid disturbing artefacts, particularly those associated with graves, as Bridget Wolki explained to Laura:

> You know the energy of the people before go into their worldly possessions. But, yeah, it was a big taboo for us. Touching or taking any of that stuff… . Everybody has their own opinion on everything so I can't speak for everybody but I can speak for my family and say we weren't allowed to touch because of bad juju would be on you, bad luck. It would bring bad weather…

These teachings led us to move away from excavation in our own work, though there are some community members who see value in it, particularly in the face of accelerated coastal erosion as a result of climate change. Because of these teachings, community members worry about what happens to artefacts after they are excavated, which was the major impetus behind our community visit to Prince of Wales Northern Heritage Centre (PWNHC). Trip participants felt the trip was important so that they could reconnect with the artefacts and see that they are well cared for. At PWNHC, Beverly Amos talked to Laura about seeing artefacts from Banks Island: "And that's a really special part. I felt like I belonged to something. It was like a part of my people, yeah, my ancestors. So that was really special".

Applying the Lessons We Have Learned

The Inuvialuit we work with, who recognize and celebrate the importance of Elders sharing their knowledge, remind us of our obligation to share what we have learned, through our relationships with them, with our broader academic communities. Over the course of the Ikaahuk Archaeology Project, Sachs Harbour community members have emphasized the importance of involving Elders and other community members in the interpretation of archaeological artefacts and sites, providing opportunities for intergenerational knowledge exchange and disseminating the results of archaeological research to communities in ways that are accessible and meaningful to them.

We are both incorporating these lessons in our current work. Moving forwards, Lisa has joined forces with a team of other researchers and Inuvialuit to pursue these ends through Phase 2 of the Inuvialuit Living History project (Hennessy et al. 2013, Lyons et al. 2012). This project is a collaboration between Inuvialuit Elders and knowledge holders, archaeologists, anthropologists, digital media specialists, and museum professionals to examine how we can most appropriately and effectively create, document, and disseminate multiple forms of knowledge about Inuvialuit history and heritage in the digital realm. The first phase of the project focussed on making the MacFarlane collection, a group of Inuvialuit ethnographic objects from the Smithsonian Institution in Washington, more accessible to Inuvialuit and other interested audiences online through the Inuvialuit Living History website (www.inuvialuitlivinghistory.com). This new phase will involve adding new collections and content to the site and reworking its aesthetics and layout to more effectively reflect and represent an Inuvialuit worldview. We recently hosted a large community gathering where Elders and knowledge holders told stories and taught youth to make traditional tools and stencil prints and shared their knowledge of Inuvialuit artefacts brought to the gathering from southern repositories. We also held a land-based culture camp where Elders and youth engaged in traditional activities, visited cultural sites, and youth documented their experiences through a range of digital media.

Laura is now conducting postdoctoral research as a contributor to the Tradition and Transition partnership between Memorial University of Newfoundland and the Nunatsiavut Government. Her project, the Agvituk Archaeology Digital Archive Project, explores best practices for knowledge sharing through the development of a digital archive containing archaeological knowledge and traditional knowledge of the archaeological site Agvituk, located within the present boundaries of the largely Inuit community of Hopedale, Nunatsiavut. One aim of this research is to lessen the community-perceived gap between youth and Elders by working with youth to interview Elders and community knowledge holders about the past and archaeology. Nunatsiavummiut youth are facing multiple challenges not limited to transgenerational trauma, food insecurity, poverty, isolation, and inadequate access to mental health care and housing. These challenges have resulted in a suicide rate in Nunatsiavut that is more than 20 times the national average. Northerners often cite greater knowledge of heritage and participation in culture as one of many ways to work towards combating these challenges (Inuit Tapiriit Kaanatami 2016; Lys 2018). The project team hopes that through strengthening relationships between Elders and youth, and supporting youth interest in their culture and heritage, archaeology can be used as a tool to promote healing.

For us, a heart-centred archaeological practice is a work in progress. It involves putting our relationships with community members at the centre of what we do and working with them towards common goals. It means being attuned and responsive to their changing needs. In the spirit of Rose (1983), this practice is about bringing the hand and heart to our "brain" work through a focus on *doing*, engaging with artefacts and collectively participating in traditional and nontraditional activities, and *caring*, tending the relationships that make that work possible. Bringing together our intellectual and emotional selves in this way calls us to action and points us to other places where we need to promote change as we rethink our working lives and try to better align them with our personal values.

Bringing a Heart-Centred Practice to Academia and Beyond

In terms of Rose's (1983) *hand*, we focussed earlier on learning through doing with Inuvialuit community members, but she also meant doing in the sense of activism and working for change. A heart-centred practice demands that we work for structural change within academia, so that it assigns greater value to all of the caring work we do in our research, teaching, and service. We need to help reshape our institutions so that they value and reward us for supporting and nurturing our community research partners, our students, and each other (see also Lyons and Supernant and Surface-Evans this volume). Academic structures have long valued research over other scholarly endeavours, prioritizing a Western rational approach to research over a more holistic one inspired by Indigenous ways of knowing and feminist approaches. They measure success (also framed as "impact") in terms of the number and quality (based on publication venue) of peer-reviewed publications. These standards influence tenure, promotion, pay, and funding success (Kasten 1984, Fairweather 2005) and devalue nontraditional outputs such as websites and videos that are often produced through community research. When Lisa started at Western, she was told by several of her senior colleagues to focus on publication over other aspects of her work and advised to put a minimum of effort into teaching, to free up more writing time. She felt very vulnerable during her pre-tenure years because of the time she was investing in building relationships in Sachs Harbour. As Monture (2009: 95) notes about researchers working with Indigenous communities:

> someone who offends Aboriginal communities, a concern often shared with me and I assume other Indigenous faculty, proceeds through the [tenure] process unchallenged. Yet someone, Indigenous or White, who works very hard at maintaining their relationships and understands those relationships as foundational for accumulation of their knowledge and expertise in the 'field' does work that earns them no university credit but is very time consuming. The result is to make invisible the work that is most important to Indigenous people and communities. And this will impact on the number of scholarly papers that an individual can produce.

In recent years, there have been some positive changes in the way funding bodies and universities evaluate scholarly merit. Many major research funding programs, emphasizing the importance of Indigenous research and knowledge mobilization to communities (e.g. SSHRC 2015, 2017) and many institutional processes for tenure and promotion, now consider nontraditional research outputs such as digital and social media contributions in their criteria (O'Meara et al. 2015). Tensions between these newly reframed expectations and highly entrenched, long-standing measures of impact can disadvantage researchers taking a holistic, caring approach since decisions are often strongly influenced by the assessments of individual reviewers, who interpret evaluation criteria differently. Lisa's recent experiences on university-wide and national multidisciplinary funding committees suggest that research impact is often still evaluated primarily based on traditional publication counts. One way to work towards structural change would be for heart-centred scholars with university appointments to advocate for the review of tenure and promotion processes within our own universities. This work will obviously fall to those of us privileged enough to have such appointments. Reframing these policies at the university level could go a long way towards educating our colleagues with a more mind-centred practice about the values and "hidden" caring work involved in community-engaged scholarship, potentially influencing their work as reviewers in other contexts. Evaluating the impact of such work is a tricky and fraught exercise, but the same is true for peer-reviewed publications (O'Meara et al. 2015). Appropriate measures of impact could be broadened to include things like reference letters from community members (Monture 2009) and the number and length of collaborative relationships.

We can also play the long game in terms of working towards change. A caring approach to teaching means prioritizing our relationships with students and teaching about the context within which archaeology operates (see also Supernant and Lyons and Surface-Evans this volume). Nurturing them to succeed in the discipline means sharing our own experiences and explicitly talking about the structures of power that shape its reward system. Lisa does this, for example, in her graduate professional development class in the section on grant writing. Sharing her experiences of the tenure process and of serving on grant committees in this class often leads to lively discussions about the kinds of research that are disadvantaged by these structures and how those structures need to change. One day, our students (like Laura!) will join the professorial ranks and be in a position to help us change our disciplinary culture. Investing in our students in this way has its own emotional rewards. Having Lisa invest the care and emotional support she did into her mentorship, Laura was able to become more confident and pursue a career she otherwise would have shied away from. For Lisa, it has been a great pleasure to watch Laura's development from a reserved undergraduate to the valued colleague and friend that she is today.

Having more Indigenous students and colleagues in the university system will also help to change it, since holism and care – for each other, for other living things, and for the land – are central to Indigenous ways of thinking and being (Cajete 2015). By working closely with Indigenous youth in our research, helping them gain practical experience and feel confident in their abilities, we can encourage them to pursue higher education. This is something we are both trying to achieve in our current work.

The care that links us with Inuvialuit community members and links them to their ancestors through their ancestors' things also calls us to turn our hands to make change to the heritage legislation that governs those objects. In most jurisdictions, including the Northwest Territories, heritage legislation is built upon Western archaeological and curatorial understandings of objects. It frames them as having value in and of themselves and prioritizes "rational" over "emotional" engagements with them. It also tends to prioritize access by "heritage professionals" over access by descendant communities. For example, our archaeological fieldwork on Banks Island required a Northwest Territories archaeological permit. The permitting process requires that all permit requests are sent to the Community Corporation and the Hunters and Trappers Committee in the community closest to the proposed work. Communities can thus control archaeological fieldwork on their traditional territories, since a permit will be denied of the community does not approve. However, if communities do not respond within 30 days, the permit is issued without community comment, so the balance of power lies with archaeologists. Moreover, the legislation stipulates that all excavated artefacts from sites in the Northwest Territories are housed at the Prince of Wales Northern Heritage Centre in Yellowknife. While community members are always welcome to visit them there, few know who to contact to gain access, and doing so requires the journey to Yellowknife. There is also no formal process to involve communities in decisions about access to archaeological collections from their traditional territories after they are excavated. Once an excavation permit is approved, communities lose all formal control of their artefacts. In practice, the Heritage Centre staff often seek community input on such matters, but community authority is not entrenched in legislation. The Inuvialuit we work with value artefacts as objects of the heart and not just of the mind – they have a profound connection with these things. As so-called experts, we need to voice our support for legislation that privileges this special relationship over any "scientific" or "curatorial" claims on those objects. Our commitment to care means that we owe this to the Inuvialuit we work with – it is one way that we can tend the flame of our relationship with them.

Heart-centred practice, then, can turn archaeologists into activists. In our case, it makes our work as much about social justice in the present as about reconstructing the past. It demands that we work to shift the values and priorities of our own discipline and academia more broadly so that they do not work counter to the aims of integrating the hand, brain, and heart. As participants in these peer-reviewed processes, we have the power to change them. Caring labour also demands that we use our expertise and our positions of privilege to help rebalance the unequal colonial power relationships within our discipline and in the policies and legislation that govern our work. It broadens our definition of what constitutes archaeology so that it is not solely about studying the past through material remains but exploring the ongoing connections between the past and present through lived experience. Because it is grounded in open, respectful relationships with the Indigenous northerners whose heritage we study, and because they value the work we do together, we find this work far more personally fulfilling than a more traditional mind-centred approach, which lacks these reciprocal connections with others. We find ourselves putting our skills to work for our Inuvialuit and Inuit partners and learning from them. We are also continually learning from each other. This act of giving and receiving, which integrates our bodies, minds and hearts, feeds our spirits and renews our commitment to our work.

Acknowledgements We are grateful to everyone in Sachs Harbour who shared with us their perspectives, knowledge, time, and friendship. Thank you to the Sachs Harbour Hunters and Trappers Committee, Sachs Harbour Community Corporation, Sachs Harbour Recreation Centre, Parks Canada, and Prince of Wales Northern Heritage Centre for supporting our work. We also thank the Social Sciences and Humanities Research Council of Canada, the Polar Continental Shelf Program, the Northern Scientific Training Committee, and the Aurora Research Institute for funding. Lisa is grateful to the Inuvialuit Living History team for the work already done and the work to come. Our thanks to Kisha and Natasha for organizing the wonderful SAA session in Vancouver, to Sonya for her thoughtful comments as discussant, and the Heart Collective (Kisha, Natasha, Sonya, and Jane) for steering this volume through the editorial process.

References

Archibald, J. (2008). *Indigenous storywork: Educating the heart, mind, body, and spirit.* Vancouver: UBC Press.

Atalay, S. (2012). *Community archaeology: Archaeology with, by and for indigenous and local communities.* Berkeley: University of California Press.

Cajete, G. (2000). *Native science: Natural laws of interdependence.* Santa Fe: Clear Light Publishers.

Cajete, G. (2015). *Indigenous community: Rekindling the teachings of the seventh fire.* St. Paul: Living Justice Press.

Fairweather, J. S. (2005). Beyond the rhetoric: Trends in the relative values of teaching and research in faculty salaries. *The Journal of Higher Education, 76*(4), 401–442.

Government of Canada. (2017). *Canada research chairs: Program statistics.* http://www.chairs-chaires.gc.ca/about_us-a_notre_sujet/statistics-statistiques-eng.aspx. Accessed 15 Oct 2017.

Haraway, D. (1988). Situated knowledges: The science question in feminism and the privilege of partial perspective. *Feminist Studies, 14*(3), 575–599. https://doi.org/10.2307/3178066.

Harding, S. G. (1986). *The science question in feminism.* Ithaca: Cornell University Press.

Held, V. (2006). *The ethics of care: Personal, political and global.* Oxford: Oxford University Press.

Hennessy, K., Lyons, N., Joe, M., Loring, S., & Arnold, C. (2013). The Inuvialuit living history project: Digital return as the forging of relationships between institutions, people, and data. *Museum Anthropology Review, 7*(1–2), 44–73.

Inuit Tapiriit Kanatami. (2016). *National Inuit suicide prevention strategy.* https://www.itk.ca/wp-content/uploads/2016/07/ITK-National-Inuit-Suicide-Prevention-Strategy-2016-English.pdf. Accessed 25 Apr 2018.

Kasten, K. L. (1984). Tenure and merit pay as rewards for research, teaching and service at a research university. *Journal of Higher Education, 55*(4), 500–514.

Keller, E. F. (1985). *Reflections on gender and science.* New Haven: Yale University Press.

Kelvin, L. E. (2011). *The Inuit-Metis of Sandwich Bay: Oral histories and archaeology.* Unpublished MA Thesis, Department of Archaeology, Memorial University.

Kelvin, L. E. (2016). *There is more than one way to do something right: Applying community-based approaches to an archaeology of Banks Island, NWT.* Electronic Thesis and Dissertation Repository, 4168. https://ir.lib.uwo.ca/etd/4168

Kennedy, J. C. (Ed.). (2014). *History and renewal of Labrador's Inuit-Métis.* St. John's: ISER Books.

Longino, H. E. (1990). *Science as social knowledge: Values and objectivity in scientific inquiry.* Princeton: Princeton University Press.

Lyons, N. (2013). *Where the wind blows us: Practicing critical community archaeology in the Canadian North.* Tucson: University of Arizona Press.

Lyons, N., Hennessy, K., Joe, M., Arnold, C., Elias, A., Loring, S., & Pokiak, J. (2012). The Inuvialuit living history project. *The SAA Archaeological Record, 12*(4), 39–42.

Lys, C. (2018). Exploring coping strategies and mental health support systems among female youth in Northwest Territories using body mapping. *International Journal of Circumpolar Health, 77*(1). https://doi.org/10.1080/22423982.2018.1466604.

Monture, P. (2009). Doing academia differently': Confronting 'whiteness' in the university. In F. Henryand & C. Tator (Eds.), *Confronting racism in the Canadian university: Demanding social justice, inclusion, and equity* (pp. 76–105). Toronto: University of Toronto Press.

Nicholas, G. P., & Andrews, T. D. (1997). Indigenous archaeology in the modern world. In G. P. Nicholas & T. D. Andrews (Eds.), *Archaeology at a crossroads: Archaeology and First Peoples in Canada* (pp. 1–18). Burnaby: Archaeology Press.

O'Meara, K., Eatman, T., Petersen, S. (2015). Advancing engaged scholarship in tenure and promotion: A roadmap and call for reform. *Liberal Education, 101*(3). https://www.aacu.org/liberaleducation/2015/summer/o%27meara

Park, S. M. (1996). Research, teaching and service: Why shouldn't women's work count? *Journal of Higher Education, 67*(1), 46–84.

Rose, H. (1983). Hand, brain and heart: A feminist epistemology for the natural sciences. *Signs: Journal of Women in Culture and Society, 9*(1), 73–90.

Social Sciences and Humanities Research Council of Canada (SSHRC). (2015). *Community engagement.* http://www.sshrc-crsh.gc.ca/society-societe/community-communite/index-eng.aspx?pedisable=true. Accessed 20 Oct 2017.

Social Sciences and Humanities Research Council of Canada (SSHRC). (2017). *Aboriginal research.* http://www.sshrc-crsh.gc.ca/society-societe/community-communite/aboriginal_research-recherche_autochtone/index-eng.aspx. Accessed 20 Oct 2017.

Steckley, J. L. (2009). *White lies about the Inuit.* Toronto: University of Toronto Press.

Chapter 8
Digging for Heart

A Meditation on Connections Between Archaeology, True Nature of the Self, and Heart-Centered Practice

Jami Macarty

To the extent there is a central argument in this chapter, it is that all archaeology can be as much about the discovery of the true nature of the self as it is about the discovery of ancient and material worlds.

Background: I am a poet, editor, yogi, a teacher of poetry and yoga, and a one-season trench facer at two archaeological sites in Tucson, Arizona.

Foreground: When I was first invited by my partner John Welch (see Chap. 2, this volume) to offer a meditation practice to archaeologists in the Archaeology of the Heart session at the 2017 Society for America Archaeology meeting, intuition guided me instantly to the classical Tibetan meditation practice *Tonglen*, outlined in *The Tibetan Book of Living and Dying* by Sogyal Rinpoche. From the Tibetan, meaning "giving and receiving" (or "sending and taking"), *Tonglen* is an ancient practice that awakens compassion and introduces us to a more expansive view of reality. In the *Tonglen* practice, we visualize "taking in" with the in breath and "sending out" with the out breath. What we "take in" (e.g. self-hate, pain of a friend or stranger, etc.) and "send out" (self-love, relief for friend or stranger, etc.) varies in accord with our intentions in each practice. The great intention of *Tonglen*, however, is to reverse our natural inclination to avoid suffering and seek pleasure. The process of "giving and receiving" liberates us from habits of avoidance and patterns of selfishness. As a result, we begin to feel love for both ourselves and others, to take care of ourselves and others, and to connect with the open dimension of the heart of reality and our true nature. From my way of thinking, a *Tonglen* practice mirrors the

J. Macarty (✉)
Simon Fraser University (Creative Writing Program) & Integrative Restoration Institute, Burnaby, BC, Canada

© Springer Nature Switzerland AG 2020   117
K. Supernant et al. (eds.), *Archaeologies of the Heart*,
https://doi.org/10.1007/978-3-030-36350-5_8

desired reciprocity among archaeologists and their colleagues, partners, and collaborators within the theory of heart-centered archaeology.

Archaeology, a study of peoples and materialities, and archaeologists, its trained practitioners, are accustomed to looking to the external world for direction and data. Archaeologists origins and participation in academe, where intellect, individuality, and disputation are celebrated, perpetuates and even habituates one-way looking—outward to the external world, to what may be received and taken. Of course, academics aren't the only ones inculcated and pressured to look outside of themselves for the meaning of life and value of their work and themselves; many of us are addicted to looking to colleagues and society for validation. According to Buddhist teachings, when we focus outside ourselves, we naturally identify with our outgoing, egoic consciousness. When we're identified with our egoic consciousness, we tend to look at the people and world around us as separate, as something that we need to attract or to avoid. It follows that if we wish to attract or avoid something, then we must view ourselves as not having or being enough already. But, what if we're already whole and one with all? What if it's our forgetfulness of our wholeness that leads our actions to become conquering and mining and consuming, our interactions to become intolerant and antagonistic? In other words, our focus on, avoidance of, grasping for, and identification with the world outside ourselves is what further obscures our inner being, our true nature.

So, all we have to do is remember our true nature, and from that ground of inner being, treat ourselves and others with tolerance and friendship. Sounds simple enough, right? That's what Buddha said, that it is "simple." Then, why do many of us lose touch with our inner being, think we're limited, act in ways that reveal our lack of self-love and self-respect, and delude ourselves about our true nature? In a word: fear. We're scared to look into our true nature. Why? Fear. It's scary to fathom the depth of our true nature. We're scared of what we may find. Fear. It's what stops us from investigating our inner being and, in turn, what keeps us identified with our outgoing, egoic consciousness.

Consider the book *What Would Buddha Do?*; in it, author Franz Metcalf applies the example of Buddha and his teachings to the problems we deal with in our everyday lives. Here, I offer my equivalent coinage: *What would an archaeologist do?* Is fear how an archaeologist approaches an archaeological site? That's not what I witnessed from the archaeologists I stood beside while looking down at a floor feature in a four by four. My experience and sensibilities suggest instead that curiosity and excitement are more fundamental motivators in and to processes of archaeological discovery. In my knowledge and imagination, archaeologists dig away from fear and toward discovery and realization, especially related to communion among groups of people, their environs, their neighbors, and their social and spiritual institutions.

So, what keeps so many of us, generally, and archaeologists more specifically, from digging toward our hearts, from conceiving our true nature? Why does it seem outlandish and improbable for empirical scientists to balance external and internal inquiry? Archaeologists, who examine how artifacts and sites arrayed in space and time speak to aspects of history, ecology, society, and humanity, seem ideally positioned to explore such questions. Why's that? Well, in Buddhism, it is said that the "local" (e.g. artifacts, features, proximal interrelations) points to, contextualizes, and connects to the "global" (e.g. ancient village sites, regional settlement systems, and perspectives accessible through archaeology's associated sciences). You see? Archaeologists are already attuned to connections between the "local" and the "global." My partner says it can be called "multiscale awareness." Cool! In Buddhism, it's called omni-dimensional awareness. The real question, it seems to me, is: what can transpire when archaeologists transfer and apply that skill to heart-centered practice (i.e. through meditation or other means)? It follows that if an individual archaeologist is practiced in connecting to her own (local) heart—the doorway to her true nature—she has the ability to connect to the global heart, the Great Heart. An archaeologist more connected to the true nature of herself will therefore be more connected to other and to the All. What potentials for self, other, and global awareness lie just below the surface?

I say, "Dig On!"

This chapter is your invitation to build your relationship, dear archaeologist, with yourself, to look in the direction of yourself. Welcome to the doorway of your heart!

Now to the how of it. Transferring the personal strengths of curiosity and excitement and the ability to perceive the global in the local will oblige and require you to look in a different direction. That is, to shift your practice of outward looking to its opposite: inward-looking.

The outward, the inward—everyday life and meditative practice—these are not two separate worlds divided by some precipitous chasm or requiring a dichotomous choice; no, these worlds inspire one another. Our true nature (aka Buddha Nature) can be compared to the nature of the sky. Whether the sky is overcast or not, whether we can see the sky or not, the sky is always there. Clouds are not the sky, just as our thoughts and emotions, attractions and aversions are not us or our true nature. Indeed, I am the sky. You are the sky. Everything else is just the weather. To write of our true nature as sky-like is, of course, only a metaphor. Buddhist teachings use metaphor to help practitioners imagine the boundlessness of their true nature, just as the editors of this volume use metaphor in their introduction to share with us the expansive, wholistic vision of and for a heart-centered archaeology.

The heart is a site unseen; archaeology is comprised of sites unseen. Our relationships to our own hearts and the hearts of others are based largely on a yearning to discover combined with an ability to conceptualize and imagine. Archaeological exploration, too, is based in discovery, conceptualization, and imagination. And, both the exploration of the heart and archaeological exploration are based on some level of trust and acceptance of mystery. To shift one's attitude toward the heart-centered requires courage, discipline, and a tolerance for subtlety. By definition, there is not and cannot be a practice more rigorous than the exploration of the true nature of self.

Meditation, the emphatically heart-centered, inward-looking practice still in the process of perfection after 5000 years teaches us how to bring a profound and pragmatic state of awareness into action within our lives. That's the whole point and purpose of meditation—to integrate awareness into every aspect and level of our lives. Through the practice—daily, small, moment-to-moment doses—of inward-looking, touching into our hearts, and the heart of reality, we may experience a deep sense of nourishment and compassion, a connection to our true nature, and to the source of life itself, the Great Heart. So, our capacity to touch into our own hearts, to be aware, and to be conscious, is an entrance point into the Great Heart.

As we turn our eyes inward and tune to our hearts, we actually become open to the ever-present love, the awareness, the pure being that surrounds us and underlies our life. The energy discovered there is both your true self, and paradoxically, it's also a protecting, enfolding energy that contains our body and even the universe itself.

***

To a *Tonglen* practice! What follows is a script of my adaptation of a *Tonglen* practice, inspired by my teachers Pema Chödrön and Sally Kempton. With written scripts, it's customary to read through the entire practice first. Afterward, you may like to record the script in your or a friend's voice. Then, listen to the practice.

Let's take a small dose! Come to your posture. Put down anything you're holding. Uncross your legs, ankles, and arms. Sit in a comfortable upright posture.

With the inhalation allow your buttocks to sink into your seat… With the exhalation feel the spinal column growing upward from that grounded base…

Have the intention to stay present with your heart.

Your attention is with the breath. You're aware of the natural movement of your breathing. You're aware of the chest wall, so that the breath feels as though it's flowing directly into the heart, drawing your attention with it.

As the breath flows in, let its gentle touch caress the outer dimensions of the heart—top of the heart… bottom the heart… left side of the heart… right side of the heart… front of the heart… back of the heart…

Deep into the body behind the breast bone, the breath entering and caressing the heart… flowing out, the exhalation, expanding the heart space in all directions…

Your focus is very soft as the breath opens the heart space. Each inhalation deepening your sense of contact, of being with the energy in the heart. Each exhalation opening and expanding the inner heart.

As thoughts arise, let them flow past you the way clouds flow through the sky.

Flowing out, the exhalation, expanding the heart space in all directions…

Breathe in for all of us and breathe out for all of us.

***

I offer this practice, as my teachers, their teachers, their teachers' teachers, their teachers' teachers' teachers have for thousands of years, asking that this meditation be of benefit to all beings and Earth.

Namaste. From my heart, I bow to you and honor the light of awareness within you.

References

Barks, C., & Green, M. (1997). *The illuminated Rumi*. New York, NY: Broadway Books.

Metcalf, F. (2002). *What would Buddha do?: 101 answers to life's daily dilemmas*. Berkeley, CA: Ulysses Press.

Rinpoche, S. (1993). *The Tibetan book of living and dying*. New York, NY: HarperCollins.

Taylor, K. (1995). *The ethics of caring: Honoring the web of life in our professional healing relationships*. Santa Cruz, CA: Hanford Mead.

Part II
Heart-Centered Encounters with the Archaeological Record

How can archaeologists draw on a heart-centered framework in their explorations and analyses of objects and material culture? The chapters in this section explore how the materiality of the past, whether through children's gravestones or a discarded wedding dress, can evoke a variety of emotions in practitioners.

Jane Baxter, whose own academic story is woven through her analysis, shares her experiences of studying childhood in the past and how our understanding of childhood within our present cultural context creates specific emotional engagements with the subject of study. Gravestones evoke a sense of loss, grief, and disruption to the expected and hoped for outcome. Objects of our own childhood create feelings of nostalgia, even as those objects become obsolete. Baxter argues that developing an archaeology of emotion, particularly one focused on love, is essential to how we connect with people in the past, for emotion is a shared human experience.

Anthony P. Graesch, Corbin Maynard, and Avery Thomas also explore the complex emotionality of archaeological engagement with material objects. They examine concentrations of urban illegal discard sites that demonstrate a tension between lawful and unlawful discard practices, which often take place in liminal or hidden spaces. Tracing a thread from the apprehension of being "caught" while studying these sites to the intimacies of a life represented in a discarded wedding dress and jacket that fit one of the researchers, Graesch and his undergraduate colleagues discuss how the detachment of the subject/object divide was blurred due to the closeness of the practitioners to the objects of study and to the individual people whose lives were represented in these discarded, yet deeply intimate, material objects.

Several chapters in this section draw on examples from archaeology of the deeper past to trace how the practitioner's context and situated knowledges can impact how we understand the archaeological record. Callum Abbott emphasizes a community of practice and situated learning approach to the study of lithics from Quadra Island, British Columbia, arguing that studying the act of making and using lithic objects, in addition to the specific characteristics of the objects themselves, connects us more deeply with ancient peoples. A heart-centered approach, which breaks down traditional binaries, allows for a different engagement with lithic technology through situated social practices of learning, doing, and making. Using a morphometric analysis of lithic debitage from archaeological sites, Abbott argues that the remarkable similarity between the assemblages from different parts of Quadra Island is a material outcome of the persistence of a community of practice over many generations.

Torill Christine Lindstrøm's chapter presents a method for interpreting emotions represented on faces represented on a Dionysiac Fresco in Pompeii, Italy. She argues that taking a semiotic approach to emotional representation allows for interpretation of the signs of either experienced or expected emotional responses. Using a tool for coding facial expression, the Facial Action Coding System, Lindstrøm categorizes the emotions in the visible faces from the fresco, arguing that the faces show a limited range, low intensity emotional expression, perhaps representing Roman ideals around composure and lack of overt emotionality.

Melanie Chang and April Nowell's chapter is a reflection on how archaeologists have conceptualized Neanderthals as either part of "us" or one of "them" throughout the history of the discipline. Whether researchers have considered Neanderthals as more or less human is dependent on the biases of the researcher and the time in which they worked. Chang and Nowell argue that Neanderthals used symbolic behavior, specifically personal ornamentation, in a way like genetically modern humans of the same time, demonstrating that they were, in fact, more like "us" than not.

Deciding whether Neanderthals were capable of symbolic behavior is not just a scientific question; it is an emotional one as well. Writing about a similar time, Leslie Van Gelder's chapter is an intimate exploration of finger flutings in painted Upper Paleolithic caves in Europe. The flutings can be connected, through analysis of hand size, to adults and children who would have been in these cave systems. Many of the paintings in these caves would have required at least two people, one to paint and one to hold the light. Van Gelder's analysis of the location of these finger flutings allows for a reconstruction of some of the activities of individuals: a parent lifting a child, two people helping each other on to a ledge, a young girl fluting with both hands as someone else holds a light for her, and a child running his or her fingers over a mammoth painting with two other companions. The intimate evidence of touch evokes emotional connections with people in the past.

Chapter 9
Emotional Practice and Emotional Archaeology

A Perspective from the Archaeology of Childhood

Jane Eva Baxter

Children Put Me in My Place(s): The Origins of an Emotional Journey

A heart-centered archaeology is one that allows us to connect our whole selves to our practice (Supernant and Lyons, Chap. 1, this volume), reminds us that "good" research does not have to be detached, and reinforces an idea recently asserted by Bader and Malhi (2019:1–2) that "personal connectedness can strengthen, not hold back (my) research." This is not the archaeology I was taught in school. I was trained in a strong tradition of materialist, scientific American archaeology during a period of post-processual critique, which in hindsight had many of the people teaching me doubling down on the "right way" to do and think about archaeology in light of these new theoretical ideas. I learned that the tangible, visible remains of people's behavior that comprised the material world could be decoupled from the cultural "epiphenomena" that resided in people's heads. This convenient dualism allowed archaeology to use scientific approaches to reveal the practices of daily life, struggle a bit with the social relationships that informed those practices, and largely discount the richly complicated intangible culture of human existence as unknowable or irrelevant to archaeological pursuits. I was also encouraged to keep my own "intangibles" away from my research as much as possible. There are still many archaeologists who see an interest in this latter aspect of human lives as "unnecessary fluff" or "empirically impossible," and the literature is filled with lingering cautionary tales admonishing archaeologists not to stray from the materialist traditions that have characterized American archaeology for generations (see Kus 2000).

When I chose the topic of children to be the focus of my dissertation research (Baxter 2000), it was met with considerable skepticism. Most of the scant literature,

J. E. Baxter (✉)
Department of Anthropology, DePaul University, Chicago, IL, USA
e-mail: jbaxter@depaul.edu

© Springer Nature Switzerland AG 2020
K. Supernant et al. (eds.), *Archaeologies of the Heart*,
https://doi.org/10.1007/978-3-030-36350-5_9

with the exception of a few pioneering works, was not filled with a sense of possibility and rather was infused with a message that discouraged archaeologists from studying children. The archaeological evidence for children simply wasn't there but even more pervasive was a sense that children weren't important enough to be deserving of archaeological study. Children weren't considered significant in the economic and social lives of their communities or as part of the cosmological and emotional worlds of those in the past, and this sensibility kept children virtually absent from archaeological inquiry for generations. My own work, while among the first studies of children, was a scientific, spatial, and statistical study designed simply to show children could be identified using archaeological methods (Baxter 2000, 2005). At the time it was important, but it didn't feel wholly satisfying.

My intellectual interest in children was paired with my own choice to be child-free. I never had a longing or desire to have children and always felt there were other things in my life I wasn't willing to compromise to do so. I have two adult stepchildren who I adore, but I am extremely happy I didn't have to raise them. The decision to not have children for a woman of my generation is a complicated one, as it is a choice that is still, albeit less so, highly stigmatized (Blackstone 2019). People's reactions often range from curiosity, to pity, to outright anger and contempt when I divulge I don't have children by choice; there is a strong popular sense in America that women are supposed to want children and something isn't quite right about you if you don't.

Contemporary American culture amplifies the importance of children in families where they are wanted including increasingly elaborate celebrations around conception, gender determination, birth, developmental milestones, and educational achievement, as well as the proliferation of ideal and essential material and experiential indulgences for children that are highly commoditized and broadcast steadily through advertising and social media. Unwanted pregnancies, the inability to conceive a child, or having a child that does not meet culturally prescribed cognitive, social, or physical milestones are couched in complex, emotional cultural discourses. The idea of collectively providing and caring for all children is a largely unrealized but often touted American ideal (Mintz 2004), and there is a dominant cultural sensibility about being fearful for children who may be harmed by dangerous adults, by peer pressure, by premature adulthood (particularly in terms of sex and violence), and by becoming too greedy and materialistic, or conversely, by not having enough (Baxter 2019a). There is a comfortable recognition that children are integral to the economic and social worlds of adults in contemporary America and that they have been so since the advent of capitalism (Jacobson 2008; Matthews 2010; Zelizer 1994).

Choices in my personal life have been amplified because of my intellectual and scholarly interests in childhood in the past. Both colleagues and those outside the field frequently ask me if having children of my own inspired my research interests on children. When I explain I am child-free and that my scholarly interest in children is exactly that, many people stop questioning. Others press on asking if I feel my studies of children in the past are a way of reconciling not having children in my own life. These aren't particularly welcome questions, but they also underscore the feminized nature of scholarship on children and an interesting paradox on how many archaeologists think and feel about children and childhood (Baxter 2015a).

My scholarly and personal relationships to children have given me a particular platform from which to view this paradox. On the one hand, scholars in many disciplines who study childhood in the past, including archaeology, have found themselves on the margins of their field because they have chosen a topic considered to be unimportant (Baxter et al. 2017). On the other hand, the culture that many of these scholars come from spends an exceptional amount of time, energy, money, and effort on children, and the same colleagues who think our work is unimportant are immersed this child-centric culture of the present. While it is obviously unrealistic to suggest all societies viewed, treated, and valued children as we do today, the lack of nuance in this past/present divide has always been striking, and I have always found it uncomfortable. This discomfort has produced change in how I think about and how I practice archaeology.

Many of the theoretical ideas that shaped my archaeological education have long been discarded but so too is treading this awkward divide about how we experience childhood in the present and how we think about children in the past. Much of the scholarship on the archaeology of childhood demonstrates adults investing in children, caring for children, and prioritizing children in their own culturally specific ways. I have come to see much of the archaeology of childhood as being the archaeology of love, of care, and of hope as people actively made choices that highlighted the importance of children in their families and communities in the moment and in their aspirations for the future. I also have transformed the way I think about myself as an archaeologist as I actively seek ways to redraw the lines in my research process that allow me to experience empathy and compassion for the humanity of my practice while maintaining an analytical rigor that is respectful of the evidence I encounter. Part of this process is giving the children I study in the past the same emotional space I am expected to give children in the present.

The Archaeology of Emotions

Navigating emotional spaces in archaeology is not new, but it also does not have a long history in the discipline (Fleisher and Norman 2016). An increasing number of archaeologists hold a desire to develop understandings of the past that focus on complex human actors while respecting the material record available for archaeological study, and emotion is providing one such avenue to do so. Fleisher and Norman (2016: 3) noted that archaeologists have tended to ascribe emotion to populations in the past in an ad hoc fashion, most particularly emotions of anxiety and stress when archaeologically visible environmental conditions or social circumstances, such as warfare, create significant disruption and change to normal patterns of living. A more systematic interest in the emotional lives of people in the past is emerging in both archaeology (Fleisher and Norman 2016; Tarlow 2012) and history (e.g., Plamper 2017; Rosenwein 2015) and is resulting in deeper theoretical and methodological considerations of how scholars can bridge the emotional divide between past and present without projecting contemporary emotional sensibilities into the past.

Perhaps unsurprisingly, much of the literature that addresses emotion in archaeology is tied to mortuary archaeology and how symbolic and ritual behavior around death reflects bereavement, sorrow, anger, and fear (e.g., Chesson 2016; Murphy 2011; Tarlow 1999). Bioarchaeology also has added to this movement by focusing on emotionally laden concepts such as care (e.g., Tilley 2015; Tilley and Schrenk 2017) and aspects of embodied human experiences such as sexuality and disability (e.g., Byrnes and Muller 2017, Geller 2017, Sievert and Brown 2016). Archaeological interests in emotion are often tied to broader conversations about the human experience and/or the need for archaeology to engage broadly with the intangible aspects of human experiences and how they articulate with the material world (Biagetti and Lugli 2016; Fleisher and Norman 2016; Harris and Sørensen 2010; Hublin 2009).

Archaeological concerns with emotion are also present in areas where archaeological scholarship about the past directly intersects with the present. Studies of looting, collecting, and the antiquities trade have explored the emotional ties that individuals have to objects from the past (e.g., Walker Tubb 2006) and the trauma associated with witnessing the destruction of shared cultural heritage as acts of war and terrorism (e.g., Kersel and Luke 2012). Archaeologists are also finding new ways of writing and presenting archaeology in academic and popular circles that directly address the emotional value of heritage and the past for those in the present (Lyons et al. 2018; Roussou et al. 2017).

Scholars engaging with emotion are integrating neuroscience and psychology into disciplinary interests to enable nuanced, situated understandings of emotion rather than being stifled by the binary debate between social constructivism and biological universalism (Plamper 2017; Tarlow 2012). All humans have emotional lives that are deeply rooted in biology, but humans also have the ability to choose how, when, where, and why to suppress (not to eliminate), to emphasize, and to express emotions as ways of communicating and connecting with the broader world. Contemporary scholarship is enmeshed in an understanding that emotions are at once biological and cultural and personal and shared (Niedenthal and Ric 2017).

Archaeological interests in emotion do not rest as much with the individual as they do with groups of people who shared emotional sensibilities. Theories that address individual relationships to emotion and those that equate emotional states, expressions, or forms to entire cultures are not as helpful as ideas about emotion that have scalar possibilities (Fleisher and Norman 2016:7–8). One such alternative is the work of Barbara Rosenwein (2006, 2015) who conducted research on societies in premodern Europe to develop the idea of emotional communities. Emotional communities are social communities that share, define, tolerate, and deplore particular emotional expressions. These communities are not equated to entire cultural groups but rather are communities that coexist in society and not necessarily in opposition. People may belong to multiple emotional communities simultaneously, and communities may wax and wane in dominance or prevalence over time. Rosenwein illustrates how emotional norms and modes of expression are fluid and are shaped by social and cultural environments. The concept of emotional communities also allows individuals to engage with multiple forms of shared expression and understandings of emotions as they move through different communities connected to different parts of their lives.

In their introduction to *The Archaeology of Anxiety*, Fleisher and Norman (2016:9–10) suggest aspects of the archaeological record where emotions may be more accessible than others. These include "evocative spaces," which through design, character, and/or use elicit emotional experiences of place. Another is ritual performance where actors are calling emotional states into consciousness as a part of a ritualized activity or event. These types of contexts are archaeologically accessible through the material record and can be tied to ideas of emotional communities who spent time in particular spaces and participated in certain ritual performances. Certainly, these do not have to be mortuary spaces or rituals, but here I'm going to specifically use mortuary studies of children in the nineteenth century as a way of integrating ideas of emotion into my archaeological study of children.

Studying the Death of Children in Nineteenth-Century America

One aspect of my work on the archaeology of childhood has been studying the commemorative practices for children in Chicago's rural garden cemeteries. I have focused my work on the earliest years of these institutions and the commemorations of individual children who predeceased the adults in their family (Baxter 2015b). I looked at how different communities in Chicago chose to commemorate children at a time of major population influx from the United States and abroad. The importance of children for establishing a family in a new place paired with high infant and childhood mortality was a challenge to families socially and economically. At the same time, the death of a child also afforded families an opportunity to stake their claim in a new city and often country as they literally and symbolically put family blood into the soil. During the course of this work, I focused my attention on the way children were treated as research subjects by different disciplines (Baxter 2013) and embarked on a small project to address how children were taught to think about death and dying in a period of high infant and child mortality (Baxter 2019b).

The rural garden cemeteries where I work are most certainly evocative spaces, as they were deliberately designed to impart many social and cosmological messages to visitors. These cemeteries emerged in England and America in the nineteenth century as a response to increasing urbanization and industrialization (see Tarlow 1999 for a discussion of these cemeteries in England). On the surface, the rationale for these cemeteries was one of hygiene. The movement of people into urban areas resulted in overcrowded city cemeteries and church graveyards that were located in congested city centers. The presence of the dead so close to the living was considered a contributor to the disease outbreaks that plagued urban populations. Rural garden cemeteries created separate spaces for the dead outside of city centers, generally located on rail lines to facilitate the movement of the deceased as well as for the transportation of mourners and visitors (French 1974).

The first such cemetery in the United States was Mount Auburn Cemetery (Fig. 9.1), and the formulaic, planned landscape initiated there was adapted to cities across America while retaining several key design features. These cemeteries were not only located outside of the city they served but were surrounded by walls and accessed through a single, gated entrance creating a sense visitors were stepping into a special, separate world. Inside were a series of prescribed pathways that twisted and turned taking visitors through carefully designed "natural" landscapes with hills, trees, lakes, and beautiful vistas, all designed to transport newly urbanized populations to a place where they could peacefully contemplate god and nature

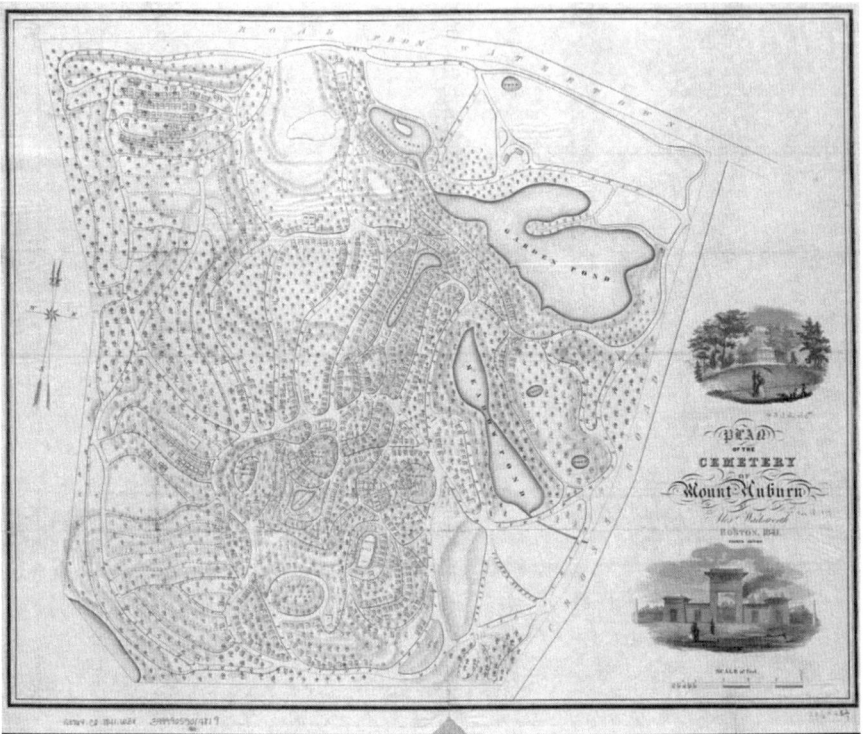

Fig. 9.1 Plan of the Cemetery of Mount Auburn by Alexander Wadsworth, 1841. Mount Auburn Cemetery is located outside Boston, Massachusetts, and was dedicated in 1831 as the first rural garden cemetery in the United States. This map illustrates the planned nature of the landscape including the exterior walls, the designed topography, the "natural" features, and the single gate leading to prescribed pathways for visitors. This formulaic landscape was the basis for rural garden cemeteries developed across the United States throughout the nineteenth century. (Image obtained through an open via Wikimedia Commons. Author and license information can be found via this link: https://commons.wikimedia.org/wiki/File:Plan_of_the_cemetery_of_Mount_Auburn_ (3720668892).jpg)

(Beder 1974). This landscape design masked the primary function of the landscape, as a place to house the dead, and emphasized its suitability for visitation by the living (Darnall 1983). Visitation, picnicking, promenading, and socializing in cemeteries became common practice (Baxter 2019b), and highly symbolic iconography and carefully chosen words and phrases on tombstones allowed people to read messages of sentiment, piety, civic duty, and bereavement as they spent leisure time in the cemetery. The rituals that produced the mortuary landscape were continued long after death through these continued rituals of visitation.

For the first time, it was possible to pre-purchase and design a family plot that would display the wealth and status of that family to visitors (Fenza 1989). The size of the plot and the number of generations it contained; the material, size, and style of the headstones; and the relative prominence of the plot location all became important features allowing visitors to read the landscape and understand the circumstances of the family in life. Ethnic communities, church congregations, wealthy elites, and working-class citizens could all determine their final neighborhood before they died, thereby replicating the social order for eternity. Transcending all other social factors, however, was an emphasis on family (Bohan 1988). As population movements and new economic modes disrupted traditional family life, the cemetery became a place where families would be reunited and where family continuity could be perpetually maintained.

Children became particularly potent symbols of home and family life during this time of upheaval and social change (Baxter 2015b, 2019a; Little et al. 1992:14), and their grave markers reflect this through designs conveying innocence, purity, and home (Snyder 1992) (Figs. 9.2 and 9.3). Messages expressed through headstone design were reinforced by children's epitaphs (Smith 1987) and consolation literature, which was a popular genre for parents at a time of high infant and child mortality (Baxter 2019b; Douglas 1975).

Rural garden cemeteries were a part of a larger movement designed to beautify and celebrate death in nineteenth-century America. Death was embraced as a part of living culture, and elaborate spaces, rituals, and language specifically to express emotions of loss and suffering when a loved one died were considered essential elements of mourning and commemoration. The "beautification of death" movement included the preservation and decoration of corpses to prolong a "lifelike" appearance, the photography of deceased family members in family portraits alongside the living, the performance of detailed rituals, and the elaboration of mortuary monuments that denied death through euphemisms of sleep, rest, and continuity with the living in images and epitaphs (Baxter 2013, 2015b, 2019b; LeeDecker 2009) (Figs. 9.2 and 9.3). Whether performative or heartfelt or both, nineteenth-century Americans placed emotions in very public spaces and contexts in the mourning process.

My time studying children in Chicago's cemeteries was a surprisingly and profoundly emotional experience for me as a researcher. My research involved solitary hikes up and down rows of graves over hundreds of acres seeking out the headstones and grave markers of infants and children and recording the details of each stone. The monuments carefully and deliberately designed to convey a family's loss and grief to cemetery visitors certainly had an effect on me, even if I was visiting

Fig. 9.2 The headstones of two children buried in Chicago's Oak Woods Cemetery. Often, older children were given more elaborate burials that emphasized the family's wealth, status, and ostensibly grief, and depicted the child as a beloved individual in the family whose loss was very particular. On the left is the memorial stone of India Kephart who died in 1882 at age 5. She's memorialized asleep with a pillow and blanket invoking a common euphemism for death and is resting in a scallop shell, which symbolizes her Christian journey through life and her baptism. India holds a doll in her arms, which symbolized home and family. On the right is the headstone for William "Willie" Omohundro, who died in 1887 at age 9. This expensive metal stone uses a budding rose to symbolize his young life and a nickname to convey endearment. The lament, "Oh What Hopes Lie Buried Here" illustrates parental investment in this child as the future of their family. (Photos courtesy of James E. Dourney)

150 years after the interment of a child. After collecting the data for this project, I couldn't go into a cemetery for several months because I found it too emotionally difficult – I was exhausted from encountering loss and grief. Sarah Tarlow (2000:20) addressed the emotional experience of conducting archaeological research in historic cemeteries when she said:

> When excavating a skeleton, many archaeologists experience some kind of emotional response such as fear, guilt, or reverence, but when confronted only with the biological fact of bones, grief is not a common response. However, conducting research in a graveyard presents one not only with the facts of a death, but with enough information to build a history, to become acquainted with something of the individual, their name, age, partner, parents, and children. Moreover, the existence of the monument itself, erected by a person or persons who experienced their loss is testimony to bereavement. It is hard to remain unaffected when one is confronted with the often explicit evidence of somebody else's sentiment.

These types of emotional responses today raise questions about the emotional communities that parents were a part of as they publicly mourned their children and erected monuments to convey appropriate sentiments of grief and loss to cemetery visitors.

Fig. 9.3 The headstones of two children buried at Crown Hill Cemetery in Indianapolis, Indiana. The same types of stones may be found in rural garden cemeteries across the United States. More simple stones such as these were used to commemorate younger children or children of less wealthy families, but they were no less sentimental. The most common image for children's headstones throughout the nineteenth and twentieth centuries is the lamb. The lamb here is for the son of M&A Borbecker, with a very simple epitaph expressing this 4-year-old place in the family. The memorial placed to commemorate 4-year-old Floyd on the right includes the simple phrase, "our darling," which concisely conveys a sense of family belonging and parental loss. (Photos courtesy of James E. Dourney)

Emotional Responses to the Death of Children

Parents constructing monuments for their children in nineteenth-century American cemeteries were doing so during a period of high infant and child mortality. The increasing concentration of populations in cities resulted in a concomitant increase in the death of children. In 1850, more than 1 in 4 children born did not live to see their first birthday. By 1900, that rate had declined to approximately 1 in 5, but 30% of deaths in America were still people under age 18 (Baxter 2019a, b). By comparison, less than 1% of American children die as infants today, and only 1.4% of recorded deaths is people under the age of 18. Addressing the emotions of nineteenth-century parents needs to account for these fundamental differences in life expectancies for children.

Parental investment in children, both emotional and material, at times of high infant and child mortality is a question that has been of interest to historians for quite some time. In his foundational work, *Centuries of Childhood*, Philippe Aries (1973) argued that parents in Medieval Europe were not emotionally invested in their children, did not offer them high levels of care, and saw childhood as something that was to be hastened rather than indulged. He argued that high infant and child mortality was the cause of these attitudes toward children and that children had to survive to a certain age before attaining a level of personhood and importance in families. This idea of equating high infant and child mortality with a lack of parental care and concern became a pervasive sensibility in historical studies more generally, particularly for other periods such as seventeenth-century America where children were not given toys and were dressed as miniature adults (Calvert 1992; Baxter 2019a). Many people still connect back to this early work and equate high infant and child mortality with a lack of parental investment, but subsequent scholarship has largely discredited this point of view.

More recent scholarship has critiqued this interpretation of parent-child relationships as a projection of modern ideals of parental love and care into the past, the use of selective data, and an absence of appropriate historical context (Catalano 2015). For example, medieval children were often described as being covered in dirt, which was interpreted a sign of neglect. Instead, the practice reflected a common belief that children would be protected against evil spirits and demons by the layering of earth on their skin (Catalano 2015). Dirty children weren't unloved or neglected; their parents were protecting them. Similarly, seventeenth-Century Puritan children were denied toys and dressed as miniature adults because adults considered the animalistic behaviors of babbling and crawling to be a danger to a child's mortal soul (Calvert 1992). Children were inchoate adults who needed to appear and act human as soon as possible, and parental efforts to hasten adulthood were acts of love and concern. An ample documentary record left by the Puritans illustrates just how much concern adults had for the young people who were to be their future (Chudacoff 2007).

Other scholars have presented evidence that high infant and child mortality actually increases parental anxiety over the death of children (Pollock 1983) and that parental emotions surrounding the deaths of children do not have to be elaborate expressions of grief to reflect genuine care and concern (Catalano 2015). Perhaps the most famous ethnographic study of parental emotion and the deaths of children is Nancy Scheper-Hughes' (1989) *Death Without Weeping*. Mothers in Brazil who were continuously birthing and losing children practiced a form of child neglect that hastened the deaths of children who were perceived to be too weak to survive. Their emotional community was one that sublimated grief and sadness at the loss of children as a way of coping with frequent child death. A careful reading of this work, however, does not indicate that these mothers were devoid of emotion. Rather than grief, more subtle expressions of care and pity were common, and other more overt and elaborated emotions were expressed elsewhere in their lives (Catalano 2015, and see Niedenthal and Ric 2017).

Parents in the nineteenth century had diverse responses to the birth and deaths of children that were largely affected by the economic and social circumstances of the family under a new capitalist system. The arrival of a child into a family required a reconfiguration of the household in terms of time and resources, and children were perhaps the most critical consideration in a family's household economy (Matthews 2010). Many mortuary monuments for children reflect this literal, material expenditure on the part of children and the loss of those investments in the future of the family (Fig. 9.2). Such sentiment about a loss of family investment and future are most often reserved for older children and in most extreme form are expressed through elaborate, highly individualized monuments.

The ability to invest in children in life and death was largely determined by the economic standing of the household. Alongside these elaborate monuments for children of more wealthy families were cultural practices such as baby farming that allowed parents to place children in the care of individuals who would neglect the child until they were dead (Behlmer 1982). This death by proxy alleviated the burden of caring for a child that could not be cared for and created a space between the parent and the act of infanticide. Other solutions such as orphanages and orphan trains allowed families to relinquish their responsibilities for children, often to institutions and other families whose care resulted in very poor outcomes for the children (Fass 2016). These practices are not indicative of a lack of parental concern or love but rather circumstances that made it impossible for parents to care for their children. Tokens left with orphans at London's Foundling Museum are one profound example of the emotional attachments parents had to the children they gave up to institutional care (The Foundling Museum 2019). These children were a part of the cumulative vital statistics of the day but would not have been afforded a commemorative marker in a local cemetery (Baxter 2015b).

Expressions of loss were not just related to material and social investment but also to sentiments of care and love. Sentimental attachment to children was a cultural sensibility that stood outside the capitalist system that structured much of family life and harkened back to a time of more traditional, ideal family values. The desire for and hope that any particular child would survive was very real even though mortality rates were high, and the death of a child was most often characterized as outside the "natural order" where parents predecease their children (Murphy 2011). In the nineteenth century, America was becoming increasingly secular, and while religious sentiments of God reclaiming a chosen innocent were not uncommon, invoking a child's place in the family was a way to make a very brief life meaningful and help make the loss more comprehensible (Baxter 2019b). Expressions of grief were tied to ideas of home and heaven but also to a child's place in the enduring institution of family life.

Grief itself was an important cultural construction in nineteenth-century America. Much like cemeteries offered a place of nature, god, and family that stood outside industrial, urban spaces, the development of an elaborate grieving process offered

Americans a way to change the rules of time. An elaborate and extended mourning culture coevolved with modernity as an effective state juxtaposed with progressive, mechanical time. Grieving allowed people to step out of the structured time of their daily lives and instead to create a temporal space aligned with a human dimension, one that was collective, repetitive, and reflective (Luciano 2009). The beautification of death movement created guidelines for families to engage in prolonged rituals of grieving that replicated ideas of time present in a pre-industrial world.

This culture of grieving took material form in the commemorative markers for children that are much more likely to convey the grief and loss of parents left to mourn rather than a concern for the child's fate after death (Smith 1987). While we know a gravestone may not represent "real" attitudes toward a deceased child and instead may reflect idealized and manipulated identities in a symbolic context, the most certain interpretation of a headstone is as an expression of attachment, loss, and grief (Haveman 1999:282, Tarlow 2000). Elaborate monuments and memorials (Fig. 9.2) are not unnecessary to express grief and loss as, with just a few words, mourners could convey parental investment in an infant or child. The presence of very small stones that simply say "baby" or "infant" has been identified as evidence for parental detachment but simultaneously illustrates a desire to express to the world that a short life happened and that the family saw that life as worth remembering (Haveman 1999; Rainville 1999: 572). At the same time, even a few words, like "little guy" or "our darling," efficiently illustrate attachment and sentiment on the part of parents and the importance of the individual in the family fold (Fig. 9.3).

The emotional communities' parents participated in when they lost a child in the nineteenth century were both a part of and in response to new social and economic worlds evolving at the time. Creating tangible and intangible spaces for expressions of grief, care, and love in the context of mourning and commemoration offered parents a way to express a sense of loss not only for a child but also for a way of life that had become lost to them. The ability to symbolically visit, connect, and reinforce the enduring continuity of family at a time when family life was being disrupted elevated the importance of children in commemorative culture. The need to make sense of a short life lost situated grief for children in the context of family where their loss represented both the real material, economic, and social care afforded to children in life and parental aspirations for their children and family in the future.

The Value of Engaging Emotions Past and Present in Archaeology

It is quite possible to conduct archaeological analyses of children and of cemeteries without a serious consideration of emotions. Headstones from the nineteenth century can be analyzed much like any mortuary assemblage encountered by archaeologists. Socioeconomic status of an individual or family can be interpreted based on the raw materials used, the quantity of that material, the amount of time and energy expended on creating the monument, and the positioning of a grave within the cemetery landscape, among other variables. Dimensions of identity can be discerned and analyzed for the cemetery population. Categorical identities such as ethnicity, gender, and age can all be interpreted using these monuments. More rare in archaeological interpretations generally are the insights into eschatological beliefs and civic values that readily can be gleaned from symbolism decoded using historical sources and inscriptions on the monuments themselves. None of these types of analyses are incorrect, or easy, or without value, but in many ways they are incomplete.

For those of use trained within the legacy of a scientific archaeology, a quest for certainty and objectivity limited the kinds of questions asked and the types of analyses considered valid, feasible, and possible in our field. Movement away from this type of archaeology has many causes, but I believe underlying many theoretical developments in the field is the ongoing realization by archaeologists that their archaeological interpretations in the past have only limited relationships to their own human experiences in the present. The desire to explore topics that amplify the humanity of archaeological subjects, the need to acknowledge and value non-archaeological ways of knowing the past, and the demand for alternative ways of communicating archaeological findings are all rooted in a dissatisfaction with an archaeology that denies the humanity of people in the past and therefore, in a way, our own too. The archaeology of emotions is one way of narrowing the gap between our own lived experiences and how we envision life in the past.

Tarlow (2012) has argued that it is important not to conflate rigorous attempts to study emotion in the past with the reflexive, emotional practice of archaeology in the present. I would agree with this distinction but also believe that if archaeology is to make the same "emotional turn" that many historians and scholars of the past are more widely embracing, archaeologists need to change how they practice archaeology. Connectedness to our own humanity, reflexivity toward our own emotional states, and an extension of human compassion that transcends time much as it transcends cultural divides in the present all make possible a different kind of archaeology where emotion is integral to the human experience past and present (e.g., Leone 2009).

References

Aries, P.. (1973). *Centuries of childhood: A social history of family life*. Translated by Robert Baldick. London: Hammondsworth.

Bader, A. C., & Malhi, R. S. (2019). How subjectivity strengthens research: Developing an integrative approach to investigating human diet on the Pacific Northwest Coast. *American Anthropologist Vital Topics Forum, 121*, 476. https://anthrosource.onlinelibrary.wiley.com/doi/10.1111/aman.13218.

Baxter, J.E. (2000). *An archaeology of childhood: Children and material culture in 19th Century America*. (PhD Dissertation). Department of Anthropology, University of Michigan, Ann Arbor.

Baxter, J. E. (2005). *The archaeology of childhood: Children, gender, and material culture.* Lanham: Alta Mira Press.

Baxter, J. E. (2013). Status, sentimentality, and structuration: An examination of "intellectual spaces" for children in the study of America's historic cemeteries. *Childhood in the Past, 6*(2), 106–122.

Baxter, J. E. (2015a). The archaeological study of children. Electronic Document, http://allegralaboratory.net/the-archaeological-study-of-children/

Baxter, J. E. (2015b). "Oh, What Hopes Lie Buried Here!:" Nineteenth century children's headstones in Chicago's garden cemeteries. In R. Kory (Ed.), *Lebenswelten von Kindern und Frauen in der Vormoderne: Archäologische und Anthropologische Forschungen in memoriam Brigtte Lohrke*. PaläowissenschaftlicheStudien Volume 4 (pp. 1–16). Berlin: Curach Bhan Publications.

Baxter, J. E. (2019a). *The archaeology of American childhood and adolescence.* Gainesville: University of Florida Press.

Baxter, J. E. (2019b). How to die a good death: Teaching children about mortality in Nineteenth Century America. *Childhood in the Past, 12*(1)., (online only now- pps. In May!).

Baxter, J. E., Vey, S., McGuire, E., Conway, S., & Blom, D. (2017). Interdisciplinarity in the study of childhood in the past. *Childhood in the Past, 10*(1), 57–71.

Beder, T. (1974). The 'rural' cemetery movement: Urban travail and the appeal of nature. *The New England Quarterly, 47*, 196–211.

Behlmer, G. (1982). *Child abuse and moral reform in England, 1870–1908.* Palo Alto: Stanford University Press.

Biagetti, S., & Lugli, F. (2016). *The intangible elements of culture in ethnoarchaeological research.* New York: Springer.

Blackstone, A. (2019). *Childfree by choice: The movement redefining family and creating a new sense of independence.* New York: Penguin/Random House.

Bohan, R. (1988). A home away from home: Bellefontaine Cemetery, St. Louis, and the rural cemetery movement. *Prospects, 13*, 135–179.

Byrnes, J., & Muller, J. (2017). *Bioarchaeology of impairment and disability: Theoretical ethnohistorical and methodological perspectives.* New York: Springer.

Calvert, K. (1992). *Children in the house: The material culture of childhood in America 1600–1900.* Boston: Northeastern University Press.

Catalano, A. J. (2015). *A global history of child death: Mortality, burial, and parental attitudes.* New York: Peter Lang.

Chesson, M. (2016). Risky business: A life full of obligations to the dead and the living on the Early Bronze Age Southeastern Dead Sea Plain, Jordan. In J. Fleisher & N. Norman (Eds.), *The archaeology of anxiety: The materiality of anxiousness, worry, and fear* (pp. 41–66). New York: Springer.

Chudacoff, H. (2007). *Children at play: An American history.* New York: New York University Press.

Darnall, M. (1983). The American cemetery as picturesque landscape: The Bellefontaine Cemetery, St. Louis. *Winterthur Portfolio, 18*, 249–269.

Douglas, A. (1975). Heaven our home: Consolation literature in the northern United States, 1830–1880. In D. E. Stannard (Ed.), *Death in America* (pp. 49–68). Philadelphia: University of Pennsylvania Press.

Fass, P. (2016). *The end of American childhood: A history of parenting from life on the frontier to the managed child.* Princeton: Princeton University Press.

Fenza, P. J. (1989). Communities of the dead: Tombstones as a reflection of social organization. *Markers, 6*, 137–158.

Fleisher, J., & Norman, N. (2016). Archaeologies of anxiety: The materiality of anxiousness, worry, and fear. In J. Fleisher & N. Norman (Eds.), *Archaeologies of anxiety: The materiality of anxiousness, worry, and fear* (pp. 1–20). New York: Springer.

French, S. (1974). The cemetery as cultural institution: The establishment of Mt. Auburn and the 'rural cemetery' movement. *American Quarterly, 26*, 37–59.

Geller, P. (2017). *The bioarchaeology of socio-sexual lives: Queering common sense about sex, gender, and sexuality*. New York: Springer.

Harris, O., & Sørensen, T. F. (2010). Rethinking emotion and material culture. *Archaeological Dialogues, 17*(2), 145–163.

Haveman, M. (1999). A sociohistorical analysis of children's gravestones. *Illness, Crisis, and Loss, 7*, 266–286.

Hublin, J.-J. (2009). The prehistory of compassion. *Proceedings of the National Academy of Sciences, USA, 106*, 6429–6430.

Jacobson, L. (2008). Parents and children in the consumer household: Regulating and negotiating the boundaries of children's consumer freedoms and family obligations. In L. Jacobson (Ed.), *Children and consumer culture in American society: A historical handbook and guide* (pp. 63–84). Westport: Praeger.

Kersel, M., & Luke, C. (2012). Editorial introduction: The archaeology of trauma. *Journal of Field Archaeology, 37*(4), 314–315.

Kus, S. (2000). Comment on Tarlow. *Current Anthropology, 41*(5), 735.

LeeDecker, C. (2009). Preparing for an afterlife on earth: The transformation of mortuary behavior in 19th century North America. In T. Makewski & D. Gaimster (Eds.), *International handbook of historical archaeology* (pp. 141–157). New York: Sprigner.

Leone, M. (2009). Making historical archaeology postcolonial. In T. Majewski & D. Gaimster (Eds.), *International handbook of historical archaeology* (pp. 159–168). New York: Springer.

Little, B., Lanphear, K., & Owsley, D. (1992). Mortuary display and status in a nineteenth century Anglo- American cemetery in Manassas, Virginia. *American Antiquity, 57*, 397–418.

Luciano, D. (2009). *Arranging grief: Sacred time and the body nineteenth-century America*. New York: New York University Press.

Lyons, N., Hoffman, T., Miller, D., Huddlestan, S., Leon, R., & Squires, K. (2018). Katzie & the Wapato: An archaeological love story. *Archaeologies, 14*(1), 7–29.

Matthews, C. N. (2010). *The archaeology of American capitalism*. Gainesville: University Press of Florida.

Mintz, S. (2004). *Huck's raft: A history of American childhood*. Belknap: New York.

Murphy, E. M. (2011). Children's burial grounds in Ireland (cillinī) and parental emotions toward infant death. *International Journal of Historical Archaeology, 15*(3), 409–428.

Niedenthal, P., & Ric, F. (2017). *Psychology of emotion*. New York: Psychology Press.

Plamper, J. (2017). *The history of emotions*. Oxford, UK: Oxford University Press.

Pollock, L. A. (1983). *Forgotten children: Parent-child relations from 1500–1900*. New York: Cambridge University Press.

Rainville, L. (1999). Hanover deathscapes: Mortuary variability in New Hampshire 1770–1920. *Ethnohistory, 46*, 541–597.

Rosenwein, B. H. (2006). *Emotional communities in the early middle ages*. Ithaca: Cornell University Press.

Rosenwein, B. H. (2015). *Generations of feeling: A history of emotions, 600–1700*. Cambridge: Cambridge University Press.

Roussou, M., Ripanti, F., & Servi, K. (2017). Engaging visitors of archaeological sites through "EMOTIVE" storytelling experiences: A pilot at the Ancient Agora of Athens. *Journal of Archaeologia E Calcolatori, 28*(2), 405–420.

Scheper-Hughes, N. (1989). *Death without weeping: The violence of everyday life in Brazil*. Berkeley: University of California Press.

Smith, D. (1987). Safe in the arms of Jesus': Consolation on Delaware children's gravestones 1840–99. *Markers, 4*, 85–106.

Snyder, E. (1992). Innocents in a worldly world: Victorian children's gravemarkers. In R. Meyer (Ed.), *Cemeteries and Gravemarkers: Voices of American culture* (pp. 11–30). Logan: Utah State University Press.

Tarlow, S. (1999). *Bereavement and commemoration: An archaeology of mortality*. Oxford: Blackwell.

Tarlow, S. (2000). Emotion in archaeology. *Current Anthropology, 41*(5), 713–714.

Tarlow, S. (2012). The archaeology of emotion and affect. *Annual Review of Anthropology, 41,* 169–185.

The Foundling Museum. (2019). The foundling hospital tokens. Electronic resource accessed March 2, 2019. https://foundlingmuseum.org.uk/collections/whats-on-display/the-tokens/

Tilley, L. (2015). *Theory and practice in the bioarchaeology of care.* New York: Springer.

Tilley, L., & Schrenk, A. A. (2017). *New developments in the bioarchaeology of care.* New York: Springer.

Walker Tubb, K. (2006). Artifacts and emotion. In N. Brodie, M. Kersel, C. Luke, & K. Walker (Eds.), *Archaeology, cultural heritage, and the antiquities trade* (pp. 284–302). Gainesville: University Press of Florida.

Zelizer, V. A. (1994). *Pricing the priceless child: The changing social value of children.* Princeton: Princeton University Press.

Chapter 10
Discard, Emotions, and Empathy on the Margins of the Waste Stream

Anthony P. Graesch, Corbin Maynard, and Avery Thomas

Introduction

On a late summer day in 2015, we park a pickup truck at the edge of an unmaintained dirt lot in southeastern Connecticut. Located on the margins of an otherwise busy shopping complex that includes a supermarket, several restaurants, and a dozen or so other small businesses, this uninviting, two-acre parcel sees few visitors. Seldom-pruned trees, bushes, and unchecked weeds form a thick, forest-like perimeter between the unpaved lot and the more heavily trafficked adjacent spaces. The ground surface is mostly compacted sediment, partly covered with colonizing grasses, potholes, and unsorted gravels, and strewn with various cultural ephemera, not the least of which are bits of broken concrete, wire, plastic wrappers, and disposable drink containers. Prominently visible at the northern extent of the lot are several discrete concentrations of identifiable household possessions marking a series of illegal garbage dumping events: furniture, old tires, half-dozen boxes of personal effects, several black garbage bags with contents unknown, and some dilapidated appliances, including an old dishwasher in which a feral cat is taking refuge (Fig. 10.1). The illegal dumping is why we came.

Our project began as an exploratory investigation into atypical or non-normative discard behavior in the contemporary, with special attention to an illegal garbage dump that had been encountered during pedestrian survey for another archaeology project. Over time, we – an anthropology professor (AG) and two (then-) undergraduate students (CM and AT) – expanded the pilot study to include four additional sites. Emerging at the center of the investigation were questions about the circumstances shaping deviation from normative discard behavior or acts of discard that circumvent municipally sanctioned garbage disposal. These questions were nested in broader interests in the ways that archaeological interventions in contemporary

A. P. Graesch (✉) · C. Maynard · A. Thomas
Department of Anthropology, Connecticut College, New London, CT, USA
e-mail: agraesch@conncoll.edu

© Springer Nature Switzerland AG 2020
K. Supernant et al. (eds.), *Archaeologies of the Heart*,
https://doi.org/10.1007/978-3-030-36350-5_10

Fig. 10.1 The vacant lot where we discovered Site 2

waste streams can be leveraged to deeper understandings of the material basis of capitalist societies as well as the destructive forces of supermodernity as revealed in discard (sensu González-Ruibal 2008). Admittedly, we were also interested in cultivating new fieldwork opportunities that could serve method-intensive archaeology curricula at a small liberal arts college. Operating from the premise that there are few substitutes for hands-on, experientially immersive learning, we set out to explore new ways to train undergraduate students in archaeological map making, photography, and other data collection techniques while simultaneously exploring core archaeological concepts (e.g., provenience, association, formation processes, etc.) with tangible examples.

Our fieldwork at five sites yielded substantial data and made evident that illegal garbage dumping is a potent site of anthropological inquiry on the margins of the contemporary waste stream. We found that field-based investigations of modern-day illegal discard are compellingly relevant and easily adapted to undergraduate archaeology courses, especially curricula that seek to demonstrate the salience of archaeology to the study of the contemporary world. Capable of reconciling qualitative and quantitative investigatory approaches, and building arguments on substantial material evidence, an archaeology of the contemporary is situated to foster unique and often impactful perspectives on, for example, the ways that discard in postindustrial, hyper-consumptive societies implicates issues of ecological toxicity, alterations in the suite of atmospheric and oceanic conditions labeled "climate change," and the behavioral foundations of an "Anthropocene" (Edgeworth 2014; Graves-Brown 2014).

In the manner in which new research projects can sometimes prompt unexpected questions and yield unanticipated results, we became aware that acts of discard have an emotional tenor that is difficult to ignore. We also discovered that the work of studying contemporary illegal discard can be a deeply affective experience for researchers. None of us knew exactly how to grapple with this aspect of the work, but we came to realize that acknowledging the ways that illegal garbage dumps materialize and elicit emotion is important to achieving deeper understandings of the ways that discards implicate behavior and meaning in other domains of every-day life. This chapter, a product of faculty-student research over several college semesters, explores some of the ways that emotion shapes contemporary discard behavior, some of the ways that emotion is part of the work of *researching* discard, and some findings that emerge only when we acknowledge the affective dimensions of discard in the contemporary as well as the past.

A Case for Discards on the Fringe

Our visits to the vacant dirt lot, or what we would later label "Site 2," feel simultaneously conspicuous and illicit. The lot sits in full view of visitors and employees at a mid-range motel located across an access road, approximately 50 meters to the west, and our presence draws the gaze of all passersby. Aside from the occasional parked tractor and semi-trailer, it's unusual to see vehicles or people in this space. To the south, an unadorned, visibly decaying building that once housed a Chuck E. Cheese franchise contributes to a sense of abandonment and marginality. AT and CM reflect on the striking emotional contrast between joyful memories of a child-centered vibrancy – birthday parties, video games, and pizza – and the melancholy of the present-day decomposition and disorder.

A red Salvation Army donation box has been placed in a corner of the lot nearest the access road and signifies the only perceptibly legitimate reason to be here. We came to inspect the garbage, but stepping out of the truck and into a space that visibly satisfies municipal definitions of "blight," we realize we are apprehensive. Given the associative circumstances – people in a space that is seldom occupied, unsanctioned piles of garbage, and a pickup truck – and in the absence of other visual cues to prompt alternative expectations for on-site behavior, we wonder if distant observers harbor suspicions about our activities.

And why not? On this day, we have done little to signal our interests as archaeologists rather than trash-dumping interlopers or scavenging opportunists, the latter of which are rarely accorded positive status in contemporary North America. During subsequent visits, we donned orange safety vests and latex gloves, but we were never really sure whether this did much to visually communicate the nature of our on-site work. Beyond crime-related forensic investigations, there isn't much of a conceptual category for the study of garbage in the milieu of twenty-first century pop culture, and anthropologists' interests in contemporary refuse are scarcely known or understood outside of focused research communities. Even within academia, and in spite of broad reverence for the innovative work of William Rathje and colleagues (e.g., Rathje 1979, 1984; Rathje and Murphy 1992), an archaeology of contemporary discard has garnered only modest respect as an intellectual pursuit. In the more recent past, research programs designed by Jason De León (2012, 2013), Robin Nagel (2013), Joshua Reno (2009, 2013), and Larry Zimmerman and students (Zimmerman et al. 2010; Zimmerman and Welch 2011) have legitimized twenty-first-century discard practices as potent sites of anthropological inquiry. Nevertheless, few archaeologists since Rathje have applied the scrutiny typically afforded ancient trash to the discards of the present.

Archaeology as a whole has been a discipline that distances itself from the present, preferring the objects and features that are no longer part of social life over the behavioral messiness of surface assemblages in the present (Graves-Brown 2011; Harrison 2011; Lucas 2004). A perceived familiarity with the forms and common usages of objects found in twenty-first century dumps and landfills has undoubtedly shaped archaeologists' attitudes about the scholarly significance of discarded modern material culture (González-Ruibal 2008). Empirically observing and documenting present-day trash is that much more challenging when the objects are not only recognizable but also readily found in the researchers' house, basement, and/or garage. How do we maintain an objective detachment when we can easily draw from emic categories in not only naming the object but also predicting the social practices in which it participates? And how do we study a material record that elicits emotional responses from the fieldworkers? Such "closeness" to our research subjects makes us uneasy when engaging an investigatory process that historically has been framed in a Western scientific praxis (i.e., processual archaeology) and oftentimes still strives for impartiality and objectivity from an ontological location beyond the culture in question (see also Baxter, this volume). Despite more than four decades of critical revaluation of archaeologists' positionality in the investigatory process, the idiom "familiarity breeds contempt" may apply to the study of self and the societies in which we forge routine life. However, this uneasiness with our relationships to the discards and material-centered practices of the present just might be marshaled to challenge the very assumption of familiarity, to acknowledge the shaping role of emotion in discard, and perhaps even to foster new analytic lenses that help us better understand how objects and assemblages have different meanings on the continua of class, gender, ethnicity, and age (Buchli and Lucas 2001; Graves-Brown 2011; Graves-Brown et al. 2013).

Studies of contemporary discard afford opportunity to examine not only patterns of consumption and waste across these continua but also a multitude of processes that shape discard decisions and, in turn, affect the materialization of those decisions in an archaeological context. To date, landfills have served as the primary venue for academic and popular studies of (mostly urban) discard behavior in the North American present (e.g., Humes 2012; Rathje and Murphy 1992; Reno 2009, 2013), although Zimmerman and students have examined discard (among other material practices) in homeless camps in St. Paul and Indianapolis (Zimmerman et al. 2010; Zimmerman and Welch 2011). Other branches of the waste stream and materializations of discard behavior remain under-investigated or altogether untapped, including illegal dumps, transfer stations, reclamation facilities, and various forms of surface assemblages that evince casual discard in public spaces.

Archaeologists, we argue, should be particularly interested in these latter sites, many of which are transitory and subject to removal, if only to better understand how the interplay between capital markets, thriftiness, moral consensus concerning appropriate discard practices, social performance, and dissent might shape the paths and processes by which various kinds of objects and materials come to be discarded. Given the impermanence of these site types, an entire spectrum of discard-related decisions and behaviors may only be accessible in the present but have bearing on interpretations of discard practices as they relate to production, consumption, exchange, and social life in the past. This said, we very much advocate for an archaeology of discard in the present, *for* the present, and perhaps even for the future (sensu Dawdy 2009; Harrison 2011). The unique conceptual and methodological toolkits that archaeologists bring to data-robust studies of discard phenomena in the present can potentially be harnessed in collaborative efforts to understand a myriad of trash-related social and environmental challenges faced by local communities, including economic mobility issues, neighborhood vitality, toxic leachate and materials pollution to waterways, and incremental body burden. Indeed, De León (2012, 2013), Zimmerman and students (Zimmerman and Welch 2011), and Chenoweth (2017) make compellingly apparent that an archaeological lens can provide insights into contemporary structural and behavioral phenomena seldom generated with other disciplinary approaches. In turn, these insights can shape public discourse and maybe even public policy (Zimmerman et al. 2010).

To this, we add that illegal dump sites and their like permit archaeologists to examine *assemblages* of discarded belongings before they are disaggregated, disarticulated, and oftentimes fragmented as a result of various sorting, reclamation, and mixing processes at points further along the waste stream. This opportunity to document the qualities and associations of objects that were collected and simultaneously dumped affords exploration of the interplay between individual decisions, object agency, and broader structural circumstances shaping acts and forms of discard. The documentation and analysis of objects in situ and still part of a dumped assemblage also afford a consideration of the emotive capacity of discards as well as the emotional contours of certain discard acts that might otherwise be difficult, if not impossible, to accomplish in landfill deposits.

Five Illegal Dumps

At the core of our study was the rigorous documentation of unsanctioned, open-air garbage dumping events at five sites, all located in New London County. This pocket of southeastern Connecticut is home to just under 270,000 people living in 24 municipalities distributed across roughly 2000 km² (770 sq. miles). Two of these municipalities are small cities, whereas the other 22 are designated as towns.

Applying US Census Bureau standards of population size and density, at least 70 percent of the county is classifiable as rural.

Four of the sites investigated were located in the town of Waterford, and one was located on the margins of the City of New London. Most of these sites were discovered during automobile-based survey of 137 km of roadway traversing East Lyme, Groton, Montville, New London, and Waterford. Our survey included roads and lots in residential neighborhoods as well as active and abandoned commercially zoned spaces, including industrial parks, access roads, and loading dock-adjacent spaces of major retail stores (e.g., Best Buy, Walmart, Home Depot). We also targeted undeveloped and interstitial spaces, including highway underpasses, bridges, utility easements, and the shoulders of less-traveled roads. Some of our survey included roads and spaces mentioned during semiformal interviews with public works employees. Importantly, our survey coverage was neither comprehensive nor exhaustive. As such, we cannot make defensible claims of representativeness with respect to the types and total number of dump sites for each municipality.

On-site documentation of dump assemblages provided opportunity to train students in the application of a familiar set of archaeological field methods, including GPS recording, assemblage mapping, photography, field notes, and cataloging. We carefully documented provenience and association, especially for the purpose of identifying discrete dumping events (Fig. 10.2). This entailed not only mapping spatially discrete concentrations of artifacts but also noting superposition in dumped assemblages. When objects were discarded in bags or boxes, we took care to preserve these associations in catalogs and field notes.

In total, we recorded 22 dumping events at the 5 sites (Table 10.1). Two of the sites (Sites 1 and 4) were defined by only a single instance of illegal garbage dumping; another 2 (Sites 2 and 5) featured 3 or 4 dumping events; and 1 site (Site 3) contained as many as 13 spatially discrete assemblages. Cataloging and analysis revealed at least four major categories of dumping behavior: the purging of objects pertaining to residential activities and practices; the discard of construction-related by-products; the dumping of organic and inorganic debris resulting from landscaping events; and, the discard of consumer goods packaging during transient uses of out-of-the way spaces (see Table 10.1). Below, we draw on data gathered at all of the sites, although much of our discussion is informed by investigations at two particular sites – Sites 1 and 2 – where assemblages originated primarily from interior residential contexts.

We turn now to highlighting some domains or areas of contemporary illegal discard where we see compelling need for attention to the ways that emotion shapes the terminus of people-object relationships. Owing to space constraints, we fall short of fully doing justice to any: some concern tensions with structural forces; some concern the experiential qualities of illicit spaces; some address conceptual and methodological reflexivities; and, all warrant deeper exploration with more robust datasets. Nevertheless, our goal is to show that considerations of emotion in archaeological studies of contemporary discard can provide for fuller understandings of material-centered practices in capitalist societies. An acknowledgement of the emotional contours of discard, we also argue, is key to creating conceptual space

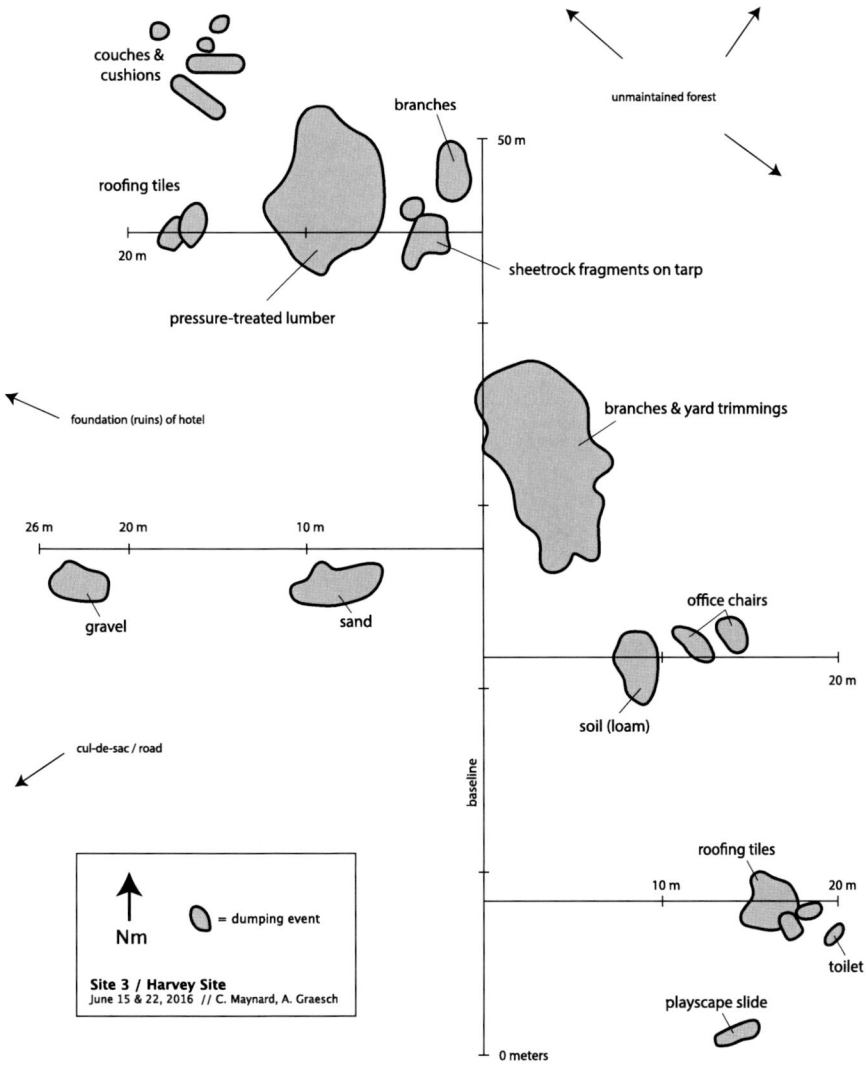

Fig. 10.2 Mapping helped students to identify discrete dumping events at Site 3

for some of the heart-centered practices advocated in and with this volume (see Supernant and Lyons, this volume; Surface-Evans, this volume). Lastly, we attempt to show how considerations of emotion are not at odds with data-driven analyses and inference. We do not make claims of universality, and given the small sample size, we do not make claims of *normative* illegal behavior or what Chenoweth (2017) refers to as the sedimentation of larger-scale processes over time. Rather, we merely attempt to understand our observations and data.

Table 10.1 Illegal dump sites and assemblage types documented during the study

Site #	Site name (informal)	Number of unique dumping events	Assemblage type(s)
1	Tank site	1	Residential
2	Vacant lot	3	Residential
3	Harvey site	13	Mixed – construction and landscaping (75%); residential
4	Miner site	1	Transient
5	Parkway site	4	Mixed – landscaping (50%), transient, and residential

Discarding Outside the Law

The potential of contemporary fringe spaces (and their associated assemblages) for shedding insights into structural forces shaping discard behavior was first highlighted by Wilk and Schiffer (1979) in their analysis of vacant lots in Tucson, Arizona. Drawing from data assembled by students in one of their courses, they suggest an archaeology of vacant lots "may reveal aspects of social structure and property relations difficult to identify by other means" (1979:535). In the same vein, we argue that the investigation of non-normative and unsanctioned garbage dumping affords an exploration of the ways that acts of elusion and illegality may emerge in tandem with (and as a response to) broader structural forces, such as the municipal regulations governing garbage disposal. In the United States, municipal laws reflect something of the socially shared, historically particularistic, and community-centered ideas about where trash should and should not be discarded, but are also shaped by the economic parameters of trash pickup, transport, and processing in a neoliberal economy. In this sense, we view acts of illegal dumping and resultant dump sites as reflecting a tension between law and everyday practice, and this tension is most evident when archaeological evidence is "read" against textual (or other) data addressing relevant legal code (Hartnett and Dawdy 2013).

Municipal regulations concerning residential and commercial garbage discard behavior vary in scope and specificity across the United States and Canada, but there is broad consensus that discard outside of municipally sanctioned garbage staging and disposal sites or without prior authorization of a municipal agency is prohibited by law. In many municipalities, there are specific limits on the size and type of objects that can be discarded through curbside pickup. Indeed, public works and sanitation departments in cities and towns often manage a list of items regarded as "special" and thus not permitted in residential curbside trash bins. For example, some materials classified as toxic or hazardous (e.g., NiCad batteries, motor oil, and scrap electronics) cannot be tossed into trash bins but are accepted for recycling without extra charge at transfer stations. Other toxic materials (e.g., insecticides, paint, varnish, and pool chemicals) are often not accepted at transfer stations but can be disposed of at 1-day, hazardous waste collection events scheduled at rotating locations. Large household objects, such as major appliances and furniture, can only be legally disposed of through the arrangement of a special curbside collection or by transporting these objects to a transfer station and paying for disposal. To discard any of these and other materials classified as "special," the homeowner or renter must either pay additional money, possess or arrange for special equipment (e.g., a pickup truck and/or trailer), coordinate the timing of disposal within a narrower range of scheduling options, or all of the above.

Suffice it to say that prior planning and investments of time and money are required to remove these items from residential properties. For some, particularly the economically disenfranchised, these are significant logistical and financial barriers to disposing unwanted objects. For others, the aggregate of these hurdles may constitute an inflection point in tolerance for government oversight of household affairs. For many, the relationship with garbage is one of reluctance, if not abhorrence (Shanks et al. 2004), and individual approaches to residential discard are defined against a backdrop of narrow, rarely flexible rules established by municipalities.

It follows that acts of illegal dumping and the resulting open-air dumps may be regarded as both an instantiation and materialization of oppositional stances to structural forces (e.g., municipal governance) that influence aspects of private, domestic life. The motivations of these stances might be seen on a continuum, ranging from economic hardship to deliberate protest. Of course, inferring motivation in the absence of interviews with dumpers is tricky, at best, but we argue that some combination of economic distress and a dissenting ideology is all the more likely to explain dumping behavior when willful violation of trash disposal regulations (in general) and illegal dumping (in particular) incur considerable risk of punitive consequences. In the United States, an illegal dumping conviction can be treated as a misdemeanor or a felony, depending on the state, and fines levied can range from a few hundred to thousands of dollars. Other outcomes often include some combination of community service, incarceration, probation, remediation, and restitution. Many communities also publish police logs in local newspapers, which afford a mechanism and venue for social shaming.

The effectiveness of these punitive measures is evident in the inverse correlation of their severity to the frequency of illegal dumping: in states and municipalities where legal consequences for dumping are light and/or weakly enforced, illegal dump sites are more widely documented (e.g., see Tunnell 2008). In Connecticut, a violation of garbage dumping laws is treated only as a civil penalty but can incur anywhere between one and ten thousand dollars in fines for every day that the offending garbage remains at an unsanctioned dump site. Equally serious is the possibility that, if found guilty, accused dumpers may forfeit the automobile used to transport objects to the illegal dump (CGS 2018: 22a-250a,c). Dump sites, then, reflect a certain willingness to assume or disregard for the risk of somewhat weighty consequences on the part of those who illegally dump. Indeed, given the premeditated arrangements required of dumping – scouting a potential dump site and loading and hauling the unwanted objects – we think it is difficult to disentangle motives centering on ideologies of elusion and dissidence from purely economic motives.

Illegal dumping in open-air spaces is not the only or even a representative measure of atypical or deviant discard practices reflecting a tension between everyday life and regulatory codes. Our conversations with public works employees made evident that people can and do dispose of materials in curbside bins that are otherwise prohibited by municipal regulations, including toxic chemicals. Furthermore, owing to how garbage is collected, transported, and processed, much of this likely happens without discovery or repercussion to the dumper. Still other illegal behaviors might include transporting and dumping possessions into steel dumpsters rented or owned by restaurants, retailers, or construction companies. In all of these cases, these expressions of nonconformity and dissent are virtually impossible to identify in the material record and manifest only (but not consistently) in instances of contamination to loads of garbage processed at recycling and reclamation centers. As all of these acts of discard are accompanied by risk of discovery and subsequent punitive consequences, there is an emotional gravity to discard that should not be ignored if we are to more fully understand the circumstances by which objects enter into the waste stream.

Illicit Spaces

Given the punitive costs, acts of illegal dumping tend to be secretive and inconspicuous, and our work at documenting unsanctioned dumps suggested that illicit activities require illicit spaces. At all of the sites in our modest study, we noted distinctive and recurring attributes of spaces targeted for garbage dumping. These include poor lighting, limited visibility from passing traffic or other forms of monitoring (e.g., security cameras), infrequent use by a general public, and easy access by automobile. Based on interviews with public works employees and our own observations, roadway dead ends, nonresidential cul-de-sacs, unmaintained dirt tracks, and the peripheries of expansive, poorly lit parking lots are among the most frequently used spaces for illegal dumping.

Some spaces come to be imbued with a durable residue or memory of dumping. Public works employees will clean up dump sites and haul garbage to transfer stations only to find that new dumping events occur shortly thereafter, suggesting that either the perceived attributes of the space or evidence of past dumping (or both) are compelling signals to prospective dumpers (also see Laundra 2011). At Site 3, for example, we documented at least 13 discrete dumping events, some of which had been around for several weeks or months, based on plant growth in and around dumped objects (Fig. 10.3). Although a possibility, we think it unlikely that each of these events is attributable to the same dumper(s). Conversations with public works employees made evident that this locale – the terminus of a dead-end road, near the ruins of a motel that operated more than two decades ago – has been a favored dumping spot for many years, likely owing to its seclusion on a street that has no

Fig. 10.3 A dead-end street where we documented Site 4

other commercial or residential destinations. Given its out-of-the-way location, this site is a lower priority for municipal cleanup and, consequently, an ideal spot for private activities or interactions.

Importantly, dump sites tend to *feel* seedy. Throughout our initial visits and subsequent fieldwork at all of the sites, we experienced various degrees of trepidation during extended time in these spaces. In two cases, our on-site fieldwork thwarted two pre-planned meetings between people arriving in separate cars with tinted windows, one of which was a police cruiser driven by somebody who seemingly had no interest in understanding our relationship to a place where illicit activities were imprinted in the material surround. As all parties departed almost immediately after arrival, we assumed that the meetings were meant to be private and the space chosen for its secluded, "backstage" affordances (Goffman 1959). Regardless of whether these affordances fully explain illegal dumping at these sites, we wager that the affective experiences of occupying these spaces are similar for both dumpers and archaeologists, alike.

Inferring Emotion in Discard(s)(ing)(ers)

An archaeology of the contemporary is as much concerned with the shaping roles of objects in the everyday social lives of living humans as it is with the generative, culturally situated processes accounting for an archaeological record in the present.

Admittedly, the distinction between these broader domains of study is complicated, especially given that the entanglements between objects and people can persist long after the point at which we might think they have come to a conclusion. Landfills, for example, have lasting repercussions – psychological, economic, toxicological, and environmental – long after their constituent objects are discarded. Although the aggregate garbage will be compacted and eventually sculpted into artificial land-forms, the transition from a systemic to an archaeological context is prolonged for as long as the refuse continues to discernibly affect people's lives, including those who live near the landfill site as well as those who labor in its operations and upkeep (u.g., see Reno 2009).

This is not a new idea, per se. Wilk and Schiffer suggested that archaeologists think about discard, or the movement of objects from a systemic to archaeological context, "as a continuum rather than an abrupt transition" (1979: 532). Like land-fills, illegally dumped objects – either singly or in aggregate (as landscape fea-tures) – may be in the early stages of becoming part of an archaeological record, but they remain in a systemic context to the extent that they still visually prompt asso-ciations of waste, blight, immorality, and poverty with/in the spaces they occupy. As both inconspicuous and conspicuous features occupying interstitial spaces on land-scapes, these features retain agency as long as they continue to elicit emotional responses (e.g., moral outrage, fear of crime, etc.), particularly from those who live next to concentrations of refuse.

Material instantiations of this distinction between archaeological and systemic contexts (as well as other site formation processes) are exceedingly useful in under-graduate archaeological training, but the assemblages found at illegal dump sites may reveal even more about the logics and affective experiences that compel illegal discard. For example, our analysis suggests that objects found in some illegal dumps may have been relegated to mostly liminal but nonetheless still affective statuses long *before* they were discarded. Site 1, for example, comprises many identifiable household objects that were likely curated on the periphery of everyday social life with the intent of later disposal (Fig. 10.4). This assemblage includes items that implicate transitions in the organization and composition of an American household (e.g., an infant car seat, a toddler mattress, crib parts, and a baby stroller), by-products from one or more home remodeling projects (e.g., window flashing, parts of a door frame, vinyl and wood trim, and scrap timber), and waste materials result-ing from automobile maintenance (e.g., used filters and 7 liters of engine oil in four plastic containers). Owing to their size or toxicity, much of the collection is not eligible for weekly curbside collection, and purging the full assemblage from home spaces would require special arrangements.

As a whole, the Site 1 assemblage suggests a discard process whereby objects were stored in a garage or basement until a change in their cumulative abundance (or something else) triggered a formal discard event. As it is unlikely that all of these objects were deemed unwanted and classified as "garbage" at the exact same time, we suggest the items were accumulated and stored with the intent of disposal at a later date. On the continuum of movement from systemic to archaeological, this is a rather gradual transition: these objects effectively entered into a liminal systemic

Fig. 10.4 Residential discards at Site 1

context *prior* to being aggregated and removed from the home. The ways that these objects impact lived experiences in liminal systemic context prior to discard, however, are different than the ways that they elicit emotional responses as postdepositional landscape features. That is, rather than connoting illegality in morally suspect spaces, liminal assemblages in home spaces are more apt to elicit stress, especially if they are perceived as "clutter."

The retention of unused and otherwise unwanted objects in contemporary American household inventories is a measurable outcome of decades of unfettered consumption. Arnold et al. (2012) have rigorously documented the extraordinary ways that homeowners use various residential spaces to store massive accumulations of consumer goods and other objects, many of which are merely newer replacements for still-functional antecedents. Material overabundance and a reluctance to part with inessential and redundant possessions have created an emotional burden, of sorts. Indeed, there is compelling evidence to suggest that high densities of objects staged for later removal, including the kinds of objects represented in our Site 1 assemblage, affectively hold sway over homeowners' physiological states. In a study of 60 self-narrated tours of home inventories, researchers found that homeowners (and mothers, in particular) who used specific sets of value-charged words (e.g., junk, overflow, messy, cluttered, chaotic, trashy, disaster, haphazard, etc.) in their narratives tended to experience higher levels of depression as measured by cortisol samples over a number of days (Saxbe and Repetti 2010). In short, sustained accumulation and, by extension, deferred discard are aspects of contemporary materiality that are measurably associated with negative emotional states.

It follows that the act of discarding can also be an emotionally layered experience, although not necessarily a *negative* experience. This idea is perhaps most evinced with the profitability of a robust home-organizing industry that emerged in tandem with historically unprecedented levels of accumulation in the United States. In this sector, self-labeled "tidying experts" and "organizing consultants" frame acts of discard as intrinsically healthful. A recently trending Marie Kondo (Kondo 2019) is particularly noteworthy for popularizing a method of home organizing that explicitly links acts of discard with emotions. By prompting homeowners to evaluate objects' intrinsic joy-sparking qualities and, when no joy is sparked, to recognize objects' histories of service, she compels an acknowledgment of materiality and, specifically, the affective relationships between people and their possessions. In the end, a perfectly usable object may be discarded into the waste stream, but the transitional process is one that is rooted in, generative of, and mediated by the sentiments of the objects' former owner.

Involuntary Dispossession

Hyper-consumerism and perceived fungibility of objects and material resources may ultimately explain much of contemporary discard behavior in present-day North America. Reno (2013), for example, discusses the sheer and relentless volume of garbage routinely interacted with by waste workers at a Michigan landfill: "No matter how personal, people will throw anything away without a thought... and people will also throw things away that are 'perfectly good'" (2013: 269). While this sentiment may ring true in some cases, there is good evidence to indicate that the process by which some people come to sever their relationship with belongings can be emotionally complicated (see above), but also that the paths by which objects enter the waste stream are many and sometimes complex.

Assemblages documented at Site 2 provide a compelling example. In aggregate, this collection comprised 129 articles of clothing, 419 personal effects, and 23 pieces of equipment and small furniture discarded in a single dumping event at the edge of the dirt lot described at the outset of this chapter. The clothing and personal effects – books, magazines, vinyl records, writing paper, toy stuffed animals, photos, greeting cards, drawing implements, paper mail, and various tchotchkes – were transported and dumped in six cardboard boxes and three black, 5-gallon garbage bags. In the aggregate assemblage, we can discern the names, partial gender identities, and social relatedness of five people in three seemingly nonoverlapping social spheres: two were married; two knew each other as friends or closer; and one was a man who, for a period of time, sought employment in the restaurant management sector (Table 10.2). Our surface investigations revealed that most boxes contained objects belonging to only one or another of the three social groupings, whereas two of the bags contained assemblages of mixed origin or ownership. Furthermore, the

Table 10.2 Objects with identifying information recovered at Site 2

Person	Number of objects	Examples of objects
SDB	65	High school ID card; invoices; employee manuals; military correspondence and transfer notice; resume; jean jacket; military-issued clothing; photos; poems; personal correspondence
JE	3	Love letters; greeting card
Both	8	Wedding invitations; wedding photos
MM	36	Invoices; tax guide; insurance policy; W-9 form; bank statements; employee manuals; work schedules; resume; personal correspondence
DF	7	Envelopes and postal packaging; personal correspondence from VH/SW
VH	4	Love letters; poetry

boxes, bags, and various bits of furniture and equipment were found intermingled and not spatially grouped by owner identity, suggesting a single rather than three discrete dumping events.

The circumstances by which these possessions were aggregated cannot be definitively ascertained, but several lines of data suggest it is unlikely that the objects were knowingly or deliberately discarded by all of their owners. First, the entirety of the boxed and bagged assemblages was eligible for and easily disposed of via curbside garbage collection. Indeed, all 36 kg (80 lbs) of clothes and the 419 boxed objects could fit in a typical 96-gallon curbside container. Given the abundance of objects with identifying information (e.g., mailed envelopes, bills, invoices), it seems unlikely that any of the five individuals who might have come into possession of the belongings of the other four would choose to add their own garbage and risk the punitive consequences of illegal dumping. Second, objects originating from two or more households were commingled in at least two identical bags, suggesting a spatial association – perhaps in a liminal systemic context – prior to collection and discard. Third, and related to the latter point, much of the corpus of written correspondence and other mailed documents dates to the mid-1990s (see Table 10.2). This likely indicates that most or the entirety of the collection resided in storage for nearly two decades. Lastly, the assemblages of personal effects comprised sentiment-laden objects marking notable life experiences and events, including weddings (e.g., invitations, cards, a wedding dress, and veil), military service (e.g., various articles of military-issued uniforms, photos), formative childhood years (e.g., photo albums, diaries, toy stuffed animals, travel-related souvenirs), intimate relationships (e.g., love letters and poetry), and remarkable achievements (e.g., a 5-month sobriety coin from Alcoholics Anonymous). Unlike other classes of contemporary consumer goods, most of these objects are regarded as deeply personal, often curated in household inventories for decades (Arnold et al. 2012) and, in the case of the wedding dress, even transmitted across generations.

Although any of the latter objects can be observed in residential curbside bins, where their discard signifies a physical and moral detachment of owner from object

(Reno 2013), the copresence of personal effects belonging to at least three house-holds likely indicates a different path by which they came to (eventually) be discarded or a process we are labeling "involuntary dispossession." The term "dis-possess" typically implies an action upon one party to deprive another of property, land, and heritage. Here, we use the term more broadly to include a myriad of cir-cumstances and processes by which people come to be alienated from possessions that they otherwise would not knowingly or willingly discard. Such processes might include environmental catastrophe (e.g., hurricanes, floods), foreclosure, confisca-tion, expropriation, and theft. In the case of Site 2, we interpret the assemblage as originating from a shelter or substance-free, multi-occupant housing where the objects may have been stored and perhaps abandoned in the face of substance recov-ery, financial insolvency, psychological afflictions, and/or legal hardship with the intention of later recovery.

Emotional Resonance in Fieldwork

While we did not intentionally embark on an exploration of the emotional contours of discard, we quickly learned that the discards of the living have the capacity to reveal vulnerability, loss, and suffering, but certainly also love, happiness, and belonging. In turn, this prompted questions about the emotive capacities of assem-blages of the past that may go untapped for archaeologists' inattention to the affec-tive facets of discard. If we can fathom emotional qualities or layers to the ways that our relationships to objects shape situated human experiences (i.e., material life), then can we also fathom emotional qualities to the *severance* of these relationships (i.e., discard)? Certainly, not all acts of discard may have deep emotional signifi-cance, but clearly some do, and some much more than others.

An exploration of the emotive capacities of archaeological records begins with an acknowledgment that the embodied and sensorially immersive acts of "doing" an archaeology of the present can elicit emotionally affective responses on the part of the researchers. Archaeology as a discipline has rarely embraced (or even encour-aged) what Tarlow (2000, 2012) labels an "introspective" approach to emotion, despite the discipline's broader strides in adopting increasingly rigorous and meth-odologically reflective approaches to studying the material record. Although vary-ing emotional states undoubtedly impact data recovery and interpretation, we focus our attention here on the generative processes accounting for affective experiences and, in turn, the extent to which an acknowledgment of emotion opens conceptual space for the development of heart-centered practices. Admittedly, this brief discus-sion is based on anecdotal data (i.e., our informal reflections on our experiences rather than careful documentation of emotional response), and the ideas raised beg for systematic study.

While working at illegal dumps, our emotionally affective experiences first and foremost derived from discovering and handling culturally familiar objects. The assemblages of photos, cherished toys, and children's personal effects were particularly moving; all three of us saw something of our own American experiences and childhoods (or those of our children) in the collections: family, home, vacation, antics, angst, love, loss, and sadness. We also encountered objects that connoted struggles with finances, health, and addiction, including several objects from Alcoholics Anonymous. Much of the assemblage of clothing items was equally as evocative. Although inclement weather had taken its toll, many of the clothes were still presentable and could easily have been found on the racks of the local Goodwill store. Most were sized for and likely belonged to a young woman, including military-issued articles, a wedding dress and veil, and a collection of t-shirts memorializing participation in a church-centered, pilgrimage-like event. After handling and cataloging these latter artifacts, one of the authors (AT) recalls a poignant reaction to finding a particular jean jacket in which the name of its owner had been handwritten with indelible marker on the interior flap (Fig. 10.5). The jacket was still wearable, still fashionable, and easily fit AT. The inscription as well as moderate use-wear on the sleeves and waistline all suggested this jacket was well-loved and, in turn, begged the question of why and how it had come to reside on a pile of discarded belongings at the edge of a vacant lot.

Our culturally and historically situated familiarity with these objects – their use in daily performance, their ritual significance, and their capacity to memorialize – established a unique sense of relatedness that we had not experienced on previous archaeological projects addressing objects and features from other cultural contexts. Importantly, this relatedness between discarded objects and the researchers invoked a profound sadness and perhaps even concern for the welfare of the objects as well as their former owners. There is a growing body of research suggesting that handling artifacts can positively affect mood and confer therapeutic affordances (Chatterjee and Noble 2009; Schaepe et al. 2017), although less is understood about

Fig. 10.5 A jacket featuring a handwritten name discovered at Site 2

negative emotional affect (e.g., sadness). Elsewhere, however, anthropologists have experienced similarly poignant emotional responses when encountering the lost, abandoned, and discarded belongings of undocumented migrants in the Sonoran desert, objects that can be linked to deeply personal narratives of individual turmoil, hardship, and grief (De León 2013, 2015, and personal communication).

Undoubtedly, our emotional responses and concerns for the objects and their owners were magnified by the fact that many of the objects could be linked to people for which we also had discovered names and other identifying information. That is, the wedding dress did not just once belong to *any* young woman; we knew her name, we cataloged some of her other belongings, and we were able to piece together some of her major life experiences (e.g., childhood memories, military service, and marriage). However, it is worth noting that one of the authors (AG) has documented tens of thousands of objects in twenty-first century American households (e.g., Arnold et al. 2012) but never experienced such a profound affective response to interacting with culturally familiar objects until studying illegal discard. That is, familiar objects in an archaeological or near-archaeological context seemingly resonate meanings in ways that are seldom experienced when handling the same culturally familiar objects in a systemic context. Accepting the idea that objects can be imbued with the residue or spiritual resonance of their owner(s) (Mauss 2011 [1925]), we suggest that the act of discard (or loss, or abandonment) is transformative in that it creates the necessary "distance" or separation of object and owner needed to establish a perceptible resonance.

Furthermore, the extent to which the archaeologist may be affected by an object's resonance is likely correlated with the researcher's relationship to the material record being studied: when researchers and stakeholders have material connections to ancestors (e.g., Schaepe et al. 2017), the affective experiences are likely that much more profound. This has certainly played out in AG's experiences of collaborating with Stó:lō-Coast Salish in subsurface archaeological investigations of nineteenth-century households in southwestern British Columbia. Whereas the handling of tool-making by-products and other frequently discarded household debris has elicited little or no emotional response on the part of AG, Chawathil First Nation collaborators often meditate on a more personal and affective connection at the point of discovery and when holding recovered objects. Mediating much of this response is local, culturally situated knowledge of *shxwelí*, or a life force present in all things and often connected with *spoleqwíth'a*, or the spirit of the ancestor responsible for making the object (Stó:lō Nation Lalems ye Stó:lō Si:ya:m 2003).

Setting aside our (dis)connections with ancestors and heritage, we submit that our team's emotional responses were also mediated by the preservation of mostly if not fully *intact assemblages* of discarded belongings. That is, had any of these objects been found in isolation (e.g., the jean jacket), we doubt the same range and intensity of emotional responses would have been realized. Assemblages of associated objects, as well as associations between objects and features, may be more durable "material anchors" for emotionally affective narratives (Hutchins 2005), if only for the fact that assemblages afford inferential arguments concerning site formation processes seldom permitted by individual objects.

Other aspects of the work also shaped our affective experiences. The fringe spaces we surveyed and inhabited during the course of the study often instilled a sense of uneasiness, illicitness, and sometimes ethical uncertainty. We encountered homelessness, abandonment, and ruination: like garbage, all are typically regarded as unsavory, undesirable, and maybe even morally inappropriate. Our search for and engagement with these spaces and subjects were directly oppositional to everyday social conventions, and we felt more vulnerable working when our actions could be observed and judged by others in the communities in which we reside. As such, we sometimes found ourselves on shaky ontological footing and incapable of projecting an intellectual authority over the work. All of this struck us as both odd and surprising, given that discards and ruins are typical subjects of archaeological inquiry. The difference, of course, is that our scholarly attention was focused on garbage of the living and in the present, where meanings assigned to discarded and abandoned objects are qualitatively different than those assigned to less familiar and oftentimes romanticized or abstracted material cultures of the past (Pétursdóttir and Olsen 2014).

Finally, our candid discussions of the ways that the archaeological work affected our emotional states were instrumental to vocalizing and exploring individual biases and assumptions that might impact the research (see also Baxter as well as Surface-Evans, this volume). These discussions also made evident that the affective experiences that emerge from archaeological fieldwork in culturally familiar settings create space for students to move beyond abstraction and cultivate a deeper-seated empathy when encountering non-Western concepts concerning the relatedness and interconnectedness of material culture and people. This empathy, we argue, is at the core of heart-centered sensibilities and practices, including the demonstration of a genuine respect for assertions of individual and community connections to the past via the archaeological record, as well as for emplacements of the past in landscapes (Surface-Evans, this volume). Although an archaeology of the contemporary can address questions, concerns, and challenges observed among and within living communities, methodologically rigorous and data-robust archaeological studies of present-day discard phenomena are also venues for deepening an understanding and respect for the emotive capacity and resonance of the material record.

Acknowledgments This faculty-student research was generously supported by a Research Matters Grant, a ConnSSHARP Fellowship, the Office of the Dean of Faculty, and the Department of Anthropology at Connecticut College. We are grateful to the employees at the Town of Waterford Public Works Department, the Town of East Lyme Transfer Station, and the Town of Montville Transfer Station for indulging our many questions and patiently discussing the nuances of illegal garbage dumping behavior. Objects and materials collected from illegal dump sites for laboratory analysis were ultimately returned to the waste stream. Morgan Kleyweg '17 enthusiastically helped with early project planning as well as cataloging the many finds from Site 2. We thank our colleagues for enduring numerous conversations about discard and the emotional experience of writing about emotion in discard. We are deeply appreciative of the editors and three anonymous reviewers for constructive critique and helpful suggestions. Of course, we assume all responsibility for any incoherency, errors, or omissions.

References

Arnold, J. E., Graesch, A. P., Ochs, E., & Ragazzini, E. (2012). *Life at home in the Twenty-First Century: 32 families open their doors*. Los Angeles: Cotsen Institute of Archaeology Press.

Buchli, V., & Lucas, G. (2001). The absent present: Archaeologies of the contemporary past. In V. Buchli & G. Lucas (Eds.), *Archaeologies of the contemporary past* (pp. 3–18). London: Routledge.

CGS: Connecticut General Statutes. (2018). Legislative Commissioners' Office. Sections 22a-250a and 22a-250c. https://www.cga.ct.gov/lco/statutes.asp. Accessed 2 Mar 2018.

Chatterjee, H. J., & Noble, G. (2009). Object therapy: A student-selected component exploring the potential of museum object handling as an enrichment activity for patients in hospital. *Global Journal of Health Sciences, 1*(2), 42–49.

Chenoweth, J. M. (2017). Natural graffiti and cultural plants: Memory, race, and contemporary archaeology in Yosemite and Detroit. *American Anthropologist, 119*(3), 464–477.

Dawdy, S. L. (2009). Millennial archaeology: Locating the discipline in the age of insecurity. *Archaeological Dialogues, 16*(2), 131–142.

De León, J. (2012). "Better to be hot than caught": Excavating the conflicting roles of migrant material culture. *American Anthropologist, 114*(3), 477–495.

De León, J. (2013). Undocumented use-wear and the materiality of habitual suffering in the Sonoran Desert. *Journal of Material Culture, 18*(4), 1–31.

De León, J. (2015). *The land of open graves: Living and dying on the migrant trail*. Oakland: University of California Press.

Edgeworth, M. (2014). Introduction. In M. Edgeworth, J. Benjamin, B. Clarke, Z. Crossland, E. Domanska, A. C. Gorman, P. Graves-Brown, E. C. Harris, M. J. Hudson, J. M. Kelly, V. J. Paz, M. A. Salerno, C. Witmore, & A. Zarankin (Eds.), *Archaeology of the Anthropocene* (pp. 73–77). *Journal of Contemporary Archaeology, 1*(1), 73–132.

Goffman, E. (1959). *The presentation of self in everyday life*. New York: Doubleday.

González-Ruibal, A. (2008). Time to destroy: an archaeology of supermodernity. *Current Anthropology, 49*(2), 247–279.

Graves-Brown, P. (2011). Archaeology: a career in ruins. *Archaeological Dialogues, 18*(2), 168–171.

Graves-Brown, P. (2014). When was the anthropocene? (and why?). In M. Edgeworth, J. Benjamin, B. Clarke, Z. Crossland, E. Domanska, A. C. Gorman, P. Graves-Brown, E. C. Harris, M. J. Hudson, J. M. Kelly, V. J. Paz, M. A. Salerno, C. Witmore, & A. Zarankin (Eds.), *Archaeology of the Anthropocene* (pp. 77–81). *Journal of Contemporary Archaeology, 1*(1), 73–132.

Graves-Brown, P., Harrison, R., & Puccini, A. (2013). Introduction. In P. Graves-Brown, R. Harrison, & A. Piccini (Eds.), *The Oxford handbook of the archaeology of the contemporary world* (pp. 1–23). Oxford: Oxford University Press.

Harrison, R. (2011). Surface assemblages: Towards an archaeology in and of the present. *Archaeological Dialogues, 18*(2), 141–161.

Hartnett, A., & Dawdy, S. L. (2013). The archaeology of illegal and illicit economies. *Annual Review of Anthropology, 42*, 37–51.

Humes, E. (2012). *Garbology: Our dirty love affair with trash*. New York: Avery.

Hutchins, E. (2005). Material anchors for conceptual blends. *Journal of Pragmatics, 37*(10), 1555–1577.

Kondo, M. (Creator). (2019). *Tidying Up*. The Jackal Group. *Netflix*. https://www.netflix.com/watch/80209464?

Laundra, K. H. (2011). The dump: a visual exploration of illegal dumping on public lands in rural America. *Online Journal of Rural Research & Policy, 6*(2), 1–34.

Lucas, G. (2004). Modern disturbances: on the ambiguities of archaeology. *Modernism/Modernity, 11*(1), 109–120.

Mauss, M. (2011 [1925]). *The gift: Forms and functions of exchange in archaic societies*. Eastford, Connecticut: Martino Fine Books.

Nagle, R. (2013). *Picking up: On the streets and behind the trucks with the sanitation workers of New York City*. New York: Farrar, Straus and Giroux.

Pétursdóttir, Þ., & Olsen, B. (2014). An archaeology of ruins. In B. Olsen & Þ. Pétursdóttir (Eds.), *Ruin memories: Materialities, aesthetics, and the archaeology of the recent past* (pp. 3–29). Oxon: Routledge.

Rathje, W. (1979). Modern material culture studies. *Advances in Archaeological Method and Theory, 2*, 1–37.

Rathje, W. (1984). The garbage decade. *American Behavioral Scientist, 28*, 9–29.

Rathje, W., & Murphy, C. (1992). *Rubbish! The archaeology of garbage*. Tucson: University of Arizona Press.

Reno, J. (2009). Your trash is someone's treasure: the politics of value at a Michigan landfill. *Journal of Material Culture, 14*(1), 29–46.

Reno, J. (2013). Waste. In P. Graves-Brown, R. Harrison, & A. Piccini (Eds.), *The Oxford handbook of the archaeology of the contemporary world* (pp. 261–272). Oxford: Oxford University Press.

Saxbe, D. E., & Repetti, R. (2010). No place like home: Home tours correlate with daily patterns of mood and cortisol. *Personality and Social Psychology Bulletin, 36*(1), 71–81.

Schaepe, D. M., Angelbeck, B., Snook, D., & Welch, J. R. (2017). Archaeology as therapy: Connecting belongings, knowledge, time, place, and well-being. *Current Anthropology, 58*(4), 502–533.

Shanks, M., Platt, D., & Rathje, W. (2004). The perfume of garbage: Modernity and the archaeological. *Modernism/modernity, 11*(1), 61–83.

Stó:lō Nation Lalems ye Stó:lō Si:ya:m. (2003). Stó:lō Heritage Policy Manual. http://www.srrm-centre.com/files/File/Stolo%20Heritage%20Policy%20Manual%20-%20May%202003%20-%20v1.2.pdf. Accessed 16 Mar 2018.

Tarlow, S. (2000). Emotion in archaeology. *Current Anthropology, 41*(5), 713–730.

Tarlow, S. (2012). The archaeology of emotion and affect. *Annual Review of Anthropology, 41*(1), 69–85.

Tunnell, K. (2008). Illegal dumping: Large and small scale littering in rural Kentucky. *Justice Studies Faculty and Staff Research*, Paper 8. http://encompass.eku.edu/cjps_fsresearch/8. Accessed 16 Mar 2018.

Wilk, R., & Schiffer, M. B. (1979). The archaeology of vacant lots in Tucson, Arizona. *American Antiquity, 44*(3), 530–536.

Zimmerman, L. J., Singleton, C., & Welch, J. (2010). Activism and creating a translational archaeology of homelessness. *World Archaeology, 42*(3), 443–454.

Zimmerman, L. J., & Welch, J. (2011). Displaced and barely visible: archaeology and the material culture of homelessness. *Historical Archaeology, 45*(1), 67–85.

Chapter 11
Lithics and Learning

Lithic Technology as Heart-Centered Practice

Callum Abbott

Introduction

This chapter explores the idea that lithic technologies are fully entangled with the social contexts wherein they are made, used, and remade. I foreground the communities whose material traces constitute the archaeological record by emphasizing the emergent co-construction and reciprocal relationships between the makers of material culture and the things they make. More than just utilitarian "tools," I define technology as the means by which people mediate social relationships through the production and use of objects and thereby embody the making and remaking of their material worlds (Dobres 2000:1). Engaging this interpretive logic through my own experience of learning to make, use, and study stone tools connects to this volume's theme of recognizing the wholeness of people in the past and the present.

Throughout this chapter, I explicitly take a *communities of practice* approach (Lave and Wenger 1991; Wenger 1998). In doing so, I challenge Cartesian notions of material culture as passive reflections of cultures "out there" and underscore the significance of "being in the world" to the lived lives and embodied knowledge of people in both the past and the present (Conkey, Chap. 17, this volume; Ingold 1993; Morgan and Eddisford 2015). Focusing attention on the ongoing processes by which knowledge spreads, skills grow, personhood emerges, and communities form transforms my objects of analysis from static nouns into active verbs such as learning, knowing, doing, making, and becoming (Ingold 2000, 2011, 2013; Lave 2011; Lave and Wenger 1991; Lyons and Marshall 2014; Nicholas 2010; Roddick and Stahl 2016; Wenger 1998).

C. Abbott (✉)
Department of Anthropology, University of Victoria, Victoria, BC, Canada

Hakai Institute, Heriot Bay, BC, Canada
e-mail: callum.w.f.abbott@gmail.com

© Springer Nature Switzerland AG 2020
K. Supernant et al. (eds.), *Archaeologies of the Heart*,
https://doi.org/10.1007/978-3-030-36350-5_11

Lave and Wenger (1991) define situated learning by placing heavy emphasis on the relationality of community-making. Their definition also fits the ethos of heart-centered archaeological practice: a holistic, open, and integrated process (Lyons and Supernant, Chap. 1, this volume). Contrary to western metanarratives that privilege product over process, both situated learning and heart-centered practice share an equal concern with process and product. It is these shared foci that unite the communities of practice approach I take here with the overall themes of this volume. My goal is to accentuate the processes by which communities of practice continually come into being—processes with emotional dynamics that simultaneously constrain and produce possibility (Crown 2016; Dilley 2010; Harris and Sørensen 2010). Knowledge perceived as "on the move" (Lave 2011:174), "in motion" (Roddick and Stahl 2016:28), that "is living [and] breathes" (Lyons and Marshall 2014:510–511) and "arises from be[com]ing" (Gosden 1994:11), is able to crosscut and confront ontologies more conventionally portrayed in binary terms. As Lave (2008:290) poetically puts it, situated learning is a "way of looking, not a thing to look for."

This chapter reports on a pilot study seeking to explore communities of lithic practice using a combination of quantitative morphometric methods and reflexive introspection akin to Welch's (Chap. 2, this volume) appreciative inquiry. By pausing to consider my own locatedness and reflecting on how to best craft my current and future archaeological practices as "agents of change," I situate a methodology for tracking the embodied gestures of working stone within a rubric of heart-centered practice.

Situated Learning as an Archaeology of the Heart

…activity and the world mutually constitute each other. (Lave and Wenger 1991:33)

In his manifesto for anthropology as a discipline of correspondence and care, social anthropologist Tim Ingold puts his finger on a humble idea that is fundamental to the arguments I make here: that it is important "to join with others" (Ingold 2017:24). These "others" may take many forms including communities, objects, technologies, materials, ideas, and histories. This process of joining needs to be done carefully because as Deloria (1969) and Zimmerman and Makes Strong Move (2008) rightfully observe, anthropologists and archaeologists can and have hurt people in our reckless assumptions of our own infallible objectivity. Therefore, interrogating and complicating one's taken for granted assumptions is a requisite component of heart-centered archaeological practice. Because humanness, according to a dualistic western ontology, is a paradox of a form of life that can realize its own essence only by transcending it (Ingold 2011:8), connecting to our own humanity through care, respect, empathy, and emotion is a method for bridging artificial divides and suspiciously convenient dualisms (Baxter, Chap. 9, this volume).

False binaries such as heart:mind, body:brain, doing:thinking, and process:product are ripe for unpacking within a relational framework (Hodgetts and Kelvin, Chap. 7, this volume). If we are not heartless archaeologists, an assertion supported by each chapter of this volume, then the same concession must also be granted to people at all places and times. In short, they too are people with fully integrated hearts, minds, bodies, spirits, environments, and histories. Considerations of holistic humanism are sorely lacking in archaeological discourses appealing exclusively to objectivity and western rationalism. I seek to unpack these conjectures using the communities of practice approach I take here.

The communities of practice literature underscores the constant socially and historically situated learning that takes place during everyday activities and how people come to know and to be via processes Lave and Wenger (1991:29) term "legitimate peripheral participation." The situated learning lens is a means of analytically engaging with the emergent processes of knowledge (re)creation within and across generations. Critically, the communities of practice concept is *not* about defining who is in and who is out (see also Chang and Nowell, Chap. 13, this volume) but rather the processes by which communities make and remake themselves. Putting this nuanced framework into action brings our full selves to our archaeological practices and counters the mind-centered approach typical of academia (Hodgetts and Kelvin, Chap. 7, this volume).

Contrary to some models of learning which posit knowledge to be transmitted as prepackaged blocks detached from historical or social contexts (cf., Fuller and Unwin 2012), understanding in practice means knowledge and skills grow relationally through situated learning enmeshed in action and embedded in life worlds (Roddick and Stahl 2016:23). Each generation must discover, grow, and learn for themselves—albeit with guidance from their predecessors (Hallam and Ingold 2014; Lave 1996). For example, Carriere and Croes' (2018) "Generationally-Linked Archaeology" helps connect descendent communities with ancestral knowledge through collaborative replicative practice. This ecological model of learning and enskilment (Walls and Malafouris 2016) positions making, sustaining, and identifying within communities of practice as key sites where social life is produced and reproduced (Roddick and Stahl 2016:3).

To this end, I would add learning and teaching to Baxter's (Chap. 9, this volume) discussion of emotion and childhood as universal human experiences. I admit that perhaps my identity as a university student for the majority of my archaeological career to date influences my fascination with learning about learning more than I discursively know. However, the fact that so many of this volume's contributors discuss the inherent relationships between what they do and how it informs their pedagogy suggests I am not alone in this regard. We are all constantly engaged in legitimate peripheral participation and situated learning that shapes us while we simultaneously shape our communities of archaeological practice. This contrasts top-down models of knowledge transmission predicated on another false binary because clearly teachers can learn and learners can teach.

While we can never fully know the communities of the past on their own terms, a communities of practice approach attentive to process (e.g., Fowles 2002; Gosden

and Malafouris 2015; Martindale et al. 2017a; Sassaman and Holly 2011) and relationality (e.g., Cruikshank 2005; Losey 2010; Watts 2013) holds promise to facilitate more holistic insights about the people whose material culture we study.
Additionally, full engagement with this approach demands reflexive introspection
by turning the metaphorical ontological mirror upon ourselves and critically considering how we shape and are shaped by our own communities of archaeological
practice.

Stone Tool Use-Lives and Lives Lived by Stone

> …practice rests upon a set of relations: relations between persons acting and relations
> between the social and material worlds. (Gosselain 2016:202)

Kakaliouras (2012:S213) observes "it is not that one way of seeing a thing is more
true than another but that the things themselves are produced, maintained, conceived of, and operate in different worlds." The relationality of these "thoroughly
entangled rather than transcendent life worlds" (Alberti et al. 2011:896) is an insight
Indigenous knowledge holders and producers have long known (Atleo 2004; Todd
2016; Turner 2005, 2014). Yet only with the recent advent of the so-called ontological turn in the social sciences (Paleček and Risjord 2012) and shifting scholarly
attention toward "being, becoming, existence, and relation" (Lyons et al. 2016:360)
are western scholars catching up by realizing "ontologies are materially constituted
and materials are negotiated ontologically" (Harris and Robb 2012:676–677). This
realization suggests that archaeological artifacts and lithic materials can "act back"
(Mathews 2014:9; Miller 2010; Pollard 2008:47; Robb 2015). If stones have life
force (Atalay, Chap. 16, this volume; Kii7iljuus and Harris 2005:123) and making
is a process of *working with* rather than a process of *doing to* materials (Bunn 2011),
the implications for archaeological analyses of lithic technologies are profound.

The relative durability of stone means these materials or "other-than-human persons" (Armstrong and Anderson, Chap. 3, this volume) can and likely do pass
through many hands during their potentially long and varied (use-)lives. From the
time of a lithic artifact's first anthropogenic modification to the moment it is excavated by an archaeologist, each hand it encounters has the potential to alter its morphology through retouch, use, breakage, repair, and recycling (Appadurai 1986;
Harrison 2010; Kopytoff 1986; Mackie 1995; Rolland and Dibble 1990). These
recursive processes of stone tool production, circulation, and consumption are inad-
equately characterized by typical archaeological models where form is arbitrarily
imposed from the mind of a maker onto a passive external environment. This linear
paradigm is the essence of the "finished artifact fallacy" previously identified by
Davidson and Noble (1989, 1993). Rather, lithic artifacts excavated from archaeological contexts are "rarely reflective of [an] end product that was imagined at the
time a nodule was originally struck" (Dibble et al. 2017:827). As Ingold (2013:41)

reminds us, it is often meaningless to ask the question of whether or not a thing is finished.

Similarly, ethnographic evidence suggests at least some skilled makers and users of stone tools are much more concerned with the angle and size of working edges relative to particular tasks at hand than the overall shape of lithic artifacts (Gould et al. 1971:154), an observation I argue is applicable to most—if not all—lithic technologies. The notion that some lithic artifacts are tools with specific functions and others are not is a dualistic imposition upon people whose lithic technologies may simply be "pieces of stone, parts of which may be used to perform certain activities" (White and Thomas 1972:278). Therefore, archaeological definitions of what constitutes a tool require broader considerations in order to avoid recapitulations of normative discourses reinforcing narratives of "rugged men doing primal things" (Gero 1991:167). As new tasks arise unexpectedly and working edges become dull, these edges must be modified accordingly. Thus their maintenance during the familiar yet occasionally stochastic interplay of skilled kinesthetic movements, fracture mechanics, and emergent needs is arguably more indicative of learned technological practices (Fig. 11.1) than the overall form of most lithic artifacts in the archaeological record. In the following section, I reflect on my own situated learning and embodied knowledge of these technological practices.

Lithic Technologies as Situated Social Practice

> Technologies need to be considered for their social implications as well as part of the 'ecology' of practices. (Angelbeck and Cameron 2014:6)

Archaeological materials and objects are sources of insight into the ways cultures were and are actively produced by human engagements with them (Stahl 2010:154). One avenue to achieve insight is to replicate objects using techniques, tools, and materials similar to those hypothesized to have been used in the past. As Weismantel (2011:314, original emphasis) states, it is a worthwhile exercise to occasionally "abandon *reading* for *playing*" because "not all objects submit to being read." This radical particularity of the experience of embodiment (Weismantel 2011:315) echoes Ingold's (2007:14) assertion that the properties of materials are "neither objectively determined nor subjectively imagined but practically experienced." Because the language we use creates modes of engagement or estrangement (Supernant 2018:146; Watkins 2006), shifting one's linguistic framing to *experiential* archaeology creates an environment conducive to holistic learning through doing in contrast to the hypothesis testing positivism of *experimental* archaeology. This subtle shift in nomenclature has the capacity to amplify the sensorial and emotional effects that the objects we encounter and materials we work with have on us (Colwell-Chanthaphonh 2004; Graesch et al., Chap. 10, this volume; Muntean et al. 2015; Zimmerman 2010).

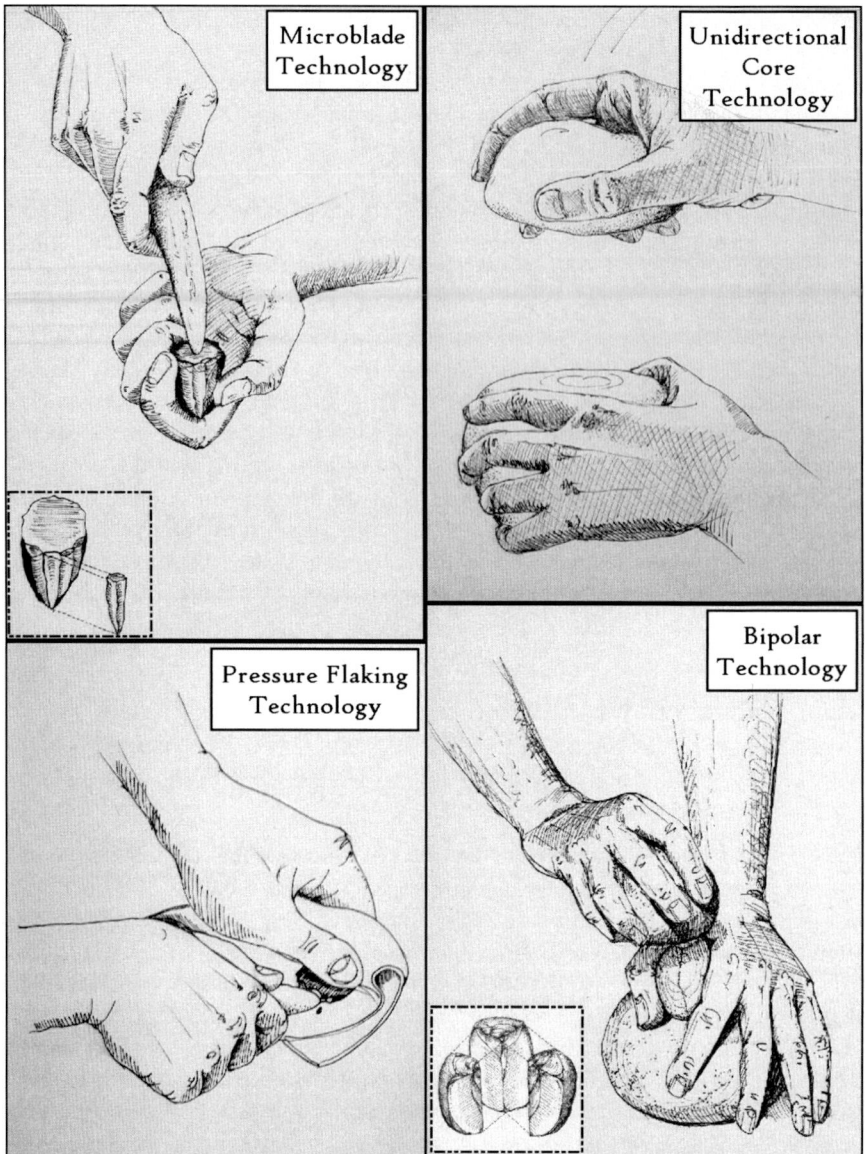

Fig. 11.1 Gestures of flaked stone tool production. Illustrations by Sharonne Specker

My initial clumsy attempts at knapping resulted in a gory melee of battered fingers, bloody legs, and randomly shaped debitage. However, through situated learning with patient mentors, my skills continue to grow. Repetitive movement fosters kinaesthetic memory that operates in tandem with improvisation and innovation, thereby "making things stick" (Barber 2007:25). For example, participation in the

Fig. 11.2 Members of the UVic Flintknapping Club sharing their embodied knowledge

University of Victoria (UVic) Flintknapping Club facilitates my enthusiasm for knapping, a concurrently insightful and enjoyable activity (Fig. 11.2).

Figure 11.2 is a photograph I took during a meeting of the UVic Flintknapping Club. The similarity of our postures is striking; we are all sitting on chairs, backs curved, and arms resting on our thighs. This is no coincidence and certainly not the inevitable outcome of deterministic tool-making evolutionary trajectories. One's bodily gestures, postures, rhythms of movement, chosen materials, and tools are all learned practices and technological choices that continually come into being through situated learning within communities of lithic practice (MacKay 2008). As a group of young adults of largely settler descent creating a setting for experiential hands-on learning by emulating past practices, our particular community of practice is obviously distanced from the myriad of alternative motivations, contexts, and needs for learning to make and use lithic technologies throughout human history. Nonetheless, ever since the first Oldowan tool was made approximately three million years ago, situated learning within communities of practice (including human-stone interactions) is the shared medium through which knapping skills grow and intergenerational knowledge is made and remade. Our corporeal and gestural "doings" (sensu Fowles 2013) are our means of corresponding with the skilled practitioners who came before us, those with whom we share our inhabited worlds, and those to come (Hodgetts and Kelvin, Chap. 7, this volume; Lyons and Marshall 2014:497–503;

Rizvi, Chap. 6, this volume; Roddick 2016). Although the focus of our knapping sessions may vary, situated learning is always taking place. In doing so, we learn not just with our minds and brains but also with our bodies and hearts.

Bourdieu's (1977:72–95) "hexis," the way people move and position their bodies in lived worlds, and "habitus," the structured and structuring dispositions and embodied principles through which people improvise their way through life, are highly relevant here because they are inculcated via bodily practices that in turn generate perception and action (Roddick 2009:83). History channels the body (Harris and Robb 2012) and motor habits such as muscle memory, posture, gestural rhythms, and handedness "bring different muscular and sensory modalities into play, creating in the process different senses of the body and relations with other bodies" (Gosden 2008:2009; see also Tringham 2013). In this way, materiality emerges through the interaction of embodied action on matter (Lucas 2012:197). A slight twist of the wrist and a micro-adjustment to one's hands, arms, posture, and breathing can transform a bloody mess into a fluid correspondence between person and stone. Fluent relational rhythms are "the creators of form" (Leroi-Gourhan 1993[1964]:309), and stone momentarily becomes liquid in the hands of a skilled knapper (Ingold 2013:44).

The purpose of this section has been twofold: first, by reflecting on my own experience of learning to make flaked stone tools, I provide a tangible example showing how material articulations of individual agency within contexts of situated social learning are fundamental processes of community-making; second, I argue that material outcomes of these fundamental processes are recorded in the "mountains of flakes" that characterize the archaeological record (Bamforth and Finlay 2008:3). I address these topics in the following section using quantitative morphometric methods.

Archaeological Lithic Debitage Morphometric Case Study

In this section I ground my theoretical framework in a morphometric case study of three archaeological lithic debitage assemblages from Quadra Island on the Northwest Coast of North America (Fig. 11.3). This case study is a form of exploratory data analysis that quantitatively describes the morphologies of 435 complete debitage flakes from three archaeological sites located in the traditional territories of the We Wai Kai, We Wai Kum, Kwiakah, K'ómoks, Xwemalhkwu, and Klahoose First Nations. I take a cue from Williams and Andrefsky (2011:871) who investigated "the influence of learning traditions and the influence of experience" between different contemporary knappers. Their study found statistically significant variability for morphological attributes such as flake length, width, and platform size between debitage assemblages made by people who learned how to make flaked stone tools in differential flintknapping traditions. These findings suggest deceptively prosaic flakes are the material manifestations of the skilled movements that detached them from a core and are the congelation of learned human gestures.

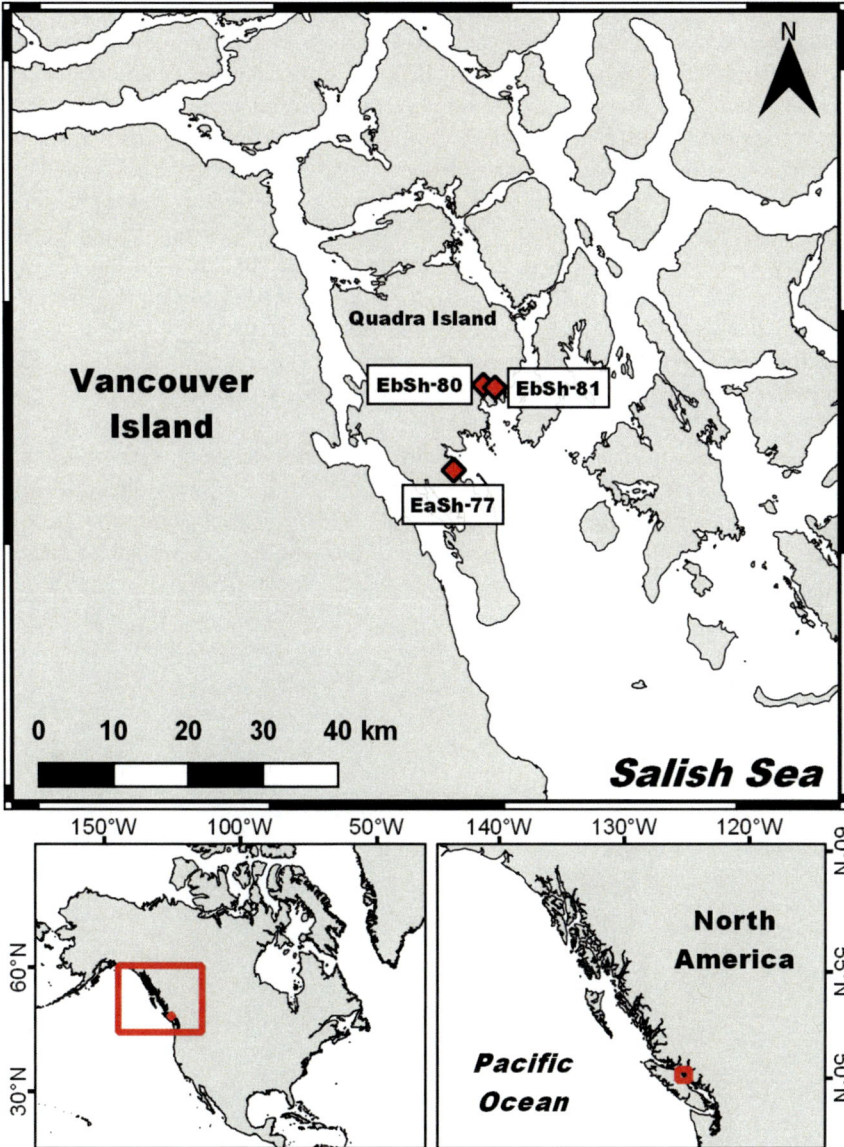

Fig. 11.3 Overview map of sampled archaeological sites. Map produced in QGIS (QGIS Development Team 2017)

I use these empirical insights to establish useful interpretive parameters for exploring the degree of gestural continuity within communities of lithic practice via their material traces observable in the archaeological record. I undertake an assemblage-scale analysis explicitly concerned with how gestural practices and embodied knapping knowledge shift or remain stable through thousands of years by focusing on places of recurrent intergenerational depositional practices whose cumulative residues manifest as archaeological deposits rather than individual artifacts, stratigraphic layers, or components. Because some may regard this research design as speculative, I emphasize that this analysis is a dynamic text that moves away from grand narratives towards a form of discourse incorporating incompleteness by design (Lucas 2012:252). Excising such grandiosity and fixedness from the archaeological narratives we craft is crucial for ensuring we do not silence alternative voices (Hodder 2018; Trouillot 1995). In short, healthy speculation guided by appreciative inquiry (Welch, Chap. 2, this volume) can lead to better questions.

The sample for this case study is derived from the Renda Rock Shelter (EaSh-77), Crescent Channel (EbSh-81), and Village Bay Lake Island (EbSh-80) lithic assemblages that respectively date to the early, mid-, and late Holocene[1] (Table 11.1). The main goal of this morphometric case study is to assess if the shapes (proxies for gestures) of the 435 flakes in the sample form distinct clusters when plotted by archaeological site (proxies for time). I conducted a principal component analysis (PCA) to transform input flake morphology variables into a lower dimensional space while retaining as much information about these variables as possible (Jolliffe 2002). Calculating eigenvector coefficients indicates the relative weight of each input morphological attribute variable onto each output principal component (Table 11.2).

Table 11.1 Summary statistics for complete debitage flakes sample. Values in millimeters

Morphological attribute	Archaeological site	n	Minimum	Maximum	Median	Mean	SD
Platform size	EaSh-77	25	2.5	41.9	7.4	13.1	11.1
	EbSh-81	258	0.6	71.0	5.5	7.8	8.4
	EbSh-80	152	0.9	73.8	6.4	9.1	9.8
Width	EaSh-77	25	3.0	44.7	10.4	14.1	10.9
	EbSh-81	258	2.9	84.0	8.8	12.2	10.5
	EbSh-80	152	2.4	77.0	9.4	13.0	11.2
Length	EaSh-77	25	5.5	75.6	16.3	21.7	19.1
	EbSh-81	258	3.0	99.0	10.5	13.9	11.6
	EbSh-80	152	3.1	68.2	10.5	14.0	11.8

Table 11.2 PCA results for three morphological attributes of complete debitage flakes

		Component 1	Component 2	Component 3
Eigenvector coefficients	Platform size	−0.571	−0.676	0.466
	Width	−0.594	−0.052	−0.803
	Length	−0.567	0.735	0.371
Proportion of variance		87.7%	8.6%	3.7%
Cumulative proportion of variance		87.7%	96.3%	100.0%

---

[1] See Abbott (2018) for more detailed descriptions of the archaeological sites, assemblages, and analysis.

Multiplying these coefficients by the original morphological attribute values (i.e., flake length, width, and platform size) and the proportion of variance value for a given component calculates a principal component score for each flake in the sample. This analysis indicates that plotting the first and second principal component scores of all 435 sampled flakes graphically represents 96.3% of their three-dimensional shapes in a two-dimensional morphospace. Discrete clustering of principal component scores may be interpreted as distinctly shaped debitage assemblages. Alternatively, overlapping principal component scores and confidence interval ellipses may be interpreted as similarly shaped debitage assemblages.

The results of this PCA demonstrate a tremendous amount of similarity between the shapes of the complete debitage flakes in the sampled lithic assemblages as most artifacts from all three archaeological sites cluster around the 0,0 morphospace coordinate and confidence interval ellipses overlap significantly (Fig. 11.4). This means that shared gestural practices across spatial and temporal contexts may be inferred. Rather than wholly separate communities of lithic practice who fashioned entirely distinctive stone tools, I argue this morphometric analysis provides evidence that the skilled makers and users of lithic technologies who inhabited these places on the landscape shared common gestures regardless of when they did so and the kinds of stone tools they made. This is a remarkable feat of kinaesthetic coordination despite a pan-Holocene temporality.

However, these findings do *not* imply that the ancestral inhabitants of these archaeological sites were incapable of cultural innovation or change. Indeed, there is strong evidence that they did just so, as inferred through macroscopic lithic analysis methods I detail elsewhere (Abbott 2018:81–125). Rather, this analysis is an illustrative case study showing that technological change took place within shared gestural repertoires spanning millennia.

In contrast to most archaeological taxonomies which typically privilege change over continuity, this morphometric analysis demonstrates considerable continuity in the shapes of sampled flakes throughout the Holocene. The principal component scores plot (Fig. 11.4) is a radical chronographic (Roddick 2017) demonstrating the utility of assembling and comparing data sets drawn from seemingly disparate spatial and temporal contexts. This kind of visualization has the capacity to surprise us and opens doors to previously unconsidered or undervalued archaeological narratives about the past. By contemplating histories in alternative terms relative to the totalizing or homogeneous time characteristic of orthodox archaeological chronologies (Lucas 2005:9–15), this morphometric analysis unsettles conventional narratives and draws attention to the shared gestures of communities of practice spanning hundreds of generations of lived human lives. In the following section, I reflect on these results and what their implications are for heart-centered archaeological practice.

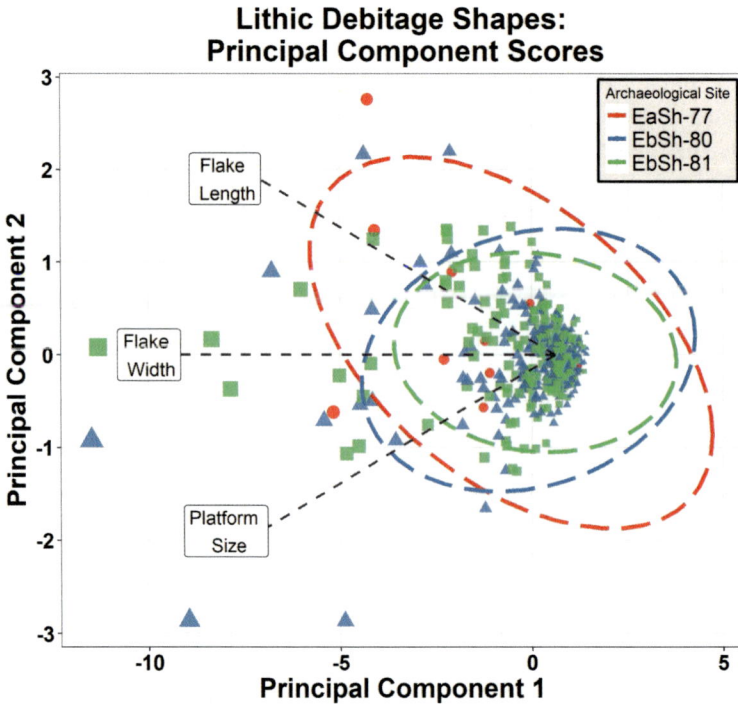

Fig. 11.4 PCA results: Component 1 and component 2 scores for morphological attributes of 435 complete debitage flakes. Plot produced in the R Statistical Computing Environment (R Core Team 2017) with the tidyverse packages (Wickham 2017)

Reflection

> ...the questions we direct at the archaeological record and the epistemologies, methods, and interpretive logics we use reveal as much about ourselves as they do about past peoples. (Martindale et al. 2016:189)

The ways we come to know the past are recursively entangled with our knowledge production practices in the present, and as Martindale and Nicholas (2014:457) keenly observe, "our views on the past are inevitably partial." In drawing on diverse literatures and methods that emphasize this inevitable partiality, my intention is to invite the reader to question their own taken for granted assumptions about what is known about lithic technologies and what is knowable by studying stone artifacts. By systematically unpacking interpretive assumptions, I aim to make very clear the need for what Lyons and Supernant (Chap. 1, this volume) call "a new space for thinking through an integrated, responsible, and grounded archaeology."

Much like shell middens are demonstrably not the piles of garbage the etymological roots of this English phrase imply (Carlson 1999; Gamble 2017; Grier et al. 2017; Letham et al. 2017; Martindale et al. 2017a; McLay et al. 2008; Menzies

2015), debitage flakes are not superfluous waste, nor are they always inconsequential by-products carelessly discarded in favour of what some archaeologists consider to be more charismatic artifacts. Ordinary objects such as "the casual flake" make up the vast bulk of archaeological assemblages, and to ignore them is to throw away most of our data (Robb 2007:2). As Graesch et al. (Chap. 10, this volume) also demonstrate with their introspective study of illegal discard sites in Southeastern Connecticut, shifting one's focus to facets of the archaeological record some may regard as unglamorous can lead to supplemental interpretive insights and, ultimately, more holistic knowledge of the past and the people who lived it. Multiple analytical foci and the fortified forms of knowledge they inspire are effective methods for bridging lofty post-processual ideals to the archaeological record itself (Ames and Martindale 2014; Baxter, Chap. 9, this volume; Lucas 2012).

The morphometric case study discussed here directs attention to the residues of the processes of stone tool production rather than just the products. By dissolving this false binary, I blur distinctions between material culture, communities, places, and times. I also highlight the relationality of the hundreds of generations whose material practices crosscut the divisive classifications used to structure many archaeological chronologies. Taken together, it is clear archaeologists would do well to continually question our own assumptions about the impermeability of any "taxonomic boundaries" (Martindale et al. 2017a:134; Chang and Nowell, Chap. 13, this volume).

The recognition that our objects of empirical study are socially produced does not, however, erase the responsibility to ethically respond to the constructed nature of our units of analysis (Trouillot 2003:128). Perhaps the greatest contradiction of questionable contemporary scholarship is the ignorance of all human struggles—including between some archaeologists and living Indigenous communities (Fowles 2016:22). Thus, effectively decolonizing contemporary archaeological practice requires the deconstruction of the many fundamental assumptions and essentialized categories arising from colonialism that premise much of what we do (Ferris et al. 2014:16; Hodgetts and Kelvin, Chap. 7, this volume; Rizvi, Chap. 6, this volume).

The results of this case study have particular resonance within the context of Northwest Coast archaeological scholarship, a literature replete with explicit and implicit focus on the orthogenetic emergence of cultural complexity among Indigenous societies of the region (Mackie 2001; Martindale and Letham 2011; Martindale et al. 2017b; Moss 2011). By assuming simplicity or inferiority as a naturalized and universal cultural evolutionary starting point, the perceived emergence of complexity among so-called complex hunter-gatherer-fishers usurps the very people whose histories we study as the primary focus. Often viewed by those who subscribe to models of progressive developmental social evolutionism as the anthropological archetype of cultural complexity, these teleologies and "seductively elegant reductionist scenarios" (Logan and Stahl 2017:1357) must only be considered with utmost reticence. As a corrective measure to this chronotope of inevitable linear progression tacitly leading to a Eurocentric ideal (Joyce 2002:34), I argue we must reframe both our questions and practices (including our visualizations of archaeological data) in ways that improve our explanations of the past as a function of being challenged (Martindale 2018:155). Recognition among data scientists that a linear model will never tell you your data are not linear (Wickham and Grolemund 2017) is an observation pertinent to Northwest Coast archaeological scholarship and archaeological practice writ large.

I began an earlier section of this chapter by invoking the ontological turn's focus on the plurality of life worlds in their unfinished processes of becoming. While the validity of these pluralities is an ongoing philosophical conversation necessarily beyond the scope of any lone voice, my more immediate aim is to emphasize that we must anticipate, acknowledge, and respect unfamiliar ways of knowing and being throughout our archaeological practices (see also Armstrong and Anderson, Chap. 3, this volume). I do not argue for universal passive acceptance of these alternative epistemologies and ontologies—some of which may deeply contradict our own—but rather the need to constantly make and maintain room for the unfamiliar even when these alternative ways of knowing and being challenge our own realities.

For me, this introspection shifts my attention to the materialities of lived lives and relationality of communities in formation as gleaned through their associated material traces. A similar disciplinary introspection also creates space to question our analytical assumptions by reflecting on how they infiltrate and shape the histories we write and the stories we tell within (and without) our own communities of archaeological practice (Atalay, Chap. 16, this volume; Conkey, Chap. 17, this volume; Joyce 2002; Lucas 2005:60–61; Swenson and Roddick 2017). The unfortunate repercussions of these constructed narratives take on a visceral intimacy when careless knowledge production practices are painfully felt by living communities. Consequently, humility, empathy, and care are essential for heart-centered archaeological practice. Such tenets are particularly important for me as a white man born on and working in unceded First Nations' territories. This is an intellectual insight I know in my mind as well as an emotion I feel in my heart.

Conclusion

In this chapter I engage my analysis with methods and a theoretical framework that enable me to surmount conventional analytical silos and eschew binaries (Logan and Stahl 2017:1395). In doing so, I connect to the broader themes of this volume by eroding culturally constructed distinctions between false binaries such as heart:mind, body:brain, doing:thinking, learning:teaching, and process:product. This volume comes at a time when archaeologists are being pushed and pushing ourselves to redefine "the boundaries that have long defined our craft" (Lepofsky and Armstrong 2018:64). During this moment of disciplinary dialogue and reinvention, we should celebrate ambiguity that destabilizes assertions of certitude (Conkey, Chap. 17, this volume). To act otherwise would be to deny ourselves the opportunity to create a more rigorous and humanistic archaeology. The heart-centered archaeological practices outlined, discussed, and reflected on by this volume's contributors are promising steps in this direction.

A communities of practice approach informed by empirical data analysis accentuates "the human in objects" (Lucas 2012:262) with humanistic rigour and rigorous humanism. This is a humble but valuable step toward redefining lithic technologies—past and present—as heart-centered practices. By situating my analysis within a rubric of reflexive heart-centered practice, this chapter helps to interrogate disciplinary assumptions and works toward redefining how we know what we know and do what we do as situated archaeological practitioners.

Acknowledgments The seeds for this paper were sown when Natasha Lyons and Kisha Supernant invited me to participate in the *Archaeologies of the Heart* symposium at the 2017 Society for American Archaeology meetings in Vancouver. I am very grateful for the invitation to contribute to such a lively, thoughtful, inspiring, and occasionally tearful meeting of archaeological scholars who put their hearts into what they do. Natasha and Kisha along with Seonaid Duffield, Jacob Earnshaw, Daryl Fedje, Quentin Mackie, Andrew Martindale, John Murray, Jacob Salmen-Hartley, Jenny Serpa-Francoeur, Ann Stahl, and three anonymous reviewers provided valuable critical feedback on earlier versions of this paper. Big thanks to Sharonne Specker for contributing her beautiful illustrations. Nicholas Waber and Daniel Stueber taught me to knap, and many others make continuing to do so both insightful and fun. Christina Munck, Eric Peterson, and the Hakai Institute staff provided much appreciated financial and logistical support. Any errors or biases are my own. Thank you to all.

References

Abbott, C. (2018). *Lithic technologies of the Discovery Islands: Materials, stone tool production, and communities of skilled practitioners*. Unpublished MA thesis, University of Victoria, Victoria.

Alberti, B., Fowles, S., Holbraad, M., Marshall, Y., & Witmore, C. (2011). "Worlds otherwise": Archaeology, anthropology and ontological difference. *Current Anthropology, 52*(6), 896–912.

Ames, K. M., & Martindale, A. (2014). Rope bridges and cables: A synthesis of Prince Rupert harbour archaeology. *Canadian Journal of Archaeology, 38*, 140–178.

Angelbeck, B., & Cameron, I. (2014). The Faustian bargain of technological change: Evaluating the socioeconomic effects of the bow and arrow transition in the coast Salish past. *Journal of Anthropological Archaeology, 36*, 93–109.

Appadurai, A. (1986). Introduction: Commodities and the politics of value. In *The social life of things: Commodities in Cultural Perspective* (pp. 3–63). Cambridge: Cambridge University Press.

Atleo, U. R. (2004). *Tsawalk: A Nuu-chah-nulth worldview*. Vancouver: UBC Press.

Bamforth, D. B., & Finlay, N. (2008). Introduction: Archaeological approaches to lithic production skill and craft learning. *Journal of Archaeological Method and Theory, 15*, 1–27.

Barber, K. (2007). Improvisation and the art of making things stick. In E. Hallam & T. Ingold (Eds.), *Creativity and cultural improvisation* (pp. 25–41). Oxford: Berg.

Bourdieu, P. (1977). *Outline of a theory of practice*. Cambridge: Cambridge University Press.

Bunn, S. (2011). Materials in making. In T. Ingold (Ed.), *Redrawing anthropology: Materials, movements and lines* (pp. 21–32). Surrey: Ashgate.

Carlson, R. L. (1999). Sacred sites on the northwest coast of North America. In B. Coles, J. Coles, & M. S. Jorgensen (Eds.), *Bog bodies, sacred sites and wetland archaeology* (Wetland Archaeology Research Project occasional paper) (Vol. 12, pp. 39–46). Exeter: University of Exeter Department of Archaeology.

Carriere, E., & Croes, D. R. (2018). *Re-awakening ancient Salish Sea basketry: Fifty years of basketry studies in culture and science* (Journal of northwest anthropology memoir series). Richland: Northwest Anthropology.

Colwell-Chanthaphonh, C. (2004). Those obscure objects of desire: Collecting cultures and the archaeological landscape in the San Pedro Valley of Arizona. *Journal of Contemporary Ethnography, 33*(5), 571–601.

Crown, P. L. (2016). Secrecy, production rights, and practice within communities of potters in the Prehispanic American Southwest. In A. P. Roddick & A. B. Stahl (Eds.), *Knowledge in motion: Constellations of learning across time and place* (pp. 67–96). Tucson: University of Arizona Press.

Cruikshank, J. (2005). *Do glaciers listen? Local knowledge, colonial encounters, and social imagination*. Vancouver: UBC Press.

Davidson, I., & Noble, W. (1989). The archaeology of perception: Traces of depiction and language. *Current Anthropology, 30*(2), 125–155.

Davidson, I., & Noble, W. (1993). Tools and language in human evolution. In K. R. Gibson & T. Ingold (Eds.), *Tools, language, and cognition in human evolution* (pp. 363–388). Cambridge: Cambridge University Press.

Deloria, V., Jr. (1969). *Custer died for your sins: An Indian manifesto*. Norman: University of Oklahoma Press.

Dibble, H. L., Holdaway, S. J., Lin, S. C., Braun, D. P., Douglass, M. J., Iovita, R., McPherron, S. P., Olszewski, D. I., & Sandgathe, D. (2017). Major fallacies surrounding stone artifacts and assemblages. *Journal of Archaeological Method & Theory, 24*, 814–851.

Dilley, R. (2010). Reflections on knowledge practices and the problem of ignorance. In T. H. J. Marchand (Ed.), *Making knowledge: Explorations of the indissoluble relation between mind, body and environment* (pp. 167–182). Oxford: Wiley Blackwell.

Dobres, M.-A. (2000). *Technology and social agency: Outlining a practice framework for archaeology*. Malden: Blackwell Publishers.

Ferris, N., Harrison, R., & Beaudoin, M. A. (2014). Introduction: Rethinking colonial pasts through the archaeologies of the colonized. In N. Ferris, R. Harrison, & M. V. Wilcox (Eds.), *Rethinking colonial pasts through archaeology* (pp. 1–34). Oxford: University of Oxford Press.

Fowles, S. (2002). From social type to social process: Placing 'tribe' in a historical framework. In W. Parkinson (Ed.), *The archaeology of tribal societies* (pp. 13–33). Ann Arbor: International Monographs in Prehistory.

Fowles, S. (2013). *An archaeology of doings: Secularism and the study of Pueblo religion*. Sante Fe: School for Advanced Research Press.

Fowles, S. (2016). The perfect subject (postcolonial object studies). *Journal of Material Culture, 21*(1), 9–27.

Fuller, A., & Unwin, L. (Eds.). (2012). *Contemporary apprenticeship: International perspectives on an evolving model of learning*. London: Routledge.

Gamble, L. H. (2017). Feasting, ritual practices, social memory, and persistent places: New interpretations of shell mounds in Southern California. *American Antiquity, 82*(3), 427–451.

Gero, J. M. (1991). Genderlithics: Women's roles in stone tool production. In J. M. Gero & M. W. Conkey (Eds.), *Engendering archaeology: Women and prehistory* (pp. 163–193). Oxford: Basil Blackwell.

Gosden, C. (1994). *Social being and time*. Oxford: Blackwell.

Gosden, C. (2008). Social ontologies. *Philosophical Transactions of the Royal Society B, 363*, 2003–2010.

Gosden, C., & Malafouris, L. (2015). Process archaeology (P-arch). *World Archaeology, 47*(5), 701–717.

Gosselain, O. P. (2016). Commentary: On fluxes, connections, and their archaeological manifestations. In E. Kiriatzi & C. Knappett (Eds.), *Human mobility and technological transfer in the prehistoric mediterranean* (pp. 194–206). Cambridge: Cambridge University Press.

Gould, R. A., Koster, D. A., & Sontz, A. H. L. (1971). The lithic assemblage of the Western Desert aborigines of Australia. *American Antiquity, 36*(2), 149–169.

Grier, C., Angelbeck, B., & McLay, E. (2017). Terraforming and monumentality as long-term social practice in the Salish Sea region of the northwest coast of North America. *Hunter Gatherer Research, 3*(1), 107–132.

Hallam, E., & Ingold, T. (Eds.). (2014). *Making and growing: Anthropological studies of organisms and artefacts (anthropological studies of creativity and perception)*. Surrey: Ashgate.

Harris, O. J. T., & Robb, J. (2012). Multiple ontologies and the problem of the body in history. *American Anthropologist, 114*(4), 668–679.

Harris, O. J. T., & Sørensen, T. F. (2010). Rethinking emotion and material culture. *Archaeological Dialogues, 17*(2), 145–163.

Harrison, R. (2010). Stone tools. In M. C. Beaudry & D. Hicks (Eds.), *The Oxford handbook of material culture* (pp. 521–542). Oxford: Oxford University Press.

Hodder, I. (2018). Big history and a post-truth archaeology? *The SAA Archaeological Record, 18*(5), 43–45.

Ingold, T. (1993). The temporality of the landscape. *World Archaeology, 25*(2), 152–174.

Ingold, T. (2000). *The perception of the environment: Essays on livelihood, dwelling and skill*. London: Routledge.

Ingold, T. (2007). Materials against materiality. *Archaeological Dialogues, 14*(1), 1–16.

Ingold, T. (2011). *Being alive: Essays on movement, knowledge and description*. London: Routledge.

Ingold, T. (2013). *Making: Anthropology, archaeology, art and architecture*. London: Routledge.

Ingold, T. (2017). On human correspondence. *Journal of the Royal Anthropological Institute, 23*, 9–27.

Jolliffe, I. T. (2002). *Principal component analysis* (Second ed.). New York: Springer.

Joyce, R. A. (2002). *The languages of archaeology: Dialogue, narrative, and writing*. New York: Blackwell.

Kakaliouras, A. M. (2012). An anthropology of repatriation: Contemporary physical anthropological and native American ontologies of practice. *Current Anthropology, 53*(S5), S210–S221.

Kii7iljuus-Barb Wilson, & Harris, H. (2005). Tlsda Xaaydas K'aaygang.nga: Long, long ago Haida ancient stories. In D. W. Fedje & R. W. Mathewes (Eds.), *Haida Gwaii: Human history and environment from the time of loon to the time of the Iron people* (pp. 121–139). Vancouver: UBC Press.

Kopytoff, I. (1986). The cultural biography of things: Commoditization as process. In A. Appadurai (Ed.), *The social life of things* (pp. 64–91). Cambridge: Cambridge University Press.

Lave, J. (1996). The practice of learning. In S. Chaiklin & J. Lave (Eds.), *Understanding practice: Perspectives on activity and context* (pp. 3–32). Cambridge: Cambridge University Press.

Lave, J. (2008). Epilogue: Situated learning and changing practice. In A. Amin & J. Roberts (Eds.), *Community, economic creativity, and organization* (pp. 283–296). Oxford: Oxford University Press.

Lave, J. (2011). *Apprenticeship in critical ethnographic practice*. Chicago: University of Chicago Press.

Lave, J., & Wenger, E. (1991). *Situated learning: Legitimate peripheral participation*. Cambridge: Cambridge University Press.

Lepofsky, D., & Armstrong, C. G. (2018). Foraging new ground: Documenting ancient resource and environmental management in Canadian Archaeology. *Canadian Journal of Archaeology, 42*, 57–73.

Leroi-Gourhan, A. (1993 [1964]). *Gesture and speech* (Le Geste et la Parole) (trans: Berger, A. B.). Cambridge: MIT Press.

Letham, B., Martindale, A., Supernant, K., Brown, T. J., Cybulski, J. S., & Ames, K. M. (2017). Assessing the scale and pace of large shell-bearing site occupation in the Prince Rupert harbour area, British Columbia. *Journal of Island & Coastal Archaeology*. https://doi.org/10.1080/15564894.2017.1387621.

Logan, A. L., & Stahl, A. B. (2017). Genealogies of practice in and of the environment in Banda, Ghana. *Journal of Archaeological Method & Theory, 24*(4), 1356–1399.

Losey, R. J. (2010). Animism as a means of exploring archaeological fishing structures on Willapa Bay, Washington, USA. *Cambridge Archaeological Journal, 20*(1), 17–32.

Lucas, G. (2005). *The archaeology of time*. London: Routledge.

Lucas, G. (2012). *Understanding the archaeological record*. Cambridge: Cambridge University Press.

Lyons, N., & Marshall, Y. (2014). Memory, practice, telling community. *Canadian Journal of Archaeology, 38*, 496–518.

Lyons, N., Schaepe, D. M., Hennessy, K., Blake, M., Pennier, C., Welch, J., McIntosh, K., Phillips, A., Charlie, B., Hall, C., Hall, L., Kadir, A., Point, A., Pennier, V., Phillips, R., Muntean, R., Williams, J., Jr., Williams, J., Sr., Chapman, J., & Pennier, C. (2016). Sharing deep history as digital knowledge: An ontology of the Sq'e'wlets website project. *Journal of Social Archaeology, 16*(3), 359–384.

MacKay, G. R. (2008). *The Ni̲i̲'i̲i̲' hunting stand site: Understanding technological practice as social practice in subarctic archaeology (Hudę Hudän series, occasional papers in archaeology no. 15)*. Whitehorse: Archaeology Programme, Government of the Yukon.

Mackie, Q. (1995). *The taxonomy of ground stone woodworking tools*. Oxford: British Archaeological Reports (BAR) International Series.

Mackie, Q. (2001). *Settlement archaeology in a Fjordland archipelago: Network analysis, social practice and the built environment of Western Vancouver Island, British Columbia, Canada since 2,000 BP*. Oxford: British Archaeological Reports (BAR) International Series.

Martindale, A. (2018). The future of history in archaeology. *Canadian Journal of Archaeology, 42*, 154–164.

Martindale, A., & Letham, B. (2011). Causalities and models within the archaeological construction of political order on the Northwest Coast of North America. In P. G. Johansen & A. M. Bauer (Eds.), *The archaeology of politics: The materiality of political practice and action in the past* (pp. 323–353). Newcastle: Cambridge Scholars Press.

Martindale, A., & Nicholas, G. P. (2014). Archaeology as federated knowledge. *Canadian Journal of Archaeology, 38*, 434–465.

Martindale, A., Lyons, N., Nicholas, G. P., Angelbeck, B., Connaughton, S. P., Grier, C., Herbert, J., Leon, M., Marshall, Y., Piccini, A., Schaepe, D. M., Supernant, K., & Warrick, G. (2016). Archaeology as Partnership in Practice: A reply to La Salle and Hutchings. *Canadian Journal of Archaeology, 40*, 181–204.

Martindale, A., Letham, B., Supernant, K., Brown, T. J., Edinborough, K., Duelks, J., & Ames, K. M. (2017a). Urbanism in northern Tsimshian archaeology. *Hunter Gatherer Research, 3*(1), 133–163.

Martindale, A., Marsden, S., Patton, K., Ruggles, A., Letham, B., Supernant, K., Archer, D., McLaren, D., & Ames, K. M. (2017b). The role of small villages in northern Tsimshian territory from oral and archaeological records. *Journal of Social Archaeology, 17*(3), 285–325.

Mathews, D. L. (2014). *Funerary ritual, ancestral presence, and the Rocky Point ways of death*. Unpublished Ph.D. dissertation, University of Victoria, Victoria.

McLay, E., Bannister, K., Joe, L., Thom, B., & Nicholas, G. P. (2008). "A"lhut tu tet Sul'hweentst (respecting the ancestors): Understanding Hul'qumi'num heritage laws and concerns for the protection of archaeological heritage. In C. Bell & V. Napoleon (Eds.), *First Nations cultural heritage and law: Case studies, voices, and perspectives*. Vancouver: UBC Press.

Menzies, C. (2015). Revisiting "Dm Sibilhaa'nm Da Laxyuubm Gitxaała (picking abalone in Gitxaała territory)": Vindication, appropriation, and archaeology. In A. McMillan & I. McKechnie (Eds.), *These outer shores: Archaeological insights into Indigenous lifeways along the exposed coasts of British Columbia* (Vol. 187, pp. 129–154). Vancouver: BC Studies.

Miller, D. (2010). *Stuff*. Cambridge: Polity.

Morgan, C. L., & Eddisford, D. (2015). Dig houses, dwelling, and knowledge production in archaeology. *Journal of Contemporary Archaeology, 2*(1), 169–193.

Moss, M. L. (2011). *Northwest Coast: Archaeology as deep history.* Washington, D.C.: Society for American Archaeology Press.

Muntean, R., Hennessy, K., Antle, A., Rowley, S., Wilson, J., & Matkin, B. (2015). ʔeləw̓k̓ʷ – Belongings: Tangible interactions with intangible heritage. *Journal of Science and Technology of the Arts, 7*(2), 59–69.

Nicholas, G. P. (2010). *Being and becoming Indigenous archaeologists.* Walnut Creek: Left Coast Press.

Paleček, M., & Risjord, M. (2012). Relativism and the ontological turn within anthropology. *Philosophy of the Social Sciences, 43*(1), 3–23.

Pollard, J. (2008). Deposition and material agency in the early Neolithic of Southern Britain. In B. J. Mills & W. H. Walker (Eds.), *Memory work: Archaeologies of material practices* (pp. 41–59). Santa Fe: School for Advanced Research Press.

QGIS Development Team (2017). *Quantum Geographic Information System* (2.18.13 "Las Palmas" ed.). Open Source Geospatial Foundation. https://www.qgis.osgeo.org

R Core Team (2017). *R: A language and environment for statistical computing* (3.4.3 "Kite-Eating Tree" ed.). Vienna: R Foundation for Statistical Computing. https://www.R-project.org/

Robb, J. E. (2007). *The early Mediterranean village: Agency, material culture, and social change in Neolithic Italy.* New York: Cambridge University Press.

Robb, J. E. (2015). What do things want? Object design as a middle range theory of material culture. In L. Overholtzer & C. Robin (Eds.), *The materiality of everyday life* (pp. 166–180). Arlington: Archaeology Papers of the American Anthropological Association.

Roddick, A. P. (2009). *Communities of pottery production and consumption on the Taraco peninsula, Bolivia, 200 BC–300 AD.* Unpublished Ph.D. dissertation, University of California, Berkeley

Roddick, A. P. (2016). Scalar relations: A juxtaposition of craft learning in the Lake Titicaca Basin. In A. P. Roddick & A. B. Stahl (Eds.), *Knowledge in motion: Constellations of learning across time and place* (pp. 126–154). Tucson: University of Arizona Press.

Roddick, A. P. (2017). Disordering the Chronotope and visualizing inhabitation in the Lake Titicaca Basin. In E. Swenson & A. P. Roddick (Eds.), *Constructions of time and history in the pre-Columbian Andes* (pp. 65–106). Boulder: University Press of Colorado.

Roddick, A. P., & Stahl, A. B. (2016). Introduction: Knowledge in motion. In A. P. Roddick & A. B. Stahl (Eds.), *Knowledge in motion: Constellations of learning across time and place* (pp. 1–38). Tucson: University of Arizona Press.

Rolland, N., & Dibble, H. L. (1990). A new synthesis of middle Paleolithic variability. *American Antiquity, 55*(3), 480–499.

Sassaman, K. E., & Holly, D. H. (Eds.). (2011). *Hunter-gatherer archaeology as historical process.* Tucson: The University of Arizona Press.

Stahl, A. B. (2010). Material histories. In D. Hicks & M. C. Beaudry (Eds.), *The Oxford handbook of material culture* (pp. 150–172). Oxford: Oxford University Press.

Supernant, K. (2018). Reconciling the past for the future: The next 50 years of Canadian archaeology in the post-TRC era. *Canadian Journal of Archaeology, 42*, 144–153.

Swenson, E., & Roddick, A. P. (2017). Introduction: Rethinking temporality and historicity from the perspective of Andean Archaeology. In E. Swenson & A. P. Roddick (Eds.), *Constructions of time and history in the pre-Columbian Andes* (pp. 3–43). Boulder: University Press of Colorado.

Todd, Z. (2016). An Indigenous Feminist's take on the ontological turn: 'Ontology' is just another word for colonialism. *Journal of Historical Sociology, 29*(1), 4–22.

Tringham, R. (2013). A sense of touch–the full-body experience–in the past and present of Çatalhöyük, Turkey. In J. Day (Ed.), *Making senses of the past: Toward a sensory archaeology* (pp. 177–195). Carbondale: Southern Illinois University Press.

Trouillot, M.-R. (1995). *Silencing the past: Power and the production of history.* Boston: Beacon Press.

Trouillot, M.-R. (2003). *Global transformations: Anthropology and the modern world*. New York: Palgrave/MacMillan.

Turner, N. J. (2005). *The earth's blanket: Traditional teachings for sustainable living*. Madeira Park: Douglas & McIntyre.

Turner, N. J. (2014). *Ancient pathways, ancestral knowledge: Ethnobotany and ecological wisdom of Indigenous peoples of northwestern North America* (Vol. 2). Montréal: McGill–Queen's University Press.

Walls, M., & Malafouris, L. (2016). Creativity as a developmental ecology. In V. P. Glăveanu (Ed.), *The Palgrave handbook of creativity and culture research* (pp. 623–637). Bassingstoke: Palgrave Macmillan.

Watkins, J. (2006). Communicating archaeology: Words to the wise. *Journal of Social Archaeology, 6*(1), 100–118.

Watts, C. M. (Ed.). (2013). *Relational archaeologies: Humans, animals, things*. New York: Routledge.

Weismantel, M. (2011). Obstinate things. In B. L. Voss & E. C. Casella (Eds.), *The archaeology of colonialism: Intimate encounters and sexual effects* (pp. 303–320). Cambridge: Cambridge University Press.

Wenger, E. (1998). *Communities of practice: Learning, meaning and identity*. Cambridge: Cambridge University Press.

White, J. P., & Thomas, D. H. (1972). What mean these stones? Ethno-taxonomic models and archaeological interpretation in the New Guinea highlands. In D. L. Clarke (Ed.), *Models in archaeology* (pp. 275–308). London: Methuen.

Wickham, H. (2017). *Tidyverse: Easily install and load the 'Tidyverse'. R package* Version 1.2.1: https://CRAN.R-project.org/package=tidyverse

Wickham, H., & Grolemund, G. (2017). *R for data science: Import, tidy, transform, visualize, and model data*. Sebastopol: O'Reilly Media.

Williams, J. P., & Andrefsky, W., Jr. (2011). Debitage variability among multiple flint knappers. *Journal of Archaeological Science, 38*(4), 865–872.

Zimmerman, L. J. (2010). Archaeology through the lens of the local. In A. Stroulia & S. B. Sutton (Eds.), *Archaeology in situ: Local perspectives on archaeology, archaeologists, and sites in Greece* (pp. 473–480). Lanham: Lexington Books.

Zimmerman, L. J., & Makes Strong Move, D. (2008). Archaeological taxonomy, Native Americans, and scientific landscapes of clearance: A case study from northeastern Iowa. In A. Smith & A. Gazin-Schwartz (Eds.), *Landscapes of clearance: Archaeological and anthropological perspectives* (pp. 190–211). Walnut Creek: Left Coast Press.

Chapter 12
Emotions in the Dionysiac Fresco in Villa of the Mysteries Outside Pompeii

Torill Christine Lindstrøm

Introduction

Emotions and emotional expressions are ephemeral phenomena and therefore hard to identify in archaeological materials and contexts. However, sometimes we "meet" prehistoric (or historic but ancient) persons, in their depictions: paintings, statues, figurines, etc. Sometimes one may think that people depicted themselves or had others do it. But mostly they depicted other individuals, gods, and mythological persons, and they made general representations of humans, not of particular individuals. The study of facial expressions in ancient depictions may tell us something about how people in the past wanted their gods and other important persons to look like, and perhaps more interestingly, how they themselves wanted to be represented and seen. Their depictions can tell us something about them, their cultures and values.

This text starts with indicating how emotions may be detected in archaeological material and how they can function as semiotics and shortly presents the nature-nurture discussion regarding facial expressions. Then the text then turns to its focus, an analysis of the facial expressions on the persons painted in a large Roman Fresco in Pompeii, called the Dionysiac Fresco, located in Villa of the Mysteries, just outside Pompeii, Italy.

I have been spellbound by this Dionysiac Fresco since I visited the Villa as a 19-year-old teenager. It was my impression that the Fresco filled the room with a special atmosphere and that its figures looked at me, as if they wanted to tell me something. They were engaged in various activities and interacted with each other. I wanted to understand what they were doing, and, as a student of psychology: What were they feeling? What were their emotions? Why were their faces depicted the way they were? This analysis endeavors to answer these questions.

T. C. Lindstrøm (✉)
Department of Psychosocial Science, Faculty of Psychology and SapienCE, Centre for Early Sapiens Behaviour, CoE Faculty of Humanities University of Bergen, Bergen, Norway
e-mail: torill.Lindstrom@uib.no

© Springer Nature Switzerland AG 2020
K. Supernant et al. (eds.), *Archaeologies of the Heart*,
https://doi.org/10.1007/978-3-030-36350-5_12

To understand their emotions, I wanted to study their emotional expressions, primarily and particularly in their faces. Emotional expressions can be signs of inner states or displays of culturally approved and expected inner states – in both cases they are *signs*. The science of signs is semiotics, and the semiotics of emotions are primarily studied within psychology and the social sciences.

A general question arose: Is it possible to find, identify, analyze, and understand emotions at all, of ancient persons based on archaeological findings as evidence? Could semiotics be a way of looking at such findings? And connected to the Dionysiac Fresco: Could it be possible to find out what emotions the persons in this Fresco expressed? Would there be a systematic way of finding this out? An instrument?

There are several classes of semiotic evidence from which we can draw reasonable inferences regarding emotions that were felt by people in former times. Regarding semiotics, I prefer to refer to the classical terminology of Peirce (1955 [1931]), where he differentiates between iconic, indexical, and symbolic signs. Iconic signs "show," in a very literal way, representations with likeness of what they signify. For instance, road signs with a drawing of a church or an elk signal that there is a church or elks in the vicinity. Indexical signs "point to," or refer to, what they signal in a less literal but usually intuitively comprehensible ways: Smoke signals fire, and deer footprints signal that there are deer in the area. In contrast, symbolic signs are arbitrary. A six-pointed star, a cross, and a half moon symbolize Judaism, Christianity, and Islam, respectively. A heart symbolizes love, and a zigzag thunderbolt symbolizes electricity. All these *symbolic* signs have some kind of reference to what they symbolize, but usually they are intuitively understood. They require some contextual or cultural knowledge; therefore, and in this way, symbolic signs may convey deeper meanings that are complex and abstract.

Considerable developments in semiotic theories have taken place since Peirce presented his theories in 1931 (Clarke 2003; Danesi 2007; Gottdiener et al. 2003). Among them, particularly semiotics regarding pictorial concepts (Sonesson 1989). However, for the present analysis, I found Peirce's theory and broad meta-concepts to be useful and sufficient. This investigation is not about the more subtle semiotics in paintings, a field where religious paintings, in particular, can be extremely complex in signs and symbols. The Dionysiac Fresco in Villa of the Mysteries certainly inspires to such a total analysis (Lindstrøm in prep) Here, the focus is on analyzing the faces of the painted persons, not their bodies, behaviors, clothes, or objects. One could argue that this procedure is a reduction of the Fresco's totality, as well as that of the persons in it. Nevertheless, I find it highly relevant also to analyze the facial expressions separately (as I elsewhere have done with their behaviors, clothes, and objects), because their faces may, in themselves, contain information that is relevant for understanding the totality of Fresco. According to a hermeneutic analysis, the parts help to understand the whole, and the whole helps to understand the parts (Ramberg and Gjesdal 2003, 2005). Adhering to this, in the discussion, the findings are explained from the broader contexts of the Fresco: the Roman society and values, as well as their contemporary Dionysiac cultic practices. So, for the present investigation and for the introductory examples below, Peirce's semiotic trichotomy of signs seems adequate and sufficient.

Archaeological Evidence of Emotions: Semiotics in Human Remains and Objects

Archaeological findings are ample with all three kinds of semiotic evidence. Even the ephemeral emotions can be traced and found represented within all the three categories of semiotic signs. Here are three examples:

In Denmark, it is reasonable to interpret the Vedbæk mesolithic burial (ca. 7000 years BP) (Nilsson Stutz 2003) of a young woman buried together with a newborn baby on a swan's wing, as signs of the emotions of deep love and great grief. This burial is simply heartbreaking. The dead bodies, their obvious close relation, and the fact that they were carefully buried together must be iconic signs of grief over deeply loved ones. Their grave goods are indexical signs of love and care for them but also of their social status. The swan's wing could be construed as a symbolic sign of hope for resurrection and recreation. In many cultures, birds symbolize spiritual and creative divine powers and connections between the human and divine realms (Campbell 1976).

Other signs of emotions connect to the many bodies found on ancient battlefields and sites of massacres. They convey several iconic and indexical signs, many of which can be connected to anger and fear but also to other emotions. Violent acts are often primarily thought of as motivated by aggression and fear but can also be performed in states of numbness or lust (Børresen 1996; Nell 2006). Terrorists' faces are notably expressionless before they act, a sign of numbness (Ekman, personal communication, 2008). Archaeologically, violent acts indicating concomitant emotions appear in signs of aggressive acts: marks on skeletons and skulls of inflicted injuries. Fear can be inferred as indexical signs of fear both from those injuries that were not momentarily lethal and from other possible iconic signs of fear and pain: open jaws and twisted skeletons. Although, admittedly, some of these skeletal distortions may have taken place post-mortem. Irrespective of the post-battle boasting of the winning warriors, strong, and often extremely unpleasant, emotions were felt by combatants on both sides of the conflicts. Battlefields are not scenes of cold and calculated well-prepared murders, but of strong and often desperate feelings. Finally, regarding symbolic signs, the bodies are not symbolic in themselves, but they may carry or be adorned with objects that express the owners' ethnicity, religion, or status in the army. Yet, these objects do not signify emotions in themselves, but might have been laden with emotionally charged meanings. Examples of these semiotics of emotions are findings of skeletons, weapons, personal belongings, and ornaments from the battlefields of the Teutoburg Forest (the Roman Varus Battlefield) (Clunn 2009) and the Tollense Valley (Bronze Age) (Jantzen et al. 2011).

More subtle signs of emotionality can be inferred from objects that are deliberately invested with aesthetic qualities beyond their functionality: made more beautiful than necessary for their practical use. For example, lithic artifacts from the ~75-ka Middle Stone Age levels at Blombos Cave, South Africa, were produced by heat-treating and minute pressure flaking, procedures that were not necessary for their practical use and functions (Mourre et al. 2010). The heat-treatment made the flint generally more malleable and made the refined pressure flaking easier. The resulting superfluous finish made these artifacts strikingly beautiful and pleasing to touch and handle. Since aesthetic experiences, through perceptual and cognitive mechanisms, give rise to emotions of pleasure and joy (Reber et al. 2004), the beauty of these ancient artifacts can be inferred to signify these positive emotions (pleasure and joy) in those who made, saw, and used them, perhaps even traded them for other goods. But are there more direct evidence of emotions? Iconic evidence? Literal icons (= "pictures")?

Archaeological Evidence of Emotions: Depictions of Faces

A particular class of evidence of emotionality is objects where people have depicted themselves, other persons, divinities, and mythological beings, either as personified portraits or statues or as "typical" representations of a particular kind of persons. Bodily postures may subtly indicate emotions, but depictions of faces reveal more concrete and precise iconic signs of emotions. Depicted faces are found in various techniques and materials throughout archaeological findings, for instance, drawings, paintings, sculpture, pottery, tapestry, embroidery, metal work, carved wood, carved stone, etc.

Sometimes the faces are made with striking emotional expressions. Yet they always show *some* kind of expression, as it can be argued that even expressionlessness is an expression that conveys a certain meaning. But when the expressions are explicit, they are often emotional, and they were likely to be recognized as such, by the people who had made them or who looked at them.

In Europe, some of the most notable examples of depicted expressions come from the classical world of the Greeks, Etruscans, and Romans (Brendel and Serra Ridgway 1995; Ramage and Ramage 1995). The Norwegian classical archaeologist and art historian L'Orange (1967) did a fascinating analysis of emotionality and personality as expressed in the sculptured portraits of Roman emperors. But his work was based on an *intuitive* analysis of these faces and his personal impressions, combined with biographical information of varying validity, about the emperors. For *systematic* studies of facial expressions, we must turn to psychology, where emotional facial expressions are systematically studied since 1969. So, I wondered: Would it be possible to analyze archaeological depictions of faces with this psychological methodology? That raised the following question:

Emotional Expressions: Nature or Culture? Or Both?

"Emotion" is a phenomenon and constructs with numerous definitions and traditions, from religion and philosophy to psychology and physiology (Scarantino and de Sousa 2018). Within psychology, the perhaps most used categorizations of basic emotions are those of Ekman and Friesen (1978), six (anger, distrust, fear, happiness, sadness, surprise); of Plutchik (1980, 2003), eight (anger, fear, anticipation, surprise, joy, sadness, trust, disgust); and the interdisciplinary primary emotional systems by Montag and Panksepp (2017), six (seeking, fear, care, anger, play, sadness). Although different, they are not incompatibly contrasting. The theory of Ekman and Friesen (1978) is, for instance, compatible with Montag and Panksepp (2016), according to the latter.

Ekman and Friesen's theory has an instrument developed from it: "the Facial Action Coding System" (FACS) (Ekman and Friesen 1978; Ekman and Rosenberg 2005). This feature renders this theory particularly useful for research. FACS is extensively used for studies of facial expressions, emotional and otherwise (Kanade et al. 2000; Kring and Sloan 2007. (FACS is described in further detail below, in the Methods section.) The FACS registers contractions in facial muscles and rests on the assumption that it is possible to identify emotions in faces because facial muscles, contractions, expressions, and emotions are part of the genetic characteristics of humans as a species (Plutchik 2003; Walton 2016). But, whether there really are universal human emotions and universal expressions of them is debated (Ekman 1992; Friedlund 1994). The idea of a human nature, with fundamental common characteristics that can be registered and measured, was challenged by the social constructivist position. It claims that human behaviors are socially situated, and knowledge about them is socially constructed (Gergen 1985; McKinley 2015). Clearly, *individuals* do have different emotional tendencies and express emotions varyingly and in varying degrees. Furthermore, different persons may express different emotions in the same kind of situations, and there are mixed emotional states and expressions, as well as suppressed emotions. These differences can also vary between *cultures*, as cultural rules and norms are learned and emotional expressions are culturally modified (Miyamoto and Ryff 2011; Tsai et al. 2007). I would add that differences in emotional expressions can be observed also between persons *within* cultures and subcultures and vary in the same persons across situations and during their life-span. Cultures also differ with regard to social control of emotions and to what extent emotional expressions are accepted in various circumstances. This means that emotional expressions are not always spontaneous expressions of inner states, but can be simply socially approved and socially appropriate *displays* of emotional expressions. Finally, both on cultural and personal levels, there are "rules," the general, usual, and normal, and "exceptions," aberrations, deviations, anything specific, unusual, or abnormal.

However, despite these cultural, social, and situational modifications, there still seem to be some common human universals with regard to emotions and their expressions, which is one reason why people from different cultures can communicate at all (Gaspar et al. 2014; Hwang and Matsumoto 2016; Niedenthal et al. 2006). Although people laugh differently, may laugh to different jokes, or laugh for different reason (joy, contempt, relief), laughter as such is relatively easy to identify. And so are many other emotional expressions.

The instrument, FACS, is the most widely used instrument for registration of facial expressions, across cultures, ages, and clinical conditions. So, given that we have this instrument, FACS, and given that humans have felt and expressed emotions through all times and cultures, would it be possible also to analyze archaeological depictions of faces with FACS? Faces from another culture and another time? Roman faces that were painted 2000 years ago?

The Villa of the Mysteries and Its Dionysiac Fresco

The Roman towns of Pompeii and Herculaneum, in Italy, are famous for many things, among them their wall paintings (Ling 1991; Mielsch 2001). They show with great accuracy and realism, animals, birds, landscapes, and architecture, but also people and gods from mythology, literature, and from real, everyday life. Pompeii and Herculaneum were destroyed under the great volcanic eruption of Mount Vesuvius in October AD 79. Before that, Pompeii was a middle-sized town with a flourishing international trade and a cosmopolitan cultural life.

The Villa of the Mysteries with its famous Fresco is located a few minutes' walk north of Pompeii centrum, close to the Herculaneum Gate on Via dei Sepolcri (Zanker 1998, p. 73). The Villa has a long history (Pisarra 2006/2007). Built around the first half of the second century BC (200–150 BC), it was originally a typical Samnite-Oscan Villa of modest size. It was refurbished and modified several times. It was an elegant Villa of considerable size with many rooms that were decorated with high-quality wall paintings and Frescos, during the Villa's Roman times. The most famous painting is the Dionysiac Fresco that was painted sometime between 60 and 40 BC in Style II phase 1b (Beyen 2013).

The Fresco is usually referred to as being "Dionysiac," because Dionysos and his partner are the central figures in the Fresco, and other persons belonging to Dionysos' entourage, Silenoi, satyrs, and a bacchant, are present. The Fresco is therefore often called the Great Dionysiac Fresco (Lindstrøm 2014; Lindstrøm in prep) It is one of the most famous Frescos from Roman antiquity.

Roman painting, as well as Roman art in general, was influenced by both Etruscan and Greek predecessors: Etruscan naturalism and Greek-Hellenistic realism (Huyghe 1962, p. 315). The Greek influences seem to have been most pronounced however, and it came from three sources: from direct contact with the Greek colonies in Campania, indirectly from Etruscan art that was influenced by the Greeks in Campania, and, finally, from direct contacts with Hellenistic Greece including the Greek regions in Asia Minor, in particular Pergamon. Roman art was characterized not only by Hellenistic naturalism and idealism but also by a strong realism, particularly with regard to facial features (Bloch 1966; Ling 1991; Mielsch 2001). Roman sculptures and paintings show facial emotional expressions, but usually only very subtly.

The Dionysiac Fresco is a typical *megalography*, a Hellenistic style of wall painting. Life-size or close-to-life-size-painted person is the criterion for a Fresco to be identified as a megalography (Vitruvius 2003, VII, 5, 2). The figures of the Fresco are ca. 160 cm high. Considering the average height of Pompeian women, 154 cm,

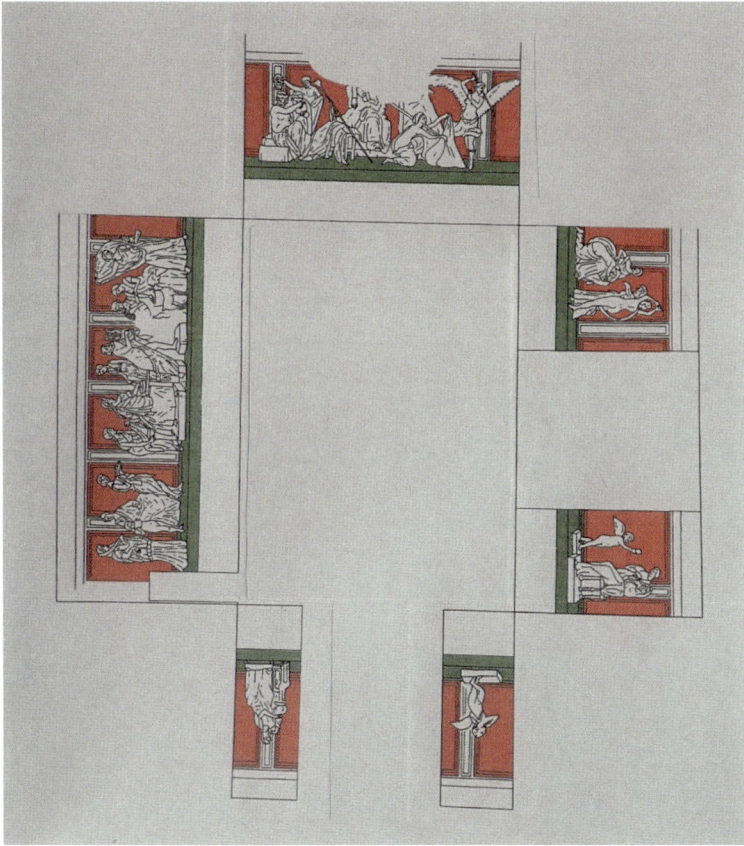

Fig. 12.1 Layout of the Dionysiac Fresco. (From Sauron 1998, with permission)

and men, 166 cm (based on skeletal remains) (History Stack Exchange (http://history.stackexchange.com/averageheight), the figures had approximately the size of the contemporary onlooker. The Fresco decorates all the walls of a *triclinium* (dining room), only "interrupted" by a large window and a large door opening (Fig. 12.1). The paintings on the four walls of the triclinium are shown in Figs. 12.2, 12.3, 12.4, and 12.5.

The approximately 2-meter-high Fresco dominates the room completely. It covers all the walls. Its life-sized figures are engaged in various activities. There are no landscapes or buildings in the Fresco to divert the onlookers' attention away from the figures. They catch all attention. There are 29 (possibly 28) persons, human and divine (or perhaps humans impersonating divinities), and 2 herbivore animals (a fawn and a goat). Of the persons, 19 are adult females, 5 are adult males, and 5 are boys. A lot of interactions are going on: Two women listen to a reading (or chanting) boy, four women are doing something with what appear to be household utensils, a Silenos plays a lyre, two satyrs take care of animals, and a woman is running while

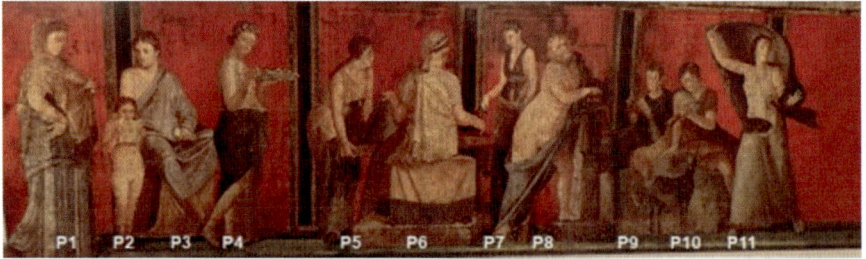

Fig. 12.2 The Dionysiac Fresco, northern wall. The persons are labelled with a "P" and a number according to their position

Fig. 12.3 The Dionysiac Fresco, eastern wall

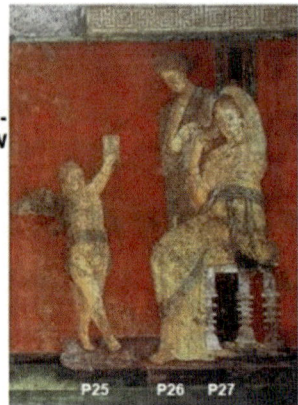

Fig. 12.4 The Dionysiac Fresco, southern wall

Fig. 12.5 The Dionysiac Fresco, western wall

looking at a Silenos who, with two satyrs, probably is engaged in a kind of divination practice (lecanomancy) (*lekanomanteia*) in a liquid within a bowl, or catoptromancy (*katoptromanteia*) a vision on the inside of a bowl (Taylor 2008: 106–08, 113–36). Dionysos rests in the arms of his partner, and a woman is about to unveil a *phallos* while looking at a winged female who is whipping a woman kneeling over another woman's lap. A woman looks at the whipping while attending a dancing woman. Two Eroses attend two women who probably are engaged in another divination practice (catoptromancy with a mirror) while doing the hair of one of them, and finally, a seated woman looks toward the last divination scene. These interactions entail many movements. Perhaps these movements are accompanied by facial expressions of emotional states?

Hellenistic art is characterized by realism in facial features and expressions and of movements. Since the Dionysiac Fresco is Hellenistic and entails many interactive movements, one should expect also to find emotional expressions on the faces of the persons in the Fresco. Earlier interpretations of emotions in the Fresco often have focused on particular persons, such as the running woman. She is generally interpreted as expressing fear and Dionysos as expressing love and excitement (De Grummond 2002). However, these interpretations have largely been done intuitively. Therefore, I wanted to investigate, in a systematic way, the faces of *all* the persons in the Dionysiac Fresco and try to identify their emotional expressions.

Methods

Data Collection

Data were quantitative registrations of the facial expressions of the persons that are painted in the Dionysiac Fresco in Villa of the Mysteries, Pompeii, registered and scored with FACS (Ekman and Friesen 1978; Ekman and Rosenberg 2005). The FACS was originally developed for registering emotions on faces of living people and from photos, films, and videos. Paintings of faces have in common with photos of faces that they are still depictions. Paul Ekman confirmed to me that FACS can be, and has been, used on paintings of faces (Costa and Corazza 2006a, b) and encouraged me to study these particular Roman paintings with FACS. Since the facial expressions of the persons in the Fresco are generally rather subtle, I was advised to register and score as Action Units (AUs) even the minor variations, particularly around the eyes and mouth (Ekman, personal communication, 27 July, 2008). The FACS scoring was conducted by three independent analysts, myself and two graduate psychology students. The students had learned the FACS manual and were instructed and tested regarding its use. Three scorers are considered sufficient when the FACS manual is used properly.

Instrument: The Facial Action Coding System

The Facial Action Coding System (FACS) is based on the structures and actions of the anatomically defined human facial muscle groups (Ekman and Friesen 1978). Both the muscle contractions, called Action Units (AUs) (Table 12.1, upper part), and their intensity (on a scale from 1 to 5) are registered. A simpler system was also developed by Ekman and Friesen, with more grossly defined Action Units that are easier to register (Table 12.1, lower part). Both systems were used here.

Although the FACS is developed to identify and register muscle contractions and their intensity which take place in moving faces (using film or video), the actual registration takes place with the help of playback and still pictures, and the instruction manual have photos to exemplify the expressions. Meaning that, still pictures can be analyzed with FACS. Although developed within psychology, it has been extensively used outside psychology, for instance, in psychiatry, criminal studies, terrorist identification, teaching, art studies, robot developments comparative ethology, and primate studies (Caeiro et al. 2012; Costa and Corazza 2006a, b; Del Giudice and Colle 2007; Ekman and Rosenberg 2005; Freitas-Magalhães 2012; Hamm et al. 2011; Lints-Martindale et al. 2007; Vick et al. 2006). Several of these studies have used photos and other still pictures. As mentioned above, FACS is also used on art (Costa and Corazza 2006a, b). Therefore, I felt confident when applying FACS to painted pictures in a Roman fresco.

Table 12.1 The FACS (Facial Action Scoring System and its Action Units (AU))

AU number	Descriptor	Muscular basis
1	Inner brow raiser	Frontalis, pars medialis
2	Outer brow raiser	Frontalis, pars lateralis
4	Brow lowerer	Depressor glabellae, depressor supercilii, corrugator
5	Upper lid raiser	Levator palpebrae superioris
6	Cheek raiser	Orbicularis oculi, pars orbitalis
7	Lid tightener	Orbicularis oculi, pars palebralis
9	Nose wrinkle	Levator labii superioris, alaeque nasi
10	Upper lip raiser	Levator labii superioris, caput
11	Nasolabial folder deepener	Zygomatic minor
12	Lip corner puller	Zygomatic major
13	Cheek puffer	Caninus
14	Dimpler	Buccinator
15	Lip corner depressor	Triangularis
16	Lower lip depressor	Depressor labii
17	Chin raiser	Mentalis
18	Lip puckerer	Incisivii labii superioris, incisivii labii inferioris
20	Lip stretcher	Risorius
22	Lip funneler	Orbicularis oris
23	Lip tightener	Orbicularis oris
24	Lip pressor	Orbicularis oris
25	Lips part	Depressor labii, or relaxation of mentalis or orbicularis oris
26	Jaw drop	Masetter, temporal and internal pterygoid relaxed
27	Mouth stretch	Pterygoids, disastric
28	Lip suck	Orbicular Orbis

Findings

The findings are shown in Table 12.2. The persons are labelled P1 to P29, meaning Person 1 to Person 29, as they are labelled in Fig. 12.2, 12.3, 12.4, and 12.5. FACS' large range of Action Units (43) and range regarding degree of intensity (1–5) give 215 different possible scorings. Despite this large number, the scorings between the raters were 56% completely identical. Another 36% had a very slight discrepancy regarding intensity (one degree) but within the same Action Units (AUs). This discrepancy was regarded as unsubstantial as it was relevant only for the intensity of the emotion, not for identification of the emotion itself. Taken together, these results gave a 92% inter-scorer agreement of emotions, meaning that there was a high reliability in the scoring and registration of facial expressions.

Of the 29 individuals depicted in the Dionysiac Fresco, only the faces of 25 (15 females and 10 males) could be analyzed, as 3 faces were disintegrated, and 1 per-

Table 12.2 Facial expressions scored by FACS as AUs and interpreted emotions

	Action Units (AU)									Final AUs	Emotion
	AU1	AU2	AU4	AU5	AU7	AU15	AU17	AU23	AU25		
Scorers (scorer 1/(versus) 2 and 3)	1/2+3	1/2+3	1/2+3	1/2+3	1/2+3	1/2+3	1/2+3	1/2+3	1/2+3		
Persons											
P 1 woman standing or walking				1/1				1/1		AU5: 1, AU23: 1	Neutral
P 2 boy reading				1/1				1/1		AU5: 1, AU23: 1	Neutral
P 3 woman seated next to reading boy				1/					1/1	(AU5: 1), AU23: 1	Neutral
P 4 woman carrying object				1?/1				1/1		AU5: 1, AU23: 1	Neutral
P 5 woman bending, holding object				2/1				2/1		AU5: 1–2, AU23: 1–2	Neutral
P 6 woman sitting, seen from behind								1/1		AU23: 1	Neutral
P 7 woman pouring liquid from a jar									1(?)/1	AU25: 1	Neutral
P 8 man with lyre (Silenos)				1/1		1/1	/1	1(2)/1		AU5: 1, AU15: 1, AU23: 1, (AU17: 1)	Sadness? ? serenity?
P 9 boy with syrinx (pan?)				1/1				1/1		AU5:1, AU23: 1	Neutral
P 10 boy or girl with fawn					1/			1/1		AU23: 1, (AU7 1)	Neutral
P 11 woman running				3/2					2/2	AU5: 2–3, AU25: 2	Fear
P 12 man sitting, holding bowl (Silenos)			1?/1	1/1					2(3)/2	AU4: 1, AU5: 1, AU25: 2	Annoyance, surprise?
P 13 man bending over bowl (a satyr?)				3/3						AU5: 3	Surprise?

Figure								AU summary	Interpretation
P 14 man standing, with mask (satyr?)		x		x			3/3	AU23: 3	Neutral
P 15 man reclining near P16 (Dionysos)					1/2		3/3	AU5: 1–2, AU25: 3	Ecstasy?
P 16 woman sitting, holding P15	x	x	x	x	x	x	x	x	Missing data
P 17 woman kneeling, arms at object						2/1(2)		AU23: 2	Neutral
P 18 woman standing behind P17	x	x	x	x	x	x	x	x	Missing data
P 19 woman standing close to P18	x	x	x	x	x	x	x	x	Missing data
P 20 woman winged, holding whip					1/1		2/2	AU5: 1, AU25: 2	Neutral?
P 21 woman kneeling over another's lap	x	1?/x	x	x	x	x	x	x, (AU1: 1)	Missing data
P 22 woman sitting, P21's head in lap	/1(2)	1/2(1)	2/2	2/2	3/3		1(?)/1	AU1: 1, AU5: 3, AU25: 1, (AU2: 1)	Surprise, fear?
P 23 woman standing, holding thyrsos			2/2	1/1	2/2	1/1		AU5: 2, AU15: 1, AU23: 1	Sadness? concern?
P 24 woman dancing ("the maenad")	x	x	x	x	x	x	x	x	Missing data
P 25 boy winged, holding mirror (Eros)					3/3(4)	1/1		AU5: 3, AU23: 1	Neutral
P 26 woman looking at mirror					2/1	1/1		AU5: 1–2, AU23: 1	Neutral
P 27 woman sitting, doing her hair					/2(1)	1/1		AU23: 1, (AU5: 2)	Neutral
P 28 boy winged, holding a bow (Eros)				2/2		1/1		AU7: 2, AU23: 1	Neutral
P 29 woman sitting			2/2	2/2	2/2		2/2	AU5: 2, AU25: 2	Neutral

Missing data (impossible to score) are marked with an X in the table

son was seen from behind. The 25 faces that could be scored can be seen either en face or in varying degrees of profiles. The facial expressions were registered as separate Action Units (AUs) according to the FACS manual. The emotion of each individual was determined based on the combination of registered Action Units, in accordance with the FACS manual. All data are presented in Table 12.2.

Few Action Units (AUs) were found in the faces, only nine, AU1, inner brow raiser; AU2, outer brow raiser; AU4, brow lowerer; AU5, upper lid raiser; AU7, lid thightener; AU15, lip corner depressor; AU17, chin raiser; AU23, lip tightener; and AU25, lips part. However, eight of these are directly connected to eyes and mouth, which are the most important areas for emotional expressions.

The intensities were low: Of possible scores ranging between 1 and 5, medium intensity level (3) was scored on seven persons, level 4 on one person only, and the rest on level 1 or 2. This means that most of the persons had rather neutral, expressionless faces, and those who showed emotions, showed them in a low degree.

Of the 24 visible faces, 17 (68%) had neutral faces with no particular emotion expressed. The seven remaining persons (28%) showed some emotional expressions, but they were so subtle that, in the table, each emotion is followed by a question mark in order to underline this fact (Fig. 12.6). Interpreted, they expressed the

P8 SADNESS, SERENITY

P11 FEAR

P12ANNOYANCE, SURPRISE

P13 SURPRISE

P15ECSTASY

P22 SURPRISE, FEAR

P23 SADNESS, CONCERN

Fig. 12.6 The seven faces with emotional expressions. Moving left to right from the top left: P8 sadness; P11 fear; P12 annoyance, surprise; P13 surprise; P15 ecstasy; P22 surprise, fear; P23 sadness, concern

following emotions: Two appeared sad or serene, Person 8 (P8) a man with lyre, commonly identified as Silenos; and sad or concerned, Person 23 (P23) a woman standing, holding a *thyrsos*. One person displayed annoyance or surprise, Person 12 (P12) a man sitting and holding a bowl, commonly identified as another Silenos. Two additional persons displayed surprise, Person 13 (P13) a man bending over a bowl, most possibly a satyr, and Person 22 (P22) a woman sitting with Person 21's (P21) head in her lap, or it is possible that she displays some fear. Another person more clearly displayed fear: Person 11 (P11) a running woman. The only possible, but not certain, positive emotion (ecstasy?) was displayed by Person 15 (P15) identified as Dionysos. He may be interpreted as expressing a state of ecstasy as his head is bent backward and his eyes are rolling upward, an expression that is found during certain ecstasy-enhancing religious practices (Alland Jr. 1962; Eliade 1974).

Discussion

This analysis of facial expressions of the persons in the Dionysiac Fresco from Pompeii suggests that they show a limited range and low intensity of emotional expressions. Most of the persons are characterized by neutral serenity and emotional control. Even the two Silenoi (P8 and P12) and the satyr (P13) are serene. Usually, they are depicted drunk and happy. That Dionysos' face indicates ecstasy is more to be expected. The amount of emotional neutrality in this Fresco is odd considering that Hellenistic art tended to be emotionally expressive and Dionysiac practices to be emotionally excessive. The very narrow range and low intensity of the registered Action Units (AUs) may be due to three causes, and these causes are not mutually exclusive:

The first is methodological. Some of the painted faces were difficult to inspect and analyze because they were "worn" after having been covered under layers of ash and soil for about 2000 years and exposed to air after they were dug out in the 1920s (Maiuri 1931).

The second possible cause is the general Roman ideal of self-composure and emotional control, for both sexes, but in particular for men. The culturally approved ideal self-presentation of a Roman man was one of being educated, eloquent, responsible, and controlled, possessing "honor," "dignitas," "gravitas," and "severitas" (Dupont 1989; Giardina 1993; Lessing and Varone 2001, p. 94). A Roman man should possess self-composure, not lose his temper, and not let his emotions show. Exceptions were emotions shown during funerals and after the Roman army had suffered defeats. But these emotions were not necessarily "felt"; they were primarily prescribed displays of the correct sentiments for these social and public occasions. So, in these connections, Roman men were not expected to express emotions, but to display feelings. According to their ideals, depictions of Roman men are indeed very serene.

Emotionality was regarded as effeminate and a sign of weakness. According to the Romans, emotionality characterized women, children, and slaves but also actors, entertainers, prostitutes, barbarians, and animals. All of these were regarded as having no proper control of themselves, no self-composure (Lindstrøm 2011). Yet, Roman freeborn women represented a middle category between Roman men and non-Romans, and ought to control their emotions. Still, women were regarded as being considerably influenced, if not governed, by their emotions, and therefore not regarded as quite rational or reliable. However, they were necessary for the reproduction of Roman citizens and therefore expected to conduct themselves accordingly, with dignity and modesty, expressing pudicitia (modesty, chastity, purity) and fides (loyalty to their husband) (Hölkeskamp 2004). In particular, women from the higher social strata were expected to exert self-control. This mixed attitude regarding women is also shown in that the paintings of women may sometimes show more emotional expressions than those of men. Children of freeborn Romans also had the ambiguous role of being "Roman" yet were still childish: emotional, immature, and unreliable. Also their faces are depicted varyingly: often emotionally non-expressive, but sometimes quite expressive.

In the Fresco in Villa of the Mysteries, the majority (24) of the persons from whom facial expressions could be registered were either female (19) or children (5). Considering the Roman ideas of emotionality, one might expect to find, at least some, more emotional expressions than what was found. This leads to the third possible cause for the low number of emotional expressions:

The Fresco has many Dionysiac elements, iconic, indexical, and symbolic signs, so it is indeed justified to call it "Dionysiac." The presence of Dionysos in the center of the Fresco is the strongest indication. But whatever is shown in Fresco, it is definitely not wild and orgiastic Dionysiac activities. This is puzzling because Dionysiac rites and cultic behaviors could be rather intense with regard to emotionality. And indeed, other Dionysiac paintings, statues, sarcophaguses, and figurines depict maenads and satyrs engaged in orgiastic dancing, and the various Dionysiac processions, often phallophoric, were definitely not characterized by serenity. It was the very transgression of the normal behaviors and of the boundary zone between the human and the divine, and to experience a transcendent state of unity and ecstatic communion with Dionysos, that was the essence of the rites and Dionysiac practices. To be initiated to the mysteries of Dionysos, to be drinking wine (incorporating Dionysos) and perhaps dancing, could lead to the highly emotionally charged states of Dionysiac enthusiasmos and mania, the "Bacchic frenzy" (bakkheia) (Henrichs 1993; Nilsson 1957).

When these orgiastic Dionysiac aspects are not found in the emotional semiotics of the Fresco, it is a possibility that the rituals shown there were connected to, or at least influenced by, the cult of Dionysos Zagreus, the Orphic Dionysos. There are several indications, signs, for this in the Fresco, of which a few are mentioned here: The serenity of the persons is a very concrete iconic sign. The total absence of wine, vines, and grapes, despite the fact that Dionysos was the god of wine, is so noteworthy that this absence can be regarded as an indexical sign. The unusual soberness of Silenos and satyrs likewise are iconic signs: Whatever the Fresco shows is not about Dionysiac drunkenness and ecstatic practices. The harmony between animals (goat and fawn) and humans (actually satyrs here, but depicted in more human forms than usual) is very special. It stands in contrast to the typical sacrifice of goats to Dionysos, the maenads' tearing apart of wild animals, and the fawn fleece that Dionysos sometimes wore. This harmony in the Fresco involves all three kinds of semiotic signs (iconic, indexical, and symbolic). It is iconic in that a harmonious tender relationship is concretely shown; it is indexical in that it refers to the absence of ritual killing; and it may be symbolic in its possible referral to Orpheus who was a "master of animals" and who attracted and tamed wild animals with his music and singing (Counts and Arnold 2010).

The elements of prophesying also can be taken to hint to Orpheus, whose head was an oracle after his death, and thus function as both iconic and indexical signs. In the Fresco, a satyr Person 13 (P13) looks into a bowl, and Person 26 (P26) looks into a mirror. The former can be lekanomanteia, prophesying based on a mirroring vision in a liquid within a bowl, or katoptromanteia based on a mirroring vision on the inside of a bowl (Gallistl 1995; Taylor 2008, pp. 106–108, 113–136). Also mirrors were used for katoptromanteia as they could be seen as magical, offering oracular answers to the future as well as giving contact with the dead (Taylor 2008). Oracular practices were often connected to Orpheusism.

Finally, the presence of a book scroll (in the reading scene), but possible two more, is also a sign on all three levels: iconic, indexical, and symbolic. They are iconic in that the book scroll(s) is concretely shown; indexical in that it/they refer to texts and reading, most likely during rituals; and symbolic in that the informed onlooker may understand what texts and rites book these scrolls symbolize, such as the Orphic Hymns (Graf 2009).

All these semiotic elements in the Fresco could be interpreted to point to the activities of an Orphic *thiasos* (cultic group, congregation), or at least, to some form of Dionysiac mysteries or Dionysianism inspired by Orphic philosophical ideas and cultic elements (Jiménez San Cristóbal 2009; Rizzo 1914). Since the majority of the persons in the Fresco are women, the Fresco could be connected to a cult for women. Dionysos was an extremely popular god, and he was a central god in Orphism and was in those contexts often called Dionysos Zagreus, representing a merged identity between Dionysos and Orpheus. The Orphic lifestyle, *bios orphikos*, demanded vegetarianism among other strict rules of conduct, but there were more moderate versions as well. Versions that were more philosophical and, we might say, more therapeutic for the individual. Therefore, it is possible that, whatever is shown in the Fresco, although clearly ample with Dionysiac components, might show, or refer to, rites that were of a more modest and restrained Orphic kind, and therefore the emotional expressions were accordingly moderate.

The lives of Roman women implied a considerable amount of strains, stresses, and challenges, regardless of social status. Roman marriage arrangements, dangerous childbirths, a high child mortality, and divorces in a society where children belonged to their father, were contextual factors that women had to cope with. They did not own their own bodies, nor had their ownership to their children. The children of slaves could even be sold by their owners (Hölkeskamp 2004). There could be a lot of fear in a woman's life. But women were permitted to assemble for religious purposes, and this could have given them sanctuaries (both literally and figuratively). So, to belong to a cultic group or community, a *thiasos*, one that was reserved for women (Jaccottet 2003), could have very positive effects for the members. The social life, contacts, and friends that a *thiasos* offered could, in addition to enhance joyful emotions, greatly enhance women's coping possibilities as they could get practical help, advice and social and emotional support, empathy, compassion, and understanding. Regarding Dionysos, he, among his many characteristics, could represent an ideal man and ideal god: According to the myths, he saved the lives of both his wife, Ariadne, and his mother, Semele. He cared for women and he loved them. He was also the god of nature and vegetation, fertility, fecundity, prosperity, and happiness. His devotees were even promised a happy afterlife after death. To belong to a Dionysiac *thiasos*, perhaps particularly one of an Orphic Dionysiac character, could have considerable fear-reducing effects and, in general, have positive effects on a woman's emotional life.

Conclusion

Most of the faces on the depicted person in the Dionysiac Fresco in Villa of the Mysteries show neutral expressions; and the facial expressions are vague in the seven persons who do express some emotionality. The three possible "causes" for the meagre expressions of emotions are not conflicting, but compatible. First, the methodological one is obvious: The data were from painted faces, in a Fresco in various stages of disintegration. Second, the Roman ideal of self-composure makes strong emotional expressions unlikely to be painted. Third, if it is true that the Fresco is inspired by Orphic Dionysianism which demands asceticism and self-discipline, restraints on emotional expressions are to be expected. But whatever the causes, I must conclude that there are not many or strong emotions shown in the Dionysiac Fresco in Villa of the Mysteries outside Pompeii. But it may show women who trusted the prospect of a good hereafter and who had reasonable satisfying lives.

To live in the Roman late republic and early empire meant to live in a society where emotionality was distrusted, disrespected, and even despised, a society where compassion and empathy were not considered ideals, whereas toughness and merciless exertion of power and control were. Cruelty and killing were popular public entertainments (*ludi circences*). To connect this Roman world to the "Heart and Emotion" theme feels a bit to blend oil and water. To study the emotions and motivations in this society with understanding, acceptance, and compassion is challenging (Lindstrøm 2010). However, even in this society, empathy, compassion, patience, gratitude, and understanding must have coexisted alongside the rough-and-tough ideals. Certain religious societies may have provided "pockets" where "Heart and Emotion" ideals could flourish and thrive. Partly because the religions themselves had an ethos with resembling ideals, and partly because close relations and social networks developed among the members. Dionysiac *thiasoi* (congregations), particularly those of Orphic Dionysianism, may have provided such venues were positive emotions and relations were encouraged and practiced.

References

Alland, A., Jr. (1962). "Possession" in a revivalistic negro church. *Journal for the Scientific Study of Religion, 1*(2), 204–213.

Beyen, H. G. (2013). *Die pompejanische Wanddekoration vom zweitem bis zum vierten Stil* (Vol. 1 & 2). Berlin: Springer. (First published in 1938).

Bloch, R. (1966). *Etruscan art.* London: Barrie and Rockliff.

Børresen, B. (1996). *Den ensomme apen. Instinkt på avveie.* Oslo: Gyldendal.

Brendel, O. J., & Serra Ridgway, F. R. (1995). *Etruscan art* (2nd ed.). New Haven: Yale University Press.

Caeiro, C. T. C., Waller, B. M., Zimmermann, E., Burrows, A. M., & Davila-Ross, M. (2012). OrangFACS: A muscle-based facial movement coding system for orangutans (pongo spp.). *International Journal of Primatology, 34*, 115.

Campbell, J. (1976). *The masks of god: Creative mythology.* New York: Penguin Books.

Clarke, D. S. (2003). *Sign levels.* Dordrecht: Kluwer.

Clunn, T. (2009). *The quest for the lost Roman legions: Discovering the Varus battlefield.* El Dorado Hills: Savas Beatie.

Costa, M., & Corazza, L. (2006a). Aesthetic phenomena as supernormal stimuli: The case of eye, lip, and lower-face size and roundness in artistic portraits. *Perception, 35*, 229–246.

Costa, M., & Corazza, L. (2006b). *Psicologia della Bellezza.* Firenze: Giunti.

Counts, D. B., & Arnold, B. (2010). *The master of animals in Old World iconography* (Series: Archaeolingua, 24). Budapest: Archaeolingua.

Danesi, M. (2007). *The quest for meaning: A guide to semiotic theory and practice.* Toronto: University of Toronto Press.

De Grummond, E. (2002). Mirrors, marriage, and mysteries. In J. H. Humphrey (Ed.), *Pompeian brothels, Pompeii's ancient history, mirrors and mysteries, art and nature at Oplontis, & the Herculaneum "Basilica"* (Journal of Roman Archaeology, Supplementary Series no. 47) (pp. 62–85).

Del Giudice, M., & Colle, L. (2007). Differences between children and adults in the recognition of enjoyment smiles. *Developmental Psychology, 43*(3), 796–803.

Dupont, F. (1989). *Daily life in ancient Rome.* Cambridge: Blackwell Publishers.

Ekman, P. (1992). An argument for basic emotions. *Cognition & Emotion, 6*(3–4), 169–200.

Ekman, P. (2008). Personal communication, at: The 12th European Conference on Facial Expression. Swiss Center for Affective Sciences. University of Geneva, Geneva, 27. – 31.07.2008.

Ekman, P., & Friesen, W. V. (1978). *The facial action coding system.* Palo Alto: Consulting Psychologists Press.

Ekman, P., & Rosenberg, E. L. (2005). *What the face reveals. Basic and applied studies of spontaneous expression using the Facial Action Coding System.* New York: Oxford University Press.

Eliade, M. (1974). *Shamanism. Archaic techniques of ecstasy.* Princeton: Princeton University Press.

Freitas-Magalhães, A. (2012). Microexpression and macroexpression. In V. S. Ramachandran (Ed.), *Encyclopedia of human behavior* (Vol. 2, pp. 173–183). Oxford: Elsevier/Academic Press.

Friedlund, A. J. (1994). *Human facial expression. An evolutionary view.* New York: Academic Press.

Gallistl, B. (1995). *Maske und Spiegel. Zur Maskenszene des Pompejaner Mysterienfrieses.* Hildesheim: Georg Olms Verlag.

Gaspar, A., Esteves, F., & Arriaga, P. (2014). On prototypical facial expressions versus variations in facial behavior: What we have learned on the "visibility" of emotions from measuring facial actions in humans and apes. In M. Pina & N. Gontier (Eds.), *The evolution of social communication in primates* (Interdisciplinary evolution research, vol. 1) (pp. 101–126). Cham: Springer.

Gergen, K. (1985). *The social construction of the person.* New York: Springer.

Giardina, A. (Ed.). (1993). *The romans.* Chicago: The University of Chicago Press.

Gottdiener, M., Boklund-Lagopoulou, K., & Lagopoulos, A. P. (2003). *Semiotics*. London: Sage.

Graf, F. (2009). Serious singing: The orphic hymns as religious texts. *Kernos, 22*, 169–182.

Hamm, J., Köhler, C. G., Gur, R. C., & Verma, R. (2011). Automated Facial Action Coding System for dynamic analysis of facial expressions in neuropsychiatric disorders. *Journal of Neuroscience Methods., 200*(2), 237–256.

Henrichs, A. (1993). "He Has a God in him": Human and divine in the modern perception of Dionysus. In T. H. Carpenter & C. A. Faraone (Eds.), *Masks of Dionysos* (pp. 13–43). Ithaca: Cornell University Press.

Hölkeskamp, K. J. (2004). Under Roman roofs: Family, house, and household. In H. I. Flower (Ed.), *The Cambridge companion to the Roman Republic* (pp. 113–159). Cambridge: Cambridge University Press.

Huyghe, R. (1962). Art forms and society. In R. Huyge (Ed.), *Larousse encyclopedia of prehistoric & ancient art* (pp. 312–320). London: Hamlyn.

Hwang, H., & Matsumoto, D. (2016). Evidence for the universality of facial expressions of emotion. In M. K. Mandal & A. Awasthi (Eds.), *Understanding facial expressions in communication. Cross-cultural and multidisciplinary perspectives* (pp. 41–56). New Delhi: Springer.

Jaccottet, A.-F. (2003). *Choisir Dionysos. Les associations dionysiaques ou la face cache du dionysisme*. Vol. I. Texte. Vol. II. Documents. Zürich: Akanthus.

Jantzen, D., Brinker, U., Orschiedt, J., Heinemeier, J., Piek, J., Hauenstein, K., Krüger, J., Lidke, G., Lübke, H., Lampe, R., Lorenz, S., Schult, M., & Terberger, T. (2011). A Bronze Age battlefield? Weapons and trauma in the Tollense Valley, north-eastern Germany. *Antiquity, 85*, 417–433.

Jiménez San Cristóbal, A. I. (2009). The meaning of βακχος and βακχευειν in orphism. In G. Casadio & P. A. Johnston (Eds.), *Mystic cults in Magna Graecia* (pp. 46–60). Austin: University of Texas Press.

Kanade, T., Cohn, J. F., & Tian, Y. (2000). Comprehensive database for facial expression analysis. *Proceedings of the Fourth International Conference on Automatic Face and Gesture Recognition (France Grenoble 2000 March 30)*. Los Alamitos: IEEE Computer Society.

Kring, A., & Sloan, D. M. (2007). The facial expression coding system (FACES): Development, validation, and utility. *Psychological Assessment, 19*(2), 210–224.

L'Orange, H. P. L. (1967). *Romerske keisere i marmor og bronse*. ("Roman emperors in marble and bronze"). Oslo: Dreyers Forlag.

Lessing, E., & Varone, A. (2001). *Pompeii*. Paris: Éditions Pierre Terrail.

Lindstrøm, T. C. (2010). The animals of the arena. How and why could their destruction and death be endured and enjoyed? *World Archaeology, 42*, 313–326.

Lindstrøm, T. C. (2011). Facial expressions (and non-expressions) in ancient Roman faces. Bollettino di Archeologia On Line. Volume Speciale. Poster Session 7, 87–96. Direzione Generale per le Antichità. Tribunale di Roma. www.archeologia.beniculturali.it/pages/pubblicazioni.html

Lindstrøm, T. C. (2014). Copy or not a copy? That's the question. El retrado privado en AVGVSTA EMERITA. Arqueologica Clásica (CIAC 2013). Merida: Museo Nacional de Arte Romano. Ministero de Educacion, Cultura y Deporte. ISBN 9788477968924, pp 47–50.

Lindstrøm, T. C. (in prep). The great Dionysiac fresco in Villa dei Misteri, Pompeii. A transdisciplinary investigation.

Ling, R. (1991). *Roman painting*. Cambridge: Cambridge University Press.

Lints-Martindale, A. C., Hadjistavropoulos, T., Barber, B., & Gibson, S. J. (2007). A psychophysical investigation of the Facial Action Coding System as an index of pain variability among older adults with and without Alzheimer's disease. *Pain Medicine, 8*(8), 678–689.

Maiuri, A. (1931). *Pompeii*. Roma: Libreria Dello Stato.

McKinley, J. (2015). Critical argument and writer identity: Social constructivism as a theoretical framework for EFL academic writing. *Critical Inquiry in Language Studies, 12*(3), 184–207.

Mielsch, H. (2001). *Römische wandmalerei*. Darmstadt: Wissenschaftliche Buchgesellschaft.

Miyamoto, Y., & Ryff, C. (2011). Cultural differences in the dialectical and non-dialectical emotional styles and their implications for health. *Cognition and Emotion., 25*, 22–30.

Montag, C., & Panksepp, J. (2016). Primal emotional-affective expressive foundations of human facial expression. *Motivation and Emotion, 40*, 760–766.

Montag, C., & Panksepp, J. (2017). Primary emotional systems and personality: An evolutionary perspective. *Frontiers in Psychology, 8*. https://doi.org/10.3389/fpsyg.2017.00464.

Mourre, V., Villa, P., & Henshilwood, C. S. (2010). Early use of pressure flaking on lithic artifacts at Blombos Cave, South Africa. *Science, 330*(6004), 659–662.

Nell, V. (2006). Cruelty's rewards: The gratifications of perpetrators and spectators. *Behavioral and Brain Sciences, 29*, 211–257.

Niedenthal, P. M., Krauth-Gruber, S., & Ric, F. (2006). *Psychology of emotion. Interpersonal, experiential, and cognitive approaches*. New York: Psychology Press.

Nilsson, M. P. (1957). The *Dionysiac mysteries of the Hellenistic and Roman age*. Acta Instituti Atheniensis Regni Sueciae 8, V, Lund.

Nilsson Stutz, L. (2003). *Embodied rituals and ritualized bodies: Tracing ritual practices in Late Mesolithic burials*. Acta Archaeologica Lundensia, Series in 8°, Vol. 46.

Peirce, C. S. (1955). [1931].). *Logic assemiotic*. New York: Dover.

Pisarra, D. (2006/2007). La Villa dei Misteri di Pompei: Documantazione d'archivio ed analisi delle fasi edilizie. Tesi di laurea. Università degli Studi della Calabria, Facoltà di Lettere e Filosofia.

Plutchik, R. (1980). *Emotion: A psychoevolutionary synthesis*. New York: Harper & Row.

Plutchik, R. (2003). *Emotions and life: Perspectives from psychology, biology and evolution*. Washington, D. C.: American Psychological Association.

Ramage, N. H., & Ramage, A. (1995). *Roman art. Romulus to Constantine*. London: Laurence King Publishing.

Ramberg, B., & Gjesdal, K. (2003, 2005). Hermeneutics: Continuations. Stanford encyclopedia of philosophy, https://plato.stanford.edu/

Reber, R., Schwarz, N., & Winkielman, P. (2004). Processing fluency and aesthetic pleasure: Is beauty in the perceiver's processing experience? *Personality and Social Psychology Review, 8*(4), 364–382.

Rizzo, G. E. (1914). Dionysos Mystes. Contributi esegetici alla rapprezentazione dei misteri orfici. Memorie dell'Accademia Archiologico di Napoli, (pp 39–101).

Sauron, G. (1998). *La grande fresque de La Villa des Mystères à Pompéi*. Paris: Picard.

Scarantino, A., & de Sousa, R. (2018). Emotion. In E. Zalta (Ed.), *The Stanford encyclopedia of philosophy*. (Winter 2018 edition). https://plato.stanford.edu/archives/win2018/entries/emotion/

Sonesson, G. (1989). *Pictorial concepts. Inquiries into the semiotic heritage and its relevance for the analysis of the visual world*. Lund: Lund University Press.

Taylor, R. (2008). *The moral mirror of Roman art*. Cambridge: Cambridge University Press.

Tsai, J. L., Louie, J. Y., Chen, E. E., & Uchida, Y. (2007). Learning what feelings to desire: Socialization of ideal affect through children's storybooks. *Personality and Social Psychology Bulletin., 33*(1), 17–30.

Vick, S. J., Waller, B. M., Parr, L. A., Smith Pasqualini, M. C., & Bard, K. A. (2006). A cross-species comparison of facial morphology and movement in humans and chimpanzees Using the Facial Action Coding System (FACS). *Journal of Nonverbal Behavior, 31*(1), 1–20.

Vitruvius, M. P. (2003). *De architechtura*. New York: The Monacelli Press.

Walton, S. (2016). *Natural history of human emotions, eBook*. Dean Street Press.

Zanker, P. (1998). *Pompeii. Public and private life*. Cambridge: Harvard University Press.

Chapter 13
Conceiving of "Them" When Before There Was Only "Us"

Melanie L. Chang and April Nowell

Introduction

Let's be honest. Most scientists who study human evolution entered the field for fundamentally romantic reasons. As Matt Cartmill put it, "The hunger for mytho-logical charters is a large part of what draws people to the study of human origins" (Cartmill 2002: 196). If we wanted to do science as a pure quest for knowledge in the service of understanding *how things work*, we wouldn't be studying human evolution. Humans are terrible models for understanding how evolution works for a lot of reasons, including the taxonomic poverty of our clade, long generation times, ethical limitations on experimental research, and a sub-par fossil record. As paleo-anthropologists, our practices belie our motivations. We follow breadcrumb trails consisting of bones, stones, and DNA to retrace our footsteps and fashion specific, elaborate, very detailed reconstructions of prehistoric events and relationships, rather than seeking to elucidate the general mechanisms (if there are any) underly-ing those events and relationships. We study human evolution for the same reasons that nonscientists watch caveman documentaries on PBS: broadly, to reconstruct prehistoric lifeways, but even more than that, because we (like those PBS viewers) desire to understand what it would have been like to *be* those long-dead people and to *live* those ancient lives.

Paleoanthropologists, not without reason, are routinely accused of storytelling (Landau 1991). As "perhaps the most multidisciplinary of all the sciences" (Henke and Tattersall 2015: vii), in paleoanthropology we routinely engage with experts in other, more-or-less related disciplines to benefit from insights in their fields. This

M. L. Chang (✉)
Portland State University, Portland, OR, USA
e-mail: mlchang@pdx.edu

A. Nowell
University of Victoria, Victoria, BC, Canada
e-mail: anowell@uvic.ca

© Springer Nature Switzerland AG 2020
K. Supernant et al. (eds.), *Archaeologies of the Heart*,
https://doi.org/10.1007/978-3-030-36350-5_13

commonly (in our experience) means bumping up against the often vague but sometimes explicit assumption that what we do is not actually scientific. One of us (meaning the authors), perhaps as an act of overcompensation, pursued a dual degree in anthropology and evolutionary biology and was therefore required to perform a thesis defense in the biology department before graduating. Evolutionary biology is not a hard science either, but biologists tend to think of themselves as more rigorous than anthropologists are and do not grapple with the emotional questions that paleoanthropologists do. During the defense, the biologists repeatedly expressed befuddlement with the questions asked by the anthropologists. And afterward, during the post-defense celebration, they wanted to know: "Why are anthropologists always asking questions that *no one* can answer?" It's a fair criticism: the questions we seek to answer are so specific and so detailed, so beyond the capacity of the available data to address, that even posing them might seem fruitless. We (the authors) like to refer to these as "time machine questions." But stretching the bounds of inquiry is the paleoanthropologist's stock in trade.

Traditional models of science demand detachment. Couple the groping, emotional nature of paleoanthropological inquiry with widespread public sentiment about the basic pointlessness of anthropology as a discipline (Gibbons 2012; Rapacon 2019), and we might have an explanation for why some researchers (perhaps overcompensating) tack so hard in the opposite direction, toward a level of detachment that we consider to be counterproductive. The treatment of the Neandertals, by all measures our closest relatives, by Paleolithic archaeologists provides many cases in point. Our perspectives on Neandertals have historically been filtered through the puzzle of whether we should consider Neandertals to be "Us" or "Them" (Drell 2000), in more than just the taxonomic sense. This soul-searching reflects a deep-seated need on the part of both scientists and the public to understand what makes us unique or "special" – those traits that distinguish us, anatomically modern humans, from both our antecedents and closest living relatives. From a researcher's perspective, the distinction may boil down to one of ethology vs. ethnography. Given that time machine (and generous funding) for observational studies, which would we be practicing? Would meeting a Neandertal be an experience like spotting a Sasquatch or observing a zoo chimpanzee behind glass? Or would it be more like meeting a new neighbor, from another country or culture perhaps, but someone with whom you share and in whom you recognize a common humanity: someone with whom you could imagine getting a bite to eat, becoming friends, maybe even falling in love?

The null hypothesis of practically all Neandertal studies of is that they were *not like us*. However, efforts to appear more rigorous by keeping our closest relatives at a figurative arm's length may actually impede scientific progress by introducing biases *against* hypotheses proposing similarities between Neandertals and modern humans. This bias (overcompensation) leads paleoanthropologists to ask questions about Neandertals and their abilities that (given our similarities, never mind the fact that they persisted for hundreds of thousands of years across a wide range of environments and occupied much of Eurasia) often seem patently ridiculous. By opening ourselves to the possibility that the Neandertals were *like us* – that they were fundamentally human – we free ourselves as scientists to generate new, explicit hypotheses that are at least as testable as hypotheses framed from the opposite and prevailing viewpoint.

In this chapter, we consider the evidence for symbolic behavior among Neandertals in the form of personal ornaments and contextualize this evidence by considering the hypothesis that these ornaments were produced and should be understood within the context of symbolically mediated social relationships. The capacity for symbolic behavior may have been shared by Neandertals and modern humans and therefore may also have characterized our last common ancestor.[1] We suggest that evidence of apparently symbolic behavior in the Neandertal archaeological record in the form of personal ornaments reflects increased interactions between Neandertal groups that occurred due to environmental changes toward the end of the Pleistocene and possibly reactions to the influx of modern humans.

The Neandertals

The Neandertals evolved at least 400,000 years ago in glacial Late Pleistocene Europe. The geographic range of the Eurasian Neandertals stretched from Wales to the Altai, northward to Siberia, and southward to Gibraltar where the last remaining members of this population disappeared from the fossil record between 40,000 and 30,000 years ago. Between 120,000 and 54,000 years ago, Neandertals also inhabited the Levant, a region that includes the modern states of Israel, Jordan, Lebanon, and Syria (Nowell 2014b). During their time on this planet, Neandertals overlapped temporally and sometimes geographically with modern human populations – with us. Recent evidence indicates that late Neandertals and early modern humans in Eurasia were exploiting similar environments, producing similar artifacts, exhibiting nearly identical subsistence patterns (Nowell 2013; Roebroeks and Soressi 2016), and at least occasionally mating with each other (Fu et al. 2015; Kuhlwilm et al. 2016; Prüfer et al. 2014, 2017; Sankararaman et al. 2016, Simonti et al. 2016; Vernot and Akey 2015).

One of the major questions in later human evolution is that of the Neandertals' demise. We overlapped in both time and space with Neandertals during the Middle to Late Pleistocene, potentially (in some areas) for at least 100,000 years. Why are we the last ones standing? How do we explain why Neandertals went extinct and not modern humans? Potential explanations often rely on the principle of competitive exclusion, which posits that when two species occupy the same ecological niche (require the same resources) in the same environment, one either goes extinct or changes through evolution to occupy an alternative niche (Banks et al. 2008; Flores 2011; Gilpin et al. 2016; Hardin 1960). Such competition is exacerbated when spe-

---

[1] This hypothesis could have implications for the symbolic capabilities of *Homo heidelbergensis*, Denisovans, and other yet-to-be discovered hominin populations of the Middle to Late Pleistocene. Indeed, recent dates for jewelry and bone points at Denisova Cave suggest that the Denisovan inhabitants exhibited symbolic behavior (Douka et al. 2019).

cies are closely related. One model that has had some staying power proposes that the ability to make and use symbols – and by extension, to communicate using symbol-based language – is unique to modern humans (e.g., Barnard et al. 2016; Chase 2003; Davidson 2014, 2016; Henshilwood 2007; Henshilwood and Marean 2003; Marean 2007; Soffer 2009; Wynn et al. 2015). Studies of mostly (but not exclusively) later Neandertal sites (i.e., <48,000 BP), however, indicate that the last of the Neandertals were, at minimum, producing artifacts (e.g., Caron et al. 2011; Welker et al. 2016; Zilhão et al. 2010) and altering faunal remains (e.g., Morin and Laroulandie 2012; Peresani et al. 2012; Radovcic et al. 2015; Romandini et al. 2014) in ways suggesting personal ornamentation. Such evidence would, if found in sites associated with anatomically modern human remains, be accepted with little question as symbolic (Kuhn et al. 2004; Romandini et al. 2014; but see Wynn et al. 2015). These archaeological indicators appear to be associated with either dramatic climate change (Müller et al. 2011) or an influx of modern humans (Higham et al. 2015; Müller et al. 2011) that constricted the Neandertal range, or both, perhaps bringing previously more widely distributed Neandertal communities into closer proximity with each other. Rather than assuming that Neandertals lacked symbolic capabilities, we suggest that it is more phylogenetically conservative to assume that Neandertals possessed behavioral patterns like those of their closest relatives, modern humans. In other words, like us.

History and the Emotional Resonance of Neandertals

As the first hominin fossils to be discovered and eventually recognized for what they were – ancient humans (Trinkaus and Shipman 1992) – Neandertals are close to us in more than a phylogenetic sense, as their discovery initiated the study of human evolution as a discipline. In the late 1850s, when the first Neandertal fossils were discovered, models of biological diversity cast modern *Homo sapiens* as a species that was unique and profoundly alone. Rudolf Virchow, the eminent pathologist and anti-evolutionist, declared the Neander Valley specimens to be nothing more than the remains of a modern human with arthritis and rickets (Virchow 1872). At the same time, the doctrine of polygenism (Nott and Gliddon 1854, 1857), which decreed that the human races (as then recognized) were in fact different species, with different origins, and different hierarchical relationships, was well-established. This view of human variation was pre-evolutionary (Linnaeus 1735) and had roots in Biblical accounts of separate creation. Prominent American polygenists included "founding fathers" of physical anthropology such as Samuel George Morton and Louis Agassiz. The polygenic model of biological diversity was challenged and largely subsumed by Darwin's theory of evolution, which established the doctrine of monogenism and the necessary interpretation that all modern humans (indeed, all living things) had a common ancestor (Darwin 1859, 1871), but elements of this perspective, particularly those involving the perceived relationships and degrees of modernity of different human groups, live on in Western scientific and political contexts.

In the early 1900s, attitudes toward Neandertals were solidified by paleoanthropologist Marcellin Boule, whose reconstructions of the old man from La Chapelle-aux-Saints, France, led him to believe that Neandertals were too unlike later Europeans and too close to them in time to be ancestral to them. He described Neandertals as qualitatively and quantitatively different from modern humans, fundamentally apelike, unable to stand and walk upright (Boule 1911–1912, *L'Homme Fossile de La Chapelle-aux-Saints*; Hammond 1982). The stereotype of a hunchbacked, grunting, monosyllabic brute, perhaps carrying a club in one hand and dragging his woman by the hair with the other, persists in the popular imagination but lives alongside another, more favorable depiction: a noble savage of the sort envisioned by the "wilderness cult" of the early twentieth century (Nash 2014) who may have been compassionate, even religious (Solecki 1971), and if shaved and dressed appropriately, would not invite scrutiny in a New York subway (Coon 1939). This Neandertal, if they lived today, among us, in a contemporary cultural context, would be just like us. Is either image correct?

Modern attitudes toward Neandertals are often surprising. Historical constructions of Neandertal biology and cognition as fundamentally primitive reflect both the scientific paradigms and cultural racism of the times in which they were originally discovered. Irish geologist William King, who named the species *Homo neanderthalensis* (thereby becoming the first scientist ever to name a prehistoric human species), described the Neander Valley fossils as "simial" and believed they resembled the skulls of chimpanzees more than those of any modern population but also likened them to Africans, Australians, and other "races" he regarded as "degraded" and "savage" (King 1864). This intellectual tradition shares its heritage with the scientific racism upon which twenty-first-century principles of white supremacy are founded (Hemmer 2017). And yet, contemporary white supremacists who view the Neandertals as essentially European, as part of their primeval heritage, often embrace genetic evidence of Neandertal ancestry, in some cases attributing the "intellectual supremacy" and "physical prowess" of Europeans to this heritage (Reeve 2016; Zhang 2016). Some "are flaunting DNA ancestry test results indicating exclusively European heritage as though they were racial ID cards. They are celebrating traces of Neanderthal DNA not found in people with only African ancestry" (Harmon 2018). Distinctions between "Us" and "Them" prove to be unexpectedly flexible.

These similarities suggest basic commonalities, and yet hypotheses regarding Neandertal behavior and cognition tend to be framed from the opposite perspective, which is considered to be the "conservative" perspective – that the Neandertals were profoundly different from modern humans, that they did not have the capacity to act in modern, human ways, defined by expressing themselves symbolically, and that they did not possess modern language (e.g., Wynn and Coolidge 2012; Wynn et al. 2015). This "conservative" perspective underlies models that portray Neandertal behavioral and material culture as largely monolithic, varying little over space and time, and being more biologically determined than those of modern humans. Nowhere is this perspective more pronounced than in discussions of Neandertal symbolic behavior.

Personal Ornaments and Evidence of Symbolic Behavior Among Neandertals

Are Personal Ornaments Symbolic?

Personal ornaments play key roles in social production and continuity, have histories that link them to ancestors, and are visible, interpretable objects conveying shared meaning (White 1992) that may, in some cases, take on identities and stories of their own beyond the life of an individual (Post and Farges 2014; White 1992). Such ornaments transmit information and signal identity at a "middle distance," conveying meaning for those close enough to understand shared meanings, but who lack intimate knowledge of a particular individual or group (Kuhn and Stiner 2007).

In a recent paper, Wynn et al. (2015:9) argue that "among extant humans at least, personal ornaments are occasionally symbols, but more often they act as indexes." For example, they describe multiple body piercings popular among university students as "rarely symbolic but they do mark perceived social identity." By extension, they reason that there is no basis for assuming that Neandertal pendants were symbolic, because such pendants can also be explained simply as indexes of group affiliation.

We disagree with this interpretation for two reasons. First, Peirce (1998:143) defines an index as "a sign which refers to the Object that it denotes by virtue of being really affected by the Object...in so far as Index is affected by the Object, it necessarily has some Quality in common with the Object, and it is in respect of these that it refers to the Object." Examples of indexes include shadows, perfume lingering in the air, cooking smells, footprints, fever (as an index of infection), bullet holes, voices, recordings of voices, smoke from a fire, a knock on a door, tree rings (as an index of age), fingerprints, signatures, and handwriting (Huening 2006; Sadowski 2009). Sadowski (2009:94), in his analysis of Peirce, argues that Peirce's description of an index as being "affected by" the object should be interpreted to mean that it "is physically *caused* by the object (sender) without which index simply could not exist. In other words, a shadow cast by a tree is not simply 'affected by a tree,' it is fully caused by it." As Peirce (1998:143) notes, an index "depends upon association by contiguity," i.e., in its origin, an index is in direct contact with its object (Sadowski 2009). This is clearly not the case for personal ornaments, which are not in "contiguous association" with membership in a social group; the concept of group membership cannot directly and physically cause an ornament to come into being in the way that a specific person causes a perfume to linger in the air in a specific location. Similarly, "while symbols cannot be signs without an interpreter, indices cannot be signs without their objects (no interpreter or 'reader' necessary) (Huening 2006)."

The specific social identity or group affiliation of an individual wearing a personal ornament cannot otherwise be deduced by an observer except through the observation of other signs that may themselves be indexical (the presence of equipment related to occupation, etc.), whereas ornaments can serve as symbols of social or cultural group affiliation even in the absence of any human wearing them. In addition, forms or representations that are themselves symbolic (e.g., writing, religious symbols such as the Hindu swastika or gammadion cross, and logos) are often incorporated into personal ornaments. In sum, personal ornaments do not have indexical relationships to either self or social group membership. In order for there to be a reason to make and wear personal ornaments, there must be a symbolic relationship – an interpreter or reader is required.

Related to this reasoning, our second objection to the classification of personal ornaments as indexes is that to argue that personal ornaments are indexes and not symbols requires making the underlying argument that both Neandertals and anatomically modern humans have (1) a sense of self, (2) a sense of group membership, (3) a sense of individual membership in that group, and (4) an understanding that material culture can be used to represent and communicate information about membership in a social group but that these capacities are present without any concept of symbols. In specific reference to personal ornaments, Mary Stiner (2014:2) writes, "most paleoanthropologists agree that the capacity for language has a deeper history in hominin evolution. Archaeological evidence has convinced many of us that Middle Paleolithic hominins possessed true (if basic) language capabilities. If correct, then the later appearance of durable art [in the form of personal ornaments] is not a proxy for the beginning of language but rather its transference into a portable medium."

Personal Ornaments in the Paleolithic

The first evidence of personal adornment, whether associated with Neandertals or with modern humans, appears relatively late in the archaeological record. Possible ornaments are known from Qafzeh and Skhul (Israel) (Bar-Yosef et al. 2009; Vanhaeren et al. 2006) and perhaps Oued Djebbana (Algeria) around 100,000 BP (Vanhaeren et al. 2006). The shells at Qafzeh are naturally perforated but are argued to have functioned as containers because they contain traces of ochre or as personal ornaments because the holes exhibit wear consistent with being strung (Bar-Yosef et al. 2009). Other relevant artifacts associated with modern humans are observed slightly later, around 77,000 BP at Blombos Cave (South Africa) (d'Errico et al. 2005) and 82,000 BP at Grotte des Pigeons (Morocco) (Bouzouggar et al. 2007). Recent studies provide evidence of personal ornamentation at a number of later Neandertal sites (<48,000 BP) and suggest that this behavior may have been present as long as 130,000 years ago (Radovcic et al. 2015) (Table 13.1).

In the past, questions were raised concerning the integrity of the Neandertal-associated potential ornaments from Châtelperronian levels at the Grotte du Renne, Arcy-sur-Cure, including whether the archaeological layers were affected by local or widespread postdepositional disturbance; whether the ornaments were intrusive and truly derived from overlying Proto-Aurignacian, Aurignacian, and Gravettian levels; and whether the ornaments were accurately dated (e.g., Bar-Yosef 2006; Bar-

Table 13.1 Neandertal-associated symbolic artifacts and signs

Site	Types of artifacts	References
Grotte du Renne, Arcy-sur-Cure	Perforated/engraved teeth, shells, bone awls	Bar-Yosef (2006), Bar-Yosef and Bordes (2010), Caron et al. (2011), Higham et al. (2010), White (2001)
Quinçay	Shells, pigments	Roussel and Soressi (2010)
Cueva de los Aviones	Shells, pigments	Zilhão et al. (2010)
Cueva Anton	Shells, pigments	Zilhão et al. (2010)
Klisoura 1	(Uluzzian) dentalium beads	Koumouzelis et al. (2001)
Grotta del Cavallo	(Uluzzian) dentalium beads	Zilhão et al. (2015)
Fumane Cave	Feather use	Peresani et al. (2012)
Combe Grenal	Raptor talons	Morin and Laroulandie (2012)
Les Fieux	Raptor talons	Moran and Laroulandie (2012)
Krapina	Raptor talons	Radovcic et al. (2015)
Gorham's Cave, Gibraltar	Abstract engraving	Rodriguez-Vidal et al. (2014)
La Pasiega	Red scalariform sign	Hoffman et al. (2018)
Ardales	Red pigment on speleothem curtain	Hoffman et al. (2018)
Maltravieso	Hand stencil in red pigment	Hoffman et al. (2018)

Yosef and Bordes 2010; Higham et al. 2010; White 2001). However, a recent detailed reevaluation of the site (Caron et al. 2011) confirmed that the Châtelperronian ornaments from the Grotte du Renne are indeed associated with Neandertals. Even more recent protein analyses of fragmentary bones at the Grotte du Renne confirm that the only hominin fossils found at the site were Neandertals (Weller et al. 2016). Other sites, including the Châtelperronian site of Quinçay, in France (Roussel and Soressi 2010), and the sites of Cueva de los Aviones and Cueva Antón, in Spain (Zilhão et al. 2010), have yielded perforated marine shells, some containing mixtures of pigments, and other evidence of body painting and personal adornment. Although debate continues over whether the transitional Uluzzian industry is associated with Neandertals or modern humans (e.g., Benazzi et al. 2011; Riel-Salvatore 2009; Zilhao et al. 2015), dentalium beads have been recovered from the Uluzzian sites of Klisoura 1 in Greece (Koumouzelis et al. 2001) and Grotta del Cavallo, Italy, as well as other Uluzzian contexts.

Ornamental feather use is suggested by bird remains found at Fumane Cave, Italy (44,000 BP) (Peresani et al. 2012). Cutting, peeling, and scraping marks are present on wing bones only, indicating the purposeful removal of large flight feathers from bird species that were unlikely to be food items. While it is possible that the feathers were used for a number of non-subsistence activities (e.g., lining for bedding or clothing), the use of feathers as personal ornaments is documented in many extant and historically known hunter-gatherer societies. The recovery of talons from large, powerful diurnal raptors at Neandertal sites including Combe Grenal (90,000 BP) and Les Fieux (60,000–40,000 BP), both in France (Morin and Laroulandie 2012), have led some researchers to speculate that the talons were worn by Neandertals and functioned in symbolic contexts (for an even earlier possible instance, see Radovčić et al. 2015).[2]

Recently, nonfigurative cave art at four sites on the Iberian Peninsula has been attributed to Neandertals. These include an engraving at Gorham's Cave, Gibraltar (Rodriguez-Vidal et al. 2014), and a number of geometric signs and one hand stencil, all in red pigment, at three sites in Spain (Hoffman et al. 2018). The engraving at Gorham's Cave is well-attributed to Mousterian archaeological layers and dated to around 40,000 years ago, but the creators of the other, red-pigmented art cannot be definitively identified archaeologically or biologically due to a lack of associated evidence. However, multiple U-Th dates at the three Spanish sites define an age range of approximately 65,000–50,000 BP. Although these dates are considered controversial by some (Pearce and Bonneau 2018), if they are correct, the artwork predates the appearance of modern humans in Europe, leaving Neandertals as the only available candidates to be the artists (Hoffman et al. 2018). Taken together, the evidence for personal ornamentation and cave art suggests that at least later Neandertals were capable of symbolic behavior.

Resource Competition and Group Identification

Most putative examples of Neandertal personal ornaments are from Southern European sites that are often interpreted as late *Pleistocene refugia* for a number of mammal species, including hominins. Southern Europe appears to have been continuously occupied by Neandertals from about 100,000 to about 39,000 BP (Higham et al. 2015), whereas Northern Europe exhibits apparent hiatuses in occupation associated with extremely cold periods (i.e., Heinrich events H4 and H5) that have been interpreted to represent either local extinctions or emigration (Roebroeks et al. 2011; Stewart and Stringer 2012). Thus, paleoclimatic and paleodemographic reconstructions suggest that northern portions of the Neandertal range experienced periodic local extinctions, while southern refugia may have been continuously occupied by other Neandertal groups (Roebroeks et al. 2011).

Ancient mtDNA and nuclear studies indicate that Neandertal populations, especially later Western European Neandertals, were characterized by low genetic variability and evidence of recent population origin (<48,000 bp) (Dalen et al. 2012; Prufer et al. 2017). These data support the hypotheses that Neandertal populations were small and that Neandertals experienced periodic bottlenecks or local extinctions during periods of glacial advance, followed by repopulation of broader regions

---

[2] Similar interpretations have been made for finds at Meged Rockshelter, an Upper Paleolithic site in Israel (Kuhn et al. 2004). These finds, being associated with anatomically modern humans, are not considered controversial.

during warmer periods, with succeeding populations perhaps founded by migrants from the southern parts of the Neandertal range.[3] Fabre et al. (2009) presented evidence for the existence of two European populations of Neandertals – one in Western Europe and one in Southern Europe. They also suggest that population sizes varied over time and that migration took place between these populations.

During periods of extreme cold and range contraction, did northern Neandertals retreat to lower latitudes and thereby encounter their southern cousins? If they did, were they welcome? According to Peterson (1986:11), "Perhaps surprisingly, there is no evidence anywhere [among modern humans] that access to the land is uncontrolled in hunting and gathering societies. Boundaries do not have to be patrolled or marked to be significant." Therefore, modern ethnographic evidence suggests that increasing population density in refugia would have led to competition among Neandertals rather than cooperation between groups, if Neandertals behaved like modern humans. Roebroeks et al. (2011) argue that Neandertal subsistence strategies that prioritized the hunting of large mammals kept Neandertal population densities low and thus would have precluded northern groups from moving south. While it is true that northern Neandertals appear to have depended on large terrestrial mammals, particularly during periods of climatic deterioration, increasing evidence suggests that Southern European Neandertals consumed a variety of foodstuffs including plants, fish, shellfish, and marine mammals (Dusseldorp 2009; Weyrich et al. 2017). Northern Neandertals following changing climates south would likely have adjusted their subsistence strategies as necessary, perhaps accounting for population migration (see Fabre et al. 2009), but there is little archaeological evidence that these would-be colonizers enjoyed long-term success (Roebroeks et al. 2011).

Factors such as resource density and resource predictability are key determinants of intergroup relationships (Roebroeks et al. 2011) or "ecological tensions" (Birdsell 1970) among modern foragers. Among "extant hunter-gatherers, [access to resources]… is highly regulated within social networks which facilitated rights of reciprocal access to more favoured areas" (Roebroeks et al. 2011:118). These networks may have been mediated by readily interpretable signals expressed through material culture. As Vanhaeren and d'Errico (2006:1107) note, "Ethnographic studies have shown that beadwork, like body painting, scarification, tattooing, garments and headdress is perceived by the members of traditional societies as powerful indicators of their ethno-linguistic identity, enhancing within-group cohesion and fixing boundaries within neighbouring groups" (see also Boyd and Richerson 1987). Even among nonhuman social species, increases in population size and intensification of resource competition can lead to concomitant increases in within-group social tolerances: "shifts in social tolerance can relatively quickly and profoundly change behavior because they allow individuals to utilize pre-existing cognitive abilities in a new set of contexts" (Cieri et al. 2014:7). Periodic forays of northern Neandertals into southern territories may have prompted southern Neandertals to codify social distinctions through material culture in ways that that they would not

---

[3] A similar model has been proposed to explain the phenotypic heterogeneity observed in Middle Pleistocene hominins commonly referred to as *Homo heidelbergensis* (Dennell et al. 2014).

otherwise and previously did not (cf. White 1992). Such artifacts may therefore be interpreted as advertisements of group affiliation that would be uniquely useful in contexts in which there are relatively high chances of meeting strangers (Kuhn et al. 2001; see also Kuhn 2014), which would be the case if Neandertals were being driven into refugia by climate change, competition with anatomically modern humans, or both.

Functional Variation and Style in Late Neandertal Artifacts

We suggest that late Neandertals invested resources in making items of personal adornment (and likely a number of other archaeologically invisible signs or symbols) primarily to distinguish Neandertal groups from each other. Such reinforcements of group identity may have helped to prevent conspecifics from encroaching on limited group territories that harbored valuable resources or perhaps simply to express affiliations that did not need to be explicitly expressed when Neandertal groups were more isolated. Although it is probably impossible to identify "style" in Neandertal artifacts that may be interpreted as personal ornaments, the classic debates regarding style in archaeology (Sackett 1973; Wobst 1977) are conceptually relevant. The model that we propose is Wobstian, in that we envision ornamental artifacts (and the stylistic forms that they assumed) as actively involved in the transmission of important social information. Similar hypotheses have already been proposed to explain variation in projectile points during the MSA (Wilkins 2010) as well as the origins of visual art itself, which Straffon (2016) argues functioned as an expression of social identity facilitating reciprocity among extended social networks, behavior that would then be selected for because it increased individual access to resources and mates. Personal ornaments represent a specific form of symbolic behavior that plays key roles in constructing and mediating social relationships in contemporary societies and that, based in part on their small size and visibility at relatively close distances (Wobst 1977), in Neandertal societies may have facilitated relationships within the relatively small-scale social networks suggested by low Neandertal population densities.

This hypothesis is an alternative to explanations that rely on "acculturation" or other possible reactions to the influx of modern humans into Europe that have previously been invoked to explain variation in Neandertal material culture (see Tostevin 2007 for a detailed discussion of this debate). Personal ornaments that were made by Neandertals before modern humans arrived in Western Europe around 45,000 BP may represent reactions to increased population densities among Neandertals themselves, even in the absence of competition due to encroachment by modern humans. Similarly, among Upper Paleolithic modern humans, there is a correlation between refuge areas during the last glacial maximum and the location and frequency of Upper Paleolithic parietal art (Straus 1991). The increase in art production is considered by Straus to be a response to the intersection of increased human population densities and severe environmental conditions in Southwest Europe at that time (Straus 1991: 270).

We recognize that effective tests of this hypothesis may currently be difficult or impossible given the limited resolution of the available data. In addition, the relationship(s) between material culture variation and factors that may be related to group identity such as linguistic affinities, patterns of intergroup relationships (affiliations and/or hostilities), extent of shared borders, and geographic distance remain(s) unclear even in ethnoarchaeological studies of modern groups for which these data are known (Lycett 2014, 2015). We believe that the value of our hypothesis lies in its shift in perspective, with a specific reframing of the last Neandertals as *people*, highlighting their similarities as the closest relatives to modern humans rather than accepting a null hypothesis of major social, cognitive, and behavioral differences between our species as argued in recent studies (e.g., Collard et al. 2016; Sandgathe et al. 2011).

It is suggestive that, according to paleoclimatic data, two unusually cold events took place during the later Pleistocene at approximately 48,000 and 39,000 BP. In addition, genetic evidence indicates that Neandertals later than 48,000 BP experienced bottlenecks or local extinctions, especially in Western Europe; along with some skeletal evidence (Rios et al. 2019), these data support the hypothesis that Neandertals may already have been on the verge of extinction before modern humans arrived (Dalen et al. 2012). While it is difficult to correlate paleoclimatic data with behavioral data, if we can take the archaeological data at face value (recognizing that many examples of personal ornamentation in Neandertals are recent finds that may be reevaluated in the future), then there is evidence of an increase in symbolically mediated cultural differentiation among Neandertal populations after 48,000 BP. However, the question of "… why they began to [exhibit symbolic behavior] at this particular time so late in their evolutionary history" remains (Kuhn 2014:145; see also Nowell 2014a; Nowell and Chang 2012). We believe that taken together, the paleoclimatic, genetic, and archaeological evidence suggest that while Neandertals exhibited many aspects of modern behavior throughout their tenure as a species, a unique set of circumstances during the Late Pleistocene may have prompted Neandertal groups to codify their unique identities in durable, visual media. It is tempting to conceptualize "others" (both prehistoric and modern) as monolithic groups, but all human populations are characterized by behavioral and cultural diversity. It is probable that this human characteristic was shared with our closest hominin relatives. In this context, variation in Neandertal material culture over space and time should be expected.

Conclusion

Questions of identity are fundamental to even the most empirical of human evolutionary studies. These questions structure the hypotheses that we, as researchers, test in ways that we, as actors embedded in specific societal contexts, may not always be entirely aware of. Whether we approach the Neandertals as if they represent "Us" or "Them" is an important distinction, because it informs the framing of our null hypotheses. As anthropologists, those of us who study the evolution of humans should, perhaps, be more reflexive and more aware of this epistemological influence than scientists who study the evolution of other species. But instead, in the name of objectivity, we often refuse to consider the more obvious null hypothesis, given that the species under investigation is so similar to our own that we were able to produce fertile offspring (Sankararaman et al. 2016): the hypothesis that we were more alike than different.

Discussions of Neandertal behavior tend to focus on the identification of species characteristics in what we might refer to as an "ethological" approach. This is understandable, because such an approach is considered to be both conservative and objective. At the same time, given the close biological relationship of Neandertals to modern humans and the likely complexity of their behavior based on this relationship, a broader, more "ethnographic" approach may be more useful. What would be the cost if we thought of them as "Us," rather than "Them?" Is this viewpoint actually less objective? Or does this perspective allow us to generate new and potentially more interesting hypotheses? Reconstructions of Neandertal population structure, behavior, and lifeways may benefit by taking into account the possibility – or rather, probability – that Neandertal populations were themselves structured by cultural or ethnic distinctions, like all known modern human populations, past or present.

As Margaret Conkey asks (Chap. 17, this volume), "what have we lost in our push to be objective?" A heart-centered approach to the study of our evolutionary past that rejects the subject/object dichotomy can free us to recognize that the emotional resonance inherent in human evolutionary studies can be as much a strength of our discipline as a weakness. Jane Goodall famously refused to refer to her chimpanzee subjects by catalog number, instead giving them names (Whiten et al. 2001). Her personal, relationship-oriented methodology revolutionized primate studies and yielded insights about our closest living relatives (with whom, again, we may be *expected* to have much in common) that may not have been gained by a more dispassionate approach.

And finally, while our primary concerns are different from those of other scientists, even other evolutionary scientists, maybe our responsibilities are, too. The expansive audience to which we speak when we pose our questions and present our findings consists not only of our academic peers but also of those PBS viewers eagerly awaiting the next NOVA documentary about human origins to tell them about where we came from and why we are the way we are. Whether we like it or not, our words reverberate to become primal explanations that can be used to excuse modern injustices and power asymmetries (in ways that studies of ancient snails or even dinosaurs cannot), what Cartmill called "the fallacy of the mythological charter – the mistaken conviction that causal explanation and moral justification are the same thing" (Cartmill 2002: 199). A heart-centered approach that humanizes the past and recognizes the importance of emotion and interconnectedness in scientific practice not only opens us to interesting new avenues of empirical inquiry; it charges us to remain conscious of our testimonial power, a consciousness that in turn, objectively and purposefully, fosters the greater good.

References

Banks, W. E., d'Errico, F., Peterson, A. T., Kageyama, M., Sima, A., & Sánchez-Goñi, M.-F. (2008). Neandertal extinction by competitive exclusion. *PLoS, 3*(12), e3972. https://doi.org/10.1371/journal.pone.0003972.

Barnard, P. J., Davidson, I., & Byrne, R. W. (2016). Toward a richer theoretical scaffolding for interpreting archaeological evidence concerning cognitive evolution. In T. Wynn & F. Coolidge (Eds.), *Cognitive models in Palaeolithic archaeology* (pp. 45–67). Oxford, UK: Oxford University Press.

Bar-Yosef, O. (2006). Neanderthals and modern humans: A different interpretation. In N. J. Conard (Ed.), *When Neanderthals and modern humans met* (pp. 467–482). Tubingen: Kerns-Verlag.

Bar-Yosef, O., & Bordes, J. G. (2010). Who were the makers of the Châtelperronian culture? *Journal of Human Evolution, 59*, 586–593.

Bar-Yosef Mayer, D. E., Vandermeersch, B., & Bar-Yosef, O. (2009). Modern behavior of anatomically modern humans: shells and ochre from Qafzeh Cave, Israel. *Journal of Human Evolution, 56*, 307–314.

Benazzi, S., Douka, K., Fornai, C., Bauer, C. C., Kullmer, O., Svoboda, J., et al. (2011). Early dispersal of modern humans in Europe and implications for Neanderthal behaviour. *Nature, 479*(7374), 525–528.

Birdsell, J. B. (1970). Local group composition among the Australian Aborigines: A critique of the evidence from fieldwork conducted since 1930. *Current Anthropology, 11*, 115–141.

Boule, M. (1911–13). *L'Homme Fossile de La Chapelle-aux-Saints, extrait des Annales de paléontologie*. Masson: Paris.

Bouzouggar, A., Barton, N., Vanhaeren, M., d'Errico, F., Collcutt, S., Higham, T., et al. (2007). *Proceedings of the National Academy of Science, 104*(24), 9964–9969.

Boyd, R., & Richardson, P. J. (1987). The evolution of ethnic markers. *Current Anthropology, 2*(1), 65–79.

Caron, F., d'Errico, F., Del Moral, P., Santos, F., & Zilhão, J. (2011). The reality of Neandertal symbolic behavior at the Grotte du Renne, Arcy-sur-Cure, France. *PLoS One, 6*(6), e21545.

Cartmill, M. (2002). Paleoanthropology: Science or mythological charter? *Journal of Anthropological Research, 58*(2), 183–201.

Chase, P. (2003). *The emergence of culture: The evolution of a uniquely human way of life*. New York: Springer.

Cieri, R., Churchill, L., Franciscus, S. E., Tan, R. G., Hare, J., & B. (2014). Craniofacial feminization, social tolerance, and the origins of behavioral modernity. *Current Anthropology, 55*(4), 419–443.

Collard, M., Tarle, M., Sandgathe, D., & Allan, A. (2016). Faunal evidence for a difference in clothing use between neanderthals and early modern humans in Europe. *Journal of Anthropological Archaeology, 44*(B), 235–245.

Coon, C. (1939). *The races of Europe*. New York: Macmillan.

d'Errico, F., Henshilwood, C., Vanhaeren, M., & van Niekerke, K. (2005). Nassarius kraussianus shell beads from Blombos Cave: Evidence for symbolic behaviour in the Middle Stone Age. *Journal of Human Evolution, 48*(1), 3–24.

Dalén, L., Orlando, L., Shapiro, B., Brandström-Durling, M., Quam, R., Gilbert, M. T., et al. (2012). Partial genetic turnover in Neandertals: Continuity in the east and population replacement in the west. *Molecular Biology and Evolution, 29*(8), 1893–1897.

Darwin, C. R. (1859). *On the origin of species by means of natural selection, or, the preservation of favoured races in the struggle for life*. London: J. Murray.

Darwin, C. R. (1871). *The descent of man, and selection in relation to sex*. London: John Murray.

Davidson, I. (2014). Cognitive evolution and origins of language and speech. In C. Smith (Ed.), *Encyclopedia of global archaeology* (pp. 1530–1543). New York: Springer.

Davidson, I. (2016). Stone tools: Evidence of something in between culture and cumulative culture? In M. N. Haidle, N. J. Conard, & M. Bolus (Eds.), *The nature of culture* (pp. 99–120). New York: Springer.

Dennell, R. W., Martinon-Torres, M., & Bermudez de Castro, J. M. (2014). Hominin variability, climatic instability and population demography in Middle Pleistocene Europe. *Quaternary Science Reviews, 30*(11–12), 1511–1524.

Douka, K., Slon, V., Jacobs, Z., Bronk Ramsey, C., Shunkov, M. V., Derevianko, A. P., et al. (2019). Age estimates for hominin fossils and the onset of the Upper Palaeolithic at Denisova Cave. *Nature, 565*, 640–644.

Drell, J. (2000). Neanderthals: A history of interpretation. *Oxford Journal of Archaeology, 19*(1), 1–24.

Dusseldorp, G. L. (2009). *A view to a kill: Investigating Middle Palaeolithic subsistence using an optimal foraging perspective*. Leiden: Sidestone Press.

Fabre, V., Condemi, S., & Degioanni, A. (2009). Genetic evidence of geographical groups among Neanderthals. *PLoS One, 4*(4), e5151. https://doi.org/10.1371/journal.pone.0005151.

Flores, J. C. (2011). Diffusion coefficient for modern humans outcompeting Neanderthals. *Journal of Theoretical Biology, 280*, 189–190.

Fu, Q., et al. (2015). An early modern human from Romania with a recent Neanderthal ancestor. *Nature, 524*, 216–219.

Gibbons, A. (2012). An annus horribilis for anthropology? *Science, 338*(6114), 1520.

Gilpin, W., Feldman, M., W., Aoki, K. (2016). An ecocultural model predicts Neanderthal extinction through competition with modern humans. Proceedings of the National Academy of Sciences, 113 (8), 2134–2139 doi: https://doi.org/10.1073/pnas.1524861113.

Hammond, M. (1982). The expulsion of the Neanderthals from human ancestry: Marcellin Boule and the social context of scientific research. *Social Studies of Science, 12*(1), 1–36.

Hardin, G. (1960). The competitive exclusion principle. *Science, 131*(1409), 1291–1297.

Harmon, A. (2018). Why White Supremacists Are Chugging Milk (and Why Geneticists Are Alarmed). *The New York Times* https://nyti.ms/2AeE3Xg.

Hemmer, N. (2017). "Scientific racism" is on the rise on the right. But it's been lurking there for years. *Vox* https://www.vox.com/the-big-idea/2017/3/28/15078400/scientific-racism-murray-alt-right-black-muslim-culture-trump. Last accessed 31 Oct 2017.

Henke, W., & Tattersall, I. (eds.) (2015). Handbook of Paleoanthropology. Berlin: Springer-Verlag

Henshilwood, C. S. (2007). Fully symbolic sapiens behavior: Innovation in the Middle Stone Age at Blombos Cave, South Africa. In P. Mellars, K. Boyle, O. Bar-Yosef, & C. Stringer (Eds.), *Rethinking the human revolution* (pp. 123–132). Cambridge: MacDonald Institute.

Henshilwood, C. S., & Marean, C. (2003). The origin of modern human behavior. *Current Anthropology, 44*, 627–651.

Higham, T., Jacob, R., Julien, M., David, F., Basell, L., et al. (2010). Chronology of the Grotte du Renne (France) and implications for the context of ornaments and human remains within the Châtelperronian. *Proceedings of the National Academy of Science, USA, 107*, 20234–20239.

Higham, T., Douka, K., Wood, R., Ramsey, C. B., Brock, F., et al. (2015). The timing and spatio-temporal patterning of Neanderthal disappearance. *Nature, 512*, 306–309.

Hoffmann, D. L., Angelucci, D. E., Villaverde, V., Zapata, J., & Zilhão, J. (2018). Symbolic use of marine shells and mineral pigments by Iberian Neandertals 115,000 years ago. *Scientific Advances, 4*, 5255.

Huening, D. (2006). Symbol, *index, icon*. http://csmt.uchicago.edu/glossary2004/symbolindexicon.htm. Last accessed 9 Nov, 2016.

King, W. (1864). The reputed fossil man of the Neanderthal. *Quaternary Journal of Science, 1*, 88–97.

Koumouzelis, M., Ginter, B., Koz£Owski, J. K., Pawlikowski, M., Bar-Yosef, O., Al-Bert, R. M., et al. (2001). The early Upper Palaeolithic in Greece: The excavations in Klissoura Cave. *Journal of Archaeological Science, 28*, 515–539.

Kuhlwilm, M., Gronau, I., Hubisz, M. J., de Filippo, C., Prado-Martinez, J., Kircher, M., et al. (2016). Ancient gene flow from early modern humans into Eastern Neanderthals. *Nature, 530*(7591), 429–433.

Kuhn, S. (2014). Signaling theory and technologies of communication in the Paleolithic. *Biological Theory, 9*, 42–50. https://doi.org/10.1007/s13752-013-0156-5.

Kuhn, S., & Stiner, M. (2007). Paleolithic ornaments: Implications for cognition, demography and identity. *Diogenes, 54*, 40–48.

Kuhn, S. L., Stiner, M. C., Reese, D. S., & Güleç, E. (2001). Ornaments of the earliest Upper Paleolithic: New insights from the Levant. *Proceedings of the National Academy of Science, 98*(13), 7641–7646.

Kuhn, S., Belfer-Cohen, A., Barzilai, O., Stiner, M. C., Kerry, K. W., Munro, N., & Bar-Yosef Mayer, D. (2004). The last glacial maximum at Meged Rockshelter, upper Galilee, Israel. *Journal of the Israel Prehistoric Society, 34*, 5–47.

Landau, M. (1991). *Narratives of human evolution*. New Haven: Yale University Press.

Linnaeus, C. (1735). *Systema Naturae* (tenth edition). *Systema naturæ per regna tria naturæ, secundum classes, ordines, genera, species, cum characteribus, differentiis, synonymis, locis.* Tomus I. Editio decima, reformata. pp. [1–4], 1–824. Holmiæ. (Salvius).

Lycett, S. J. (2014). Dynamics of cultural transmission in Native Americans of the High Great Plains. *PLOSOne, 9*(11), e112244.

Lycett, S. J. (2015). Differing patterns of material culture intergroup variation on the High Plains: Quantitative analyses of parfleche characteristics vs. moccasin decoration. *American Antiquity, 80*(4), 714–731.

Marean, C. (2007). Heading north: An Africanist perspective on the replacement of Neanderthals by modern humans. In P. Mellars, Boyle, O. Bar-Yosef, & C. Stringer (Eds.), *Rethinking the human revolution* (pp. 367–379). Cambridge: MacDonald Institute.

Morin, E., & Laroulandie, V. (2012). Presumed symbolic use by diurnal raptors by Neanderthals. *PLoS One, 7*, e32856. https://doi.org/10.1371/journal.pone.0032856. pmid:22403717.

Müller, U. C., Pross, J., Tzedakis, P. C., Gamble, C., Kotthoff, U., Schmiedl, G., et al. (2011). The role of climate in the spread of modern humans into Europe. *Quaternary Sciences Review, 30*(3–4), 273–279.

Nash R. F. (2014). *Wilderness and the American Mind* (5th edition). Yale University Press.

Nott, J. C., & Gliddon, G. R. (1854). *Types of mankind*. London: Trubner and Company.

Nott, J. C., & Gliddon, G. R. (1857). *Indigenous races of the earth*. Philadelphia: JB Lippincott and Company.

Nowell, A. (2013). Cognition, behavioral modernity and the archaeological record of the Middle and Early Upper Paleolithic. In G. Hatfield & H. Pittman (Eds.), *The evolution of mind, brain, and culture* (pp. 236–262). Philadelphia: University of Pennsylvania Museum of Archaeology and Anthropology Press.

Nowell, A. (2014a). Comment on "craniofacial feminization, social tolerance, and the origins of behavioral modernity" by R. L. Cieri, S. E. Churchill, R. G. Franciscus, J. Tan, B. Hare. *Current Anthropology, 55*(4), 433–434.

Nowell, A. (2014b). Reversals of fortune: Neandertals and modern humans in the Levantine Middle Paleolithc, a view from the Druze Marsh, North Azraq (Jordan). In *Jordan's prehistory. Past and future research* (pp. 23–34). Amman: Department of Antiquities of Jordan.

Nowell, A., & Chang, M. L. (2012). *Symbolism in Late European Neanderthals: detection and evolutionary context. Presented in session designated as the Wiley-Blackwell symposium.* Portland: American Association of Physical Anthropologists meetings.

Pearce, D. F., & Bonneau, A. (2018). Trouble on the dating scene. *Nature Ecology and Evolution.* https://doi.org/10.1038/s41559-018-0540-4.

Peirce, C. S. (1998). Collected papers of Charles Sanders Peirce. In C. Hartshorne & P. Weiss (Eds.), (pp. 1931–1958). Bristol: Thoemmes Press.

Peresani, M., Fiore, I., Gala, M., Romandini, M., & Tagliacozzo, A. (2012). Late Neandertals and the intentional removal of feathers as evidenced from bird bone taphonomy at Fumane Cave 44 ky B.P., Italy. *Proceedings of the National Academy of Sciences, 108*, 3888–3893. https://doi.org/10.1073/pnas.1016212108.

Peterson, N. (1986). *Australian territorial organization*. Sidney: University of Sidney.

Post, J. E., & Farges, F. (2014). The Hope diamond: Rare gem, historic jewel. *Rocks and Minerals, 89*, 16–25.

Prüfer, K., Racimo, F., Patterson, N., Jay, F., Sankararaman, S., Sawyer, S., et al. (2014). The complete genome sequence of a Neanderthal from the Altai Mountains. *Nature, 505*, 43–49. https://doi.org/10.1038/nature12886.

Prüfer, K., de Filippo, C., Grote, S., Mafessoni, F., Korlević, P., Hajdinjak, M., et al. (2017). A high-coverage Neandertal genome from Vindija Cave in Croatia. *Science*. https://doi.org/10.1126/science.aao1887.

Radovčić, D., Sršen, A. O., Radovčić, J., & Frayer, D. W. (2015). Evidence for Neandertal jewelry: Modified white-tailed eagle claws at Krapina. *PLoS One, 10*(3), e0119802. https://doi.org/10.1371/journal.pone.0119802.

Rapacon, S. (2019). 15 worst college majors for a lucrative career. *Kiplingers* https://www.kiplinger.com/slideshow/business/T012-S001-worst-college-majors-for-a-lucrative-career-2019/index.html. Accessed Feb 2019.

Reeve, E. (2016). White nonsense: Alt-right trolls are arguing over genetic tests they think "prove" their whiteness. *Vice News* https://news.vice.com/en_us/article/vbygqm/alt-right-trolls-are-getting-23andme-genetic-tests-to-prove-their-whiteness

Riel-Salvatore, J. (2009). What is a 'transitional' industry? The Uluzzian of Southern Italy as a case study. In *Sourcebook of Paleolithic transitions* (pp. 377–396). New York: Springer.

Ríos, L., Kivell, T. L., Lalueza-Fox, C., Estalrrich, A., García-Tabernero, A., Huguet, R., et al. (2019). Skeletal anomalies in the Neandertal family of El Sidrón (Spain) support a role of inbreeding in Neandertal extinction. *Scientific Reports, 9*, 1967. https://doi.org/10.1038/s41598-019-38571-1.

Rodríguez-Vidal, J., d'Errico, F., Pacheco, F. G., Blasco, R., Rosell, J., Jennings, R. P., et al. (2014). A rock engraving made by Neanderthals in Gibraltar. *Proceedings of the National Academy of Sciences, 111*(37), 13301–13306. https://doi.org/10.1073/pnas.1411529111.

Roebroeks, W., & Soressi, M. (2016). Neandertals revised. *Proceedings of the National Academy of Science, 113*(23), 6372–6379.

Roebroeks, W., Hublin, J.-J., & MacDonald, K. (2011). Continuities and discontinuities in Neandertal presence: A closer look at Western Europe. In N. Ashton, S. Lewis, & C. Stringer (Eds.), *Ancient human occupation of Britain* (pp. 113–124). New York: Elsvier.

Romandini, M., Peresani, M., Laroulandie, V., Metz, L., Pastoors, A., Vaquero, M., & Slimak, L. (2014). Convergent evidence of eagle talons used by late Neanderthals in Europe: A further assessment on symbolism. *PLoS One, 9*, e101278. https://doi.org/10.1371/journal.pone.0101278. pmid:25010346.

Roussel, M., & Sorressi, M. (2010). La Grande Roche de la Plématrie à Quinçay (Vienne). L'évolution du Châtelperronien revisitée. In J. Primault (Ed.), *Jacques Buisson-Catil* (pp. 203–219). Préhistoire entre Vienne et Charente - Hommes et sociétés du Paléolithique, Association des Publications Chauvinoises, mémoire 38.

Sackett, J. R. (1973). Style, function and artifact variability in Palaeolithic assemblages. In C. Renfrew (Ed.), *The explanation of culture change* (pp. 317–328). Duckworth: The Old Piano Factory.

Sadowski, P. (2009). *From interactions to symbols: A systems view of the evolution of signs and communication*. Amsterdam and Philadelphia: John Benjamins Publishing.

Sandgathe, D. M., Dibble, H. L., Goldberg, P., McPherron, S. P., Turq, A., Niven, L., & Hodgkins, J. (2011). Timing of the appearance of habitual fire use. *Proceedings of the National Academy of Sciences, 108*(29). https://doi.org/10.1073/pnas.1106759108.

Sankararaman, S., Mallick, S., Patterson, N., & Reich, D. (2016). The combined landscape of Denisovan and Neanderthal ancestry in present-day humans. *Current Biology, 26*(9), 1241–1247. https://doi.org/10.1016/j.cub.2016.03.037.

Simonti, C., Vernot, B., Bastarache, L., Bottinger, E., Carrell, D. S., Chisholm, R. L., et al. (2016). The phenotypic legacy of admixture between modern humans and Neandertals. *Science, 351*(6274), 737–741. https://doi.org/10.1126/science.aad2149.

Soffer, O. (2009). Defining modernity, establishing rubicons, imagining the other—and the Neanderthal enigma. In M. Camps & P. Chauhan (Eds.), *Sourcebook of Paleolithic transitions* (pp. 43–64). New York: Springer.

Solecki, R. (1971). *Shanidar: The first flower people*. New York: Knopf.

Stewart, J. R., & Stringer, C. B. (2012). Human evolution out of Africa: The role of refugia and climate change. *Science, 335*, 1317–1321.

Stiner, M. (2014). Finding a common bandwidth: Causes of convergence and diversity in Paleolithic Beads. *Biological Theory, 9*(1), 51–64.

Stratton, L. M. (2016). Signaling in style: On cooperation, identity and the origins of visual art. In F. Panebianco & E. Serrelli (Eds.), *Understanding cultural traits: A multicultural perspective on cultural diversity* (pp. 357–373). New York: Springer.

Straus, L. G. (1991). Southwestern Europe at the last glacial maximum. *Current Anthropology, 32*(2), 189–199.

Tostevin, G. (2007). Social intimacy, artefact visibility and acculturation models of Neanderthal–modern human interaction. In P. Mellars, K. Boyle, O. Bar-Yosef, & C. Stringer (Eds.), *Rethinking the human revolution: New behavioural and biological perspectives on the origin and dispersal of modern humans* (pp. 341–358). Cambridge: MacDonald Institute.

Trinkaus, E. & Shipman P. (1992). The Neandertals: Changing the image of mankind. Knopf.

Vanhaeren, M., d'Errico, F., Stringer, C., James, S. L., Todd, J. A., & Mienis, H. K. (2006). Middle Paleolithic shell beads in Israel and Algeria. *Science, 312*(5781), 1785–1788. https://doi.org/10.1126/science.1128139.

Vernot, B., & Akey, J. M. (2015). Complex history of admixture between modern humans and Neandertals. *American Journal of Human Genetics, 96*(3), 448–453. https://doi.org/10.1016/j.ajhg.2015.01.006.

Virchow, R. (1872). Untersuchung des Neanderthal-Schädels. *Zool.- Ethnol, 4*, 157–165.

Welker, F., Hajdinjak, M., Talamo, S., Jaouen, K., Dannemann, M., David, F., et al. (2016). Palaeoproteomic evidence identifies archaic hominins associated with the Châtelperronian at the Grotte du Renne. *Proceedings of the National Academy of Science, 113*(40), 11162–11167. https://doi.org/10.1073/pnas.1605834113.

Weyrich, L. S., Duchene, S., Soubrier, J., Arriola, L., Llamas, B., Breen, J., et al. (2017). Neanderthal behaviour, diet, and disease inferred from Ancient DNA in dental calculus. *Nature*. https://doi.org/10.1038/nature21674.

White, R. (1992). Beyond art—Toward an understanding of the origins of material representation in Europe. *Annual Review of Anthropology, 21*, 537–564.

White, R. (2001). Personal ornaments from the Grotte du Renne at Arcy-sur-Cure. *Athena Review, 2*, 41–46.

Whiten, A., Goodall, J., McGrew, W. C., Nishida, T., Reynolds, V., Sugiyama, Y., et al. (2001). Charting cultural variation in chimpanzees. *Behavior, 138*(11), 1481–1516.

Wilkins, J. (2010). Style, symboling, and interaction in Middle Stone Age societies. *Explorations in Anthropology, 10*(1), 102–125.

Wobst, H. M. (1977). Stylistic behavior and information exchange. In C. E. Cleland (Ed.), *Papers for the director: Research essays in honor of James B. Griffin* (pp. 317–342). Ann Arbor: University of Michigan.

Wynn, T., & Coolidge, F. (2012). *How to think like a Neandertal*. Oxford: Oxford University Press.

Wynn, T., Overmann, K. A., & Coolidge, F. L. (2015). The false dichotomy: A refutation of the Neandertal indistinguishability claim. *Journal of Anthropological Sciences, 94*, 1–22.

Zhang, S. (2016). Will the alt-right promote a new kind of racist genetics? The Atlantic. https://www.theatlantic.com/science/archive/2016/12/genetics-race-ancestry-tests/510962/. Last accessed 31 Oct 2017.

Zilhão, J., Angelucci, D. E., Badal-García, E., d'Errico, F., Daniel, F., Dayet, L., et al. (2010). Symbolic use of marine shells and mineral pigments by Iberian Neandertals. *Proceedings of the National Academy of Sciences*. https://doi.org/10.1073/pnas.0914088107.

Zilhão, J., Banks, W. E., & d'Errico, F. (2015). Analysis of site formation and assemblage integrity does not support attribution of the Uluzzian to modern humans at Grotta del Cavallo. *PLoS One*. https://doi.org/10.1371/journal.pone.013118.

Chapter 14
Who Holds Your Light?

Revealing Relationships Through a Forensic Approach to Upper Paleolithic Cave Art

Leslie Van Gelder

Introduction

A Thought Experiment

Imagine living with a group of 20–30 individuals for a year and only interacting with those people for the whole year or perhaps 2 years. What if you were born into that group and they were made up of your family, your best friend, the boy you always fancied, or the girl who set your heart aflutter? Imagine that you slept near some of them; that you knew who chewed loudly and who ran faster than you. While you might not have always known their thoughts, simply as a function of being together in so many varied circumstances, you would have come to anticipate each other in a way that some of us today might know of a little in our interactions with our close family, our spouses and children, or someone with whom we have regularly shared a sports team or a guitar lick. But can we imagine the intimacy we might have with every member of our group if we were predominantly in the company of the same group of people without interaction with too many others for days, weeks, years, and decades?

I begin this chapter trying to imagine the relational landscape of the people I study in Upper Paleolithic caves because they inhabited a relational world that bears little resemblance to my own or to most people today. The small hunter-forager groups of the Upper Paleolithic would have had a completely different sense of longevity of relationships, a predictability and knowledge of each other in varied physical contexts, and likely a greater embodied intimacy born from sharing physical tasks such as hunting and foraging, child care, food preparation, as well as art and music making and simply the day-to-day nature of life.

L. Van Gelder (✉)
Senior Contributing Faculty, Walden University, Minneapolis, MN, USA

© Springer Nature Switzerland AG 2020
K. Supernant et al. (eds.), *Archaeologies of the Heart*,
https://doi.org/10.1007/978-3-030-36350-5_14

225

CRO-MAGNON ARTISTS OF SOUTHERN FRANCE
The procession of Mammoths in the Cavern of Font-du-Gaume. One of the Murals in the Hall of the Age of Man
Painted by Charles R. Knight, under the direction of Henry Fairfield Osborn

Fig. 14.1 Charles R. Knight, 1920, Cro Magnon Artists Painting in Font de Gaume

I also want to ground this discussion in this image painted by Charles Knight in 1920 (Fig. 14.1) following his trip to the cave of Font-de-Gaume, near the village of Les Eyzies-de-Tayac-Sireuil in the Dordogne Region of France where he envisioned the experience of the cave painters of the time. In Knight's wall-sized painting, a central male artist standing at full height paints a mammoth while beneath him crouches another man holding a stone lamp to illuminate the panel for him. To their right, another artist bends low to complete the tusks on a mammoth while another crouching man holds a stone lamp for him casting the light. It is part of the American Museum of Natural History's collection, and while Knight's depiction of many aspects of the world of the cave artists is likely not accurate (most especially the absence of any women or children), it helps to frame the question of who were the people who held the light for the cave artists when they needed two hands to work.

The question of the relationship between the painter and the light holder is of great interest here, as it captures something essential about the potential to shift our approach to how we look for relationship evidence in the archaeological record and how we might consider methods to approach the question of what does it mean to engage in an archaeology of the heart.

Since 2001, I have been studying finger flutings – lines drawn on the soft surfaces of Upper Paleolithic caves with fingers. Finger flutings can depict figurative images, such as mammoths and rhinoceros in Rouffignac Cave in Southwestern France or deer in Las Chimeneas Cave in Cantabrian Spain, and symbolic images such as tectiforms in Rouffignac; but generally they are largely nonfigurative lines that are found in as many as 56 caves in modern-day France, Spain, and Australia. Unlike art created with ochre or charcoal, finger flutings contain unique forensic data because they can capture the imprint of a finger fluter's hand including the width of the fingers used to mark soft surfaces on the wall.

As Pastoors et al. (2015) note in similar research attempting to discern individuals through footprints, "Human hand and footprints are the most personal, non-substance-based remains left from our Pleistocene ancestors. Under ideal conditions, a short period of time in the life of a single person may be recorded in a plastic surface by such an imprint. No other findings are so clearly linked to a short individual moment" (p. 551). In their work, they invited modern-day Ju/'hoan San trackers from Tsumkwe (Namibia) to view four Upper Paleolithic caves in Southern France and describe the individuals they could identify from the footprints. Their work, like ours in finger flutings, yields not only a forensic story of numbers of individuals but also begins to tell the story of how they engage in relation with each other.

In this chapter, I explore the possibility of uncovering something about the nature of the relationships among the people whose embodied marks we find on the ceilings and walls of the caves by looking at methods for identifying individuals, asking questions around shared spaces and intimate embodiment, and finally exploring the role of illumination in identifying individuals who might be present but not visible in the residue they leave behind. As an archaeology of the heart, I take into consideration emotion, care, and reciprocity; the capacity to see evidence of intimacy and relationships among specific individuals in a cave context helps to create a fuller understanding of who these people were and the relationships in the lives they led.

While few other researchers have had data that can enable such a granular approach to individuals and their behavior in the caves, the desire to know more about individuals and their actions has long been a goal of researchers, especially in the hope of trading grand narrative theories for more specific ones (Gamble, 1999, 2007; Fritz et al. 2015). As Mithen (1990) noted nearly 30 years ago, "There is a methodological challenge here -- to relate the decision-making processes of individuals to the archaeological record. It is a challenge that appears to have been ignored or wished away by others who advocate a concern with individual action in prehistory" (p.3).

My late husband and research partner, Kevin Sharpe, and I began this work by attempting to identify individuals through their finger flutings. Though I am the sole author of this paper, from 2001 to 2008, Kevin was an essential part of this research, and when I refer to "we" in sections, it is to honor the work that we engaged in together.

Our early work focused on developing a methodology that emphasized the recognition and identification of unique individuals (Sharpe and Van Gelder, 2004, 2005, 2006a, b, c, d; Van Gelder and Sharpe, 2009; Van Gelder 2016). I highlight this because it was a deliberate choice as it was a method designed to respond to a specific question. Kevin's central question regarding the finger flutings was, "Is this writing?" By what means would we be able to understand if it was or wasn't?

Panels in both Koonalda Cave, South Australia, and Rouffignac Cave, France, with their regularity and frequency of directionality in largely vertical lines had prompted this line of inquiry. To answer that question required asking an earlier question which was, "If this is writing, who wrote it?" That question was driven by the idea that if each fluting had been drawn by a different individual it might have a different meaning and significance than if an entire panel was drawn by a single individual.

We weren't giving preference to one being considered more likely to be writing than another, but the question of authorship and also whether or not panels had been created contemporaneously or with time gaps also played a role in our thinking.

Thus, rather than go down the road (which we could have) of trying to work out by what criteria we could consider line markings as a form of writing, we turned our focus to the study of individuals and the relationships between and among them in the context of each cave. By asking relationship-oriented questions, we opened ourselves up to an archaeology of the heart.

Methodology

Our methodology is based on establishing the width that a stream of flutings made with three fingers held together leaves (Fig. 14.1). When a person marks with two fingers, we cannot be sure which two fingers they are (though it is fairly difficult to mark solely with middle and fourth fingers). The rationale for using three fingers is that identifying whether right or left hand was used is less essential, as regardless of hand, they are the same three middle fingers (thumbs and pinkie fingers leave very distinctive marks). In experimental work with modern populations, we discovered a less than 2 mm margin of difference in bilaterality of hands, and thus we take into account that margin of difference in applying measures to unique individuals. The vast majority of finger flutings are also done with three or four fingers (Sharpe and Van Gelder 2006b; Van Gelder 2015b).

Studying modern populations, we were surprised to discover that while in families the overall shape of a hand favored one parent or another, but not both, the three-fingered width differed for individuals in the same family. Research into children's hands proved especially useful where we discovered that no measure of 33 mm or smaller was found in a person over the age of 7. Flutings under 30 mm were only found among children aged 5 and younger (Sharpe & Van Gelder, 2006a; Van Gelder, 2015a).

However, we did come across children who had an adult-sized finger width when fluting (though a child's finger length) so we could only say that the small-sized finger flutings were children, but it is possible that so, too, were some of the larger. We also observed that sex was not a predictor of finger fluting width and we equally had males and females with large finger fluting widths.

We did and continue to apply Manning's 2D:4D ratio in caves where we have clear profiles of finger length in an attempt to sex hands despite the known controversies that have been involved in its applications in handprint studies (Snow, 2006, 2013). Of the 15 caves studied to date, this has only been possible in Rouffignac and Gargas as conservation of flutings in other caves has not yielded the same level of clarity of finger profiles.

Within the cave, when we encounter a panel of flutings, we are looking at signs of embodiment. A finger fluting is the residue of an encounter of a human body and a soft cave surface. It could catch in time a moment when a person reached out to steady him/herself against a wall because of an uneven surface (we generally find only modern examples of this, which in itself speaks to a great level of agility among the fluters), or it captures not only the motion of their hands but that of their lower bodies. For instance, in Gargas Cave in Southern France, we have flutings that were made ostensibly by jumping and also long meandering flutings capturing someone's walking around the inside of a conical shape created by a ceiling crevasse dragging fingers along the contours of the wall. In Rouffignac's Chamber A1, there are lines that may have been made by holding hands up and swaying at the hips.

In our data collection, we look at the height of the fluting from the floor, the length of the stream, its width, depth, finger top profile, and whether or not any of the flutings intersect with other flutings in a panel. We are especially interested in flutings where there is a weaving effect of superposition – one beneath with another individual's overtop and the first overtop again as that helps to establish a greater likelihood that the flutings were created at the same time.

A fuller discussion on the findings from hand studies and our specific identifications of individuals within caves in France, Spain, and Australia can be found in the following references and can offer the reader a much more in-depth explanation as to how we have been able to arrive at a degree of individual-level specificity about certain finger flutings in these caves which will serve as a central part of the following section of this chapter (Sharpe & Van Gelder, 2004, 2006a, b, d; Van Gelder & Sharpe, 2009; Van Gelder 2015a, b, 2016).

Results and Interpretation

Our initial interest in discovering the unique identities of finger fluters in each cave led us to the examination of relationships between and among fluters. In ten European caves studied in depth to date (Table 14.1), no cave has had a single finger fluter, and no chamber's finger flutings have been created by a single artist. In each

Table 14.1 Total numbers of individuals and largest and smallest panel group sizes of ten European caves

Cave	Smallest panel size	Largest panel size	Total number of individuals
Castro Urdiales	4	4	4
El Castillo	2	3	4
El Cudon	2	2	4
El Juyo	1+	1	1 (likely 2 but not more than 3)
El Salitre	1+	2	2
Gargas	1 (child held up)	5	7
Hornos de la Pena	2	2	2
Las Brujas	2	2	2
Las Chimeneas	2	6	7
Rouffignac	2+	6	8/9

case, there are at least two individuals, and in some cases as many as six, appearing on the same panel. Koonalda Cave, in South Australia, may have the largest number of fluters with just a 1 m × 1 m panel sampling identifying as many as 16 individuals including children.

Pastoors et al.'s (2015) work in using modern-day trackers to try to interpret footprints in four caves has yielded a similar demographic of small multi-aged groups of both males and females. Their findings from Fontanet Cave in Southern France potentially describe a larger group. Among their findings, they note that a 28-year-old woman walked in the cave with three children. They point out in their explanations of the heel prints found in the cave of Tuc d'Audoubert in Southern France that two males carried clay for modeling the bison sculptures in the chamber and that also found knee imprints correlating with finger flutings in the clay surface (p. 559). They posited that the change in the depth of their footprints suggested that these two individuals had carried the clay to the area where they had crafted the bison. The trackers noted that the males walked on their heels which they believed was a deliberate act so as to insure that they did not make their identities recognizable to others with their clear footprints (Pastoors et al. 2015, p. 559). In Pastoors et al.'s (2015), and my own, I am beginning to be able to discern individuals' actions and behaviors and from here then able to begin to consider the emotional aspect of relationships among individuals in the groups that visited the caves.

Four Stories of Relationships

To highlight the possibility of looking at archaeological evidence through the lens of relationships, I give four examples of relationships between two or more individual's stories told through the finger flutings and why considering embodiment – where the people are physically located and what they are doing in their proximity to each other – might offer more information about the level of the intimacy of their relationship with each other.

All of the following examples take place in dark caves where those who entered would have had to have brought their own light source and would have had to have had enough fuel in the form of a lamp or torch to be able to come out of the cave again, too. Lamps were generally carved in stone. Deer tallow was burned with a juniper wick because it does not produce smoke (de Beaune, 1987). A lamp made of stone the size of a fist could adequately hold a deer tallow candle steady as a walker moved on uneven surfaces, even with the agility of a child as young as 5 (Van Gelder, 2019, In press).

1. In Las Chimeneas Cave in the Monte Castillo Cave System in Puente Viesgo, Spain, finger flutings are found in four different zones of the cave. A total of eight individuals have been found in the cave, including two to three children. Their flutings comprise both figurative and nonfigurative images. In the center chamber of the cave is a circle of 2 m in which a series of five deer have been drawn on the walls in charcoal. Nearby are abstract lines also drawn in charcoal.

Four meters up a long high sloping wall above and to the left of the deer are six streams of finger flutings. To reach the site in modern times required using as a step ladder to bridge the distance from the floor to the start of the slope and then a 3 m climb. At the top of the slope is a naturally rounded ledge where one or two people could presumably sit side by side, very closely.

In measuring the flutings, we discovered that they had been made by two different individuals (38 and 44 mm). In this difficulty to reach the spot, it would require crawling or pulling oneself up to handholds to arrive at the ledge. Having a partner would be advantageous to take turns holding and passing a handheld stone lamp. If both sat on the ledge at the same time (which seems the most likely scenario), their bodies would have leaned against each other in the smallness of the space. It is possible that they also could have held each other around the waist to provide more stability as each reached across an empty space and upward to make the flutings themselves.

2. In Gargas Cave in the Haute-Pyrenees Department of France, the Zone de Crevasse has many flutings which were drawn by three individuals. A tall, likely left-handed man (multiple instances of his flutings are drawn only with the left hand in the cave) with a 41–43 mm three-fingered measure, a smaller female with a 34 mm finger measure, and two children, one a male with a width of 26–28 mm and the other an infant with a width of 22 mm. Given the height of the flutings from the floor (over 1.5 m), neither of the children could have reached those heights on their own and would have had to have been lifted up (Fig. 14.2).

Along the inside of a long crevasse are the flutings of the young boy with the 26–28 mm measure. Passing from that crevasse to an adjacent one, the female (34 mm) who was likely holding him on her hip (based on the height and the long uninterrupted lines of fluting that follow the steps of someone walking but not pausing in their steps) put her hand up over the crevasse to protect her head as she passed through, leaving behind the marks of all five fingers of her left hand. When she emerged on the other side of the crevasse, she drew lines with her left hand, the young boy drew lines with his right at the same height and higher, suggesting that the boy rested on her hip as they drew.

If she is drawing with her left hand, or protecting their heads with her left hand while the boy is on her right hip, either she is holding the boy and the lamp with her right hand (which is precarious but possible), or the third member of the party, the adult male, who has not drawn anything in this section of the cave but may still be present, is there to hold the light. Alternately the light has been placed on the floor, but this seems the least likely as it would restrict the mobility that seems clear in both crevasses. Either the fluters would have had to step over an open flame to create flutings in these locations or to place the light on the floor behind them would create so much shadow as it is doubtful they would be able to see. In some seasons there is also open water on this floor, and again, it is less likely that they would put their lamp into a puddle on the floor than have someone else hold the light for them.

This scene shows the physical closeness of the female and the child. The questions of who is holding the light when both of her hands are occupied raise further questions as to who else is present but not leaving marks. This panel, like many

Fig. 14.2 Measuring the three-fingered width of a finger fluting stream

others, raises the question of can we consider what kind of relational activity it shows when one person holds a light for another? Is it possible to explore the physical and emotional relationships of someone who is holding another on her hip?

3. Chamber A1 in Rouffignac Cave, in the Dordogne Region of France, appears as a cacophony of finger flutings in seven alcoves of a low-ceilinged chamber where clay has risen with flooding in the distant past, and the finger flutings reveal the yellow limestone beneath the red clay. At least five of the eight individuals identified in the cave fluted this chamber (22 mm, 28 mm, 34 mm, 38 mm, 41 mm), including three children (22 mm, 28 mm, 34 mm). Similar Gargas, at least one of the smallest children (but likely all three) had to be held up to flute the ceiling.

One of the fluters, 28 mm, a likely 4–5-year-old female, drew lines with both hands at the chamber entrance. She repeats a similar gesture of a simultaneous right/left hand fluting in four different chambers of the cave located nearly 0.6 km apart. The tectiform she created in Chamber H1, a low-ceilinged chamber, also has the same style of fluting where two hands begin to flute in concert with each other.

Although always in the company of other fluters, what is striking about her flutings is that she must have a companion who, in these instances, holds the light for her so that she can make her marks, as there is no evidence of fire on the floor. Most fluters flute with one hand or the other, but she has multiple instances where she flutes with two hands simultaneously. Only in Chamber H1, where the marks were likely made while sitting (as they are just over a meter off the floor), could she have put her lamp on the floor to make her markings with enough light cast to provide clarity.

Her fellow person in these instances is invisible in terms of the marks made because we do not know if the light holder is also a finger fluter, or is simply present, but by looking at the embodied nature of how these lines were made, we are left with the relational question also posed in Gargas. Who is holding her light? Who is that person in her emotional landscape, to her to want to do so for her? As with the other children in Chamber A1, who is lifting them up to reach the ceiling to create their flutings?

4. Rouffignac has the largest collection of finger flutings in a European cave and has multiple examples of intimacies among members of the group. In the Voie Sacrée section of the cave, an engraved panel called the 5 Mammoth Frieze also has finger flutings made over top of engravings of mammoths.

Three streams of finger flutings cross the mammoth on the right side of the panel (Fig. 14.3). Beginning more than a meter to the right of the panel, the lines are drawn by three individuals, 38 mm at the highest, 34 mm in the middle, and 28 mm in the lowest lines. This is the only example of long horizontal lines drawn while walking in Rouffignac.

Fig. 14.3 Flutings by two individuals in Grotte de Gargas, France, male child (left) and adult male (right)

In examining these lines, we see three people together, 38 mm taller, presumably older from the adult-sized hand, and found in the company of 34 and 28 mm in multiple instances in the cave. It is possible to picture the three walking together in the way that children sometimes do, running their hands along the wall. The wall has preserved their different heights and their shared path in this low-ceilinged space where the five mammoths had been engraved. Captured in the left side of the panel is the small handprint of 28 mm where she leaned momentarily into the wall.

In seeing their interactions together preserved in the wall, a series of questions arise about the relationship between these three young people. How closely together did they walk through this chamber? Did they each hold a light or was one light enough to illuminate the space between them? Did they see the engraved mammoths when they drew over them, or did their light not illuminate the images at all? Did it matter if they drew over the mammoths?

These are only four examples of intimate moments in the caves, but there are many others as each cave studied has places that show at least two people fluting each panel. That these particular examples largely involve children is perhaps not surprising as in modern times, too, we are more attuned to seeing intimacies between children and others. In instances (and in other places in Rouffignac Cave, most notably panel G4 and the Rhino Panel of the Voie Sacrée) in Rouffignac and Gargas caves, multiple members of the group have fluted together in close proximity where the younger members of the group (28 and 30 mm) appear to have been held up at hip height so that their flutings are higher than those of the adults (Fig. 14.4). In studying the embodied relationships among these individuals, can we begin to ask questions that help us to glean any sense of their emotional relationships with each other?

In thinking about the question raised by the idea of an archaeology of the heart, I propose that we begin to consider in our archaeological practice, looking for evi-

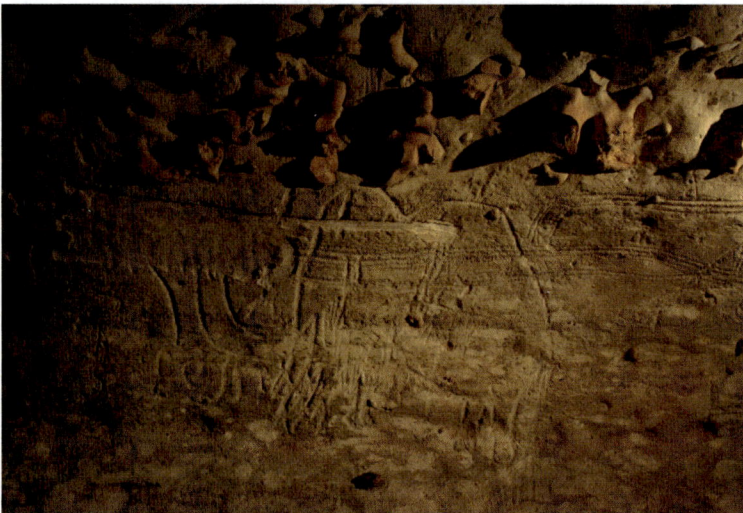

Fig. 14.4 Right side 5 Mammoth Frieze Panel. Note three horizontal streams of finger flutings at different heights

dence for relationships and intentionality in behavior in the production of cave art. Perhaps the key is to begin with a method that asks first questions of individuality, embodiment, and illumination. For instance, when approaching analysis of a drawing, we are asking the following questions: to achieve this drawing of a mammoth on that ceiling, where did the artist have to stand or lie? Could he/she do so unsupported? Where was the light that allowed for his/her hands to be involved in making this creation?

And perhaps most importantly, who might also be present at this scene who is offering support but does not make a physical mark? Can we account for or begin to understand their presence?

The combination of attempting to identify unique individuals, where they went, with whom, and how they physically created what they did begins to help us shed light on the relationships among cave artists. We have found that asking the question of "who holds the light?" opens avenues to understanding how the relationships between individuals played out in the caves.

As most of us know from our own lives, the impact of those who have physically or metaphorically held the light for us is profound. Perhaps, as is often the case in our world, too, in our quest for understanding materiality, we have become so focused on the individual who appears to have produced the singular physical final object that we have discounted the contribution of the community who have created the conditions for that to take place.

It may be that we, as archaeologists, unconsciously fall into the trap of assuming the society of the past is similar to that of the present (Lorblanchet & Bahn, 2017). Instead, we might benefit from thinking about the world of hunter-forager people of the past when they would have lived with the same small group of people most of the time: eating, sleeping, traveling, making love, raising families, and moving through the world together with an intimacy we struggle to imagine today (Wolff 2001) where nuance of relationship would be an ongoing act of co-creation. I do not speak of this as a romanticizing but simply a different worldview, and in that worldview, an archaeology of the heart would recognize and explore what nature writer Barry Lopez calls "an intimate knowing," not only between and among people in a group but also within the natural world in which they found themselves. Lopez articulates this as "one of the most striking differences between indigenous cultures and out culture is their love of our attachment and our fear of it. In traditional cultures, people strive to be included in a set of relationships, to ground their identity in a set of relationships..." (Tydeman, 2013, p.131).

My hope is that as we become researchers more attuned to the power of community, intimacy, and relationship in an through a heart-based and relational archaeology practice, we will begin to develop methodologies to look for relationships among members of past and present communities to come to understand and value the power of those who hold the light and their impact on us all. Having the courage to look for intimacy in the past and present by asking questions that might not have been considered "scientific" before all the more encourages us to ask the deeper questions of what it is to be human, to be vulnerable, to be willing to go into a dark cave not knowing what might be there and, in the companionship of others, to make our small mark upon the world and together to explore and continually find our way.

Acknowledgments I give thanks for the assistance of many people and organizations who have contributed to this work and have held the light for me. Kevin Sharpe, Frédéric Goursolle, Nicolas Ferrer, Jessica Cooney, Keryn Walshe, April Nowell, Gustavo Sanz Palomero, Raul Gutierrez Rodriguez, Eduardo Palacio Pérez, Roberto Ontañon Peredo, the Plassard Family (Rouffignac), the Mayor and Commune of Aventignan (Gargas), the Gobierno de Cantabria Consejeria de Educación Cultura y Deporte (Cantabria), South Australian Museum (Koonalda).

References

de Beaune, S. (1987). Palaeolithic lamps and their specialization: A hypothesis. *Current Anthropology, 28*(4), 569–577.

Fritz, C., Tosello, G., & Conkey, M. (2015). Reflections on the identities and roles of the artists in European Paleolithic Societies. *Journal of Archaeological Method.* https://doi.org/10.1007/s10816-015-9265-80.

Gamble, C. (1999). *The Palaeolithic societies of Europe*. Cambridge: Cambridge University Press.

Gamble, C. (2007). *Origins and revolutions. Human identity in earliest prehistory*. Cambridge, UK: Cambridge University Press.

Lorblanchet, M., & Bahn, P. (2017). *The first artists: In search of the world's oldest art*. London: Thames and Hudson.

Mithen, S. (1990). *Thoughtful foragers: A study of prehistoric decision making*. Cambridge: Cambridge University Press.

Pastoors, A., et al. (2015). Tracking in caves: Experience based reading of Pleistocene human footprints in French caves. *Cambridge Archaeological Journal., 25*(3), 551–564.

Sharpe, K., & Van Gelder, L. (2004). Children and Paleolithic 'art': Indications from Rouffignac Cave, France. *International Newsletter on Rock Art., 38*, 9–17.

Sharpe, K., & Van Gelder, L. (2005). Techniques for studying finger flutings. *Society of Primitive Technology Bulletin., 30*, 68–74.

Sharpe, K., & Van Gelder, L. (2006a). Evidence of cave marking by Paleolithic children. *Antiquity, 80*(310), 937–947.

Sharpe, K., & Van Gelder, L. (2006b). Finger flutings in Chamber A1 of Rouffignac Cave, France. *Rock Art Research., 23*(2), 179–198.

Sharpe, K., & Van Gelder, L. (2006c). A method for studying finger flutings. In P. C. Reddy (Ed.), *Exploring the mind of ancient man: Festchrift to Robert G. Bednarik*. New Delhi: Research India Press.

Sharpe, K., & Van Gelder, L. (2006d). The study of finger flutings. *Cambridge Archaeological Journal., 16*(3), 281–295.

Snow, D. (2006). Sexual dimorphism in Upper Paleolithic hand stencils. *Antiquity, 80*, 390–404.

Snow, D. (2013). Sexual dimorphism in European Upper Paleolithic cave art. *American Antiquity, 78*(4), 746–761.

Tydeman, W. (2013). *Conversations with Barry Lopez*. Norman: University of Oklahoma Press.

Van Gelder, L. (2015a). Counting the children: The role of children in the production of finger flutings in four Upper Paleolithic caves. *Oxford Journal of Archaeology, 34*(2), 120–131.

Van Gelder, L. (2015b). The role of children in the creation of finger flutings in Koonalda Cave, South Australia. *Childhood in the Past: An International Journal, 8*(2), 149–160.

Van Gelder, L. (2016). Evidence of collaboration among art makers in twelve Upper Paleolithic Caves. In R. Bednarik et al. (Eds.), *Paleoart and materiality: The scientific study of rock art* (pp. 195–203). Oxford: Archeopress.

Van Gelder, L. (2019). *Shedding light on illumination and embodiment among European Upper Paleolithic cave artists* (In press).

Van Gelder, L., & Sharpe, K. (2009). Women and girls as Upper Paleolithic cave 'artists': Deciphering the sexes of finger fluters in Rouffignac Cave. *Oxford Journal of Archaeology, 28*(4), 323–333.

Wolff, R. (2001). *Original wisdom: Stories of an ancient way of knowing*. Rochester: Inner Traditions.

Part III
From Seeds to Blossoms: Reflection and Discussion

We encourage you to reflect on the work in this volume and to consider ways to integrate these practices into your own scholarship, research, teaching, fieldwork, management, and activism. To aid in this process of taking the seeds in this volume and nurturing them into blossoms and fruit for the future, we include the following three pieces that provide reflection and commentary on the volume's themes and ideas. We invite you to engage beyond the written word with a multimedia meditation by Ruth Tringham that welcomes you into her layered experience of archaeology. You can immerse yourself in her multimedia work through this volume's online space. We also encourage you to read Ruth's written piece on slow archaeology, considering the life stories she is able to create through closely observed layers. There you will experience Tringham's exploration of the layers of her emotional engagement in archaeology over a career of several decades.

Sonya Atalay offers a heart-centered vision for the future of archaeology. She shares teachings about the "heart-berry," the strawberry, through the Haudenosaunee story of Sky Woman and the Anishinaabe story about life after the flood. Weaving this storytelling throughout her chapter, Atalay reflects on the themes of the chapters, the volume, and heart-centered practice through an Indigenous lens, tracing how we draw on deep roots of Indigenous knowledge and storytelling to support the growth of heart-berry blossoms through nurturing and care and how we bring forth the fruit of our endeavor through deep connection, relationality, collaboration, and love.

The final word of the volume, the epilogue, is Margaret Conkey's reflections on an archaeology of the heart. Thirty years ago, Meg Conkey and Ruth Tringham, together with a host of colleagues who transformed the discipline through their work on engendering archaeology (Gero and Conkey 1991), argued that the people we study in the past are not "faceless blobs" (Tringham 1991). Now, nearly 30 years later, Conkey encourages us to recognize that archaeological practitioners themselves are also not faceless blobs. Other fields of research in the sciences, social sciences, and humanities are experiencing a turn toward the heart, care, love, and empathy – Conkey notes that such a turn in archaeology is necessary for an engaged, relevant, and better future, for our discipline and beyond.

References

Gero, J. M., & Conkey, M. W. (Eds.). (1991). *Engendering archaeology: Women and prehistory.* New York: Wiley-Blackwell.

Tringham, R. (1991). Households with faces: The challenge of gender in prehistoric architectural remains. In J. Gero & M. Conkey (Eds.), *Engendering archaeology: Women and production in prehistory* (pp. 93–131). Oxford: Basil Blackwell Pubs.

Chapter 15
Closely Observed Layers: Storytelling and the Heart

Ruth Tringham

At Çatalhöyük ……

I have had a professional lifetime of heartfelt experiences as an archaeologist, especially on excavation projects. This chapter is about my most recent stories and experiences during the excavation of a 9000-year-old Neolithic house (Building 3) at the settlement mound of Çatalhöyük in west-central Turkey (Tringham and Stevanovic 2012). All the houses at Çatalhöyük were built of sun-dried mud brick whose wall surfaces and clay floors were repeatedly plastered in white clay. The walls of the houses had no openings for windows or doors (or so it seems), and access to the interior was by ladder from a hole in the flat roof (Hodder 2006: chapter 5).[1]

Inside the house, the layers of the dead/past/ancestors and – above them – the layers of the living are not separated from each other but are closely woven together as part of the same labyrinth. The portal from one to the other and the key to understanding their connection are the lids with which the burial pits are closed. We archaeologists understood this from the moment that we identified the lid of the final burial of Building 3, a young boy of 3–4 years old in a basket (Feature 617); for us who came to excavate their history, this was our first Neolithic burial (Figs. 15.1 and 15.2).

> RET Diary entry August 17, 1999: "I had an earthquake dream last night. I woke to find out that there had been a huge earthquake in Istanbul many thousands of miles to the north …..Mira started work on the burial (F.617) today, starting with the white plaster lid that we recognized two days ago by its plaster-but-not-plaster floor appearance."

---

[1] This is a video of Mirjana Stevanovic leading a tour of Building 3 as if she were its proud resident: https://vimeo.com/337032483

R. Tringham (✉)
University of California, Berkeley, CA, USA
e-mail: tringham@berkeley.edu

© Springer Nature Switzerland AG 2020   239
K. Supernant et al. (eds.), *Archaeologies of the Heart*,
https://doi.org/10.1007/978-3-030-36350-5_15

Fig. 15.1 Photo of the burial lid of F.617. A demonstration of how difficult it is to recognize a burial lid at Çatalhöyük. Note the red-painted wall next to the lid. (Unless otherwise stated, these images are all copyrighted to members of the Çatahöyük Research Project, licensed with a Creative Commons 2.5 license)

Fig. 15.2 Mirjana Stevanovic removing the lid of Feature 617 on August 17, 1999. (Unless otherwise stated, these images are all copyrighted to members of the Çatahöyük Research Project, licensed with a Creative Commons 2.5 license)

Hunting the Burial Lids

The Neolithic custom of burial at Çatalhöyük is to dig a pit, often over a meter deep, through the layers of plaster and clay floors of the living house. The pit is narrower at the top than lower down; the deceased is laid at the bottom of the pit, which is then filled in with soft dark earth to the level of the plaster floor from which it was cut. After tamping down the soil of the fill, the top of the pit is then covered with a 5 cm layer of clay plaster that is very close to the consistency and color of the floor plaster itself, but it is not identical. This is the lid. The join is smoothed over so that it is very difficult – unless you know or remember – to tell where the burial opening is (Figs. 15.3 and 15.4).[2]

As archaeologists, who poke and probe into these secrets, we want to know where the burial opening is. But we don't want to wait to come across it by accident, plunging through the unrecognized lid into the grave pit, because the lid holds the key to much more than the discovery of the resting place of the residents. It tells us about the sequence of their dying, and it tells us about their death becoming a trigger for events in the life of the living house. From a burial lid, we can track the new

Fig. 15.3 The cross-sectioned lid of Feature 631 built up to be level with the bottom of floor 2 on the northeast platform. On the right (south) edge of the pit, the boundary between the lid and the floor #2 plaster layer can be clearly seen. (Unless otherwise stated, these images are all copyrighted to members of the Çatahöyük Research Project, licensed with a Creative Commons 2.5 license)

---

[2] This video is a discussion of Ruth Tringham with Mirjana Stevanovic about the burial lids and the red-painted walls surrounding some of the burials: https://vimeo.com/336739527

Fig. 15.4 Ruth Tringham, Lori Hager, and Basak Boz working out the sequence of the lids of burial pits cutting through the platform Feature 162 in 2000. (Unless otherwise stated, these images are all copyrighted to members of the Çatahöyük Research Project, licensed with a Creative Commons 2.5 license)

plaster that is laid over the lid and its surrounding platform floor, as it creates a new floor surface over the rest of the house; we can track new configurations within the living house – new walls, new oven locations – that are created on that new floor after specific burials. The interpretation of such sequences and associations is full of ambiguity, which can be expressed in a wonderful multitude of small stories. But it provides a way of connecting the living house with the passing history of its occupants (Fig. 15.5).

Closely Observed Layers

I cannot escape the ambivalence I feel as I carry out my research in this 9000-year-old building that is also the resting place of its residents. I am excavating – revealing – layers that have hidden this place from prying eyes for 9000 years. By the time I and my team have finished the project, we have not only revealed their hiding places but we have displaced them. Worse still, that place that we revealed has almost been forgotten by the archaeologists themselves. That is a very big responsibility of destruction.

A partial exoneration of my heartlessness in this respect is provided by the heart-felt care with which we carried out the destruction. James Mellaart first excavated at the Çatalhöyük East Mound during four field seasons (1961–1963, 1965), a total

Fig. 15.5 Aerial photo of Building 3 in 2001, where the continuous white floor can be seen from burial platforms on the right to the "kitchen" on the left (south). Jason Quinlan is suspended from the roof of the BACH shelter. Michael Ashley, perching even higher, is taking this photo. (Unless otherwise stated, these images are all copyrighted to members of the Çatahöyük Research Project, licensed with a Creative Commons 2.5 license)

of 226 working days in which his team excavated close on 200 buildings, a rate of almost 1 a day (Balter 2005:26–27). By contrast, our BACH (Berkeley Archaeologists @ Çatalhöyük) project completed the entire excavation of Building 3 in seven 6-week seasons (1997–2003) and a further 10-year preparation of the materials for publication (Tringham and Stevanovic 2012). This is considered very slow, by most standards. But we were not to be hurried for the sake of "efficiency"; we had a very ambitious aim that demanded a slow pace.

Our work proceeded by the definition and excavation of "units," each one identified and recorded as a unique depositional event, perhaps a layer, perhaps a pit edge, perhaps a human skeleton, each one contributing to a massive two-dimensional scheme of the stratigraphy and history of Building 3 – its Harris matrix.[3]

Our project was based on the premise that a building was constantly being modified throughout its occupation by the practices and rhythms of its occupants as well as by the vagaries of weather and entropy (Stevanovic 2012, Hodder 2006:16–17), just as Stewart Brand (1994) has described for modern residential buildings. Our aim in analyzing the architectural features and identifying the sequence of

---

[3] This video uses the north-central platform (Feature 162) and the final burial (Feature 617) of Building 3 at Çatalhöyük to explain how single-context excavation and the Harris matrix work: https://vimeo.com/337158036

Fig. 15.6 Micromorphological section of floor plaster layers in 2002. (Unless otherwise stated, these images are all copyrighted to members of the Çatahöyük Research Project, licensed with a Creative Commons 2.5 license)

depositional events was to construct the history of Building 3 in order to lay the groundwork for creating the stories about the lives of its residents. The key to tracking the history of the houses, as in any archaeological situation, is the observation of the stratigraphic sequence of layers of deposition; in the case of Building 3 (Fig. 15.6), as in all Çatalhöyük houses, this means observations of the very thin layers created by the residents in their regular (annual?) re-plastering of walls and floors that was a necessity to keep the house alive.

The floor of Building 3 was re-plastered as a single event, in most cases one that was not associated with significant changes. But sometimes, it would involve major changes such as adding or removing a raised platform or reconfiguring its shape and boundary on the new floor, removing a relief sculpture on the wall, adding or taking down a partition wall, blocking and/or removing old storage bins and creating new ones on their stubs, and – significantly – changing the location of the house oven. We defined such major remodeling associations on a floor as "phases" in the history of the house. And we wondered whether such "phase events" were triggered by the death and burial of a resident of the house (Stevanovic 2012:77). A minor but significant event almost definitely associated with some of the burial events of the north-central platform (F.162) was the repeated painting of the walls in red that surround them (Stevanovic 2012:92).

We identified eight phases in the occupation of Building 3 and at least two phases of its gradual abandonment and collapse in the Neolithic (Fig. 15.7), covering a period of perhaps 60 years, 9000 years ago (Stevanovic 2012:51–56).The Neolithic occupation was followed by a 7000-year "rest" with a subsequent short-lived

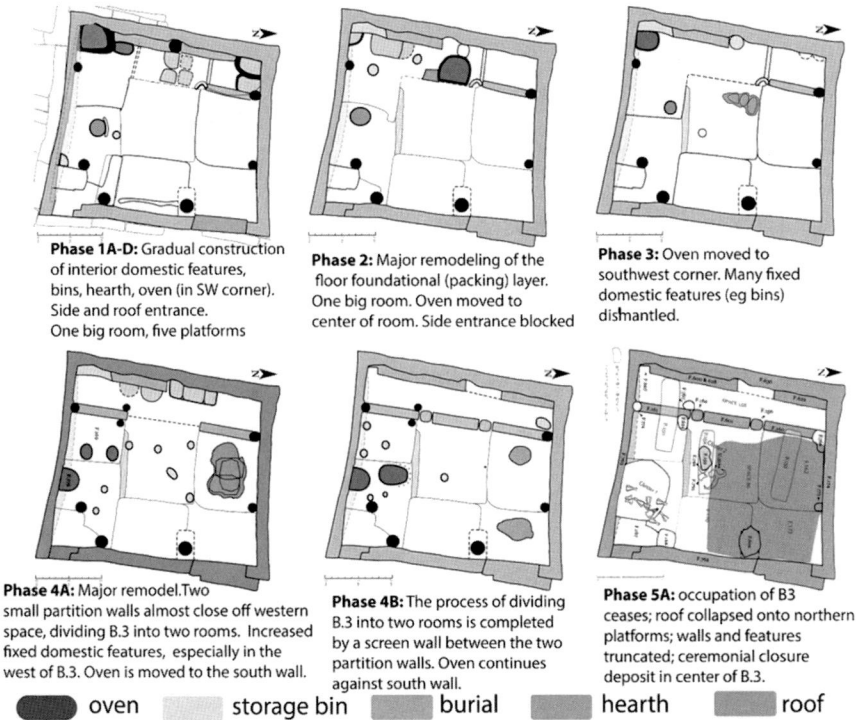

Phase 1A-D: Gradual construction of interior domestic features, bins, hearth, oven (in SW corner). Side and roof entrance. One big room, five platforms

Phase 2: Major remodeling of the floor foundational (packing) layer. One big room. Oven moved to center of room. Side entrance blocked

Phase 3: Oven moved to southwest corner. Many fixed domestic features (eg bins) dismantled.

Phase 4A: Major remodel. Two small partition walls almost close off western space, dividing B.3 into two rooms. Increased fixed domestic features, especially in the west of B.3. Oven is moved to the south wall.

Phase 4B: The process of dividing B.3 into two rooms is completed by a screen wall between the two partition walls. Oven continues against south wall.

Phase 5A: occupation of B3 ceases; roof collapsed onto northern platforms; walls and features truncated; ceremonial closure deposit in center of B.3.

● oven   storage bin   burial   hearth   roof

Fig. 15.7 The life history of Building 3 in six concentrated layers. (Copyright 2019 Ruth Tringham and Mirjana Stevanovic)

reopening in a series of first-third century AD burial events. Then Building 3 fell into another deep sleep, until – 2000 years later – its exhumation and annihilation in the name of post-processual knowledge of the past.

Heartfelt Archaeology

Such tracking demanded very slow and detailed excavation, starting with the scraping of the layers of plaster flooring and the thin layer of clay "packing" that lay beneath each one; it demanded corresponding slow and detailed visual and alphanumeric documentation of every event (aided immensely by digital technology).

This detail of field practice resonates with Bill Caraher's (2013, 2016) "Slow Archaeology":

> Slow archaeology evokes the practice of archaeology as a craft. It prioritizes an embodied attentiveness to the entire process of fieldwork as a challenge to the fragmented perspectives offered by workflows influenced by our own efficient, industrialized age. While recognizing that craft and industrial approaches to archaeology are not mutually exclusive in the dirty realities of fieldwork, the last eighty years of archaeological scholarship and practice have tended to celebrate the potential of industrial technology in archaeological practice at the expense of more integrated approaches associated with pre-industrial, craft production. (Caraher 2013:45–46)

Shawn Graham in his Electric Archaeology blog has suggested – and I agree – that Slow Archaeology is not the prerogative of field archaeology but applies also to the digital work that goes into field and post-field archaeology.

> To get the digital stuff to work involves a constant cycle of feedback and productive failure. 'Digital archaeology' is sometimes the slowest archaeology around. There's nothing inherent in the craft aspect of 'slow' archaeology that isn't also true of digital work. Digital work is inefficient in my view – it never works the first time. That's its strength. It allows us to fail faster, and that's where the illusion of 'efficiency' comes from.........'.[4]

Eric Kansa, writing from the viewpoint of digital data collection and archiving, emphasizes the ethical need for *careful* curation:

> The most important value of research data does not center on its scale, efficient collection, or even efficient interoperability. Rather, a slow data approach can highlight how data collection, management, and dissemination practices need to be considered integral to the larger ethical and professional conduct of research.....Slow archaeology captures the notion that we as a professional community should emphasize excellence in the research process, including taking time for thoughtful consideration, not simply high-throughput and efficient production of tangible research outcomes. Slow data is basically the digitized aspects of slow archaeology. (Kansa 2016:466)

All of these authors are promoting an archaeological practice that is organized more along craft lines than the specialized, standardized, assembly-line factory workflow of industrialization. Such practice is not dependent on size of project, nor whether it is paperless or paperful, but on care, attention, and detail of work. None of these authors explicitly mentions whether or not such a practice is more heartfelt or affective, although Shawn Graham approaches with the *quasi* haiku at the end of his blog:

> 'Go slow, go with care,
> make through thinking and think through making,
> employ a method of hope,
> engage in the art of inquiry.
> Play.'[5] (RET: I have re-arranged the line breaks)

What they write, however, does resonate with the original inspiration for this chapter – George Saunders, who finds the heart in the specifics of people's stories and the careful versioning of "slow writing." One morning in July 2016, I was woken as usual by "Morning Edition" on our public broadcasting station KQED. I was barely awake and trying to block out the dramas of the presidential campaign, when I heard a fragment of an interview with George Saunders – fiction and non-fiction writer, essayist – about an article he had just written for the *New Yorker* called "Who Are All These Trump Supporters?"(Saunders 2016). This is the fragment that inspired me:

> You know, as a fiction writer, one of the things you learn is God lives in specificity. You know, human kindness is increased as we pursue specificity… as you revise you always are making it better by being specific and by observing more closely. ….In the process, the piece gets more big-hearted, more fair, it includes more things and more people.[6]

---

[4] Shawn Graham's blog post is published at: https://electricarchaeology.ca/2017/03/20/slow-archaeology/(accessed 5/1/2019).

[5] https://electricarchaeology.ca/2017/03/20/slow-archaeology/

[6] The text and recording of the complete broadcast can be accessed at: http://www.npr.org/2016/07/09/485356110/in-search-for-answers-author-george-saunders-covers-trump-campaign

The Zen of Excavating

I think that George Saunders' idea of specifics and versioning applies to the way in which we scrape through the layers of dead people's life and death debris at Çatalhöyük.[7] Some of the team, especially Lori Hager and Mirjana Stevanovic, are more skilled and experienced than others. However, at first, when our team from UC Berkeley started the project in 1997, none of us had excavated in mud brick and plaster. We were all trained on wattle-and-daub architectural remains in very different contexts (Tringham and Stevanovic 2012). I swallowed my pride and learned like a nervous apprentice, watching others more experienced than I and trying it out for myself (Fig. 15.8).

Fig. 15.8 The zen of excavating at Çatalhöyük in 2001: (**a**) Ruth Tringham. (Unless otherwise stated, these images are all copyrighted to members of the Çatahöyük Research Project, licensed with a Creative Commons 2.5 license), (**b**) Ruth Tringham and Tish Prouse. (Unless otherwise stated, these images are all copyrighted to members of the Çatahöyük Research Project, licensed with a Creative Commons 2.5 license), (**c**) the BACH team. (Unless otherwise stated, these images are all copyrighted to members of the Çatahöyük Research Project, licensed with a Creative Commons 2.5 license)

---

[7]This video expresses the aura of contemplation and focused concentration that surrounds excavation of layers in Building 3: https://vimeo.com/336477361

Then we the apprentices showed the new learners the Zen of excavating that involves both specifics and versioning: if you can't work out the problem, leave it, have a coffee, and come back; or change position and work from another angle; or change hands; ask someone else what they think. Repetition and patience, white on white, no shortcuts, don't look for the immediate solution, don't dig holes, keep it clean and level, and so on. Meanwhile, inside my head, my mind is joyfully busy, making sense of the layers, using all my senses and intuition to plan where my hands-with-trowel should go next, respectfully fearful of the responsibility of the decision. This is how (for me) specificity engenders the heart and passion in archaeological practice.

Post-excavation study and publication preparation involves yet more versioning, until, as Saunders writes (2005, 2016, 2017), what emerges (we hope, but do not always succeed in producing) is not a false consensus of "what happened," but a transparent expression of the ambiguity of the past (in our case, the history of Building 3) as represented in the archaeological record (Tringham and Stevanovic 2012). The constrictions of printed publication make this a challenging ambition.

But in the ether of the Cloud and other areas of the Digital World, there are endless opportunities to continue the slow versioning of the interpretation of the source materials of an archaeological project – if they have been curated with care, as Eric Kansa (2016) advises. And, as an example, I end here with just one of the many versions of the life history of Building 3, from the point of view of one of its fictional residents.

Dido's Life

Unlike the neighboring and slightly later Building 1 that had 55 burials beneath its floors, only 10 people were buried under the floor of Building 3: 2 older adults, 2 teenagers, 3 toddlers, 1 baby, and 2 adult skulls of indeterminate age and sex. Except for the skulls and two toddler boys, each burial was a separate event. The earliest burial occurs in the second half of the history of Building 3 (Phase 3) and is of a baby (Feature 757) in a basket under the central floor of the building. It was followed by the burial of two young boys in the same place. None of these Phase 3 burials are capped by lids. In the subsequent two phases (4A and 4B), however, all the burials were capped by lids. The final burial of a child (Feature 617) triggered (or so we surmise) the closure of Building 3 (Phase 5A) in a ceremony that involved the placement of two skulls on the floor in the center of the building and the partial collapse of its roof to cover the platforms where the burials had occurred (Fig. 15.9).

In Fig. 15.9 I have charted the sequence of burials and noted which ones might (in one scenario) have triggered the remodeling that helps us to distinguish different phases in the history of Building 3. The analysis of human remains, on the basis of which this chart has been created, is published in detail by Lori Hager and Bashak Boz (2012); their chapter is an excellent example of respectful, caring, and careful archaeology. They describe their aim in and the process of "refleshing" the remains (the illustrations were created by John Swogger) as you see them in these charts (Hager and Boz, 2012:300; also see Hawkes and Molleson 2000): "The images

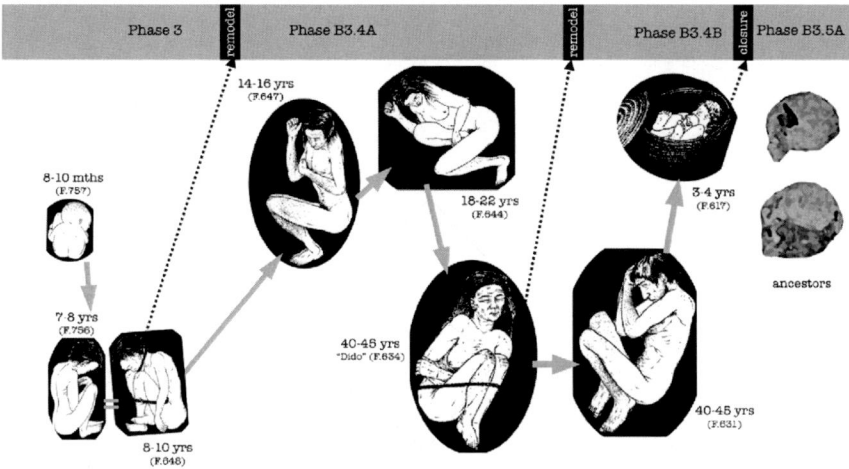

Fig. 15.9 The sequence of burials in Building 3, noting which ones might have triggered the remodeling that helps us to distinguish different phases. (Copyright 2019 Ruth Tringham)

(reconstructions) represent the principal characters in the story of Building 3, and seeing them as people rather than as skeletons gives us a sense of who they might have been, young or old, male or female. The reconstructions help us see the people who in death, and perhaps in life, were directly linked to Building 3" (Hager and Boz 2012:300).

In this quote, I am reminded of Jane Baxter remarking in her chapter in this book of the strong emotional empathy that archaeologists will have as a response to children's and young people's deaths as "disruptive, transgressive, and outside the expected (or hoped for) natural order of things" (Baxter, Chap. 9, this volume). Even though these burials are many thousands of years prior to those discussed by Jane Baxter, I nevertheless find strong resonance with the emotional affect engendered by the specifics of the archaeological record (including something as mundane as a burial lid) and the careful imagining of details of life and death for which there is little or no tangible evidence.

There is a myriad of small stories that rise up out of the debris of the dead residents in Building 3. I come now to the closely tethered but high-flying flights of imagination that bring light and sound to the silent archaeological remains. I have considered the story of "Dido," the mature 40–45-year-old woman, whose death probably triggered the remodeling of Building 3 in which the active space of the building diminished by closing off access to the western "storage" room, in many versions in many different formats (e.g., Tringham 2015a, b).[8]

---

[8] The very first version was a 1-minute video of Lori Hager excavating Dido's skull in 2000 which I set to background music of Dido's Lament in Purcell's opera *Dido and Aeneas*, in which Dido sings: "Remember me, but forget my fate." After that, the name Dido for the burial Feature 634 remained.

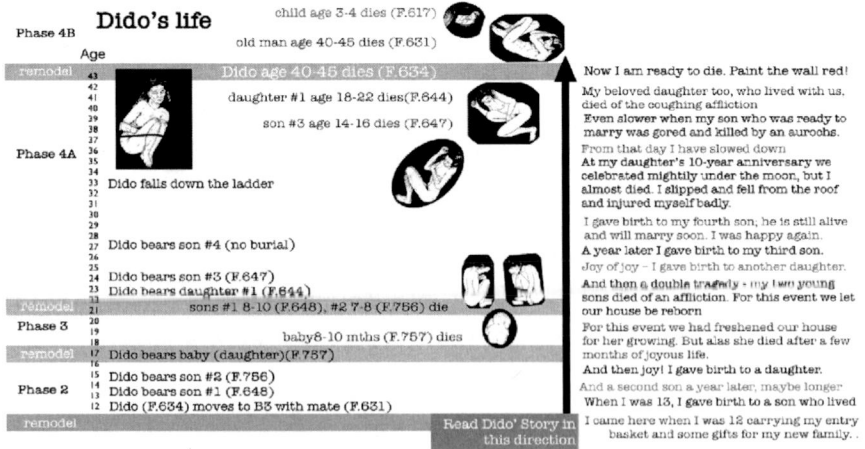

Fig. 15.10 Dido's life story. (Copyright 2019 Ruth Tringham)

In this version (Fig. 15.10), I pose the possibility that all the dead young people are the offspring of the two older individuals. Working this out brings me face to face with the life of Dido in an uncanny – and quite emotional – way. At the same time, it is a complex algebraic problem to work out the sequence of births and deaths of the Building 3 residents. And there still remains a small mystery of who gave birth to the 3-year-old child (F.617) in the final burial event of Building 3, and who buried him? Dido begins her story: I came here when I was 12. The house I came to live in was not new, but they had made it stronger and more elaborate for us newly betrothed. I have had a long life that I mark by the births and deaths of my loved ones, and a few events in between…..Now read on in the figure.

Versioning Continues

This version of the story will be frozen by the constrictions of the printing press. But already another version is appearing in an online repository of Dido's story that resides, for the moment, in a temporary collection.[9] The next version may well incorporate an experiment of using emotional nonverbal vocalizations (Tringham 2019). Narratives in the Digital World are never closed or finite. Different versions in different formats online can draw endless, ever richer, more multisensorial narratives from the research base, formats that move, speak, sing, and sigh, that surprise with their juxtapositions, and that enchant the eye (Fig. 15.11). All of these are waiting our heartfelt creativity to get to know the past residents of the earth.

---

[9] All the media (mostly videos, so far) that are relevant to this chapter are currently gathered together in an online Vimeo Showcase: https://vimeo.com/showcase/5980186. Readers should be warned that the videos in this Vimeo Showcase are the only ones in Ruth Tringham's online video archive that are guaranteed not to show images of human remains.

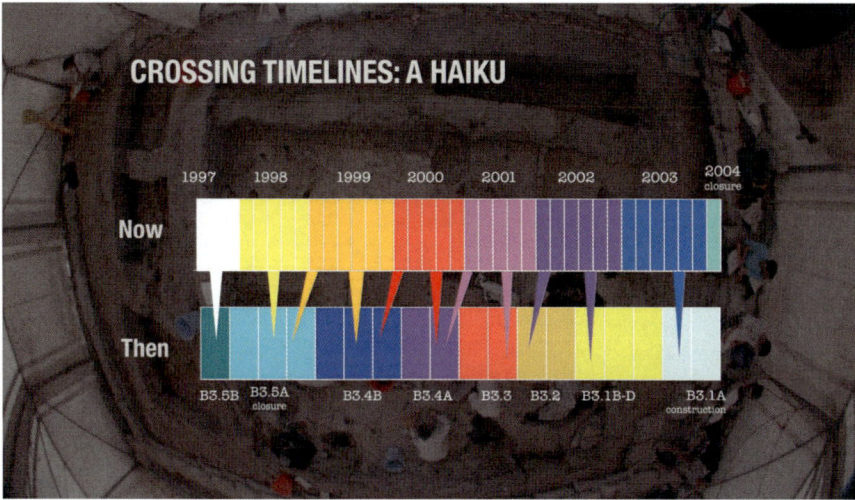

Fig. 15.11 Crossing Heartfelt Timelines: A Haiku. (Copyright 2019 Ruth Tringham)

Crossing Timelines Haiku[10]

Timeline "Now": the BACH project from start (1997) to filling in (2004), archaeologists peering back from left to right, into the life history of Building 3.

   Timeline "Then": Neolithic residents of the house from construction to closure, living forward from right to left.

   At some point, in my mind, these timelines cross;

   That,

   Makes my heart beat faster at its possibilities.

References

Balter, M. (2005). *The goddess and the bull*. New York: Simon and Schuster/the Free Press.

Brand, S. (1994). *How buildings learn*. New York City: Viking Press, Cham.

Caraher, W. (2013). Slow archaeology. *North Dakota Quarterly, 80*(2), 43–52.

Caraher, W. (2016). Slow archaeology: Technology, efficiency, and archaeological work. In E. Walcek-Averett, J. Gordon, & D. B. Counts (Eds.), *Mobilizing the past for a digital future: The potential of digital archaeology* (pp. 421–442). Grand Forks: The Digital Press of the University of North Dakota.

Hager, L., & Boz, B. (2012). Death and its relationship to life: Neolithic burials from building 3 and space 87 at Çatalhöyük. In R. Tringham & M. Stevanovic (Eds.), *Last House on the Hill: BACH area reports from Çatalhöyük, Turkey (Çatalhöyük vol.11)* (pp. 297–330). Los Angeles: Cotsen Institute of Archaeology Publications, UCLA.

---

[10] A more dynamic version of this haiku can be found at https://vimeo.com/337175758

Hawkes, L., & Molleson, T. (2000). Refleshing the past. In I. Hodder (Ed.), *Towards reflexive method in archaeology: The example at Çatalhöyük* (pp. 153–166). Cambridge: McDonald Institute of Archaeological Research.

Hodder, I. (2006). *The Leopard's tale: Revealing the mysteries of Çatalhöyük*. London: Thames and Hudson.

Kansa, E. (2016). Click here to save the past. In E. Walcek-Averett, J. Gordon, & D. B. Counts (Eds.), *Mobilizing the past for a digital future: The potential of digital archaeology* (pp. 443–474). Grand Forks: The Digital Press of the University of North Dakota.

Saunders, G. (2005). The Battle for Precision. *The Guardian* (March 19, 2005 issue).

Saunders, G. (2016). Who are all these Trump supporters? *The New Yorker* (July 10 issue).

Saunders, G. (2017). What writers really do when they write. *The Guardian* (March 4, 2017 issue).

Stevanovic, M. (2012). Summary of results of the excavation in the BACH area. In R. Tringham & M. Stevanovic (Eds.), *Last House on the Hill: BACH area reports from Çatalhöyük, Turkey (Çatalhöyük vol. 11)* (Monumenta Archaeologica 27) (pp. 49–80). Los Angeles: Cotsen Institute of Archaeology Publications, UCLA.

Tringham, R. (2015a). Dido and the basket: Fragments towards a non-linear history. In A. Clarke, U. Frederick, & S. Brown (Eds.), *Object stories: Artifacts and archaeologists* (pp. 161–168). Walnut Creek: Left Coast Press.

Tringham, R. (2015b). Creating narratives of the past as recombinant histories. In R. M. Van Dyke & R. Bernbeck (Eds.), *Subjects and narratives in archaeology* (pp. 27–54). Denver: University Press of Colorado.

Tringham, R. (2019). Giving voices (without words) to prehistoric people: Glimpses into an Archaeologist's imagination. *European Journal of Archaeology, 22*(3), 338–353. https://doi.org/10.1017/eaa.2019.20.

Tringham, R., & Stevanovic, M. (Eds.). (2012). *Last House on the Hill: BACH area reports from Çatalhöyük, Turkey (Çatalhöyük vol.11)*. Los Angeles: Cotsen Institute of Archaeology Publications, UCLA.

Chapter 16
An Archaeology Led by Strawberries

Sonya Atalay

Sky-Falling Woman and Muskrat Diving

I set out to read these chapters and draw together what I see as key themes and important points that run through them, and what struck me over and over again was how beautifully these themes and points connect with Anishinaabe teachings about strawberries. Sarah Surface-Evans mentions these "heart berries" in her chapter, and these papers illustrate many of the lessons we are gifted with and meant to learn from strawberries. With the teachings of strawberries in mind, I thought I would start by sharing a story; there are actually two stories here. One is the Haudenosaunee Sky Woman story, and the other is a related Anishinaabe story about life after the ice melted resulting in a great flood.

My friend and colleague, Robin Kimmerer, shares a beautiful version of the Sky Woman story in her book, *Braiding Sweetgrass: Indigenous Wisdom, Scientific Knowledge and the Teachings of Plants* (2015), adapted from the published version by Joanne Shenandoah and Douglas George (1996). In reading Kimmerer's work, I began thinking more deeply about the power of the Sky Woman teachings to inform our contemporary research methods and practices. I continued to reflect on traditional Anishinaabe stories and the ways we can draw on their lessons today, to help guide our work and practice in the contemporary world.

These lessons and the powerful relevance and necessity of these traditional stories for today's world circled around again, reminding me again and further strengthening the connections that I had recognized earlier. The stories and their teachings were literally brought to life before my eyes when, in October 2015, I was fortunate to witness Kahente Horn-Miller, a *Kanien'kehá:ka*/Mohawk scholar and activist, share a performative interpretation on the Amherst College campus of the Sky

S. Atalay (✉)
Department of Anthropology, University of Massachusetts Amherst, Amherst, MA, USA
e-mail: satalay@umass.edu

© Springer Nature Switzerland AG 2020
K. Supernant et al. (eds.), *Archaeologies of the Heart*,
https://doi.org/10.1007/978-3-030-36350-5_16

Woman story as adapted from her doctoral dissertation research (2009). In both her performance (2015) and her dissertation, Horn-Miller demonstrates the relevance of the Sky Woman story for our contemporary world. Her performance, aptly titled "We Are Here and She Is In Us: Revisiting the Sky Woman Story" reveals the hardships and healing that are necessary for moving Sky Woman's world, and ours, forward. Here's a summary of the story as I heard it during her performance.

Sky Woman lives among the sky people. She is pregnant and one day sees a giant hole in her world that was created by an uprooted tree. She jumps into the hole and falls for a very long time. The animals in the world below, which is our world on earth, see her falling. They talk among themselves, trying to decide what to do, how they can help her.

As Sky Woman falls, she grasps onto trees and plants, grabbing handfuls of seeds, including corn, beans, and squash, that will come to nourish the people of Turtle Island, and sacred plants of tobacco and strawberries, both powerful medicines (Fig. 16.1). Geese decide to help Sky Woman; a flock of them fly over to catch her and help break her fall. Sky Woman rests on their backs as they fly together. The animals below are trying to decide on a place where Sky Woman can come to rest. At that time, there is water covering the land.

This next part of the story caught my attention because it is similar to a story that Anishinaabe people also carry – it's the "Earth Diver" story, which takes place at a time when melting waters create a great flood and animals must work to find land among the floodwaters. In both the Sky Woman story and the Anishinaabe Earth Diver story, the animals take turns diving down to find soil. Many animals lose their lives without success. Eventually muskrat volunteers dive under the waters in search of earth, an idea that some of the animals think is ill-planned, because muskrat is

Fig. 16.1 "Sky Woman's story". (Painting by Nia:wen Owisokon Lahache, Turtle Bay Art Studio, Kahnawake, Canada)

Fig. 16.2 Muskrat diving. (Photo credit: *Fire and Water: Ojibway Teachings and Today's Duties*. Ningwakwe Learning Press (2011))

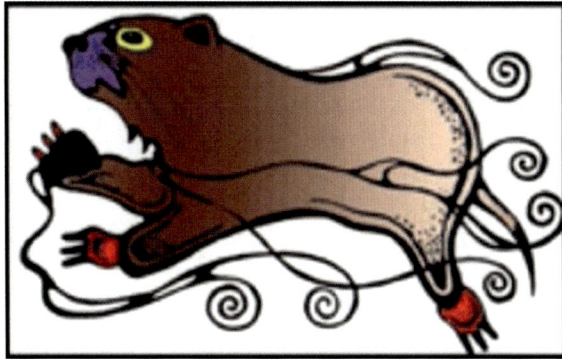

small and not the best of swimmers. The animals doubt muskrats' ability to succeed where so many have failed. Muskrat dives down, and after a very long time, when many of the animals had lost hope, he emerges. His lifeless body floats to the surface, holding a tiny paw full of soil (Fig. 16.2). The animals place the earth on the back of a turtle, who volunteers to hold it, and as Sky Woman gently dances on that soil, it expands and circles outward to become "Turtle Island," the name many Native peoples use to refer to North America.

Sky Woman then gives birth to the baby she carried during her fall through the hole in the sky world – a daughter. They live happily on Turtle Island, and eventually her daughter becomes pregnant with two sons. One son has many good qualities, such as kindness, care, empathy, compassion, and humility. The other son has negative traits – he's arrogant, stubborn, selfish, and angry. The son with the negative traits causes a difficult birth for Sky Woman's daughter, and she dies in childbirth. In her telling, Robin Kimmerer (2013: 23) describes what happens next, explaining Sky Woman's connection to the origin of strawberries. As the story continues, Sky Woman's daughter is buried, and, in the place where her body is put to rest, several of the most important plant medicines sprout up from her body. Sweetgrass from her hair, tobacco used to communicate with the spirit world from her head, and, importantly for our considerations of heart-based practices, strawberries grow from her heart.

For me, the stories shared by Kahente Horn-Miller and Robin Kimmerer are not simply beautiful, old "folk tales." I agree with Horn-Miller when she professes, and embodies in her performance (2015), that Sky Woman is in us and is still gifting us with lessons today. Kimmerer writes (2013:9): "In the public arena I've heard the Skywoman story told as a bauble of colorful 'folklore.' But, even when it is misunderstood, there is power in the telling." Kimmerer describes sharing the story with her students and she asks them: "Can they, can we all, understand the Skywoman story not as an artifact from the past but as instructions for the future?" I echo the sentiment in Kimmerer's question. I see many of the lessons that were given through these stories to the Haudenosaunee and Anishinaabe peoples reflected in the chapters of this volume, and I see in these stories a path forward for archaeology.

As Chelsey Armstrong and Eugene Anderson show so clearly in their chapter, heart-centered practices are part of efforts and conversations of relevance in other disciplines. We, as archaeologists, have allies in other fields – we can and should seek out others, colleagues and allies, who are working toward heart-centered practices in their disciplines and their communities so we can learn from each other. We can also begin working with them to form collaborations in which we share practices and develop projects across disciplines. There is excellent work to draw on from colleagues in other academic fields and also from communities of practice. As Armstrong and Anderson note: understanding Indigenous ontologies in the Indigenous Nations we work with will help us build heart-centered archaeologies and ultimately a better practice. As we delve into and further explore these areas of new connections and interconnectedness, we will find ways of weaving "ecologies of the heart" (Anderson 1996) into our archaeologies.

Armstrong and Anderson give us several clear methods forward. Perhaps part of what archaeologists can begin to practice is an understanding of how to appropriately consider and engage with some *landscapes*, *sites*, and *artifacts* as "beings that are other-than-human," and, as they so rightly state in their chapter, these other-than-human beings are worthy of respect and good treatment. I would like to see us also more actively engage together in acts of "backcasting" as Armstrong and Anderson describe. We can explore and imagine ideal archaeological futures in which heart-centered practices and community-based research with Indigenous and local communities are regular parts of practice, in both academia and cultural resource management.

I hope at least a few readers of this volume will join me in what I have called "Imagining Decolonial Research Futures" (Atalay 2018). Can we imagine ourselves as Sky Woman, falling into a new world, bringing along seeds and medicines that will help us to create a new world? One that grows from our strengths and doesn't take for granted oppressive, unjust, and exploitative practices of our current world. How can we nurture and care for these seeds allowing them to grow and thrive, to provide us with healing gifts that improve our research methods and practices? Through creative narratives, art, and other creativity-based practices, might we more actively and collaboratively work to imagine the decolonial, giving ourselves space to dream the world we want to see. Can we use these creative endeavors as a means to consider, as individuals and in relationship with each other and our community partners, how to plant and nurture the seeds that we hope will grow and thrive in that new world?

Allow yourself to image for a moment a day of teaching, a fieldwork season, or how you might plan aspects of your next research project in a decolonial research future.

Lisa Hodgetts and Laura Kelvin demonstrate in their chapter that we can and must acknowledge colonial histories of our discipline while also considering what is possible and how a different archaeology is possible. Meg Conkey asks us to consider what archaeology may be like in 20 years, and she confesses to hoping for a future archaeology in which "heart takes over." Like Conkey, I also hope for a future in which we see an archaeology that takes "its humanistic goals seriously while not relinquishing its rigor nor its commitments to its audiences…," and as she argues, I also feel this is not just about archaeology but about science more broadly and about the way we engage in the practice of research and teaching. We absolutely need more "open and affective research practices." Miigwech, sincere thanks, to the contributors in this volume for moving us closer toward that future.

In the most recent issue of the *Canadian Journal of Archaeology* (2018), even more of our colleagues have engaged in acts of backcasting as they consider archaeology 50 years into the future as a way to celebrate the 50th anniversary of the Canadian Archaeological Association. Shane Donnelly Hall (2015) uses the concept of speculative futures in asking students to think creatively about human adaptation to the global environmental crisis. From Donna Haraway's (2013) discussion of "speculative fabulation" to feminist speculative fiction of Ursula K. LeGuin, scholars, writers, and artists are utilizing speculative practices in vibrant and engaging ways.

Anthropologists have begun to actively utilize speculative approaches, as we see in the volume *Anthropologies and Futures: Researching Emerging and Uncertain Worlds* (Salazar et al. 2017), where the focus is on methods of researching future peoples, cultures, and worlds. As Juan Francisco Salazar (2017) notes in his chapter in that volume, "Across a range of social sciences, particularly those inflected by phenomenology, object-oriented ontologies and feminist new materialism, the speculative is being taken up as a practical-theoretical approach to reconceptualizing problems and seeing more imaginative propositions."

How might future archaeologies nourish us all, intellectually and emotionally, in body, mind, and spirit. I hope you'll consider sharing your imaginings, I invite you allinanopen-endedcall:https://blogs.umass.edu/satalay/imagining-decolonial-research-futures/

Indigenous Research Concepts

I see in these stories of Sky Woman, the Muskrat Earth Diver, and the origin of strawberries many of the key concepts of Indigenous pedagogy and Indigenous research theories and methods. This is knowledge known and cared for over a very long time, millennia, and it's exciting to see it now being considered and applied in relation to research and teaching methods in western institutions of higher education. These forms of traditional Indigenous knowledge are foundational in JoAnn Archibald's *Indigenous Storywork* (2008), Shawn Wilson's *Research Is Ceremony* (2009), and in the work of other Indigenous scholars, some of which Natasha Lyons and Kisha Supernant discuss in their chapter. Many of those theoretical concepts and methodological approaches are nicely articulated in this conceptual model of the Indigenous research paradigm by Lori Lambert (Fig. 16.3), which are described in Lambert's scholarship (2014) and directly relate to the mission of the American Indigenous Research Association (2019). Lambert's model is also heart-centered, and many of the chapters in this volume map on to multiple aspects of this paradigm.

Indigenous Research Paradigm: A Conceptual Model

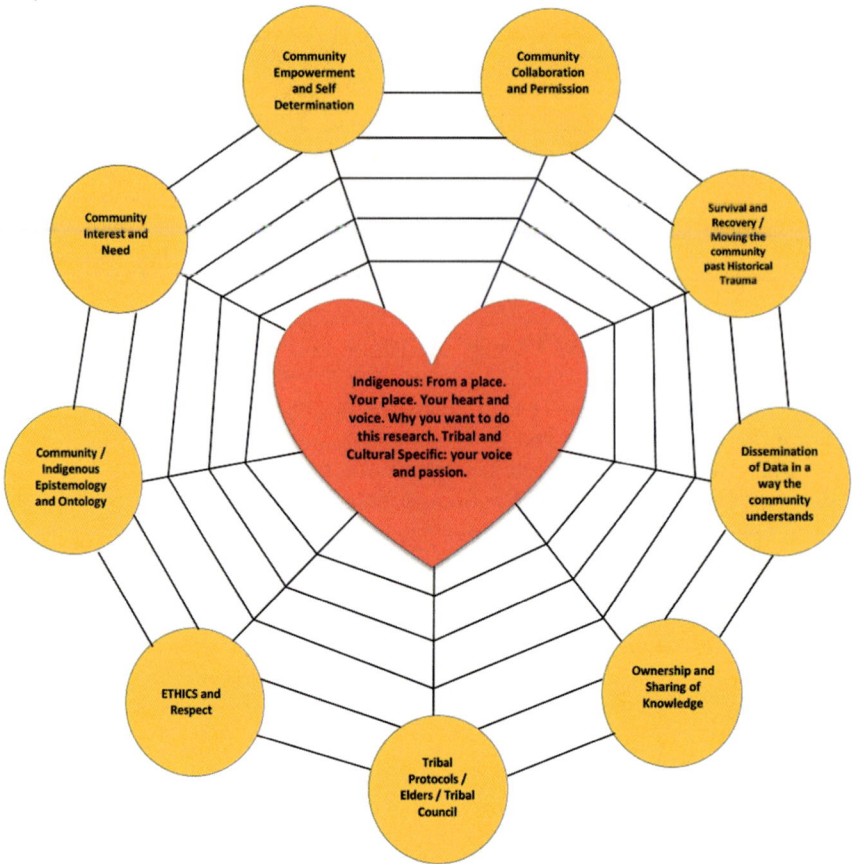

Fig. 16.3 Indigenous research paradigm: a conceptual model developed by Lori Lambert. (American Indigenous Research Association Website (2019))

As Sarah Surface-Evans noted in her chapter, for Anishinaabe peoples, strawberries are referred to as the "heart berry." In our Anishinaabe language, strawberries are "ode'iminan" or "heart seed/berries." Some say this is because they are shaped like a heart, but the traditional teaching about them is that they are, in fact, a powerful heart medicine. Not just the juicy delicious fruit that we eat but also the green stems, which are edible and are a traditional medicine used to treat diabetes and heart disease. This is a teaching shared in Anishinaabe Midewiwin ceremonies, taught to children and youth, as elders remind them to eat the *entire* berry, leaves, and all. I remember one of our elders, George Martin, gently passing on that lesson to my 2-year-old son who had only eaten the red fruit and was holding the green leafy top in his hand. George asked my son: "Are you saving the best part for last?"

As I said, I see many of the key points and themes from the chapters of this volume reflected in the story of Sky Woman, the Earth Diver, and the ode'imin (strawberry). If we think about the geese who came together to catch Sky Woman, it speaks to what many of the authors of these chapters discuss about collaboration and partnership. Several Anishinaabe stories include geese, and often these are stories meant to give lessons about partnership and collaboration. This connection made me curious about geese and their practices, so I did some reading about geese. As you've likely seen before, geese fly in V patterns; this is because they take turns in the lead position, each helping to break the harsh winds as they lead the way for the others. As the leader gets tired from taking the brunt of the wind, another of the geese takes her place, allowing her to rest for a time. Working together, the geese all take a turn leading, knowing that it is through relationship and the process of relationality that they all achieve their goal and travel safely to their destination. We see the importance of collaborative practice, shared responsibility, and working collectively with each other and community partners to achieve a common goal.

In their respective chapters, Sarah Surface-Evans and Uzma Rivi both discuss some of the challenging, difficult aspects of heart-centered practices. For example, Rizvi (Chap. 6, this volume) notes that this work brings us to engaging in difficult power relations and that we must face emotions of betrayal. Surface-Evans (Chap. 1, this volume) addresses how an "epistemology of the heart" can be seen as reflecting or implying weakness, and she points to the reality of emotional burnout. Several chapters demonstrate that anger and frustration can be embraced as they push us and inspire us to work for lasting social change. Love, respect, and care can be the grounding toward relieving the weariness of those who have been disenfranchised by federal and state governments and by our own disciplines.

I see these aspects reflected in the more difficult birth of the second twin that Sky Woman's daughter birthed. Through that part of Sky Woman's story, we are reminded to be vigilant and mindful, as there are real challenges and difficulties arising from this sort of heart-centered work. I very much appreciate Rizvi's open discussion about betrayal and the need for us to ask ourselves what we promised and what was promised to us as a way to ensure that we follow through on what is implied and promised in our collaborative partnerships.

Many of the chapters in this volume reflect the need for *balance* – of being soft yet strong, humble but knowing and holding your place. As Sarah Surface Evans remind us: being taken seriously is a real concern and something feminist scholars have taken up and continue to help us think through. We need renewed consideration of how this differs among the genders. How can we find balance between being firm yet flexible, nurturing while maintaining boundaries? And the need for balance extends to the limits we put on our work lives as we find ways to effectively balance our work life with truly restorative breaks and time away from work. We need to put these forms of balance on our "to-do" list, to keep in mind as we continue our work, developing and exploring heart-centered practices and methods.

Balance and the *intersectionality* of the body, mind, spirit, and emotion are present throughout many of these chapters. When the authors in this volume initially presented their papers in a session at the 2017 Society for American Archaeology meetings, Jami Macarty led us in a meditative practice halfway through the set of papers (Macarty, Chap. 8, this volume). Ms. Macarty reminded us in our meditation that the mind and emotion are not separate. In her chapter, Uzma Rizvi touches on this intersectionality when she speaks about the way the intellectual aspects of her work in Rajasthan, India, required emotional labor. Ruth Tringham (Chap. 15, this volume) shares the way her senses are interwoven with her intellectual work. In her work on children, Jane Baxter (Chap. 9, this volume) demonstrates the importance of giving the same emotional space for children in the past as we give to them in the present. Thinking of emotional responses beyond those connected with humans, past and present, Baxter also reminds us of the emotional value that many archaeologists feel for heritage sites and places in the present and the deeply emotional responses we feel when such places are damaged or threatened.

We might also consider the importance and benefits of limiting aspects of our senses in some contexts, such as being mindful or working in silence rather than talking or listening to music while working with ancestral remains or materials that communities view as sacred objects. Callum Abbott also refers to the balance of body and mind when he discusses learning through doing. Many of us who engage in archaeological field work can certainly relate to the enjoyable intersection of mind and body that archaeology brings. We often hear colleagues speak about their initial draw to archaeology because it allowed for combination of physical work of the body with intellectual work of the mind. There are many of us for whom the words from John Welch's chapter deeply resonate, as he notes, archaeology "illuminated pathways for my emphatically kinaesthetic predispositions in thinking, imagining, and creating—hyperactive routes to contribution less open in more sedentary and purely cerebral fields."

Overall there is so much *love* in the stories I shared at the start of this chapter. Love and thinking, planning with hope and forethought for others, looking ahead to future generations. Though she's a stranger, the animals care for Sky Woman as family, knowing she is pregnant and carries humans, seeds, and medicines. There is also so much love in the chapters in this volume, love even in the midst of anger, pain, and weariness. Love for the communities we partner with, love for ancestors – both the intellectual "ancestors," those mentors we learn from in contemporary times; love for the ones whose homes, lands, and materials we study; and acknowledgment that peoples, families, and community members of long ago also loved. They loved each other, their waters and lands, these places, and materials we study. And, as Ruth Tringham explored in her contribution and John Welch so delightfully explores in his chapter, a willingness to say those "three little words" in admitting a love for the field of archaeology.

Looking back to these origin stories as we simultaneously look forward and begin imagining decolonial archaeological futures, what archaeology might be, I find it comforting to consider that from Sky Woman's turmoil and suffering, new life begins. We are reminded of her initial fall and the seeds she grabbed on the way down. Those seeds provide gifts for the people – gifts that grow from her daughter's physical body after death, medicines from her heart, as well as plants that will nourish the bodies of those ones yet to come. And medicines from her physical body that allow humans to connect and heal in spirit and emotion. As we engage in imagining the speculative futures of the archaeologies we'd like to see, and as we work toward making those futures a reality across the very different realms and spaces where archaeology is practiced (CRM, academia, communities, etc.), I see many viable seeds in these chapters. In nurturing those seeds, we grow together, resulting in sustainable sources of sustenance and medicines. The work we put into heart-centered archaeologies will bear fruit through new ideas, methods, and practices.

Seeds

Patience is one seed. We see in Uzma Rizvi's chapter that it takes time and a sustained commitment to learn with and from communities. Archaeologies of the heart sprout, grow, and thrive when we slow down our habits and can nurture relationships. This includes our relationship with ourselves. Taking time for our own self-care leads to better work and healthier archaeologists. We also see in many of these chapters ways in which we are all still experimenting and exploring. We need to honor the time and patience it takes to learn and develop new methods. Our habits of practice need to be adjusted, to make the process slower. As we move with care and intention toward new ways of practicing, we also need to find patience with those who at times may seem stuck in and clinging to a very different archaeology of years past.

Emotions are seeds. As Natasha Lyons and Kisha Supernant note in their chapter: considering the whole person, past and present, including when working with our students, is so necessary. As you can see from the figures in this chapter, artists have depicted the stories of Sky Woman, and they portray the emotions of those involved. In her performance, Kahente Horn-Miller certainly presents the emotions, along with the logic and critical thinking of Sky Woman and the animals and other beings involved in the Sky Woman story. Lindstrøm's chapter presents us with a way to think about emotions in frescoes. She shows us the complexities of interpreting emotions across time and cultures and makes us consider what variabilities exist in facial expressions and culturally understood emotions. As Lyons and Supernant discuss, I have also found that students learn best when they can bring their whole selves, including their emotions, to spaces of learning. I have watched with awe and deep happiness as they respond and engage like never before when space is opened up for them to do so in the classroom. Anthony Graesch, Corbin Maynard, and Avery Thomas give us clear and meaningful examples of the way engaging with archaeological objects impacted their students and themselves. Jane Baxter's analysis (Chap. 9, this volume) shows how archaeologists have, at times, made assumptions about emotion in ad hoc ways, such as in their presumptions of stressful emotions among people experiencing environmental shifts or uncertainty. Baxter argues persuasively for ways that archaeology of emotion helps narrow the gap between our own lived experience and how we envision life in the past. Her work encourages us to consider more "subtle expressions" of care and emotions.

Graesch et al. and Baxter's chapters reveal archaeology as a powerful tool for connecting people with objects and places, as a practice that helps us to cultivate empathy with and respect for cultural concepts, including emotional and spiritual connections, that people have with the places and materials (even discard!) that archaeologists study. In their consideration of the long-standing interest in Neanderthals, Melanie Chang and April Nowell consider the relationships between modern humans and Neanderthals and the role that emotion plays in the interest of studying Neanderthals. They propose that archaeologists' concerns about our own fate as humans may explain the "persistent emotional resonance" of Neanderthals.

Meg Conkey urges us to consider the emotions and spirit of our work. She reminds us that we can and do resist being faceless blobs by acknowledging our personal and emotional lives in our archaeological practices. Ruth Tringham's written contribution and her multimodal piece on this volume's website explore these emotions – including joy, surprise, delight, excitement, imagination, and the feeling of one's heart beating faster from the practice of our craft. I particularly appreciate and inspired by her attention to and highlighting of the "celebration of ambiguity" and "multisensorial embrace." I feel so fortunate to have been raised by these two and the other amazing women at UC Berkeley as these types of conversations were part of the "talk around the dinner table" every day at Berkeley's Archaeological Research Facility. I recognize that most archaeologists may not have this as part of their training, but among those who do we see, these ideas embodied in their professional practice as they flourish and blossom in their careers. They are then able to similarly impart these practices as they train students.

Empathy and *compassion* are common themes and important seeds in our struggles for justice and to create a more just future. We have to acknowledge that others may not share a love for archaeology; they may experience it with fear, trauma, and anger. This acknowledgment must enter into our practice. Lisa Hodgetts and Laura Kelvin shared with us in their chapter what many of us who do community-based archaeology have also experienced: difficult challenges in Indigenous communities, climate change, pain, and loss. A heart-centered practice can help ensure that we resist what Eve Tuck (2009) refers to as "damage-centered" research. Instead, as we see with Hodgetts and Kelvin and so many others in this volume, heart and hope are what we can center.

Focus and *care* are seeds. Natasha Lyons and Kisha Supernant consider this in thoughtful ways in their chapter, prompting me to ask: How might we observe and act with care and with concern for others, even when you don't share their views or their plight? And can we also be open to and acknowledge the forms of care that come our way? Uzma Rizvi models this as she calls our attention to the care her community partners have for her, for her protection and safety. Care is necessary for building relationships, as Lyons and Supernant discuss. Jane Baxter's work on the archaeology of childhood reminds us that these studies have to consider love, care, and hope in our understandings of people in the past. She demonstrates clearly how devoid most current analyses are of emotion and shows through her discussion how this can productively be addressed.

Lisa Hodgetts and Laura Kelvin remind us that our practice is an "act of the heart" that involves *care*, just as teaching does. They point out that "care" is thought of as acceptable in teaching (when it's done by women), but care is forcefully separated from "research." They also show us that it doesn't need to be. Their chapter reminds us how our teaching can have rippling effects when we teach to the whole student. Hodgetts and Kelvin as well as Callum Abbot highlight the power of archaeology to engage students in "learning through doing."

In his presentation at the 2017 Society for American Archaeology (SAA) panel in which many of these chapters were initially presented, John Welch reminded us to see our limits and recognize when we are wrong. He called us to be brave as we go forward to explore something different. What we learned in these chapters can help us move beyond the fear of not being able to say for certain what emotions, sensations, or embodied experiences peoples of the past may have had. Bravery to venture out in new areas helps move us beyond plateaus, even when it is uncomfortable or even frightening. Welch also reminded us that we will make mistakes – the work throughout these chapters shows us the capacity we have, with open hearts, to understand, learn, move past, and forgive. Reading these chapters, I remind myself and all our readers: Minewebzhida! Let's be kind! Indeed, let's be kind, to each other, our community partners, and also to ourselves, along the way as we explore this new path.

Stories are seeds. In the pages of this volume, so many stories are shared. Callum Abbot shared one of my favorites in discussing his excellent blackstone. In Ojibwe, stones are relatives – grandfathers and grandmothers – so I have to acknowledge the lessons of that stone. We see personal stories shared such as those generously shared by Lisa Hodgetts and Laura Kelvin, and as we see in their chapter that storytelling is a powerful research method and a valuable part of community-based archaeological practice. We learn so much from the stories shared in these chapters, from the humans and also from other-than-human beings. I have been excited to see that scholars have started to acknowledge this animacy in their research and publications. I am thinking here most specifically of the 2015 article "Co-becoming Bawaka" published in the Journal "Progress in Human Geography" in which the land – Bawaka Country in Australia – is the first co-author of the piece (Bawaka Country et al. 2015).

The chapters and scholarship presented in this volume all remind us about the importance of stories and of "storywork" in Indigenous method and theory (Archibald 2008, Archibald et al. 2019). They also call us to reflect on authorship, who is present or absent(!) and who has a voice. The stories in these chapters inspire me and helped me feel brave to frame my discussion in this chapter through storytelling. Storywork is an essential aspect of Anishinaabe cultural traditions of knowledge production and mobilization (Atalay 2018). In preparing my comments for the 2017 SAA session that led to this edited volume and in writing this chapter, I also reflected back to my archaeological training and recognized that it was Meg Conkey, Ruth Tringham, Christine Hastorf, and Rosemary Joyce who, during my graduate work at UC Berkeley, inspired me to incorporate storywork into the archaeology I envisioned and practiced. And it was Ruth Tringham who inspired me to put storywork into my teaching, showing through her own creative-based research practices that it is acceptable to bring art and beauty into the stories we tell in academic spaces. Evidence of her skill as a storyteller and creative gifts are evidenced in her contribution to this volume and most notably in her online contribution. From my mentors and from Indigenous scholars like JoAnn Archibald, through observing and learning from my elders in Midewiwin ceremony, I learned that storywork is a rigorous method.

One benefit of stories is that they remind us to use our senses. Smells, color, sounds, tastes, and how these relate to pleasure, joy, fear, or excitement bring life and relatability to every good story. Considering multiple senses through narrative, storywork, or art (as evidenced in the image of Sky Woman's story in this chapter) all deepen our engagement with the past. These senses need not be provable; they are useful to think with. Most notably in this volume, Leslie Van Gelder draws the lines for us to connect how love, embodiment, and senses – such as light, acoustics, and touch – bring such essential beauty to our realms of archaeological knowledge.

We need to allow ourselves time and intellectual space to imagine the peoples of the past as having those sensations and experiences, and ourselves recognize the fulfillment and enjoyment we feel by engaging in such creative acts. I felt such joy in looking at a "double map" shared by Meg Conkey in her presentation during our SAA session, just as I feel hope when imagining Sky Woman descending toward Turtle Island, carrying seeds that will take root and create a different world. This envisioning of an embodied past is productive as it also encourages us and makes space for us to also begin visioning possible futures. Here is a speculative future: one in which archaeology and the academic world more broadly is deeply infused with heart-centered practices.

Relationality is another fundamental seed. Relationships are essential – they are at the center; they form the heart that pumps life into all of these practices. Natasha Lyons and Kisha Supernant, as well as Callum Abbott, all stress this interconnectedness in their chapters. In engaging in the work of heart-centered practices, as Abbott says, we are "resisting artificial binaries." These are practices that recognize and truly value our connections while still respecting our diversity. Centering relationality, while resisting binaries and divisions, extends beyond our relations with other people. Chelsey Armstrong and Eugene Anderson demonstrate this in their discussion of "land and kin," rightly pointing out that taking these broader forms of relationality seriously and with rigor is essential for the survival of us all. So, the way in which we live, research, and teach matters because it can be absolutely critical for determining if we get to live.

Strawberries remind us of this. They model the importance of relationality and connection. Strawberries send out runners, spreading out and entangling themselves productively with others, something we must also do with our community partners, with our colleagues, and with our students. Strawberries would not exist without the entanglement of those runners, the leaves, their unseen microbes, water, and pollinators all working in relationship. In enjoying the gift of these tiny, sweet heart berries – viewed as the leader of the berries, because they are the first that grows and ripens each year – we have to also acknowledge these multiple unseen networks and relationships, showing that we value their role in bringing us such beautiful gifts.

Nurturing Seeds and Growing Together: Gifting and Healing Medicines for Archaeological Futures

Robin Kimmerer's (2013) discussion of the Sky Woman story highlights the gifts that strawberries give us. They are small but powerful gifts from nature, sweet treats but also medicine. This echoes lessons feminist archaeologists have been telling us and continue to teach: we speak and listen, we teach and learn – all of these are gifts. These recognitions and acknowledgments of *gifting* are in stark contrast to much of the planning and practices in our institutions is extractive, focused on taking rather than giving, an important point made by Chelsey Armstrong and Eugene Anderson. Such extraction is what capitalism demands, and, if we stop, pause, and reflect, I hope we can all see and sense in the core of our beings that it is something very wrong to treat land and water and sacred places as *things* with extractive, consumptive, transactional value, rather than as animate beings, as relatives, that we engage with through principles of gifting.

We learn from Tanya Hoffman that listening is an important part of relationships. Listening is a gift: one we must remember to give and to enjoy when it's given to us. As Tanja Hoffman's chapter shows so clearly, our work as community-based archaeologists depends on it. As people who engage with the heritage of others, allowing others space to speak and gifting them with our active listening become an essential part of any archaeology of the heart.

Humility and, perhaps more unexpectedly, also discomfort are both essential. As Tanja Hoffman and Uzma Rizvi show us in their chapters, these are also valuable gifts, ones we give to ourselves as they help us learn and grow as human beings. I agree with Hoffman about the personal benefits and would also add that, as archaeologists who want to learn, cultivate, and nurture heart-centered practices and one another, we need to continually remind ourselves (and gently each other) that we and our intellectual interests should not be what's centered in these forms of archaeological work. We hold steadfast and with care a commitment to "understanding *with*" as we engage with care in peoples' heritage.

In her descent, Sky Woman grabs seeds and medicines that she carries to Turtle Island. Her daughter, after her death, provides the people with several important medicines and foods that grow from her body. Medicine is a gift that is sometimes found in surprising places. As I noted previously, strawberry leaves are edible and a powerful heart medicine. One of the most powerful gifts of strawberries is something most people cut off and throw away. Heart berries remind us, like the twins born to Sky Woman's daughter, that there is bitter, along with the gift of the sweet. As we nurture seeds of heart-centered practices and grow together, we should remember that challenges and struggle are a regular part of these practices. Rather than avoiding mention or minimizing our mistakes and "failures," we can reflect, learn, and share our stumbles with each other, as this will help improve our practice. Recognition and acknowledgment of the necessary imperfection in our practice bring balance to our work.

Natasha Lyons and Kisha Supernant share some of the healing potential of heart-centered archaeology in their chapter, as they discuss their work with Indigenous youth. Schaepe et al. (2017) also focus on the contribution archaeology can make to community well-being in their recent article "Archaeology as Therapy." As they detail, archaeology has great potential to elicit and confirm connections, and such "interconnections endow individuals and communities with identities, relationships, and orientations that are foundational for health and well-being." This resonates deeply with the vision and hope I have for community-based archaeology and heart-centered practices. These findings parallel what I have seen in my current work that explores the intersections and potential relationship of archaeology with public health (Atalay 2019). I am partnering with Native communities to reclaim tangible and intangible cultural heritage while striving to understand the role community-based archaeology can play in health and well-being, with a particular focus on how it can contribute to healing from historical trauma and unresolved grief. I am excited to think together with, provide support for, and nurture a collective of heart-centered archaeologists in an effort to help grow and sustain a future that involves archaeology as medicine.

In thinking about how we nurture seeds to grow our discipline together, teaching is critical. Natasha Lyons and Kisha Supernant bring this topic to our attention in their chapter. Over the past decade, I have also explored contemplative pedagogy practices – a field with surprising and encouraging growth in recent years – and incorporated a range of these concepts and approaches into my teaching. For those with interest in heart-centered archaeology, there is much to learn from contemplative pedagogy as well as from Indigenous, feminist, and queer pedagogical approaches.

Another important contribution made throughout these chapters that is also significant in the Sky Woman and Earth Diver stories is the importance of remembering our ancestors and their sacrifice, their humanity and their struggles, and the incredible gifts and medicines that come from those. I noticed with interest when these chapters were presented in the 2017 SAA session how presenters took time to acknowledge and thank in a caring, even loving, thoughtful way those who inspired them and taught them. We do this regularly in acknowledgments of books and in our citations, but it felt different when it occurred in our face-to-face setting at a professional conference, and something in that deeply resonated with me. That experience in our SAA session and reading the resulting chapters made me appreciate, remember, and have a deeper love for the ones who taught me and taught us all so much: my mentors who I have mentioned already as well as Amy Lonetree, Alison Wylie, Trish McAnany, Joan Gero, George Nicholas, Anne Pyburn, Richa Nagar, Linda Tuhiwai Smith, and so many other feminist and Indigenous studies scholars – just some of the talented, brilliant scholars I have had the pleasure to learn from and with. It is such a gift to have the opportunity to thank all of them here.

Bearing Fruit: New Practices and Processes in the Way We Do Research

I want to share a secret now: the work presented by the authors in this volume made me fall in love with archaeology again. I had read them all, several times in fact, in the weeks leading up to our SAA session where they were first presented.

I read them all again as we prepared this edited volume. They gave me comfort when I badly needed it – they are so rich, so vulnerable, so *human*! So many times during our conference session where they were first read aloud I had to keep myself from standing up, yelling out a big "hoowaah!" or "Geget kwe!" (Ojibwe for "so true, girl!"). I felt that same enthusiasm and deep connection with the lessons in this work throughout the process of producing this volume. That was from engaging with the work of the volume contributors, but it was also from the way my co-editors and I engaged in collaborative work with each other. Process matters! It is some of the most sustaining and healing fruit we will bear. Miigwech – sincere thanks to the authors, co-editors, participants in our SAA session, and to all those who take up the challenge of exploring new ways of practicing archaeology for gifting me with that excitement, hope, and inspiration. In recent years, for a number of reasons, I have not felt the joy, the passion, and the feeling of having my mind, spirit, hands, and emotion joyful occupied with archaeology. Working on this volume changed that. It really inspired me and gave me so much hope for the future.

These chapters are part of what I hope to see more of in archaeology – talking about, struggling with, and learning from these sorts of challenges – with emotions, care, love, and our senses. Learning and working together, in partnership, with deep respect, kindness, patience, and understanding. These can be our research medicines! It is through these that we discover, recognize, and nourish interconnectedness. And these are medicines that are desperately needed in our capitalist patriarchal society that puts more emphasis on extraction, separation, and alienation than it does on gifting, relationality, and a socially just and loving society. Thank you for thinking here with us, through these chapters, and in your own work, about how we can make lasting structural changes to transform ourselves, our practices, our discipline, and our institutions. It is through these practices that we plant further seeds, nurture them, and watch them bear fruit, as the tendrils spread and we transform our discipline.

I close by calling attention to something I think of often and have written (Atalay 2012) and spoken about frequently: compassion. I see that we have so much compassion for our community partners and not always so much understanding for ourselves and for each other. Recently, I have been writing about compassion, interconnectedness, and collaboration as essential practices that are necessary to help our world that is in crisis. In doing so, I have been thinking about Anna Tsing's (2015) book, *The Mushroom at the End of the World*, in which she talks about us beginning to see the ruins of a postcapitalist society. She discusses mushrooms as being a small, overlooked economic hope when large systems that exploit fail. As Tsing demonstrates, mushrooms require collaboration, reminding us that everything touches and is connected with everything else. They require care in gathering, and they can't be mass scaled.

Anna Tsing sees hope in mushrooms in postcapitalist ruins; I see hope in strawberries. I would like us to envision a future for archaeology in which the lessons and wisdom of the heart berry lead our way (Fig. 16.4).

Fig. 16.4 Ode'iminan. Wild strawberry forest. (Image by Jasmin Sessler from Pixabay.com)

References

American Indigenous Research Association. Mission. https://www.americanindigenousresear-chassociation.org/mission/spider-conceptual-framework/. Accessed 7 Mar 2019.

Anderson, E. N. (1996). *Ecologies of the heart: Emotion, belief, and the environment*. Oxford: Oxford University Press.

Archibald, J. Q. (2008). *Indigenous storywork: Educating the heart, mind, body, and spirit*. Vancouver: University of British Columbia Press.

Archibald, J.Q., Lee-Morgan, J.B.J., and De Santolo, J. (eds.) (2019) Decolonizing research: Indigenous storywork as methodology. London: Zed Books.

Atalay, S. (2012). *Community-based archaeology: Research with, by and for indigenous and local communities*. Berkeley: University of California Press.

Atalay, S. (2018) Imagining Decolonial Research Futures. https://blogs.umass.edu/satalay/imagin-ing-decolonial-research-futures/. Accessed 7 Mar 2019.

Atalay, S. (2019). Braiding strands of wellness: How repatriation contributes to healing through embodied practice and storywork. *Public Historian, 41*(1), 78–89.

Bawaka Country, Wright, S., & Suchet-Pearson, S. (2015). Co-becoming Bawaka: Towards a rela-tional understanding of place/space. *Progress in Human Geography, 40*(4), 455–475.

Donnelly Hall, S. (2015). Learning to imagine the future: The value of affirmative speculation in climate change education. *Resilience: A Journal of the Environmental Humanities, 2*(2), 39–52.

Haraway, D. J. (2013). SF: Science fiction, speculative Fabulation, string figures, so far. *Ada: A Journal of Gender, New Media, and Technology, 3*. https://adanewmedia.org/2013/11/issue3-haraway/.

Horn-Miller, K. (2009). *Sky Woman's Great Grand-daughters: A Narrative Inquiry into Kanienkehaka Women's Identity*. Dissertation filed September 2009, Concordia University.

Horn-Miller, K. (2015). We Are Here and She Is In Us: Revisiting the Sky Woman Story. Performance at Amherst College, October 2015.

Kimmerer, R. (2013). *Braiding sweetgrass: Indigenous wisdom, scientific knowledge and the teachings of plants*. Minneapolis: Milkweed Editions Press.

Lambert, L. (2014). *Research for indigenous survival: Indigenous research methodologies in the behavioral sciences*. Lincoln: University of Nebraska Press for Salish Kootenai College Press.

Salazar, J. F. (2017). Speculative fabulation: Researching worlds to come in Antarctica. In J. F. Salazar, S. Pink, A. Irving, & J. Sjöberg (Eds.), *Anthropologies and futures: Researching emerging and uncertain worlds* (pp. 151–170). London/New York: Bloomsbury Publishing.

Salazar, J. F., Pink, S., Irving, A., & Sjöberg, J. (2017). *Anthropologies and futures: Researching emerging and uncertain worlds*. London/New York: Bloomsbury Publishing.

Schaepe, D. M., Angelbeck, B., Snook, D., & Welch, J. (2017). Archaeology as therapy: Connecting belongings, knowledge, time, place, and well-being. *Current Anthropology, 58*(4), 502–533.

Shenandoah, J., & George, D. (1996). *Skywoman: Legends of the Iroquois*. Santa Fe: Clearlight Publications.

Tsing, A. (2015). *The mushroom at the end of the world: On the possibility of life in capitalist ruins*. Princeton: Princeton University Press.

Tuck, E. (2009). Suspending damage: A letter to communities. *Harvard Educational Review, 79*(3), 409–427.

Wilson, S. (2009). *Research is ceremony: Indigenous research methods*. Toronto: Fernwood Publishing.

Chapter 17
Epilogue When Does the "Heart" Take Over? Some Reflections on Archaeologies of the Heart

Exploring the Role of Emotion and Spirit in Archaeological Research and Practice

Margaret W. Conkey

I am wondering what archaeology will be like in 20 years: will many sites still be more or less intact or will they have been destroyed? Will our noninvasive methods get even better so that excavations will be few and far between? Will archaeologists have decided that there is the most merit in "writing from the heart" and not taking that "God's eye view" that prevails today? Will scholars be rewarded for accepting and celebrating ambiguity rather than primarily for assertions of certitude? Will there actually be retractions when an original claim is shown to not obtain? Will research papers and reports be co-authored with our collaborators, even if they are not recognized scholars or so-called experts? Will the public continue to be interested in archaeology, even if they realize that it's not an Indiana Jones enterprise? Will archaeologists be recognized as premier critical thinkers who can help us all gain a deeper understanding of the multiple ways humans have been and can be "in the world"? As I listened to the papers in the symposium that led to this volume, I had many such questions race through my mind, and in some ways, I was already hearing a different archaeology – an archaeology that took its humanistic goals seriously while not relinquishing its rigor nor its commitments to its audiences that are far more expansive than what one could imagine. I began to hope – if not root – for an archaeology when the "heart" takes over, when heart-centered research was a specific "method," one as powerful and important as a processual approach or a so-called post-colonial approach, but not one limited to a certain camp or school or set of followers. When does heart take over?

M. W. Conkey (✉)
University of California, Berkeley, Berkeley, CA, USA
e-mail: meg@berkeley.edu

© Springer Nature Switzerland AG 2020   271
K. Supernant et al. (eds.), *Archaeologies of the Heart*,
https://doi.org/10.1007/978-3-030-36350-5_17

What is it that "heart-centered research" brings to archaeology in the early twenty-first century? Most references to heart-centered activities or projects are in the domain of the health sciences, as this description of the practices offered at the Ohio State Integrative Medicine program:

> Heart-centered practices can evoke healing and positive emotions, which broaden and build compassion, forgiveness, gratitude and loving-kindness (extending goodwill for safety, health, peace and happiness).

But maybe archaeology can – and should? – do the same things: evoke healing and positive emotions that, in turn, can build compassion and gratitude? This does not sound like the vision statement of most archaeological research centers or projects that are more likely to be aiming to "better understand the human past" "to foster cross-disciplinary research and training," "to provide a long-term perspective on human adaptations," or to try to solve a specific problem or question: "when did farmers come into a valley? How did a culture survive a serious drought? What processes led to a more complex sociopolitical organization? Why did a certain technology develop and/or be replaced? On and on... But the question that this volume raises—and gives some answers! -- is "what have we lost in our push to be objective?"

How can we humanize the past so that the "human" is us, the researchers, as much as attending to putting people into the past? While some 30 years ago, we were confronting the fact that our subjects in the past were often only the now-famous "faceless blobs" (Tringham 1991), perhaps we are now – at last – confronting that we, the researchers, are the "faceless blobs" who do not appear in the research process or in the resulting narratives. We continue to be seduced by telling from the "god's eye" perspective, which, admittedly, has encompassed wider frames of reference (such as in the explosion of landscape scale studies and "beyond the site"), but we have not yet deeply engaged with the ways in which our own emotions, personal situations, and perspectives figure into the choice of a research problem or project or into the ways we engage with the other people in the project, be they other project participants or any of a multiplicity of local, on-the-ground "stakeholders," community members, or those with vested interests in what we do. How do we select the methods of research and analysis and where are "we" in the ways we represent the outcomes and to what audiences? In trying to grapple with these challenges, especially when a field like archaeology still feels it needs to justify itself as a science, to be treated as a science, and to be rewarded as a science, I want to turn to several inspirations and commentaries that might help us better accept – and celebrate – not just the ever present (but often suppressed) ambiguity of our archaeological inquiries (Gero 2007) but also the research and practices that are heart-centered that do offer a way to "evoke healing and positive emotions, which broaden and build compassion, forgiveness, gratitude, and loving-kindness (extending goodwill for safety, health, peace, and happiness)."

Lessons from Others: 1, Dov Seidman via Thomas Friedman

I confess that I had not known who Dov Seidman was until I read about him in an editorial by Thomas Friedman in the New York Times (4 January 2017). Friedman was drawing on Seidman's research and writing (e.g., Seidman 2007) in making a case that, despite the "relentless march" of technology whereby machines are both outworking us but also perhaps outthinking us, we need to have heart and to engage fully with empathy. Seidman has suggested that this current technological revolution of ours in the twenty-first century is "as consequential as the scientific revolution" was, beginning in the sixteenth century with Galileo and Copernicus, which, itself, led to the practices of science as we know them: how we have – even in archaeology – drawn on science and reason to "navigate forward." These centuries embraced the human-centered notions of "I think, therefore, I am," after Descartes. But Seidman pushes on us to respond to the question of the times: "What does it mean to be human in an age of intelligent machines?" The answer from Seidman, according to Friedman, is "the one thing that machines will never have: 'a heart'." The message to archaeology (among many others) is that, as Seidman puts it, our self-conception has to be rephrased from "I think, therefore, I am" to:

> I care, therefore, I am; I hope, therefore I am; I imagine, therefore I am; I am ethical, therefore, I am; I have a purpose, therefore, I am; I pause and reflect, therefore, I am. (Seidman, quoted by Friedman 2017)

Friedman himself points out that even jobs with much technical component "would benefit from more heart." He calls these positions STEMpathy jobs. So, for archaeology, why are we not a STEMpathy field, with empathy as central to our work as our science is? In this volume we begin to see how this can be, how the empathy actually renders the science better, as much as the science can provide a more caring and even heart-centered archaeology.

Lessons from Others: 2, Hayden White

It was the recent and sad notice that the provocative historian, Hayden White, had passed away (March 2018) that reminded me of what a superb interlocutor he would and should be for archaeologists. White took the controversial stand that while historical facts can be verified (or not!), the stories that were made from them were all "fictions." The stories we tell about the past are made from what we impose on them through such things as what White called "emplotment." That is, we choose the type of plot for our facts and observations, and the choices we make are "inevitably ethical and political" (Doran cited in Genzlinger 2018). That is, we can choose to incorporate and tell (the story) with and from the heart or from other perspectives and stances. We are finding, as archaeology expands its ethical reach, that stories with and from the heart have enormous resonance with many communities, including our own professional circles – as these papers demonstrate. Who can resist such narratives?

We are urged to read that White essay from 1996: "Storytelling: Historical and Ideological." As one reviewer of White's work once wrote (Day 2010), White's

> essays are an antidote to the philistine and sinister demands that we forget the past. In history [read, in archaeology] we don't just remember the dead, we do their remembering for them. And that's an awesome responsibility.

And it is that responsibility, one that we all must not only acknowledge but shoulder and keep central in our practices and in our storytellings, that is why an archaeology with and from the heart, in all its many possible manifestations, is a most crucial enterprise.

Lessons from Others: 3

Unlike the previous lessons, this is a domain of thought that cannot be so easily summarized nor focused on an individual scholar or writer. It is another and long paper that would encompass this domain of thinking, scholarly, and otherwise. However, it is a domain of thought that both inspired the papers in this volume and is one that is making for an ever-better archaeology, namely, the expanding corpus of thought that is under the umbrella of feminist and Indigenous principles and practices. These are not "separate" archaeologies, such as "feminist archaeology" (see Wylie 2007), that one can either select to pursue or not – they are ways of doing archaeology, ways of defining the research problems, the practices to be developed and carried out, the audiences involved, and the kinds of stories to be told. They are, in a way, a macroscale version of White's emplotment. And they are, as rooted as archaeology is in being a science, one manifestation of archaeology as a field in STEMpathy. As the volume editors stressed in their call for the papers that led to the conference session that, in turn, led to this volume: "Feminist and Indigenous models of research and wellbeing invite us to fully utilize our emotional, spiritual, intuitive, and spiritual selves, as well as our best intellectual and rational selves, in our research pursuits."

We see many such models of research in these papers. These ongoing and emergent models in the discipline demand to be interrogated as to how they have developed and implemented and with what outcomes. This is a project larger than the one at hand here, but it is one next step forward. As archaeologists – and our collaborators – work towards clarifying, defining, and evaluating our ways of doing, the principles and practices that are inspired, mobilized, and informed by the range of feminist and Indigenous thought should generate more archaeology that is heart-centered. While we are not alone in this endeavor to take on more open and affective research practices (e.g., Elliott and Culhane 2017), this volume is an elegant and inspirational start.

In concluding, I want to share an anecdote that, interestingly enough, was published in the most science of US-based science journals, SCIENCE magazine, but as one contribution to a section called Life in Science. This is, according to the editors, "an occasional feature highlighting some of the humorous or unusual day-to-day realties that face our readers" (see after Beardsley 2016). To me, and to those in this volume, this categorization of the anecdote as "unusual" and as in a separate category from the "real science" of the journal reminds us we have much work to do.

Respect for the Ancients (Beardsley 2016 – reproduced with permission)

> I am finishing the day's field notes by the light of a kerosene lamp on the Micronesian Island of Kosrae, home of the archaeological site of Safonfok, when two Micronesians on my field crew approach my tent and ask me to escort them to the latrine. These local men, who are fishermen in the village when not working on my project, know that this remote terrain was abandoned long ago by their ancestors. They have a deep respect for the ancient history of archaeological sites and the ghosts and spirits that inhabit them.
>
> It is common to ask permission of the local spirits for safe entry into an archaeological site or passage through a remote area. The men do this quietly, sometimes under their breath, sometimes with a ritual. (One man removed his shoes when we entered the jungle). The night, it is believed, belongs to the spirits and the ghosts—you don't walk around without a purpose, you don't whistle (the language of ghosts is heard as a whistle), you don't call out someone's name (a ghost may take the name and use it to trick you by luring you into a treacherous place), and you don't walk in the center of a path (this is where ghosts walk).
>
> Because I work in ancient places filled with ghosts, I have developed a reputation on this island as someone who is not afraid of anything. The men who have come to my tent trust me to provide safe passage between camp and the latrine. As we walk through the darkness, we are serenaded by night birds, croaking frogs, and buzzing insects. We quietly talk about the coral fish hooks for which Safonfok is known, and they share the island's traditional lore as told to them by their grandfathers. I spend my days uncovering ancient artifacts, but sometimes it is at night when history seems to come alive.

References

Beardsley, F. (2016). Respect for the Ancients. *Science Magazine, 354*(6317), 1242.

Day, G. (2010, November 25). Review of the fiction of narrative: Essays on history, literature and theory 1957–2007 by Hayden White. *The Times Higher Education.*

Elliott, D., & Culhane, D. (Eds.). (2017). *A different kind of ethnography: Imaginative practices and creative methodologies.* Toronto: University of Toronto Press.

Freidman, T. L. (2017, January 4). From hands to heads to hearts. *New York Times.*

Genzlinger, N. (2018, March 10). Hayden White, Historian who explored how past is created, dies at 89. *New York Times Obituaries.*

Gero, J. (2007) Honoring ambiguity, problematizing certitude. *Journal of Archaeological Method and Theory*, special issue: Doing Archaeology as a Feminist, Margaret Conkey and Alison Wylie, eds, 14, 311–327.

Seidman, D. (2007). *How: Why how we do anything means everything* (2011 2nd ed.). New York: Wiley.

Tringham, R. (1991). Households with faces: The challenge of gender in prehistoric architectural remains. In J. Gero & M. Conkey (Eds.), *Engendering archaeology: Women and production in prehistory* (pp. 93–131). Oxford: Basil Blackwell Pubs.

White, H. (1996). Storytelling: Historical and ideological. In R. Newman (Ed.), *Centuries' ends, narrative means* (pp. 58–78). Stanford: Stanford University Press.

Wylie, A. (2007). Doing archaeology as a feminist: An introduction. *Journal of Achaeological Method and Theory*, special issue: Doing Archaeology as a Feminist, Margaret Conkey and Alison Wylie, eds, *14*, 209–216.

Index

© Springer Nature Switzerland AG 2020
K. Supernant et al. (eds.), *Archaeologies of the Heart*,
https://doi.org/10.1007/978-3-030-36350-5

Manufactured by Amazon.ca
Bolton, ON